KT-495-642

# *The Complete Guide to Accelerating Sales Force Performance*

# The Complete Guide to Accelerating Sales Force Performance

Andris A. Zoltners, Ph.D
Prabhakant Sinha, Ph.D
Greggor A. Zoltners

American Management Association
New York • Atlanta • Boston • Chicago • Kansas City • San Francisco • Washington, D.C.
Brussels • Mexico City • Tokyo • Toronto

*Special discounts on bulk quantities of AMACOM books are available to corporations, professional associations, and other organizations. For details, contact Special Sales Department, AMACOM, a division of American Management Association, 1601 Broadway, New York, NY 10019.*
*Tel.: 212-903-8316 Fax: 212-903-8083*
*Web site: www.amacombooks.org*



*Library of Congress-Cataloging-in-Publication Data*

*Zoltners, Andris A.*
*The complete guide to accelerating sales force performance / Andris A. Zoltners, Prabhakant Sinha, Greggor A. Zoltners.*
*p. cm.*
*Includes index.*
*ISBN-10: 0-8144-0650-5*
*ISBN-13: 978-0-8144-0650-2*
*1. Sales management. 2. Sales personnel. I. Sinha, Prabhakant. II. Zoltners, Greggor A., 1964– III. Title.*

*HF5438.4.Z65 2001*
*658.8′1—dc21* *00-067628*


*Printed in the United States of America.*



*Printing number*

*10 9*

To Alfreds and Berta,
whose love and support enabled me to acquire the
knowledge to write this book.
—AAZ

To Anita, Pria, and Meera,
the family in Evanston, and to my parents, aunt, and uncle,
who started this journey from Paltuhata and Jogapur.
—PS

To my family.
—GAZ

# Contents

# Preface

Sales forces represent a major investment for many firms, with the largest sales forces spending billions of dollars a year to deploy and support tens of thousands of direct salespeople. Sales force costs range from one to forty percent of sales, and for many companies, the largest part of the sales and marketing budget is spent on sales staff salaries, expenses, incentives, information systems, and other support systems and structures. Sales forces make up about ten percent of the global workforce. Field selling is an important factor in the world economy with several trillion dollars spent on sales forces and sales force materials.

The power of the sales force rests on its role in sales creation, on its being the public face of the company, and on the fact that it is entrusted with the most important corporate asset: the customer. There is not a sales force anywhere that cannot seriously hurt its company's performance. At the same time, there is not a sales force anywhere that cannot significantly enhance its company's position. More salespeople will generate more sales than fewer salespeople. A motivated sales force will sell more than an unmotivated sales force. A well-trained, well-coached sales force will sell more than its undisciplined counterpart. The quality of the selling organization has a direct effect on a company's sales and profitability.

Sales forces are constantly faced with opportunities and challenges, both internal and external. Several examples of the forces that require sales force change are shown below.

Forces of change for sales forces

| | *Opportunities* | *Challenges* |
|---|---|---|
| Internal | • Realizing product or customer synergies through mergers<br>• Launching a new product<br>• Using insights from high performance territories to improve low performance territories | • Integrating disparate sales forces in a merger<br>• Dealing with a maturing product line<br>• Reversing low or declining productivity |

| | Opportunities | Challenges |
|---|---|---|
| External | • Entering an emerging new market<br>• Exploiting expanded markets due to deregulation<br>• Using emerging channels to better meet customer needs | • Adapting to customer consolidation and increased customer sophistication<br>• Adjusting to product commoditization and price pressure<br>• Reacting to new global competitors |

Faced with opportunities and challenges, sales forces have to deal with two broad types of issues as they seek to accelerate their performance.

*Alpha issues* are those that require immediate attention. *Beta issues* are less urgent and occasionally the source of the problem may not even be clear.

There is a sense of urgency around alpha issues that requires action:

- A merger necessitates the integration of two sales organizations.
- Customer consolidation has rendered the current sales force structure unfeasible.
- A new product launch in a new market raises issues of sales force structure and size.

A productivity hunt can identify beta issues, such as:

- Turnover of good people has increased significantly.
- Customer retention is good, but new customer acquisition is flagging.
- The sales force is unmotivated.
- Territory goals are not motivating the proper behavior.

Beta issues can also deal with specific sales force processes:

- The incentive plan is encouraging too much effort on the existing products and not enough on the new ones.
- Many departments in a company are dealing with the same customer, but the lack of coordination is creating customer confusion.

- Sales managers are spending too much time doing administrative tasks and not enough time providing training, coaching, and feedback.

All sales organizations are forced to deal with alpha issues. The best sales forces never ignore beta issues. They understand that today's problem will become tomorrow's disaster, and that behind every problem is a performance enhancement opportunity. Proactive companies engage in regular productivity hunts to continuously improve their sales forces. This book is for managers who want to accelerate the performance of their sales force and for students who want to better understand sales forces.

## Background of the Project

In 1976, professors Prabha Sinha and Andris Zoltners first applied their quantitative skills in a consulting project for a selling organization. They helped a pharmaceutical firm size and structure its sales force. This first project grew into a global consulting company, ZS Associates, with more than 400 employees and sales force consulting experience in over sixty countries. ZS Associates has developed numerous competencies that address such issues as go-to-market strategy, sales force size and structure, sales force productivity assessment, compensation, customer relationship management, sales territory alignment, using information effectively, targeting, resource allocation, performance evaluation, and recruitment. Projects addressing these issues in over twenty industries have solved pressing problems and added many hundreds of millions of dollars to their clients' profits. Concurrent with their consulting work, Sinha and Zoltners continued teaching sales force theory and practice to M.B.A. students and sales executives at the Kellogg Graduate School of Management at Northwestern University. They have developed an extensive library of teaching materials, conceptual frameworks, and sales force insights over two decades. They had been discussing a book on sales forces for over ten years, but their busy schedules had precluded significant progress. Finally, writer Greg Zoltners provided enough additional assistance to permit the book to proceed.

## Its Place in the Literature

Sales forces, although a critical marketing channel for many companies, are underrepresented in publications compared to other, more trendy topics like advertising, database marketing, marketing channels, consumer behavior, business-to-business marketing, and technology. Sales forces, which combine individualistic sales personalities with complex issues involving pay for performance, data-based customer targeting, proper performance evaluation, and new technology, are a source of power and a significant managerial challenge for both executives and managers. Sales force managers combine art with science more than managers in many other managerial areas. This book provides a structure for sales force decisions, educates, and serves as a sourcebook of practical ideas for managers.

*The Complete Guide to Accelerating Sales Force Performance* provides education the way a textbook does, but it also provides guidance. It advises, similar to a sales manager's manual, and it seeks to provide the sales manager with an understanding of the entire sales force system by presenting frameworks for sales force design and performance enhancement. It is definitely not the written version of a motivational speech. Neither is it about the art of selling. Nor is it a personal improvement guide for a salesperson. Rather, it is a managerial guide to the sales force system. It provides the thinking frameworks and practical insights that can be useful in enhancing the management of a selling organization. The book melds sales management science with practical insights.

The authors are consultants, academics, and businessmen. They have worked all over the world with sales forces of all sizes in many industries, and they have published academic papers about their research. They have sold consulting services, managed others who sell consulting services, helped companies manage salespeople, and taught students about managing salespeople. This book contains the knowledge and wisdom gained from twenty five years of experience in the sales force arena. The frameworks have been used repeatedly, and they work. Often, the material is common sense, organized in a straightforward way; other times it is barely the beginning of a solution. When solving problems in the real world, one sees all levels of solution elegance and degrees of implementation ease. Sales forces are the unruly beasts of the management forest—crucial because of the sales they create, yet hard to control and change because they are about people dealing with other people.

## Main Themes

The first chapter describes how to determine the role of the sales force in the ideal go-to-market strategy. The concepts in this chapter are especially important in an Internet-assisted world. The second chapter provides a framework to assess the effectiveness of a selling organization and explains how sales are the consequence of various sales force success drivers, such as sizing, hiring, training, deployment, and compensation. Subsequent chapters examine the sales force drivers. In addition, the chapters examine best practices and strategies and then present a process for determining a performance enhancement strategy for the particular driver. Each chapter ends with some concluding observations. For example, in the chapter on compensation, different compensation plans are described and the conditions that favor each one are explained. A compensation design process is shown, and some compensation caveats are presented. The chapters also incorporate sections that describe how the Internet will affect each sales force success driver.

## Audience

*The Complete Guide to Accelerating Sales Force Performance* is written for two categories of readers. The first is the business community, especially sales managers, top managers, salespeople who want to advance professionally, divisional presidents, and business owners. For this group, this book is a go-to reference manual.

The second target audience is students in universities. Sales force management is universally taught in undergraduate, graduate, and executive business school programs. There is a sales force management class or mini-class offered in most business programs. This book provides a comprehensive view of the significant decisions faced by any selling organization. The material in its chapters has been used in M.B.A. classes and executive programs at Kellogg for over twenty years.

## Key Industries Cited

The authors have personally consulted for several hundred companies in over fifty countries in many industries. Industry experience includes work for companies in the biomedical, chemical, computer, consumer products, durable goods, electronics, financial services, medical supplies and equipment, industrial distribution, information services, insurance, media and information, office equipment, oil, paper, pharmaceutical, technology, telecommunications, and utility industries.

The text provides many industry illustrations. Best practices and theories from many sales forces have been extracted and generalized for any sales force.

## Acknowledgments

We have worked with many fine companies over the years. Without them, we would not have discovered much of the material in the book. Because of confidentiality, many of them must remain nameless, but our thanks go to those who are constantly trying to improve the productivity of their sales forces.

We would like to thank Northwestern's J. L. Kellogg Graduate School of Management for providing a fertile environment for ideas to flourish. Thanks go to our M.B.A. and executive students, whose lively classroom discussions kept our theoretical exuberance in check. The material in the book has benefited tremendously from its use with students in executive courses at the Allen Center of Kellogg. We are grateful to our colleagues at Northwestern and elsewhere who supported us academically and as friends.

We would also like to thank the people of ZS Associates, a consulting firm that provides a laboratory for the ideas and research for many of the topics in the book. The consultants at ZS contributed to the book through their creativity and through their evaluation of our concepts. It has been our pleasure to work with some of the finest consultants and businesspeople on the planet. Special contributions came from Samantha Alfassa, Jaideep Bajaj, Julie Billingsley, Maneesh Chandra, Jeff Foland, Songjun Luo, Murali Mantrala, Kathryn McKay, David Mogul, Mike Moorman, Abhijit Nimgaonkar, Jean-Jacques Raoult, Richard Schuerger, Kathy Schwenk, Nancy Smith, Marshall Solem, and Chris Wright. We would like to thank Iraj Ajir and Jeff Blakely of Pfizer Pharmaceuticals, who helped with the chapters on training and performance management. Thanks also go to Marilyn Murphy of the IBM Corporation, who helped with the go-to-market chapter.

We owe very special thanks to a trio of research and editorial superstars, Sally Lorimer, Jill Wittwer, and Linda Kluver. Sally Lorimer applied her sales force expertise in reviewing every chapter for content and clarity. She rewrote many sections where she felt improvement was needed. She also researched and organized the Internet content that appears in most chapters. Her research improved the quality of the book substantially. Jill Wittwer edited our work thoroughly. She has suggested thousands of changes to various drafts of the manuscript. Her knowledge and skill facilitated a straightforward exposition of complicated and sometimes confusing ideas. Linda Kluver developed all of the book's illustrations. Her careful attention to detail made her proofreading nearly superhuman. Alice Manning provided a final editing of the book. It is only with the help of these fine collaborators that this book can be in your hands today.

It is time to put our feet to the floor and begin to accelerate sales force performance.

# *The Complete Guide to Accelerating Sales Force Performance*

# Chapter 1

# The Role of the Sales Force in the Go-to-Market Strategy

A world-class sales force is a powerful asset for any company, but using a direct selling organization is just one of a whole range of options for going to market. This chapter will help you decide when to use a sales force and when to use other marketing instruments, such as advertising, telesales, and the Internet, to reach your market. The chapter presents a complete framework for determining what role a sales force should play in a firm's go-to-market strategy.

From this chapter you will learn:

- How to partition your customers into meaningful groups so that marketing efforts can be prioritized and customized for individual market segments
- How to determine the essential work required to serve the needs of each market segment
- How to find the most efficient and effective way to deliver the essential work to each market segment
- How to decide whether to use a direct (company-owned) or an indirect (outside) sales organization

## Introduction

Sales forces represent a major investment for most firms. In the United States, nearly 12 percent of the total workforce is employed in full-time sales occupations. With over a trillion dollars spent on sales forces and sales force materials, field selling is an extremely important factor in the U.S. economy. Sales forces cost companies anywhere from 1 to 40 percent of sales. The companies with the largest sales forces spend billions of dollars to support tens of thousands of direct salespeople. For many companies in business-to-business markets, the largest part of the sales and marketing budget is spent on sales staff salaries, bonuses and commissions, expenses, and infrastructure costs.

The significance of the sales force goes beyond its cost. The sales force is the most *empowered* group of people within the firm. It represents the company publicly and is entrusted with the company's most important asset: its customers. It does its work independently, with little direct supervision.

The sales force *creates sales*. It is not just an expense; it drives the top line. More salespeople create more sales than fewer salespeople. A motivated sales force sells more than an unmotivated sales force. A well-trained, well-coached sales force sells more than its undisciplined counterpart. The ingenuity of the selling organization has a direct effect on the company's sales and profitability.

The sales force is a *force*. There is no sales force that could not seriously hurt its company's performance, and there is no sales force anywhere that could not significantly enhance its company's position. The sales force is an integral part of the product and the value that a company brings to its customers. In the pharmaceutical industry, physicians have consistently ranked the Pfizer sales force at the top of the industry. It is not surprising, therefore, that when Parke-Davis launched its blockbuster cholesterol-lowering drug, Lipitor, it entered into an alliance with Pfizer. Soon thereafter, Searle sought Pfizer's assistance to sell its state-of-the-art arthritis medication, Celebrex. In both cases, the Pfizer sales force has proved to be a powerful asset for the products.

This book focuses on how to develop and maintain a world-class sales force. But first, the role of the sales force in the firm's go-to-market strategy must be determined.

The use of a direct selling organization—people hired on a permanent basis to sell in person to customers—is only one option for going to market. In addition to direct sales forces, advertising and promotion, telemarketing, value-added resellers, and the Internet can all play roles in connecting with customers and creating sales. Some companies rely entirely on face-to-face direct sales forces; some rely on telephone call centers. Some companies sell primarily through the Internet; some feel that their customers like the social interaction a salesperson brings. Some companies use telemarketing, the Internet, and in-person sales forces all at the same time. Figure 1-1 illustrates the diversity in go-to-market strategies.

**Figure 1-1.** Varied Go-to-Market Strategies.

| *Company* | *Account Teams* | *Industry Teams* | *Geographic Sales Force* | *Inbound Telesales* | *Outbound Telesales* | *Internet* | *Advertising* | *Partners* |
|---|---|---|---|---|---|---|---|---|
| Large computer manufacturer | Global account teams with product specialists for very large accounts or accounts with a multicountry presence | For industries with critical mass | For large customers in nontargeted industries | For customer support | For small-sized opportunities | For non-business consumers and small orders, and for order processing for everyone | To consumers and trade | Partners and value-added resellers in vertical markets where partners enhance the product |
| Large chemical company | Direct sales force to key accounts | | | For orders and customer support | | | To trade | |
| Pharmaceutical company | Key account managers for group purchasing, managed care, and integrated healthcare networks | | For physicians | For customer service and information hotlines | | | To physicians and consumers | For all distribution |
| Industrial distributor | Major account team for very large accounts | | For nonmajor accounts; retail sales force at company-owned branches | To support all accounts | To service small accounts | For order processing—customized for large accounts, generic for small accounts | | |

Go-to-market strategies are changing all the time. For example, the emergence of the Internet as a sales channel has affected the way Dell Computer sells personal computers to business accounts. Many of Dell's business customers now place orders through an on-line configuration and ordering system, rather than through a salesperson. Sales channels are changing even in nontechnical industries. In 1980, the primary way to generate demand for pharmaceutical products was to use a sales force to detail products to physicians. By 2000, many other sales channels had also become important. End consumers may now be approached directly through television and print advertising. Symposia and meetings are increasingly important for reaching doctors who do not want to see pharmaceutical salespeople. In contrast, in the electric utility industry, which is facing deregulation, the role and importance of salespeople has increased significantly.

## A Framework for Developing a Go-to-Market Strategy

A go-to-market strategy defines the *activities* and the *participants* that connect a firm to its customers and prospects. Figure 1-2 provides a list of go-to-market activities. The list is divided into two parts. The first part highlights the activities that comprise the customer attraction and retention process. Salespeople are candidates to engage in these activities. The second part shows several other channel functions that, while important, are not typically part of a salesperson's responsibility. This chapter discusses the role of the sales force in the customer attraction and retention activities.

Figure 1-3 describes potential participants in a go-to-market strategy. Such a strategy involves designing and managing an effective portfolio of participants or partners who help the firm to connect with its customers and prospects and create sales. Sales force involvement in the go-to-market strategy is of two types: direct selling and indirect selling. A direct sales force is people hired by a company on a permanent basis to sell to customers face to face. Indirect selling involves the use of salespeople who are part of another organization, such as a value-added reseller, dealer, distributor, or agent, or a rental sales force. As mentioned previously, there are many alternatives to direct and indirect sales forces, including advertising and promotion, trade shows, direct mail, telephone sales, and the Internet.

Developing a go-to-market strategy that chooses from the set of potential participants must be a customized endeavor for any company.

**Figure 1-2.** Go-to-Market Activities That Connect a Firm with Its Customers and Prospects.

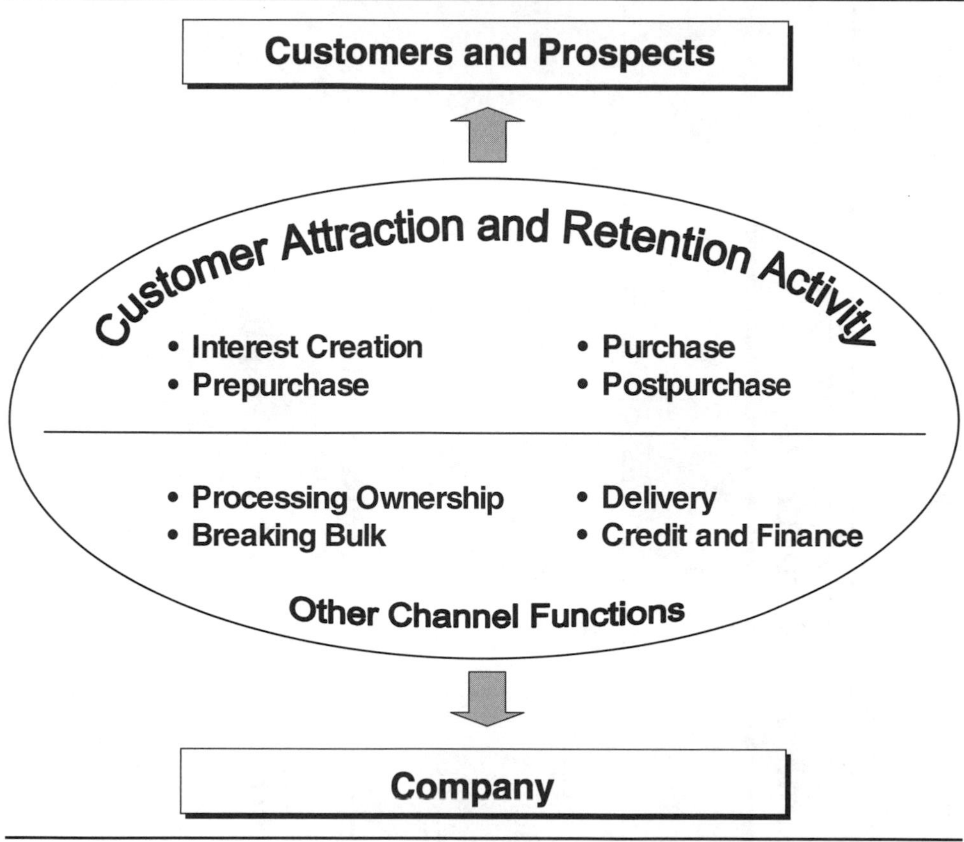


The go-to-market strategy framework described in Figure 1-4 provides a methodology for determining the role of a direct sales force in a company's go-to-market strategy. As the figure shows, a company's market is divided into multiple market segments, or groups of customers with common characteristics. The go-to-market strategy may be different for each market segment. Determining the right approach for each segment involves three basic steps:

- *Analysis* of the business environment to determine the essential work required to serve each segment
- Evaluation of *efficiency and effectiveness* to determine which go-to-market participants should perform each piece of the essential work
- Identification of *company-specific capabilities* to determine whether to use a direct or an indirect sales force

**Figure 1-3.** Potential Participants in a Firm's Go-to-Market Strategy.

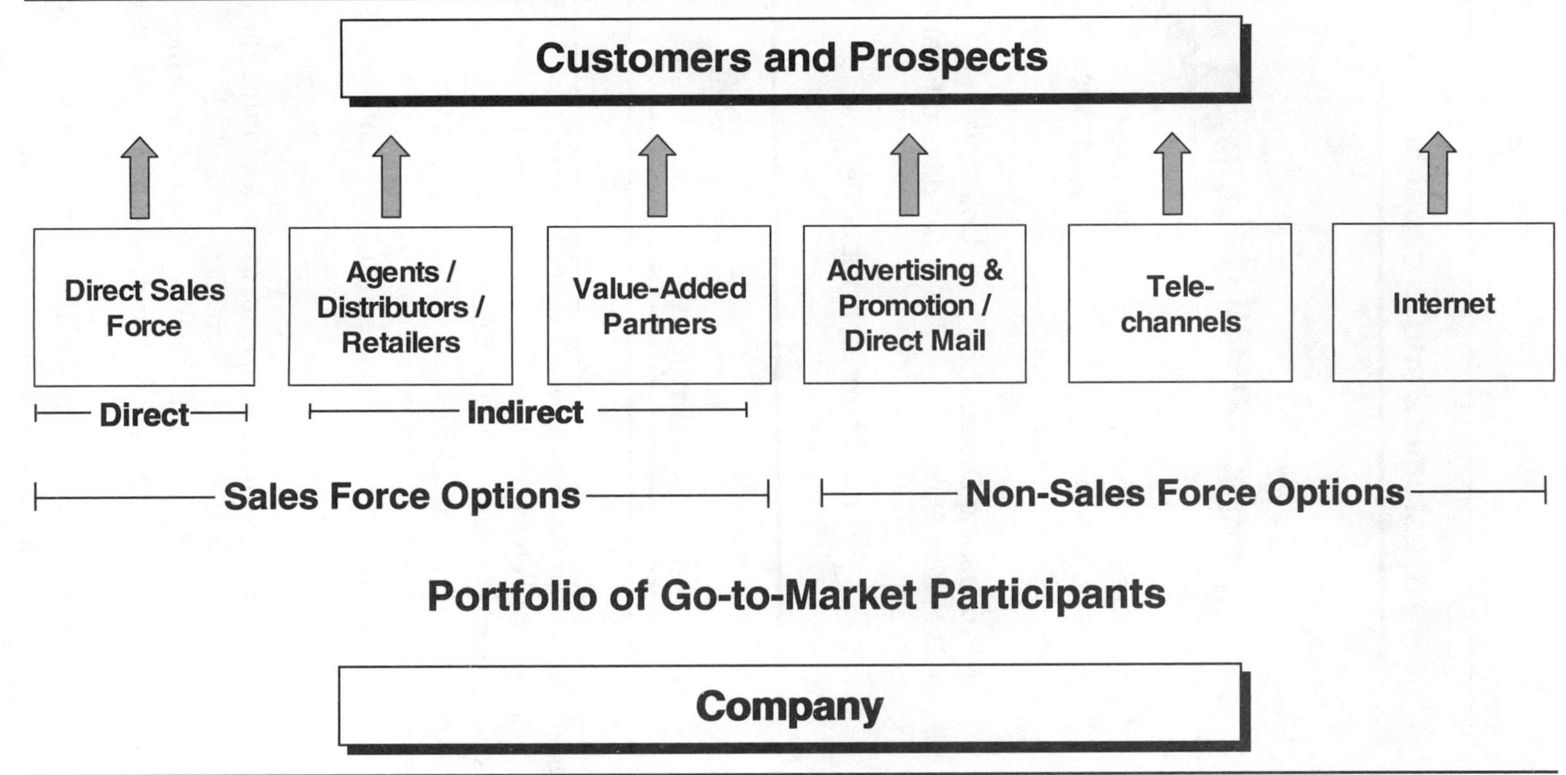

**Figure 1-4.** Go-to-Market Strategy Framework.

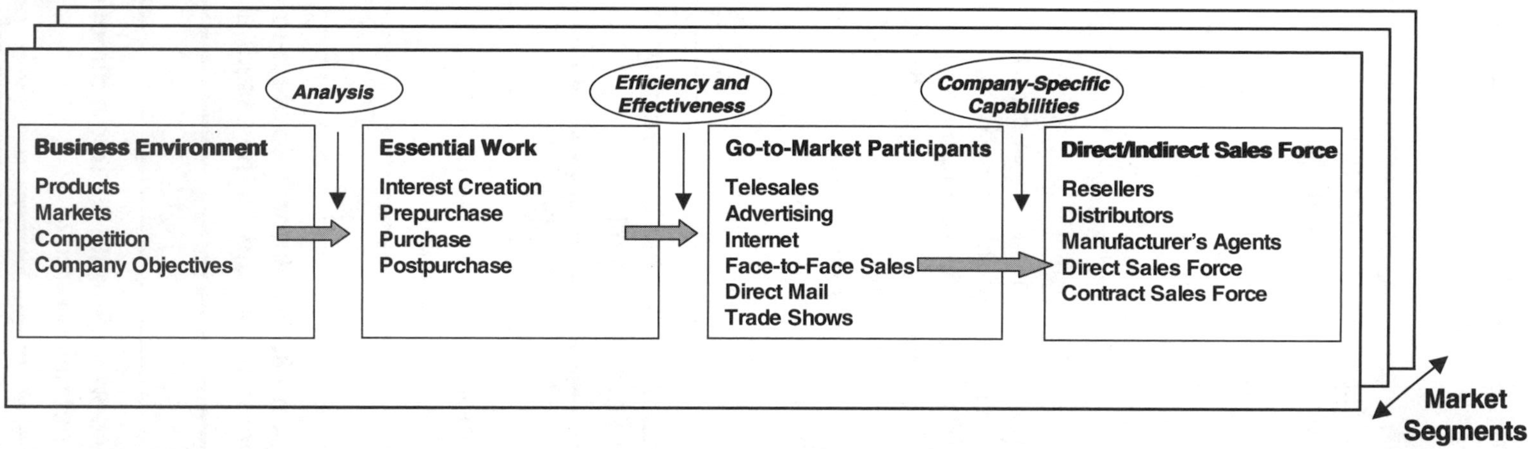

*Analysis*

*Efficiency and Effectiveness*

*Company-Specific Capabilities*

**Business Environment**

Products
Markets
Competition
Company Objectives

**Essential Work**

Interest Creation
Prepurchase
Purchase
Postpurchase

**Go-to-Market Participants**

Telesales
Advertising
Internet
Face-to-Face Sales
Direct Mail
Trade Shows

**Direct/Indirect Sales Force**

Resellers
Distributors
Manufacturer's Agents
Direct Sales Force
Contract Sales Force

**Market Segments**

Within this framework, the process of determining a go-to-market strategy involves answering the four major questions shown in Figure 1-5.

First, the go-to-market decision can be different for different market segments. For example, major accounts will be served best by a national account team, while small rural customers can be reached more efficiently by an outbound telesales group. Developing an effective market segmentation is therefore the first step in the process. This involves evaluating factors such as industry, customer size, customer buying behavior, and geography.

The second question focuses on the definition of essential work for each market segment. Essential work includes all the tasks a company must perform to meet the needs of its customers and prospects. Essential work can be subdivided into interest creation, prepurchase activity, the purchase itself, and postpurchase activity. Each company must create awareness of and interest in its products and services, perform presale activities such as generation and qualification of leads, close the sale, and complete postsale responsibilities, including demand fulfillment, after-sale service, and market feedback for strategy development. All of these activities are part of essential work.

**Figure 1-5.** Steps for Defining a Go-to-Market Strategy.

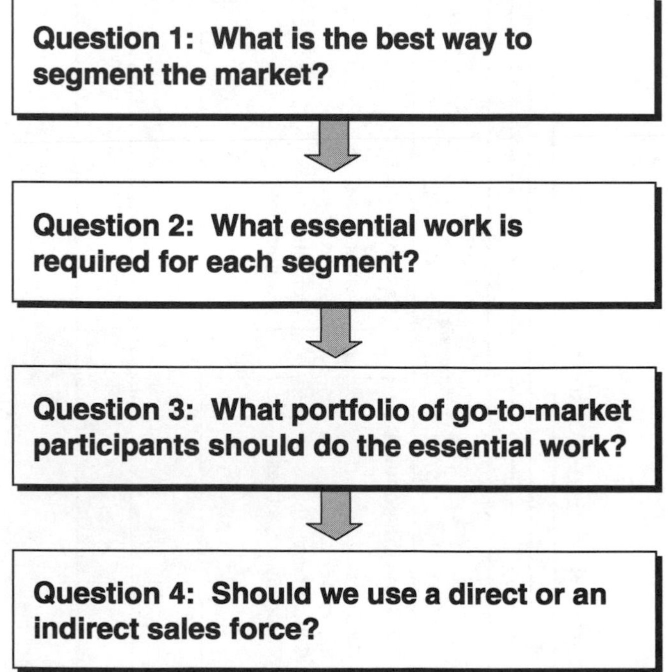

The third question centers on the selection of go-to-market participants to perform the essential work. One or more marketing instruments may be most suitable for each element. Efficiency and effectiveness guide this choice. For example, a telephone sales call is less expensive (more efficient) than a direct in-person sales call, but it is usually less effective. Advertising is great at creating awareness, but it is of little use for problem solving, getting customer feedback, or handling objections. The sales force has particular advantages and disadvantages compared to other instruments for accomplishing the various elements of essential work.

The final question involves the direct versus indirect decision. If a face-to-face sales force is the best marketing instrument given the considerations of efficiency and effectiveness, then company-specific capabilities indicate whether it should be direct (part of the company's own organization) or indirect (part of an outside organization).

The following sections of this chapter describe how to address each question in the go-to-market decision process.

## Question 1: What Is the Best Way to Segment the Market?

Any company's customers are heterogeneous, with varying needs and requirements. Market segmentation involves identifying different groups of customers with similar characteristics. Diverse customers are partitioned into smaller groups with common characteristics. Heterogeneity of the entire market becomes homogeneity by segment.

Segmentation provides companies with opportunities to increase their effectiveness. It would be easier to treat all customers the same way, but it is much more productive to prioritize customers and to customize products, services, positioning, and selling effort for individual segments.

Segmentation varies depending on the product sold. Baby diapers and adult diapers are very similar to manufacture, but they have very different selling processes. Most baby diapers are sold at retail with significant advertising support. Most adult diapers are sold in bulk to nursing homes via a selling organization.

Geographic segmentation is useful for some products but not for others. Sales of building supplies vary strongly with geography. Different exteriors and building materials are required for different locations. Sales of office supplies do not vary strongly by geography. Envelopes and pens are needed everywhere. Thus, geography would be a useful segmentation variable for building supplies, but not for office supplies.

Market segmentation approaches for developing go-to-market strategies commonly rely on sorting and aggregating customers using factors such as the following:

- *Industry:* What business is the customer in?
- *Customer size:* How big is the customer? What is the sales potential of the account?
- *Customer behavior:* Who are the key buying decision makers? Is the customer an innovator, a follower, or a laggard? Has the customer used our product already? Does the customer buy from a competitor? How much does the customer purchase now? Is the customer responsive to selling effort?
- *Geography:* Where does the customer reside?
- *Application:* How does the customer use our product?
- *Benefits:* What benefits does the customer seek?
- *Customer capabilities:* What knowledge, skills, and capabilities does the customer want its suppliers to provide?
- *Usage situation:* In what situations is our product used? How important is our product to the customer?
- *Contribution to profitability:* How much money can be made selling to this customer?

The best approach to segmentation for developing go-to-market strategies is one that generates segments whose members require similar customer attraction and retention activities, and hence similar essential work. For example, some segments may be made up of customers who need significant servicing, while others are made up of prospects who initially want to learn about the company's products. Some segments may need a consultative selling approach, while others need a transactional approach. Some segments should be ignored completely.

Figure 1-6 shows market segmentation dimensions for five companies that redesigned their go-to-market strategy. In each case, the essential work for customers and prospects within each market segment was very similar.

Sometimes the segmentation may consider only the economic value of a customer. In this go-to-market strategy, accounts and prospects are ranked in terms of opportunity, and then the most affordable selling tool is used for each account and prospect. If the incremental

**Figure 1-6.** Market Segmentations.

| *Business* | *Segmentation Dimensions* |
|---|---|
| Automobile insurance | • Account type (individual households, business/corporate accounts)<br>• Customers preferring standard vs. nonstandard plans |
| Paper products | • Customers preferring a consultative sales approach<br>• Customers preferring a transactional sales approach |
| Mass media—newspaper | • Account size (national, large, small, individuals)<br>• Type of ad (classified, display)<br>• Industry (automotive, department store, fashion, movies)<br>• Geography (local or regional) |
| Ground transportation and logistics | • Standardized services (van, bulk, specialized, multimodal, brokerage)<br>• Engineered services (dedicated, logistics) |
| Business forms | • Account size (major, regional, telesales accounts)<br>• Industry (automotive, finance, health care, retail/wholesale)<br>• Geography (region of country) |

value of a customer's business is less than the cost of calling on that customer, an alternative way of reaching the customer is required. In a scenario like this, very small rural customers get agents. Small urban customers get dealers. Medium-size customers get an inside sales force using telemarketing and direct mail. Large customers get a direct sales force. Very large customers get national account management.

Even if a company can afford a sales force, maybe it should not use one. Some very profitable customers do not need face-to-face coverage by an expensive salesperson. Instead, they should have access to a special customer service telephone number or a Web page.

## Question 2: What Essential Work Is Required for Each Segment?

From the first time a customer hears about a product, to the closing of the sale, to the very last service call, many interactions with the selling company take place. Essential work consists of all of the activities required to serve a customer properly. Every contact the customer has with a company and its products is a chance for the company's offering to shine. All aspects of the interface between a firm and its customers help to "sell." Salespeople are only part of this interface for most companies, and they perform only some of the essential work.

## Types of Essential Work

Essential work is divided into four activities: interest creation, prepurchase, purchase, and postpurchase. These parallel the chronology of a sale and are shown in Figure 1-7. Good postpurchase interaction can lead to interest creation because it supports a continuing business relationship with the customer.

**Interest Creation.** Only customers who want to buy will buy. Prospects must learn about the benefits of the product and the company. Interest creation includes:

- Prospecting and identifying potential customers
- Generating leads
- Generating traffic (inbound calls)
- Identifying purchase influencers, both internal and external to the customer
- Creating awareness of the product, the need for the product, and the company
- Providing information about the company's products and services

**Figure 1-7.** Essential Work.

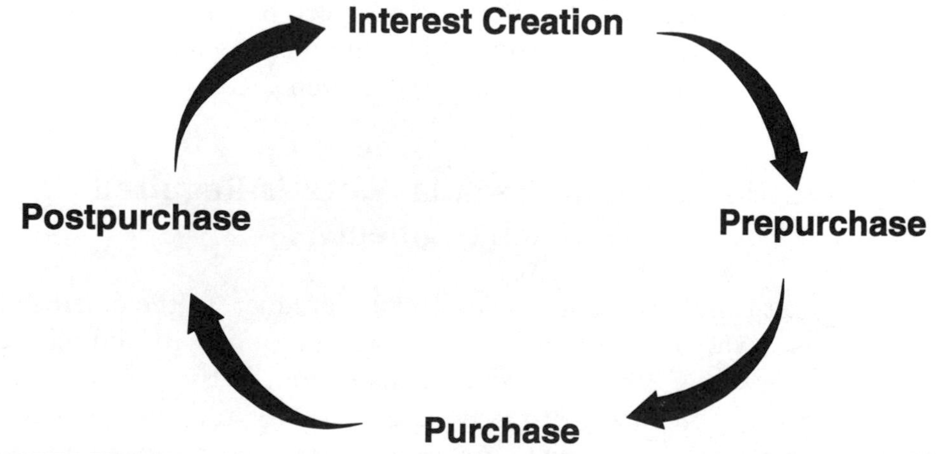

- Identifying potential selling partners and informing them of the company's capabilities

Interest creation functions are frequently performed through marketing instruments such as trade shows, direct mail, and advertising. But salespeople can prospect as well.

**Prepurchase.** During the prepurchase phase, customers and prospects are considering and evaluating competitive product offerings. Prepurchase activities include:

- Explaining features and benefits
- Qualifying customers/prospects
- Assessing customer/prospect needs
- Cooperating in problem solving
- Demonstrating company and product capabilities
- Comparing the company's product offering to competitive or substitute offerings
- Listening

**Purchase.** Purchase is the final flurry of activity culminating in a purchase. It is the activity most likely to involve direct salespeople. Purchase activities include:

- Persuading, negotiating, and finalizing terms
- Bidding
- Writing proposals and documentation
- Closing (asking for the business)
- Writing orders and reorders

**Postpurchase.** The essential work does not end with the purchase. The product must be delivered, installed, and serviced. Questions need to be answered, information about new features communicated, and bills sent and collected. Postpurchase activities include:

- Monitoring inventory
- Delivery
- Installation
- Checking order status
- Handling complaints and returns
- Developing joint customer marketing programs

- Performing customer market analysis
- Training
- Introducing new products and technologies
- Providing financing
- Collecting payments

Postpurchase activity is frequently unpopular among salespeople because incentive compensation plans often pay for the order and not for service. However, these activities build commitment, which leads to a business relationship and future sales. Whoever performs postpurchase activities is very close to the customer and can identify customer needs and problems as they arise.

## The Customer's View of the Offering

To a customer, the physical product itself and the means by which it is sold and maintained can be indistinguishable. Many of the items listed as part of essential work can also be considered part of the product offering. Sometimes the essential work is actually part of the extended product. For example, inability to deliver on time and lack of good service can disqualify a product from consideration. A copier makes copies, but a copier backed by a good service organization is running 99 percent of the time. A supplier of antilock braking systems to General Motors is providing the product, but is also assuring its availability at the right time in the assembly process. Further upstream, the supplier is also providing engineering assistance in integrating the product and its assembly with other automobile components. In the case of automobile insurance, some companies tout the ready availability of a local agent as a product advantage as compared to insurance sold over the telephone or over the Internet. Every customer buys a particular number of units, in a particular place, with a particular delivery date. Elements of the essential work merge with the physical product to become the complete product/service offering.

In some cases the essential work emerges as a new product. Service packages sold alongside a product are a good example of this. American Airlines' SABRE system for airline reservations was a beehive of interest creation, prepurchase, purchase, and postpurchase activity for the airline. Then the airline spun it off as a separate product, and it now has a higher market value than the airline itself.

The essential work activities for a broker of consumer products working at retail and a major newspaper are summarized in Figure 1-8.

**Figure 1-8.** Examples of Essential Work.

| *Company and Customers* | *Interest Creation* | *Prepurchase* | *Purchase* | *Postpurchase* |
|---|---|---|---|---|
| Consumer products broker working at the retail level. | Assess and record shelf presentation for over 100 SKUs, 4–26 times per year.<br>Suggest opportunities for performance improvement to the retailer. | Demonstrate new product lines with key decision maker.<br>Explain advertising programs that support products. | Review orders and upcoming promotions with store manager or category manager. | Verify that packages have not expired.<br>Clean shelves and fill all pegs with products.<br>Count inventory held in back of store.<br>Use store inventory counter to measure actual inventory in stock and reconcile records.<br>Record activities at store into handheld computer; upload nightly. |
| Large newspaper selling advertising to advertisers and advertising agencies in person and by telesales. | Generate leads (marketing department).<br>Cold call on prospects (account managers). | Make formal presentations.<br>Have informal discussions.<br>Inform about what sections of paper (sports, business) and locations (page placement) are available at what price.<br>Provide statistics and demographic information such as reach, coverage, and advertising payback. | Negotiate size of ad, placement, length of run, and price. | Provide art assistance for small customers who do not do their own artwork (production department).<br>Coordinate with client or advertising agency for receiving advertising materials.<br>Correct any errors for subsequent print runs. |

## Ways of Determining Essential Work

Customers have an array of needs, and these needs determine the essential work. All customers need to find products that satisfy their needs and identify suitable suppliers. For example, customers need to have their questions answered, and they may require demonstrations, evaluations, or engineering advice. Additionally, they may need delivery and installation, or they may need repairs, replacements, and service. Finally, customers need a reasonable price or appropriate financing, or both.

Different customers have different product evaluation processes. Some customers require suppliers to first sell a product at a high level, then sell it to individual departments. Other customers are decentralized and allow suppliers to sell to any department at any time.

When interacting with a customer, a selling company may become involved with many different people who have different roles. There are people who use the product, those who pay for the product, those who evaluate the product, and those who approve the purchase. One person could fill all these roles, but the process usually involves many hands.

Whatever the variety of customer needs, buying processes, and purchase influencers, the selling company must decide what work is required to meet those needs. In addition, it must assess the financial opportunity that can be realized by performing the work. Some segments may require essential work that is too costly for the financial opportunity that the segment provides. The seller must look for cheaper, nontraditional ways to perform the work if it wants to do business profitably with those segments.

When defining essential work, frameworks such as the one shown in Figure 1-9 are helpful. In this example, both customer needs and customer size/opportunity determine what essential work is appropriate for each customer segment.

Companies can use several sources of information to determine the essential work required for each market segment. Asking customers is a good place to start. Other good sources of input include salespeople, channel partners, and consultants. Finally, cross-sectional studies identifying "best practices" of companies in similar situations provide valuable insights.

Once a careful analysis yields a catalog of essential work, the next step is to decide which go-to-market participants should do it.

**Figure 1-9.** A Framework for Defining Essential Work.

| Customer Size and Opportunity | | |
|---|---|---|
| Large | **Account Maintenance**<br>Continue high-quality service<br>Automatic rebuy (EDI)<br>Prompt delivery<br>Enhance value proposition<br>Relationships<br>Friendship | **Effectiveness Selling**<br>Solve and consult<br>Cooperation<br>Customization<br>Integration<br>Partnership |
| Small | **Efficiency Selling**<br>Take orders and assure distribution<br>Consider self-ordering (lower price) | **Targeted Selling**<br>Quick needs assessment and solution<br>Explain features and benefits<br>Economic evaluation |
| | **Low Information, Low Solution Needs** | **High Information, High Solution Needs** |

**Buying Process**

## Question 3: What Portfolio of Go-to-Market Participants Should Do the Essential Work?

Once the most appropriate go-to-market activity, or essential work, has been determined, the next question is who will do it. Figure 1-3 provides several candidates: advertising and promotion, direct mail, face-to-face sales (including agents, value-added partners, and a direct sales force), telechannels, and the Internet. An old-fashioned door-to-door salesperson does almost all of the essential work. He or she creates interest, qualifies the customer, makes the sale, delivers the product, and collects the bill. Modern selling requires a hybrid approach. Grainger, an industrial products supply wholesaler, lets customers order through many channels, including a catalog, direct mail, telesales, the Internet, a direct sales force, and Grainger branch stores.

Some essential work should be done by the sales force, and some should not. Figure 1-10 shows examples of the participants in several go-to-market strategies.

It is easy to preserve and maintain conventional business practices, but careful consideration of who performs the essential work can lead to a breakthrough in business methods. In 1916, Memphis entrepreneur Clarence Saunders opened the first self-service grocery store. In his Piggly Wiggly store, clerks no longer picked out and packed up the items on each customer's grocery list; instead, the customers picked out their

**Figure 1-10.** Examples of Go-to-Market Participant Selection.

| *Business* | *Market Segmentation* | *Go-to-Market Participant Selection* | | | |
|---|---|---|---|---|---|
| | | *Interest Creation* | *Prepurchase* | *Purchase* | *Postpurchase* |
| Automobile insurance | Individual households | TV, billboards, agents, Internet | Agents, telesales, Internet | Agents, telesales, Internet | Teleservice, Internet, direct service reps |
| | Business/corporate accounts | Direct sales, agents, Internet | Direct sales, agents | Direct sales, agents | Direct service reps, agents, teleservice, Internet |
| Paper products | Customers preferring a consultative sales approach | Direct sales, distributors | Direct sales, distributors, technical support | Direct sales, distributors | Direct sales, customer service, technical support/manufacturing |
| | Customers preferring a transactional sales approach | Distributors | Distributors | Distributors | Distributors, customer service, technical support/manufacturing |

**Figure 1-10.** Continued.

| Mass media—newspaper | National and large accounts | Mass media, billboards, direct sales | Direct sales, market researchers | Direct sales | Direct sales, customer service |
|---|---|---|---|---|---|
| | Small businesses/ individuals | Mass media, billboards | Telesales | Telesales | Telesales |
| Ground transportation and logistics | Standardized services (van, bulk, specialized, multimodal, brokerage) | Direct sales, mass media, billboards, information on company trucks, independent agents | Direct sales, independent agents, telesales/ customer service | Direct sales, independent agents, telesales/ customer service | Direct sales, telesales/ customer service |
| | Engineered services (dedicated, logistics) | Telesales/customer service (leads), direct sales | Direct sales | Direct sales | Direct sales, telesales/ customer service |
| Business forms | Major accounts | Direct sales | Direct sales | Direct sales | Direct sales |
| | Regional accounts | Direct sales, telesales | Direct sales | Direct sales | Direct sales |
| | Telesales accounts | Direct sales (referral), direct mail, telesales (prospecting) | Telesales | Telesales | Telesales |

groceries themselves. In a more current example, many sellers now have Web sites that allow customers to manage their own sales orders, a task formerly done by the seller.

Cost is traditionally a key driver in choosing how to go to market. Each component of essential work must be performed by at least one go-to-market participant if products are to be sold to and used by the end customer. There is a cost for whoever does the work. Looking at the costs leads to efficient decisions about who should perform the work.

However, costs are only half of the equation. The quality of the essential work matters as well. Sales forces cost more than other marketing instruments, but they are highly effective at carrying out many aspects of essential work. They can generate sales in cases where other methods provoke no response.

The tension between long-term and short-term decision making also has an impact on the best go-to-market strategy. Some activities that are currently unprofitable may pay off in the long run if the customers are good long-term prospects. Life insurance salespeople do not generate as much sales revenue from younger prospects early in their careers as they do from older prospects with higher-paying jobs. But good relationships with less valuable customers end up as good relationships with very valuable customers.

The concepts of efficiency and effectiveness provide a natural framework for examining the costs and benefits of alternative go-to-market approaches.

## Efficiency and Effectiveness

A company spends money for marketing instruments that perform essential work. These marketing efforts create sales. The more customer contact that is created for the money spent, the more *efficient* a marketing instrument is at performing its work. The more results created per unit of exposure, the more *effective* the marketing instrument is. Another way to look at this is to say that the goal is to improve the selling expense/sales ratio, either by cutting expenses or by increasing sales. Efficient work choices cut expenses. Effective work choices increase sales. Figure 1-11 shows these relationships.

Efficiency and effectiveness are important in determining who does the essential work. Efficiency measures the number of contacts with customers that can be made through any of the available go-to-market participants. A company can buy a lot of postcards for the cost of one

Figure 1-11. The Role of Efficiency and Effectiveness.

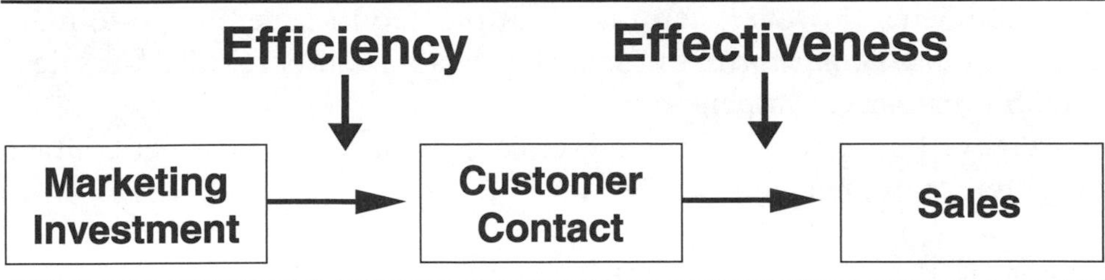


television advertisement. A sales force visit costs more than a telephone call. Effectiveness is a measure of the sales that arise from each customer contact using the available go-to-market participants. A sales force visit costs more than a telephone call, but it is more likely to produce a sale.

There are many options for performing essential work. The appropriate choice is the one that provides the best efficiency/effectiveness mix. Figure 1-12 captures the approximate trade-off between efficiency and effectiveness for various go-to-market partner choices.

As Figure 1-12 shows, a specialized sales force is most effective, but it is least efficient. Mass advertising is most efficient, but it is least effective. Everything else falls somewhere in between. Any given essential work situation requires a certain level of skill, or effectiveness.

Figure 1-12. Efficiency and Effectiveness for Go-to-Market Participant Choices.

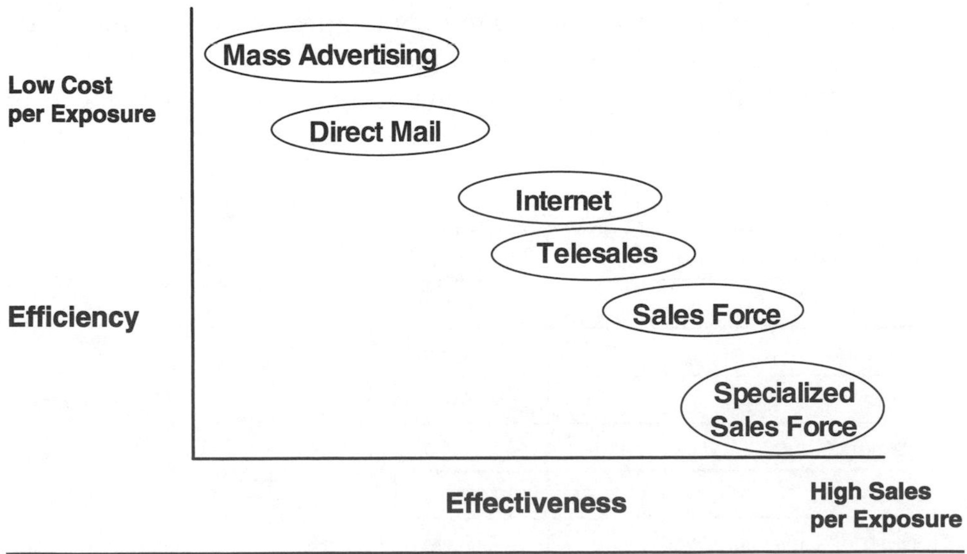

Given this effectiveness, there is a go-to-market participant that is most efficient. However, certain situations require specific go-to-market participants. If a formal proposal or evaluation is required, a salesperson must appear in person.

Figure 1-13 illustrates the significant variation in cost per contact for different marketing instruments.

## Managing Hybrid Go-to-Market Participant Portfolios

Most companies use a variety of go-to-market participants to deliver essential work to customers. Sometimes different participants are used for different customer segments. For example, many companies use the sales force to sell to large accounts, outbound telesales to sell to medium-sized accounts, and direct mail with an inbound phone number for small accounts. In other cases, different participants are used for different elements of the essential work for the same customer. For example, Cisco Systems, a telecommunications hardware provider, encourages customers to place orders over the Internet, even when a Cisco salesperson is involved in product configuration and pricing. Finally, different go-to-market participants can complete the same type of essential work for the same customer. For example, a customer of the industrial products supply wholesaler Grainger can order from a salesperson, over the telephone, or over the Internet on different purchase occasions.

Hybrid participant portfolios will become more prevalent in the future. The common choice for many companies is to use one go-to-market participant as the primary contact with the customer and use other participants as backups. Evolving technology helps make this possible. For example, many Dell PC customers begin the transaction

**Figure 1-13.** Average Cost per Contact to Reach Business Markets.

| | |
|---|---|
| Specialized business publication | $ 0.32 |
| Internet | $ 0.98 |
| Direct mail | $ 1.68 |
| Business letter | $ 13.60 |
| Telemarketing | $ 31.16 |
| Trade show | $162.00 |
| Industrial sales call | $277.00 |

*Source:* Penton Media, PRO Reports No. 303A, 1997.

on the Web, but finish the purchase on the phone. This is because telephone and Web integration technology routes people who have problems ordering over the Web to the phone for telesales assistance.

Go-to-market coordination also leads to successful hybrid participant portfolios. Customers who are uncomfortable with a value-added reseller can seamlessly receive a visit from a dedicated in-house salesperson.

Field force compensation can become an issue with hybrid go-to-market participant portfolios. When components of essential work migrate from salespeople to telemarketing or sales assistants, the variable component of a salesperson's compensation is likely to be affected. For example, one company had traditionally paid salespeople a bonus for finding new accounts. Then primary responsibility for new account prospecting shifted from the direct salespeople to a telesales group. As a result, the company had to adjust the compensation plan for direct salespeople to offset the lost bonus opportunity.

## The Four Major Go-to-Market Participants

The portfolio of go-to-market participants that is most appropriate for each customer segment and type of essential work depends upon a number of factors. This section briefly examines each of the major go-to-market participants: advertising and promotion, call centers, the Internet, and sales forces. Each of these has special characteristics, and each has different effectiveness and efficiency profiles for different customers and different types of essential work.

**Advertising and Promotion.** Advertising and promotion (A&P) consists of instruments like direct mail, newspapers, trade publications, magazines, television, cable, and radio. A&P is inexpensive per contact and is a good way to generate awareness and interest. A&P also helps with postpurchase rationalization: Customers are reassured by advertising that they chose correctly. Because A&P is often competing in a noisy environment, share of voice can be a concern. A&P is efficient, but it is not always very effective. If it is combined with telemarketing or in-person sales, however, it can provide an effective one-two punch.

**Call Centers and Telesales.** Telemarketing, telesales, and call centers all use the telephone as a means by which the company can contact customers or customers can contact the company. A call center is a location where customer calls are made or received. A telemarketer can perform all the work a salesperson performs that does not require a personal presence. For example, a telemarketer can close a sale, but he or she cannot deliver the product.

Like those of in-person sales, the costs of telesales are largely labor-driven. Wages are roughly 70 percent of total costs. Telesales is more efficient than an in-person sales force, but it is also less effective. For gauging customer reactions, voice feedback is not as rich as combined voice and visual feedback.

For call centers, inbound and outbound calls are distinct. Sometimes they are separate departments in a company, because the essential work they perform is so different. For example, inbound calls usually involve only postpurchase work, such as customer or product service. Occasionally a sale might be made as an add-on from such a call. Outbound calls usually focus on prepurchase activities, such as generation and qualification of leads. Essential work activities performed by call centers include:

- Inbound customer service calls
- Information requests
- Generation and qualification of leads
- Order taking
- Appointment making
- Satisfaction surveys
- Small sales
- Calls on geographically remote customers
- "Farming," or handling of existing accounts

When used in combination with other sales channels, call centers provide several benefits. Because face-to-face sales calls are expensive and multiple sales calls are typically required to close a sale, telemarketing provides a cheaper alternative. On average, telemarketing costs are less than 12 percent of the costs of a personal sales call. This allows more frequent contact with customers. Also, the good generation of leads by a call center for an in-person sales force means less time wasted on nonproductive face-to-face calls.

Call centers can also be used exclusively to reach small or out-of-the-way customer segments. Some customers may be too small to justify the cost of a face-to-face sales call. Others may be remotely located and therefore prohibitively expensive to visit in person. Geographic location is not an obstacle on the telephone.

Call centers also provide technological benefits. For example, many banks and insurance companies can automatically leave messages on voice mail overnight. Also, very detailed customer phone databases have been developed. These databases can flag optimal times to call and the likelihood that the customer will donate or buy. Perhaps the most powerful technological benefit of call centers is institutional memory, manifested by the integration of computers and telephony. A computerized system assists with each phone call. For example, an incoming number is identified, and the customer's call is sent to the same telesalesperson who handled that customer's last call. This person will also have specific customer information appear as a "screen pop" right at his or her workstation. The most recent address appears for verification. This institutional memory saves effort for both customers and telesales personnel.

Developing and maintaining a computerized system to handle inbound calls requires a serious commitment to infrastructure. Reliability is very important, because it is critical that the system for inbound calls run smoothly once a phone number is published. Many systems are very customized and hard to upgrade, although this will change as telecommunications products become more standardized. For example, many companies find it difficult to add phone lines or to change the information displayed on a screen pop. For this reason, many companies outsource their inbound customer service calls and use in-house staff for outbound sales calls.

Telephone sales and the Internet will become more closely integrated as technology improves. Already, a button on a Web site that offers "Call me up" can quickly put a call center in contact with the customer. The combination of the personal touch on the phone and the easy access to information on the Web is a potent one.

**The Internet.** As a medium for sales, the Internet provides significant benefits. It breaks through barriers of time and distance as a go-to-market participant. It brings benefits such as twenty-four-hour, seven-day availability (24/7), worldwide reach, improved efficiency, new means of communication, and expanded information capacity.

Internet-based applications can appear daunting, because companies often assume that Web delivery of essential work is a major undertaking. However, many variations in delivery of essential work are possible. Many companies start by doing only a small amount of essential work on the Web—specifically, interest creation. Most companies have a Web page that provides product and service information, descriptions, and specifications. Some companies put a portion of their catalog on-line, but require customers to order by phone or mail and pay by check. Most make e-mail or phone contact easy, and many can direct the customer to a dealer or a catalog site that offers their products.

The efficiency benefit of the Internet is the savings from automated processes that cut the costs of interaction. Automated processes allow faster transactions with less processing cost and more efficient distribution. On-line systems can provide quotes or capture and adjust order information. Good systems ensure parts compatibility and tighten connections throughout the manufacturing and distribution process, providing savings for all parts of the production and delivery chain. They reduce sales order errors and decrease the number of change orders, reducing rework. Reordering can be very easy with a system in place. More efficient service can increase customer retention.

The Internet provides a new medium for communication. E-mail is a rapid method of communicating with customers. However, because it is a written medium, literacy is more important. Also, e-mail misses the nuances that are important for effective communication. "Send my order right away" could be a message from an angry customer or a businesslike one. In addition to e-mail, teamwork support and groupware applications such as Lotus Notes allow better coordination between customers, suppliers, and different company departments. Chat rooms and support groups for customers allow customers to help each other and allow the company to monitor customer problems and sentiment.

The Internet also has effectiveness benefits. The company becomes very accessible to customers. The Internet captures orders and provides information twenty-four hours a day. Reach is increased because geographic boundaries are eliminated. When transaction speed is important, computer interfaces are faster. A customer can look up complicated specifications in a database just as fast as a salesperson can. The Internet can configure products while minimizing errors. A salesperson can solve a customer's problem, but an information-rich Web site allows the customer to quickly solve his or her own problems. Because of the impersonality of the Internet, collecting objective feedback is easy. Salespeople may seem intrusive compared to the passivity of an on-line order form. Also, there are no personalities on the Web that can rub a customer the wrong way. Furthermore, Web pages can be given "personality" to match the needs of a customer.

Web communication is fast, and the capacity for information in many forms is large. Video clips and pitch reels can be made available. Large product lines can be searched easily with an on-line catalog. The "dumb" computer can recall and display all sorts of minutiae that previously only highly trained salespeople could make available. Number crunching, searching, sorting, and remembering are easy for a computer. The computer can keep track of which parts of a site are most popular and how customers travel through the site. This kind of feedback allows better sites to be developed.

Business-to-business e-commerce sites can be hosted by the buyer, the seller, or a neutral party. As Figure 1-14 shows, the degree of market fragmentation influences who the most likely host of a Web site will be. For example, Cisco Systems is one of only a few suppliers of telecommunications hardware. A wide variety of customers can purchase Cisco's products. Thus, Cisco has used its seller power to set up a seller-centered site where its many potential buyers can get product information and place orders. General Motors and Ford, on the other hand, are part of a concentrated industry with many potential suppliers. As a result, they both have used their buyer power to set up buyer-centered sites that attract prequalified suppliers. Plasticsnet and e-STEEL are examples of neutral sites, or e-hubs, that bring together many buyers and many sellers of products in specific vertical markets. Finally, in markets with only a few buyers and a few sellers, the type of e-commerce site that emerges depends upon which market participant—a buyer, a seller, or a neutral party—makes the first move to develop the site.

The Internet has created a number of market-making mechanisms. On-line catalogs, auction, exchange, and barter are the different price-setting mechanisms used in transactions over the Internet. These mechanisms maximize the chance that a customer's need for speed, availability, and best price will be realized.

Companies must overcome a number of obstacles in order to exploit the Internet's power in the delivery of essential work. First, existing channel and retail relationships can impede on-line selling. If a company that traditionally sells its products through retail outlets begins to sell directly to consumers on-line, the retailers may be angry

**Figure 1-14.** Market Fragmentation and E-Market Evolution.

| *Sellers* | *Buyers:* Concentrated | *Buyers:* Fragmented |
|---|---|---|
| Concentrated | Channel Power Goes to the First Mover | Seller-Centered Sites |
| Fragmented | Buyer-Centered Sites | Public Hubs |

because they will lose business. For example, the channel power residing with tens of thousands of insurance agents is slowing the insurance industry's move to the Internet. Second, lack of technological infrastructure can be a problem. Computer hardware and expertise can be expensive, and the start-up costs can be prohibitive for companies that do not have people with the needed programming skills. Finally, legal jurisdiction in cross-border selling can be an issue in highly regulated industries.

The Internet can participate in all phases of essential work. Figure 1-15 shows examples of how essential work from each phase can be delivered via the Web.

For some software products, all of the essential work can be done on-line. The product can be discovered, purchased, delivered, and repaired on-line using updated files. Even customer training can be done on-line.

**Sales Forces.** Sales forces are good at complex, difficult, and important tasks. Salespeople provide a two-way social interaction. They listen, assess needs, provide solutions, reduce complexity, handle objections, create value, and provide long-term continuing service. They are the putty that fills all holes. Salespeople can work cooperatively with go-to-market partners. They enhance the product itself. Salespeople create "sticky" relationships—customers like the value creation and attention and stay loyal.

The sales force serves as an information-gathering resource for the firm. It can identify competitive actions and evaluate new product introductions. It can solicit customer criticism of a product and competitive products, facilitating new product development. Salespeople are frequently called on to forecast future sales.

**Figure 1-15.** How the Internet Participates in Essential Work.

| *Essential Work Phase* | *Example of Web Delivery* |
| --- | --- |
| Interest creation | • Advertising-like attributes on a company's web page<br>• E-mail |
| Prepurchase and purchase | • E-commerce buying sites |
| Postpurchase | • Automated reordering<br>• Monitoring of transaction, billing, and shipment information<br>• E-mailed feedback and customer discussion groups that facilitate market research |

In general, the sales force is very effective but not efficient. It is a very flexible and thorough go-to-market participant, but it is costly. Figure 1-16 provides cost estimates for sales forces in different industries.

The sales force can perform all aspects of the essential work, but because of its cost, it often should not. It can engage in activities that have differing levels of efficiency and effectiveness. For example, pharmaceutical representatives can discuss drug profiles in detail with a physician, leave samples with a receptionist, or do both in the same trip. When considering whether the sales force is appropriate for certain aspects of essential work, remember that the customer is essentially paying for the sales force. Is the service the sales force provides worth its cost? Would the customer pay for the salesperson if there were a separate charge?

Sales forces are generally too expensive to use for interest creation, but there are exceptions. If customers are firmly entrenched with a competitor, the use of the sales force may be necessary. Cold calling may be the only way to find and reach some customers. Impersonal mass media are likely to be ignored by tough customers. It is inefficient for the sales force to simply drop off printed material, but the sales force can follow up on printed material effectively.

Sales forces typically perform prepurchase activity well. For large customers with complicated buying processes, they may be the only choice. Prepurchase essential work can be quite involved, including product evaluations, customer need identification, or design work. In consulting, specialized preparation is often required. The consultant is both the product and the best possible salesperson.

While not usually as effective as an in-person sales call, telemar-

**Figure 1-16.** Cost per Sales Call.

Cost of an average sales call: $164.70
By industry:

| | |
|---|---|
| Services | $242.24 |
| Industrial manufacturing | $202.19 |
| Wholesale/distribution | $113.30 |
| Manufacturing | $ 95.05 |
| Retail | $ 79.70 |

Costs include compensation, benefits, and T&E costs.

Republished with permission of Bill Communications, Inc., from *Sales & Marketing Management,* Michele Marchetti, September 1999; permission conveyed through Copyright Clearance Center, Inc.

keters and the Internet provide an alternative, less expensive way to perform prepurchase activity. Ironically, the use of these methods often permits more sales force activity. For example, if telemarketing and the Internet generate viable leads and improve targeting, then the sales force can be more effective and justify its cost.

Because closing a sale may be challenging, sales forces are typically more effective than other go-to-market participants at purchase activities. Being "live" gives them insight into the needs, preferences, and thinking of the customer. A salesperson adapts quickly and can anticipate questions during negotiations.

In many industries, hybrid go-to-market strategies are being developed and the role of the sales force is being restricted, or squeezed, as shown in Figure 1-17. The sales force primarily provides the purchase function for big customers. Other participants perform the other essential work.

Relationships are built in the postpurchase phase. The sales force can provide excellent service and create a barrier to switching through rapport with the customer. When an account must be protected, a salesperson can be very effective at retaining it. The direct sales force has a role in identifying customer complaints and keeping in touch with market needs. Salespeople can see changes coming in an industrial setting that might not be noticed otherwise. For postpurchase activity, efficiency suggests that the sales force allow other participants to fill in whenever possible. Some companies have established the role of sales assistant in an attempt to achieve efficiency gains in the postpurchase phase. The sales assistant is responsible for all of the administrative, nonselling activities.

The sales force provides a critical link for companies making the transition to selling through telesales and the Internet. It can train customers to order on-line and evaluate them for the best telesales follow-

**Figure 1-17.** Sales Force Squeeze.

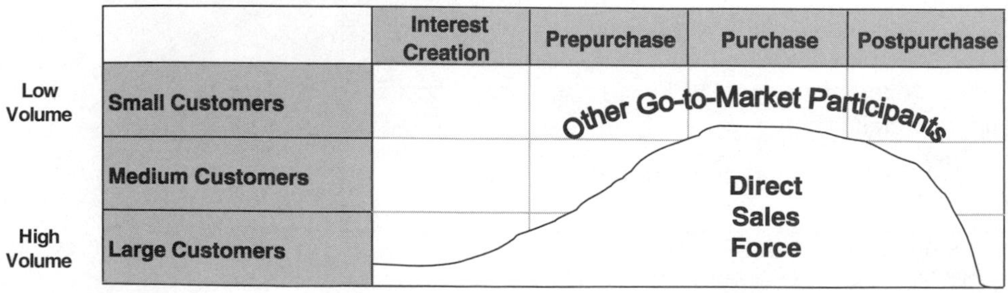

| | | Interest Creation | Prepurchase | Purchase | Postpurchase |
|---|---|---|---|---|---|
| Low Volume | Small Customers | | | | |
| | Medium Customers | | | | |
| High Volume | Large Customers | | | | |

Other Go-to-Market Participants

Direct Sales Force

up. Enabling new customer habits can be a complicated sale in itself. In companies with broad, complex product lines and many customer segments, hybrid go-to-market participant portfolios are the norm, as shown in Figure 1-10. The salesperson does some of the essential work, but other participants do complementary work for the same customer segments and most of or all the work for other segments. For example, telesales performs the prospecting, the transactions are processed over the Internet, and the salesperson manages the customer and the entire process.

## Question 4: Should We Use a Direct or an Indirect Sales Force?

Once a company has decided to use a face-to-face selling organization to perform some of the essential work, another question emerges: Should the selling be done by a company sales force, or should the company employ a selling partner? Outsourcing options include agents, manufacturer's representatives, resellers, distributors, and a contract sales force.

The outcome of the direct/indirect decision is rarely one or the other. Frequently, companies that use distributors have salespeople who co-sell with the distributors and may even call on some market segments without the distributors. For example, in selling an IBM server, an IBM direct salesperson initiates contact and completes the prepurchase activity. Then the salesperson turns the selling process over to a reseller business partner, who completes the purchase and postpurchase activities. IBM may provide technical support. The responsibilities for each component of the essential work are shown in Figure 1-18.

The level of company-specific capabilities required for success in the selling process determines whether to sell directly or indirectly. Every company has special, unique capabilities vested in its people,

**Figure 1-18.** IBM and Reseller Business Partner Share Essential Work.

| *Interest Creation* | *Prepurchase* | *Purchase* | *Postpurchase* |
|---|---|---|---|
| IBM | IBM direct salesperson | Business partner (reseller) | Business partner does delivery and installation<br>IBM may provide technical support |

products, and systems. These specific capabilities reside in three areas that are important for the direct/indirect decision: marketing, information, and financial. Figure 1-19 summarizes the marketing, information, and financial factors that favor a direct or an indirect sales force, and Figures 1-20 and 1-21 summarize the advantages and disadvantages of outsourced and direct selling.

## Sources of Indirect Salespeople

If a company decides that indirect selling is the appropriate way to perform some of the essential work, it must locate a suitable source of indirect salespeople. Several good sources are:

- Purchasing agents
- Noncompeting companies in the same industry
- Indirect salespeople already used by the company
- Trade magazine editors and salespeople
- Advertisements
- Trade associations of salespeople, such as the Electronic Representatives Association or the Manufacturers' Agents National Association (*Agency Sales* magazine, 3130 Wilshire Blvd., Los Angeles, CA 90010)
- Directories, such as *National Trade and Professional Associations of the United States* (Columbia Books, 734 15th St., N.W., Room 601, Washington, DC 20005) or *Verified Directory of Manufacturers Representatives* (Manufacturers' Agent Publishing Co., 663 Fifth Ave., New York, NY 10022)

A number of factors must be considered when deciding which source of indirect salespeople is best. First of all, product line compatibility is important. A good partner carries noncompeting, complementary product lines and has a compatible quality and price reputation. Other important considerations include the percentage of the partner's attention the manufacturer's product will receive, the relative dependence of the partner on the product line, and the compatibility of territories and customers. In addition to compatibility, the potential partner's enthusiasm for the manufacturer's product and its track record are important. Also, the potential partner's management practices, such as the way its salespeople are paid (salary versus commission), turnover rates, and training, must be considered. The final consideration is the services that the partner will provide, such as market infor-

**Figure 1-19.** Factors Favoring a Direct and an Indirect Sales Force.

| | *Favoring a Direct Sales Force* | *Favoring an Indirect Sales Force* |
|---|---|---|
| Marketing factors | Important potential customers are large and easily identified. | The market is fragmented and customers are difficult to find or understand. |
| | Buying is centralized and customers are homogeneous. | Buying is decentralized and customers are heterogeneous. |
| | The company has strong knowledge of local markets and good access to local distribution and customers. | The company lacks local market knowledge or access to local distribution and customers. |
| | The company has a broad product line and can offer a large assortment to customers. | The company has only a few products. |
| | Most competitors sell directly and there is no potential partner with significant marketing expertise in the industry. | Many competitors sell indirectly and there is a good potential partner who has significant marketing expertise in the industry. |
| | The company's name and reputation will improve the selling effort. | The company is not well known and respected. |
| | Products are complex, unique, technical, new, differentiated, intangible, or customized. | Products are easily understood commodities that have been around a long time. |
| | The selling cycle is long and orders are typically large. | The selling cycle is short and orders are typically small. |
| | The company wishes to carefully control selling effort. | It is not necessary to tightly control selling effort. |
| Information factors | The company needs information about customers for maintenance, servicing, or technical support. | Ongoing support activities are not important and the company does not need customer information. |
| | Supply of the product is not assured. | Supply of the product is assured. |
| | Monitoring sales performance is difficult. | Monitoring sales performance is easy. |
| | The company wishes to encourage salespeople to perform activities with long-term payoff, such as getting feedback from customers for new product development. | Short-term rewards are sufficient drivers of sales force behavior. |
| | Sales forecasting is difficult—the environment changes constantly. | Demand is predictable and the selling environment is stable. |
| Financial factors | The company can sustain some financial risk. | Controlling the cost of sales and minimizing financial risk are important goals. |
| | The need for the sales force will be sustained over time. | The need for the sales force is temporary or inconsistent. |
| | The market is very competitive—a reseller is likely to substitute competitive products at the end of the distribution agreement. | The market is not very competitive—the threat of competitive substitution at the end the distribution agreement is small. |
| | The company has experience with billing and collecting. | The company does not have a good billing and collecting system in place. |

**Figure 1-20.** Advantages and Disadvantages of Outsourced Selling.

| *Advantages* | |
|---|---|
| Customer relationships | A partner can have selling skills, customer relationships, or local knowledge that the company might not have. |
| Financial risk | Partners limit selling risk for the manufacturer because they can keep the manufacturer's selling costs at a certain percentage of sales. A salesperson's time is shared across products and is not as expensive. |
| Product assortment | Partners can offer many products and can thus usually offer the advantage of scale economics. A distributor offers one-stop shopping and a full line for bundled buying. |
| Variable capacity | Peak capacity needs can be met with indirect selling. Rent-a-reps and part-timers add flexibility, but can be less reliable than a full-time sales force. |
| Performance | When many manufacturer's representatives are available, the competition between them and the threat of replacement can create superior performance. |

| *Disadvantages* | |
|---|---|
| Conflict | Channel members can have incompatible goals, aims, and values. Conflict can occur over which customers should be served, which territories should be covered, which functions and duties should be performed, and which technology and sales aids should be used. Some partners "can't be bothered" to use a supplier's hot new marketing programs. Some supplier may have difficulty complying with in-stock and delivery commitments. |
| Control | Indirect channels are not as controllable as a direct selling force. Business partner salespeople will engage in activities that maximize their own income. These activities do not necessarily maximize the partner company's income, and they most certainly do not maximize the manufacturer's income. Business partners are in business too and can be expected to sell the products that are profitable for them. |

**Figure 1-21.** Advantages of Direct Selling.

| | |
|---|---|
| Control | A direct sales force legitimizes the employer's authority to examine inputs—for example, number of calls and customer lists. There is increased control of sales force capability, product information, and pricing. There is increased coordination, especially in terms of product resource allocation. The appropriate sales force resource allocation to strategic products can be achieved more readily. |
| Strategic advantage | A dedicated sales force can provide a strategic advantage over the competition. It can focus on key markets and products and customize its activity more readily than resellers. Direct salespeople enjoy job security and are dedicated to a single company. |
| Branding | A strong brand can create customers who prefer to deal directly with the producing company. This may limit the ability to use business partners. |

mation and feedback, stocking, customer service, seminars, and trade show attendance.

## Conclusion

Constant attention to the go-to-market strategy will keep the strategy fresh. Product, market, and customer conditions indicate what essential work needs to be done for each customer market segment. What essential work is required and who can perform what part of it need constant reappraisal. The efficiency and effectiveness of the various go-to-market participants determine how the essential work gets performed. Company-specific capabilities determine whether direct or indirect selling organizations are used. The rest of this book focuses on the field selling organization and provides insights into how to create and manage a highly effective sales force.

# Chapter 2

# Sales Force Assessment and Strategy

This chapter presents a sales force productivity framework that can be used to evaluate the status of a sales organization and develop a comprehensive statement of strategy.

In this chapter, you will learn:

- What key questions to ask when assessing your sales force
- How the *sales force productivity drivers*—the decisions sales managers make and the processes they use—affect the entire selling organization
- How to measure, both qualitatively and quantitatively, five key dimensions of your selling organization: the productivity drivers, people and culture, sales force activity, sales force results, and company results
- What measurement tools or "health checks" are useful in assessing your sales force
- How to use the results of sales force assessment to develop a comprehensive statement of sales force strategy

## Sales Force Strategy

Typically, sales forces follow a strategy. It can be succinct ("Grow sales 15 percent this year," "Make eight calls a day," or "Launch the new product vigorously") or more complex ("After a merger, create a new sales force and decide sales force size and relocations. Implement a new structure, culture, compensation plan, automation system, recruiting program, and training program. Do this efficiently and effectively without losing any sales").

To establish a sales force strategy, a company must determine the current status of the selling organization. If the sales force is performing poorly, an aggressive sales force strategy may be required. Unfortunately, determining the condition of the sales force is not easy. Consider the following story: The company president asks the vice president of sales, "How good is our sales force?" The vice president pauses for a minute and then answers, "We are very good." The president pursues the question, asking, "How do you know?" "Because we made our sales goal the last seven years," the vice president answers.

Does seven years of goal attainment make a sales force "very good"? Consider the following example. Several years ago, one region of a power tool company had an incredible fourth quarter, and hence an excellent year. The region exceeded goal by a phenomenal amount and attained star status. However, a sales analyst pointed out that the region included Miami and that Hurricane Andrew had created an artificially heavy demand for the company's products. In this case, the region's performance was not due to the sales force.

Sales force strategy statements vary widely across companies and industries, but four kinds of statements are common. First, a company may place emphasis on *results*. In this case, strategy means achieving sales, profit, market share, or customer satisfaction goals. Second, a company may focus on *activities* and *behaviors*. This sales force strategy includes making more calls, calling on new accounts, developing relationships, servicing existing customers better, engaging in more marketing research activity, or coordinating with channel partners such as distributors, a telemarketing team, or value-added resellers (VARs). Third, a company may state its strategy in terms of *people* and *culture*. The focus is on enhancing the skills, knowledge, and capabilities of the sales force and altering the norms and values that guide the sales force's work-style choices. Finally, a company may focus its strategy on *sales force investment* and *sales force decisions*. This strategy might include increased investment or reduced expenditure for the selling organization, a sales force reorganization, a new compensation plan, a new productivity enhancement program, or a training initiative.

Many sales force strategy statements combine elements of the four types of dimensions. Since there is wide variation in the elements that make up sales force strategy, a natural question is: "How should a sales force strategy be defined?"

Some companies with excellent performance have only average selling organizations. Most companies are not sure how good their selling organizations are, since sales forces are complex and there are many metrics. Is a sales force successful when it attains its sales goal? When customers give the company high customer satisfaction scores? When it has low sales force turnover? When expenses are under control?

This chapter discusses many aspects of a successful selling organization, including the components of a selling organization, sales force productivity drivers, measuring and assessing a sales force, and determining an effective strategy.

## The Components of a Selling Organization

Every selling organization can be viewed in terms of three basic components, shown in Figure 2-1.

First, there is the *sales force investment* in salespeople and sales support. Costs associated with salespeople include salesperson compensation, sales manager compensation, and benefits. Sales support costs include the costs of hiring, training, sales aids, sales meetings, sales data, sales systems, and laptop computers. The total annual cost may be several hundred thousand dollars for a small selling organization with just a few salespeople or several billion dollars for a large, multilevel sales force.

The sales force investment buys the company "feet on the street" that deliver the second component, *sales force activity*. Salespeople spend time traveling, preparing to sell, meeting face-to-face with customers or channel partners, performing administrative duties, and engaging in professional development activities. The main component of sales force activity is the company-adopted selling process—the essen-

**Figure 2-1.** The Basic Components of a Selling Organization.

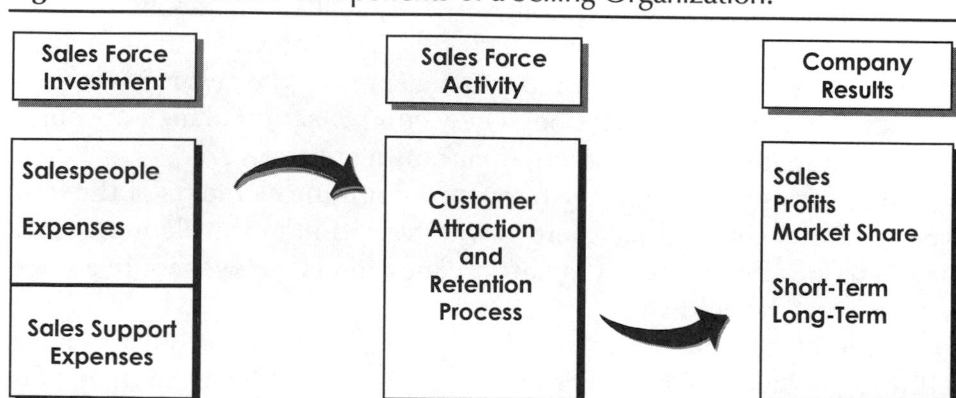

tial work. The selling process includes activities such as lead generation, prospecting, needs analysis, solution development, proposal presentation, negotiation, installation, customer service, and account maintenance and expansion. In this framework, the selling process is called the *customer attraction and retention process.*

Sales force activity is directed at a marketplace, which responds by producing *company results*, the third component. Measures of company results include sales, profits, and market share. Results can be measured in terms of absolute levels, percent of goal attainment, or growth over last year. It is useful to evaluate these statistics from both a short-term and a long-term perspective, because sales force decisions affect both time frames.

A successful selling organization *efficiently* converts selling costs into *effective* selling activity that drives significant company results. Each of these three components—selling costs, sales force activity, and company results—can be measured to establish sales force efficiency and effectiveness. People and culture and the customer are the two final components of this conceptualization of the sales force. They are added in Figure 2-2.

A company's ability to convert sales force investment into effective sales force activity is directly related to its *people* and its sales force *culture*. Competent, highly motivated people working in a "success" culture engage in the right activities. A company's sales force activity is acknowledged by its *customers* in either a positive or a negative way to generate company results. These two components—people and culture and customers—are more ambiguous than the other three components of the selling organization model, and their measurement is more challenging.

**Figure 2-2.** All the Components of a Selling Organization.

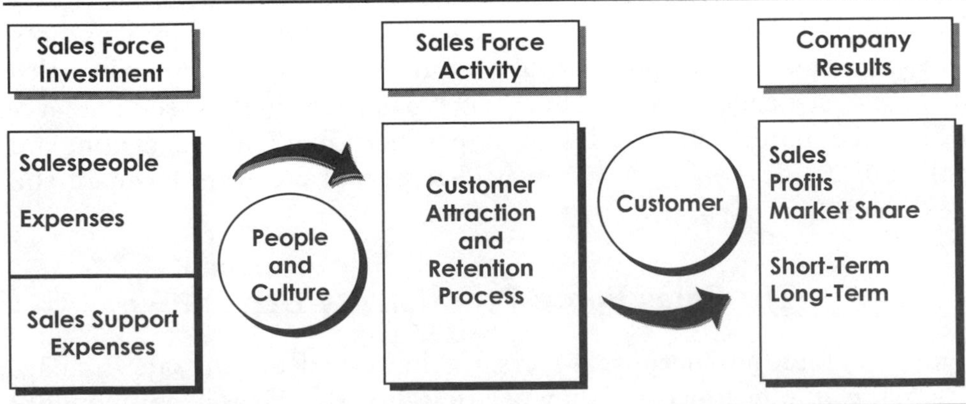

The five components within this framework provide a basis for assessing any selling organization. The framework organizes the questions used to evaluate a sales force:

| | |
|---|---|
| **Sales force investment** | Are our costs too high?<br>Is the sales force sized correctly? |
| **People and culture** | How good are the people?<br>Is personnel turnover too high? Too low?<br>Does the company have a "success" culture? |
| **Sales force activity** | Is customer coverage adequate?<br>Does the sales force call on the right people?<br>Does the sales force use the most appropriate customer attraction and retention process? |
| **Customer** | Does the sales force meet customer needs?<br>Do customers continue to buy from the company? |
| **Company results** | Can the company increase sales, market share, or profits?<br>Does the sales force generate enough new business? |

Signs of sales force success are recognizable. A sales force is successful if its costs are under control and if it has highly motivated salespeople, a positive sales force culture, appropriate selling activity, high customer satisfaction, and significant sales and profits. Finally, a sales force is successful if returns per unit of activity are high and if activity levels are high relative to costs.

The sales force productivity framework shown in Figure 2-2 is descriptive and diagnostic. It allows a company to assess the productivity level of its selling organization, but it does not tell the company how to increase sales force productivity. To improve productivity, the sales force investment component must be expanded to include the managerial decisions that drive sales force productivity. These decisions are called the *sales force productivity drivers* and are introduced in the next section.

## The Sales Force Productivity Drivers

The sales force productivity drivers are the basic decisions sales managers make and the processes they use that directly affect all components of the selling organization. They fall into four categories. The *sales research* category includes the processes of data collection and analysis, which enable the selling organization to understand customer buying behavior and to segment, prioritize, and target its markets. The *sales force investment and organization* category includes decisions on the appropriate size for the sales force; the best sales force organizational structure; the best deployment of sales force resources across products, markets, and activities; and the right sales territory alignment. These are the decisions top management is most interested in. The *people* category includes selection (recruitment and promotions), training and development, coaching and supervision, defining and assessing selling competencies, motivation programs, and personnel evaluation and progression systems. These decisions strongly affect the interaction between the sales force and the customer. The person the customer sees is the result of hiring, training, and the "success" atmosphere that the sales manager creates and fosters. These decisions have the greatest impact on sales success. The *sales systems* category includes management decisions that directly affect the efficiency, effectiveness, and job satisfaction of salespeople and hence affect customers indirectly. Compensation, incentives, benefits, sales force data, tools and processes, customer relationship management systems, and other productivity enhancement programs are decision areas that are included in this category.

Figure 2-3 expands the components of a selling organization shown in Figure 2-2 to include the productivity drivers. Notice that customer and company results are a consequence of company factors and the environment as well as the sales force. The power tool company that exceeded sales goals because of Hurricane Andrew is a good example of the effect that environmental factors can have on company results.

The sales force productivity drivers are the roots of a causal link that ultimately leads to company sales and profits. They are the decisions that, if made correctly, keep costs in line, create a successful culture, establish the right activity to satisfy customers, and drive positive company results. A sales force is successful if:

- Sales research functions create an understanding of buyer behavior. Effective market segmentation, assessment, and prioritization are performed.
- The investment in the sales force is appropriate. The sales force has the best size and structure and is deploying its resources optimally across its products and markets.

**Figure 2-3.** The Components of a Selling Organization, Expanded to Include the Sales Force Productivity Drivers.

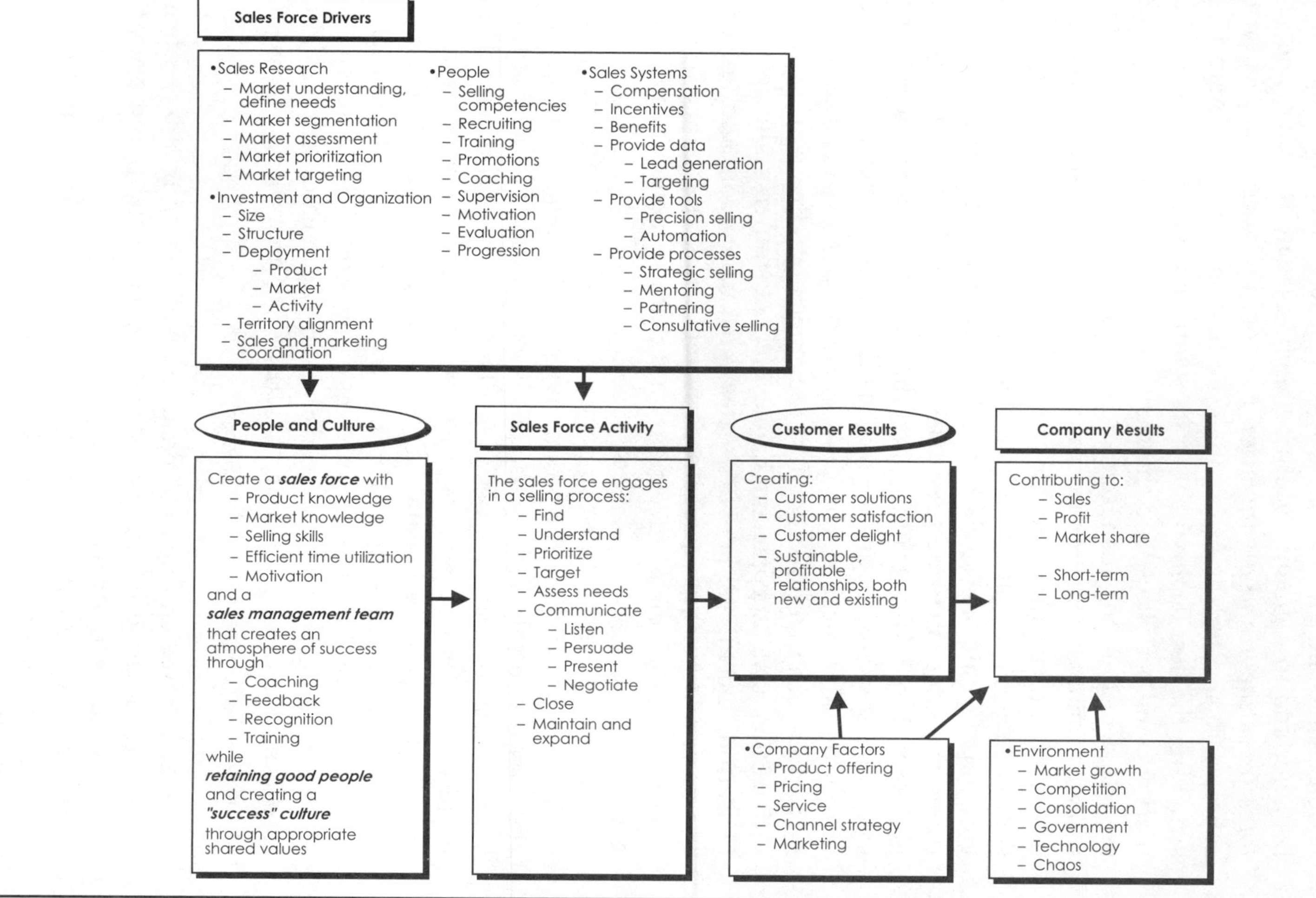

- Salesperson development is planned through powerful programs of recruiting, training, coaching, and career path development.
- Sales systems provide data, tools, and processes for accurate compensation plans and effective customer selling approaches.

The sales force productivity framework provides five dimensions on which to assess the effectiveness of a selling organization, one for each component. A sales force can assess its productivity drivers, its people and culture, its activity, its customer results, and its company results. Since the sales force productivity drivers ultimately determine the success of a selling organization, any sales force effectiveness evaluation must examine the drivers carefully.

Some components of sales force productivity are easier to measure than others. The next section provides a discussion of measures companies have used to assess their sales forces. This is a good place to start, since, as William Hewlett, co-founder of Hewlett-Packard, put it, "You can't manage what you can't measure."

## Measuring Sales Force Productivity

Each of the components of a selling organization is measurable to some extent. Sales force investment, sales force activity, customer results, and company results are usually the easiest to measure. Cost, sales, and profit data are maintained in the corporate accounting system. Activity data can be obtained through self-reporting mechanisms, from customer surveys, or from sales managers who travel with the sales force. Most companies seek customer feedback to monitor their operations and to get information that they can use for continual improvement. About 10 to 15 percent of companies survey their customers to determine sales force performance. The productivity driver and people and culture components are more difficult to measure, but a number of companies have made progress in measuring these areas. Figure 2-4 shows some of the measures companies use to assess how well their sales forces are performing.

Each area of sales force productivity can be measured. Measuring sales force productivity is valuable because these measures provide a basis for improvement programs. Most companies do not attempt to measure every area, since extensive measurement requires significant amounts of data and the effort can become expensive. The following sections describe how each component is measured.

Figure 2-4. Sales Force Measurement.

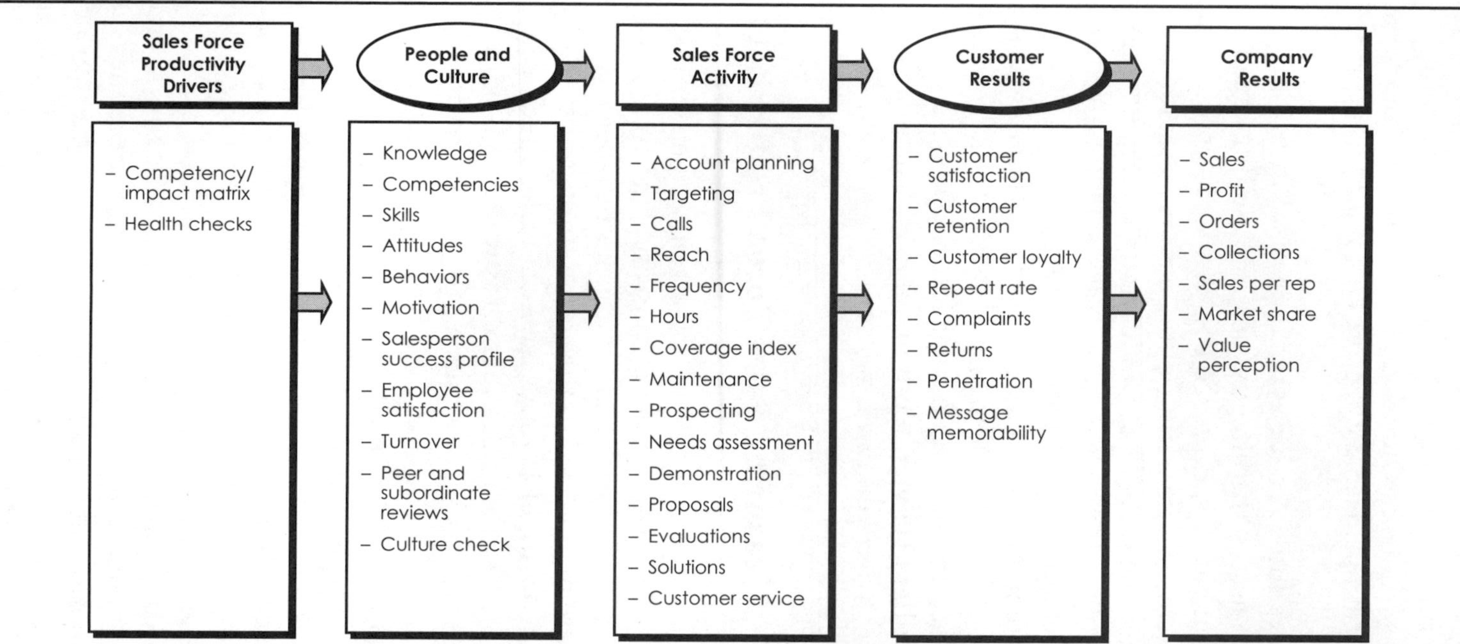

## Measuring Sales Force Productivity Drivers

Measuring sales force productivity drivers involves examining the significant sales management decisions or processes. As Figure 2-3 demonstrates, there are many drivers. Two measures of these productivity drivers have proved useful: *competency* and *impact*. First, each decision or process is evaluated in terms of how competent, or how good, the selling organization is at that decision or process. Second, each decision or process is evaluated in terms of the impact the decision or process has on the selling organization's ability to succeed. An assessment and prioritization matrix, the *competency/impact matrix,* can be developed using these two measures as the axes. Such a matrix for a transportation services sales force is presented in Figure 2-5.

This matrix is a valuable tool for assessing the current status of the sales force productivity drivers. The position of each driver on the matrix suggests a specific action that should be taken. For example, a productivity driver in the "low importance–high performance" quadrant can be maintained at its current level for the time being. Productivity drivers in the "high importance–high performance" quadrant need to be monitored closely to ensure that performance stays high. Those that fall in the "low importance–low performance" category should also be monitored in case the importance of the driver increases over time. Top priority goes to productivity drivers with low performance and high importance for sales force success. These areas present the greatest opportunity for productivity gains. Considerable improvement is possible for the transportation company in Figure 2-5.

The matrix requires measurement of both the impact and the current competency of relevant sales force productivity drivers. Methods for this type of measurement have been developed and continue to improve as more selling organizations adopt this approach.

Both quantitative and qualitative measures can be used to assess competency and impact. There are many quantitative measures, but territory-level analysis has proved very useful for many of the sales force productivity drivers. If salespeople do not allocate their time effectively, they need to improve their targeting. If high performers are underpaid and low performers are overpaid, the compensation plan needs to be revisited. If some sales territories have significant workload and others do not have enough work to keep the salesperson busy, the sales territories need rebalancing.

**Qualitative Measures of the Sales Force Productivity Drivers.** Qualitative data can be used to assess both the impact of productivity drivers

**Figure 2-5.** The Organization Recognizes the Importance of the Sales Effectiveness Drivers and the Opportunity for Improvement.

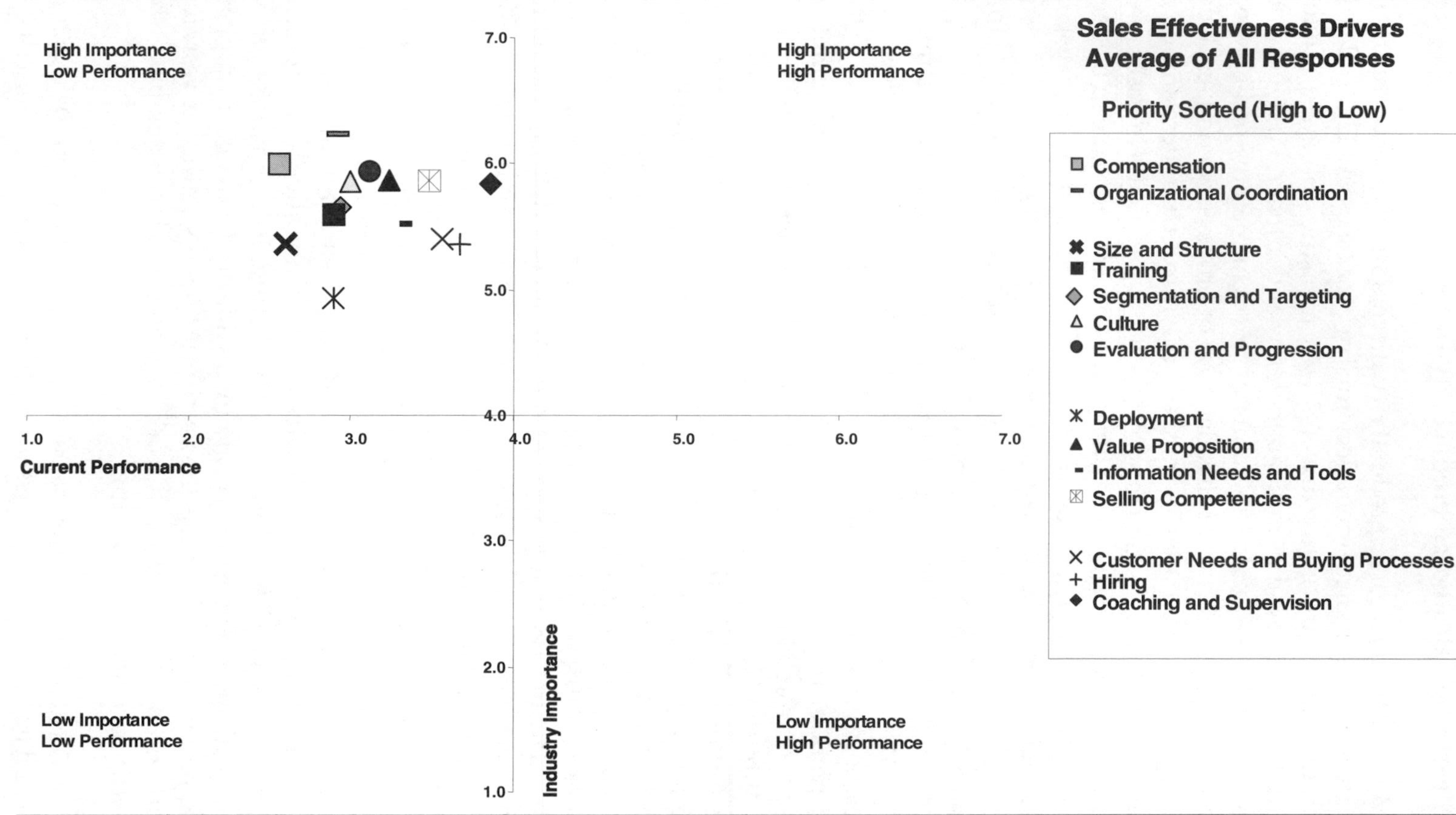

and the organization's current competency. Sources of qualitative data include interviews with salespeople and managers and days in the field with salespeople. One- or two-day workshop sessions with experienced sales and marketing managers are a popular way to gather qualitative data. Managers hear the results of field interviews and are presented with quantitative data. Then they are asked to assess the organization's competency and the impact of their sales force productivity drivers. Figure 2-6 shows how account managers at one pharmaceutical company viewed the impact of some of their sales force productivity drivers.

Questionnaires like the one in Figure 2-7 can be used to assess competency in a workshop setting.

**Another Qualitative Benchmark.** Over the last ten years, more than 1,000 sales and marketing executives have attended sales force productivity programs run by the authors at the Kellogg Graduate School of Management. Each executive group ranked the sales force productivity drivers in terms of their impact on the ability of the sales force to succeed. Overwhelmingly, the top choices have been recruitment, training, and the first-line sales manager. These are the "people" drivers from our Sales Force Productivity Framework. The general conclusion is that sales forces succeed because of their people. Interestingly, when working with individual companies, the authors have found that many managers feel they are "good enough" at recruitment, training, and executing the sales manager's role; most feel that they do not need to improve on these dimensions.

**Quantitative Analysis for Determining the Impact of Sales Force Productivity Drivers.** Most organizations try to obtain quantitative measures whenever possible. They feel more confident in their decisions if the data are objective and free of bias. A number of companies have developed quantitative methods for evaluating the impact and current competency of their sales force drivers.

One pharmaceutical company performed a clever analysis to determine impact scores for its sales force productivity drivers. It calculated competency scores for several of its sales forces within and across countries. These competency measures were correlated with several productivity measures, such as sales per person. A high correlation coefficient suggested that the productivity driver was related to sales success and hence had high impact. A low correlation coefficient suggested that the driver was not related to sales success and thus was of low importance.

**Figure 2-6.** Example of Sales Force Productivity Survey Results on Impact.

| *Please rate the following areas according to their ability to improve sales effectiveness.* | Not Important | Somewhat Important | Important | Very Important | Extremely Important | Average Rating (s.d.) |
|---|---|---|---|---|---|---|
| Improved information for targeting | 1 | 2 | 3 | 4 | 5 | 4.8 (0.4) |
| Improved compensation plan | 1 | 2 | 3 | 4 | 5 | 3.9 (1.0) |
| Improved product knowledge | 1 | 2 | 3 | 4 | 5 | 3.9 (0.8) |
| Improved selling skills | 1 | 2 | 3 | 4 | 5 | 3.9 (0.8) |
| Better sales tools and sales support | 1 | 2 | 3 | 4 | 5 | 3.3 (1.0) |
| Improved salesperson hiring process | 1 | 2 | 3 | 4 | 5 | 3.2 (0.8) |
| Improved recognition programs | 1 | 2 | 3 | 4 | 5 | 3.1 (1.2) |
| More time with immediate supervisor | 1 | 2 | 3 | 4 | 5 | 2.4 (0.9) |

**Figure 2-7.** The Sales Force Effectiveness Inventory.

| *Productivity Driver* | *C* | *B* | *A* | *Your Grade* |
|---|---|---|---|---|
| Customer needs, buying process definition | Customer needs and buying process are understood at an intuitive level | Customer needs are researched periodically and understood | Customer partnerships enable a continual assessment of customer needs and definition of the best way to meet them | |
| Market segmentation | No formal market segmentation has been done | A general segmentation is specified, but it is not research-based | A precise, well-researched market segmentation has been developed | |
| Channel design | The current channel strategy may have been appropriate in the past, but it is no longer appropriate for the current environment | There is a recognized need to develop a channel strategy that meets market segment needs; work is in progress | A clear and appropriate channel strategy for each market segment has been developed | |
| Sales force strategy | Strategy is imprecise; sales force is on its own to sell however it can | Sales strategies are defined, but their effectiveness is not fully understood or universally applied | Effective and tested customer attraction and retention strategies are in place and universally applied | |
| Sales force organizational structure | The current sales force structure may have been appropriate in the past, but it is no longer appropriate for the current environment | There is a recognized need to develop a new sales force structure that better meets customer needs and is consistent with sales force strategy; work is in progress | The sales force structure clearly and appropriately meets market and corporate requirements | |

*(continues)*

**Figure 2-7.** Continued.

| *Productivity Driver* | *C* | *B* | *A* | *Your Grade* |
|---|---|---|---|---|
| Sales force size | Company management is not aware that the sales force is not sized correctly to meet market opportunities cost-effectively | Upsizing or downsizing is anticipated | The sales force is right-sized; a profitability and coverage analysis has demonstrated the need for the current size | |
| Hiring | The hiring process is based exclusively on ad hoc interviews with the first-line sales manager and the national sales manager | The hiring process incorporates several effectiveness-enhancing approaches, such as behavioral interviewing or candidate testing | The hiring process uses a formalized, well-founded process including candidate profile definition, appropriate applicant pools, effective candidate selection processes, and effective attraction schemes | |
| Training | Training consists mostly of ad hoc approaches implemented by field sales managers | Some good training programs exist, but they are not consistently applied | Professional programs are in place and are applied consistently; training needs are continually reassessed, and program content and methods are adapted appropriately | |
| Sales manager | Sales managers are either warhorses or comets that have been selected using an ad hoc process; managers receive little or no professional development training | A sales manager selection process incorporates several effective concepts, e.g., candidate testing; some professional development exists, but it is not consistently applied | A well-developed selection process produces successful managers; managers continue to learn and grow professionally; the sales manager role evolves as market conditions change | |

| Compensation | The plan is complex and leads to unanticipated behavior, rewarding the territory and not the salesperson | The plan meets some company, customer, or salesperson criteria, but some improvement is required; improvement plans are underway | The plan is simple, is consistent with marketing strategy, ensures that the customer will be treated appropriately, is fair, and rewards the high performers | |
|---|---|---|---|---|
| Sales force tools and data | Few data are available, most progressive salespeople use their own computers, and the sales force is on its own to sell however it can | Databases are under development; the sales force is testing a few automation tools with some success; customer information is passed on when a new salesperson takes the job | Cost-effective database tools are available for such tasks as identifying customer needs, targeting, effective time management, performance evaluation, and providing value-added services for customers | |
| Total sales force productivity | Reactive studies of the productivity drivers are initiated when sales results are below expectation | Ongoing program development in several productivity driver areas, but mostly directed at "putting out fires" and "pet projects" | The productivity drivers are evaluated on an ongoing basis; areas of improvement are identified; best practices are researched and communicated, and a continuous improvement program has become part of the culture | |

The outcome of this analysis appears in Figure 2-8. This analysis could also be done across companies in the same industry. External benchmarking, however, requires cooperation among a group of companies.

**Quantitative Checks for Assessing Competency on Sales Force Productivity Drivers.** There are several quantitative checks, called *health checks,* that can be used to assess the organization's competency on a sales force productivity driver. Health checks are defined as data-based analyses that take at most two to three months to complete. They have been developed for almost all of the sales force productivity drivers. Three examples are presented here.

*A Targeting Health Check.* The health check shown in Figure 2-9, from the national accounts sales force at a large paper company, compares average hours per month per account (line graphs) with potential and actual sales per account (bar graphs). The analysis suggests that insufficient effort is being allocated to segment B and too much effort is being allocated to segments C, D, and E. Hence, targeting can be improved.

*A Compensation Health Check.* Each dot in the scatter diagram in Figure 2-10 represents a salesperson working for a large industrial distributor. Each salesperson has an associated performance score and an incentive payout score. The position of each dot indicates the salesperson's performance and incentive payout. The scatter of the dots represents the extent to which the current incentive compensation plan rewards performance with an appropriate payout. A 100 percent pay-for-performance plan would have all the dots on or near a line running from the southwest to the northeast. A plan does not pay for performance if too many dots appear in the northwest (overpaid category) or southeast (underpaid category) quadrants. This plan has 146 territories (about 10 percent of all territories) in the underpaid category and 21 territories in the overpaid category. It appears that there is room to improve this plan.

*A Sales Territory Alignment Health Check.* Each dot in the scatter diagram in Figure 2-11 represents a field salesperson for a cosmetic company. The workload, expressed in hours of face-to-face time required to cover all of the accounts in each territory, is calculated for each salesperson. The time ranges from 375 to 1,980 hours across the sales force of 205 salespeople. The salespeople are sorted from the one requiring the most

**Figure 2-8.** Correlation of Performance on Several Qualitative Dimensions with Key Business Outcomes.

| | | *Correlation Coefficient with* | | |
|---|---|---|---|---|
| *Driver* | *Driver No.* | *Sales/Rep* | *Sales/SF Cost* | *Sales/M&S Cost* |
| Assertiveness | 1 | **0.84** | **0.92** | **0.88** |
| Improvement | 2 | **0.70** | 0.57 | 0.36 |
| Communication | 3 | **0.83** | 0.61 | 0.47 |
| Hiring | 4 | 0.42 | 0.30 | 0.05 |
| Training | 5 | 0.53 | −0.09 | −0.24 |
| Coaching/supervision | 6 | 0.59 | 0.09 | −0.11 |
| Understanding customers | 7 | **0.91** | **0.72** | 0.54 |
| Customer segmentation | 8 | 0.52 | 0.56 | 0.23 |
| Precision selling | 9 | 0.52 | 0.25 | −0.08 |
| Understanding competitors | 10 | 0.35 | −0.04 | −0.25 |
| SF investment planning | 11 | −0.46 | −0.53 | −0.65 |
| New product launch process | 12 | 0.60 | **0.79** | 0.53 |
| Organizational structure | 13 | 0.69 | 0.52 | 0.31 |
| Information management | 14 | −0.27 | −0.20 | −0.50 |
| Compensation/incentives | 15 | 0.33 | 0.20 | −0.20 |
| *Selected Aggregate Drivers* | | | | |
| Culture | 1, 2, 3 | **0.84** | **0.73** | 0.59 |
| Human resources management | 4, 5, 6, 17 | 0.48 | 0.18 | −0.13 |
| Targeting/micromarketing | 7, 8, 9 | 0.68 | 0.52 | 0.21 |
| *Total Qualitative* | **All** | 0.64 | 0.45 | 0.13 |

SF = Sales force
M&S = Marketing and Sales force
***Correlations shown in bold type are statistically significant.**

**Figure 2-9.** Quick Check Example: Effort Allocation and Account Potential Analysis.

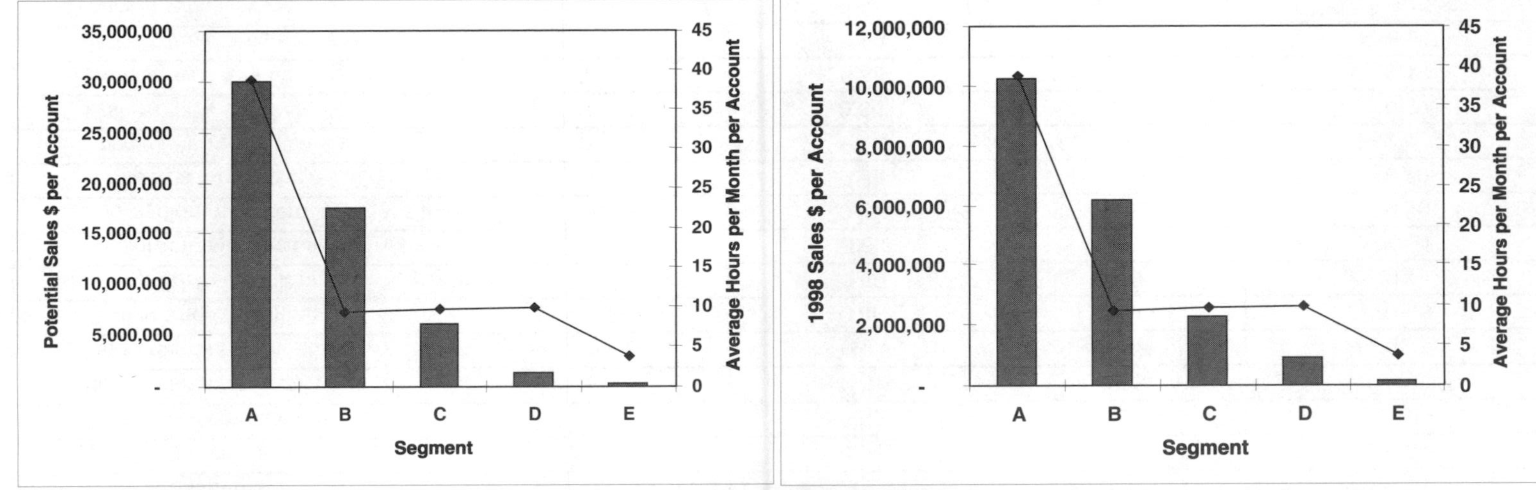


| Account Segment by Potential Sales | Potential Sales per Account | # of Accounts | Average Sales per Account ($) | Average Hours per Month per Account | Average Annual Cost to Service* | Estimated Annual Contribution |
|---|---|---|---|---|---|---|
| A | > $25MM | 4 | 10,239,416 | 38.8 | 29,100 | 994,842 |
| B | $10MM–$25MM | 6 | 6,158,113 | 9.2 | 6,900 | 608,911 |
| C | $2MM–$10MM | 20 | 2,276,984 | 9.6 | 7,200 | 220,498 |
| D | $500K–$2MM | 17 | 894,275 | 9.8 | 7,350 | 82,078 |
| E | < $500K | 12 | 147,703 | 3.7 | 2,775 | 11,995 |

* Assuming fully loaded account manager cost of $150,000 and a product gross margin of 10 percent.

◆ = Hours

**Figure 2-10.** Quick Check: Compensation.

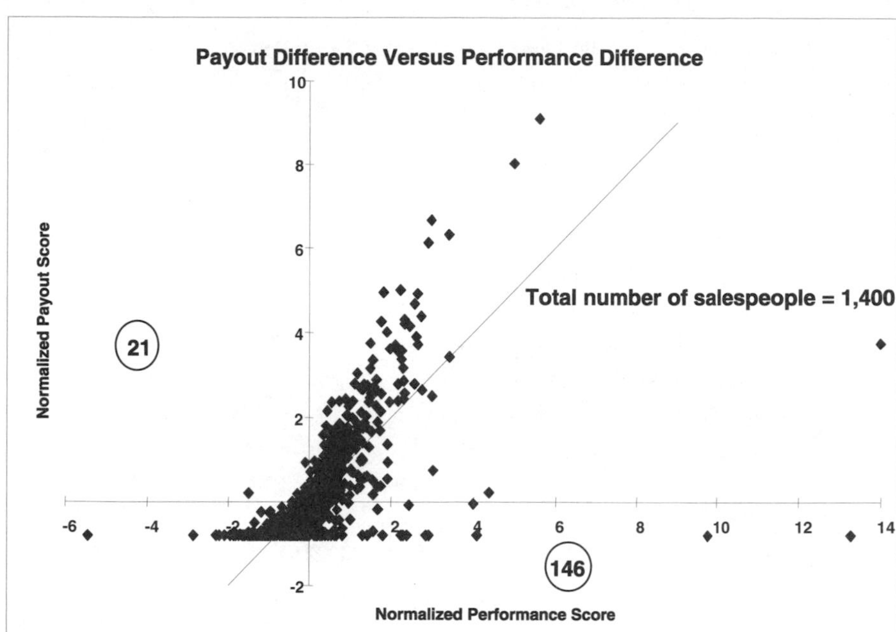


- Circled number represents number of salespeople in that quadrant.
- Normalized score is the number of standard deviations from the average.
- Performance is based on a blend of goal achievement, market share, and manager assessment.
- Payout is the incentive or nonsalary component of the total pay.

Correlation coefficient = 0.66

time to cover his or her accounts to the one requiring the least time. The salesperson needing the most time is labeled number 1, the one needing the second most is labeled 2, and so forth. The ideal workload is estimated to be 1,000 hours per year for each salesperson. Anyone who has more than 1,150 hours of workload cannot adequately cover all of the accounts in his or her territory. Anyone with fewer than 850 hours of workload has too little to do. The company is not utilizing its resources appropriately if there are too many territories that are either too large or too small. The scatter diagram shows that 65 territories are too large and 55 are too small. This misalignment costs the company millions of dollars annually.

Figure 2-12 summarizes the measurement possibilities for the sales force productivity drivers.

## Measuring People and Culture

If a sales force is to thrive, it must have good people and an appropriate culture. How good are the people in a selling organization? In a recent

**Figure 2-11.** Quick Check: Territory Alignment.

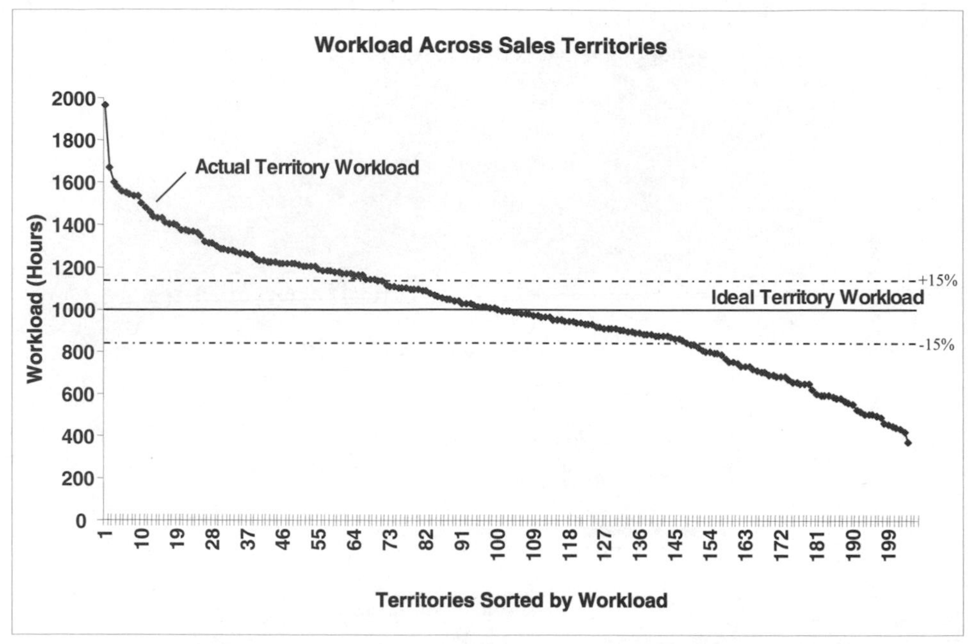


survey, when men were asked if they thought that they were "above average" athletically, 96 percent responded that they were indeed above average. What is more startling, 80 percent thought that they were in the top 25 percent of all men athletically. It should be clear from this study that a sales force survey would not provide reliable data to answer this question.

It is also clear that there are "people" differences across selling organizations. Just as some athletic teams and coaches are very talented while others are mediocre, some sales forces have talented salespeople with exceptional managers while others are mediocre. Tests are one of the best ways to assess salespeople; they can be used to monitor the knowledge and skill levels of the sales force. Turnover is a good measure of motivation. The first-level sales manager is a critical component

**Figure 2-12.** Some of the Sales Productivity Driver Measurement Possibilities.

| | *Competency* | *Impact* |
|---|---|---|
| Quantitative Data | Health checks | Correlation analysis |
| Qualitative Data | Competency/impact questionnaires<br>Workshops, days in the field with salespeople, interviews | |

in the evaluation process. He or she needs to know whether his or her direct reports are motivated and have the skills and competencies they need if they are to succeed. Regrettably, many companies have too many weak sales managers.

Sales managers also need to be assessed. How often do companies assess their sales management teams? Not very frequently. Usually companies rely on sales results to evaluate sales management. It is valuable to determine how managers contribute to salesperson growth, culture formation, and customer satisfaction. Peer and subordinate reviews (sometimes called 360-degree reviews) are a good measurement tool for this purpose. The most progressive selling organizations use them.

The culture is the genes of the organization. It is the unwritten rules that guide the behavior of the firm's salespeople and sales managers as they encounter familiar or new situations. A culture consists of norms, values, and actions that help an organization do its work effectively. There are as many sales force cultures as there are selling organizations. Some are empowering; others are controlling. Some are focused on short-term results; others are focused on long-term results. Companies with different cultures can succeed in the same industry. The pharmaceutical industry has more than 100 global competitors with selling organizations. Their sales force cultures differ across companies and across countries. Some are "homespun" and 100 percent salary. Others are aggressive and have highly leveraged compensation plans. In spite of these cultural differences, many selling organizations have been successful in this industry.

However, although different selling cultures can coexist in the same industry, it is likely that in a given industry, some cultures will be more successful than others. The marketplace and the competitive environment strongly influence the cultures that survive. It is hard to envision a "salary-only" life insurance sales culture, for example.

A culture check can be employed to measure a culture. The culture check attempts to discern the norms, values, and work style of the selling organization. Potential modules of a culture check are listed in Figure 2-13. A complete discussion of sales force cultures appears in Chapter 15.

## Measuring Activity

Salespeople are expected to do the right things in order to get the sale. Depending on the industry they are in, they influence customers and

**Figure 2-13.** Potential Modules for a Sales Force Culture Check.

**A Sales Force Culture Check**

- A choice survey—salespeople and sales managers describe their value and work-style choices. Salespeople and sales managers articulate what they believe to be the organization's unwritten rules.
- Sales force productivity driver study—study sales force productivity driver decisions for culture clues.
- Study culture statements made by management. Observe the level of consistency between what management says and what it does.
- Study the reward systems. Management rewards essential values and workstyles.
- Listen to the stories. Who are the heroes? What are the legends?
- Study the communication style.

prospects in a variety of ways. They generate leads and call on customers or prospects, by phone or in person. They bid on business, write proposals and letters, take orders and service customers, demonstrate their products or leave selling aids; they may even work with customers to integrate their products into the customers' products and processes. They target accounts and call on the appropriate individuals in a customer's organization. Sales force activity can be tracked to see if the sales force is doing the "right stuff."

Measurement of sales activity is a hotly debated topic. Some sales managers like to know (and even control) what the field force does. These managers usually design detailed call reporting systems and have salespeople fill out activity reports stating what the salesperson has accomplished during each reporting period on a regular basis. Companies that implement call reporting systems have an immediate record of the sales force's activity.

In contrast, some sales managers believe that the sales force should be completely empowered. They feel that the sales force needs to drive sales results and that measuring its activities is a distraction. However, valuable activity measures can be obtained even in the totally self-managed selling organization. Sales force activity questionnaires can be administered without much intrusion. Figure 2-14 provides the results of an activity survey administered to a newspaper advertising sales force. Notice the large proportion of time devoted to nonselling activities.

Sales activity measures do have drawbacks. The most important is the assumptions about what causes sales success. Which particular sales force activity causes sales to occur? Are high call frequencies effective? Is account development more important than account mainte-

**Figure 2-14.** Quick Check: Salesperson Selling Time.

| *Type of Activity* | | *Activity* | *Percent of Time* |
|---|---|---|---|
| Selling | 34.6% | 1. Active selling to advertisers (face-to-face/phone) | 22.8% |
| | | 2. Active selling to nonadvertisers (face-to-face/phone) | 10.7% |
| | | 3. Entertaining advertisers and nonadvertisers | 1.1% |
| Servicing | 40.8% | 4. Developing presentations and proposals | 4.6% |
| | | 5. Account planning | 4.4% |
| | | 6. Account maintenance and customer service | 8.5% |
| | | 7. Insertion orders | 8.4% |
| | | 8. Creative and layout work | 4.9% |
| | | 9. Dealing with production problems | 4.0% |
| | | 10. Dealing with credit, billing, and collection problems | 6.0% |
| Administration | 16.8% | 11. Meetings | 3.0% |
| | | 12. Paperwork and administration | 7.6% |
| | | 13. Training | 2.0% |
| | | 14. Travel (to/from accounts) | 4.2% |
| Other | 7.8% | 15. Other | 7.8% |
| Total | | | 100.0% |

nance? The activities that are easy to count and measure may not be the ones with the biggest impact on sales. A simple call count gives no indication of the quality and effectiveness of the sales presentation. One really good presentation is better than ten half-hearted ones. Also, most activity measures are self-reported and therefore subject to the vagaries of human memory and honesty. Did a sales representative really mention a particular product during a particular sales call? Even the salesperson may not know for sure. Moreover, a company may require specific call frequencies for certain customers and prospects. A salesperson who knows that a prescribed frequency isn't right for a particular account will call on that account with the prescribed frequency anyway if he or she knows that the call frequency will show up on a report. Most organizations manage to overcome these drawbacks. The activities that are most important to sales success are determined by studying the best salespeople. A culture of professionalism and honesty with good communication between the field and management keeps activity goals meaningful and reports accurate.

### Measuring Customer Results

Customer results are a good measure of sales force success. Through successful interaction with customers, the sales force creates customer solutions, customer satisfaction, and sustainable profitable relationships. Customer retention rates, repeat rates, loss ratios, penetration, message memorability, and complaints have been used to evaluate customer relationships. The following example demonstrates an innovative approach to measuring customer results that is customer-initiated. The major accounts of an industrial manufacturer scored all of their suppliers (including those selling entirely different products from the manufacturer's) on a scale of 0 to 100 and shared these statistics with the manufacturer. These customer scores were aggregated across all of the manufacturer's major accounts, and the manufacturer used the average of the scores as a measure of customer satisfaction.

Customer results measures tend to be industry- and company-specific. Some customer measures can be out of date because improved results take time to show up. Customer satisfaction is a more immediate measure and one that is popular among U.S. companies. Surveys are one way to measure customer satisfaction. It is important to write a survey that explicitly extracts the impact that the sales force has on customer satisfaction. Frequently, customers think of products and pricing when they reflect on their satisfaction. When designed and administered properly, customer satisfaction surveys determine if a sales force is adding value for its customers.

Figure 2-15 presents the various levels of customer interaction

**Figure 2-15.** A Customer Interaction Flow.

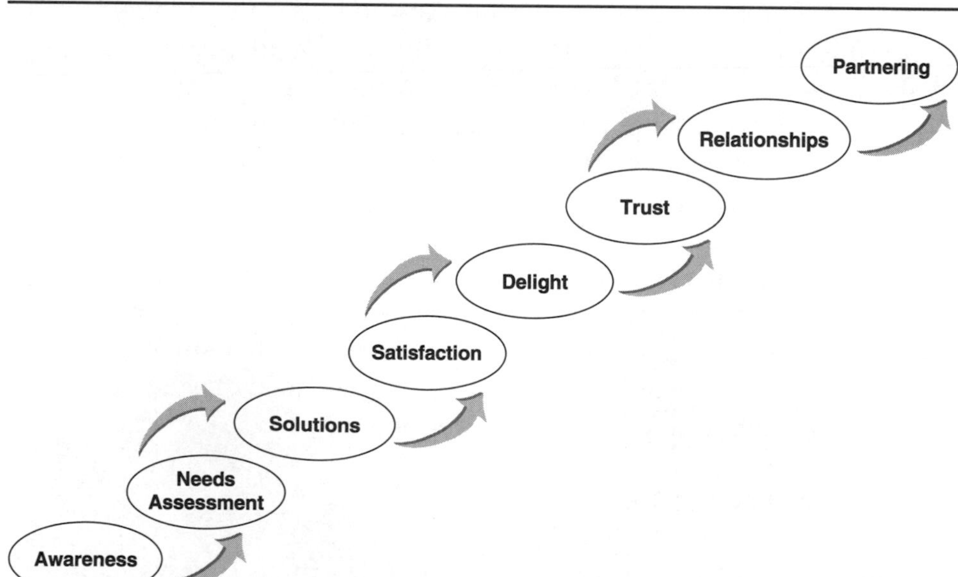

flows. Adapting these levels to any specific sales force situation guides customer measurement.

The basic level is a sale—a solution to the customer's problem. Customer satisfaction comes from a solution—a filled need. Delighted customers are hard to lose, and relationships form when steady customers buy at profitable prices and intend to be customers in the future. Partnering involves more in-depth steps of data sharing and business integration. Survey results can be obtained for any of these levels. Two examples appear in Figure 2-16.

The average customer satisfaction score for the entire sales force and the distribution of satisfaction scores can be obtained from the ratings of the individual salespeople. The information collected in the second survey in Figure 2-16 is beneficial because it also provides a measure of how competitors' sales forces are performing.

### Measuring Company Results

Sales and profits are important corporate metrics. Top management is evaluated in terms of its success relative to these measures. Most companies understand that the sales force is a significant contributor to the achievement of corporate objectives. Consequently, any sales force assessment process must include measures of company results.

Sales and profits are the measures used most frequently to assess the financial achievement of a selling organization. These measures can be expressed in four ways. They can be stated in absolute levels: Sales are $500 million. They can be conveyed as a percentage of goal attainment: Sales were 10 percent above expectations. They can be expressed relative to the prior year's performance: Sales grew 30 percent over last year. Finally, they can be compared to the competition: Market share is 22 percent. Corporate strategy dictates which perspective is most important and should be used to influence sales force behavior. On occasion, sales is not the best measure of sales force performance. For example, if sales lag orders, it is better to track results as soon as orders are written, rather than when the accounting department records the transaction.

However, it is important to stress that the sales force is not the only contributor to the development of sales. There are many other influences. Statistical studies conducted by the authors with several hundred selling organizations suggest that the one-year impact of the sales force on sales at the territory level is anywhere from 20 to 90 percent, depending on the industry. For example, if a salesperson has a

**Figure 2-16.** Two Examples of Customer Satisfaction Surveys.

Example 1:
How would you assess your interaction with John Smith?
Please rate the following statements from 1 to 7.

| | Strongly disagree | | | Neither agree nor disagree | | | Strongly agree |
|---|---|---|---|---|---|---|---|
| | 1 | 2 | 3 | 4 | 5 | 6 | 7 |
| **He presents himself in a professional manner.** | | | | | | | |
| **He understands my needs.** | | | | | | | |
| **He knows his products well.** | | | | | | | |
| **I trust him.** | | | | | | | |
| **We have established a mutually beneficial relationship.** | | | | | | | |

Example 2:
Rank-order the salespeople from each of the four companies in order of their abilities on each of the following dimensions.

| Best = 1<br>Worst = 4 | ABC | **US** | MNO | XYZ |
|---|---|---|---|---|
| **Professionalism** | | | | |
| **Understanding of my needs** | | | | |
| **Product knowledge** | | | | |
| **Trust creation** | | | | |
| **Development of a mutually beneficial relationship** | | | | |

**Figure 2-17.** Determinants of Company Sales, Profits, and Market Share.

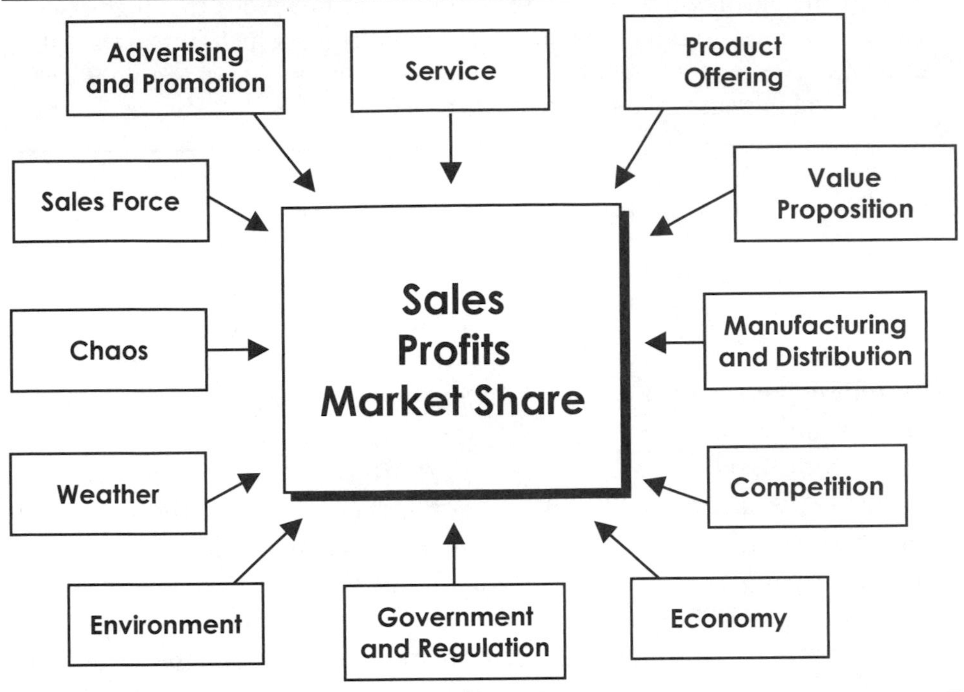


$1 million territory, that salesperson's efforts are creating only between $200,000 and $900,000 of territory sales for that year. The rest is due to the cumulative product/service strength (sales carryover from prior years' activity) and the other factors shown in Figure 2-17.

A sales force assessment that looks only at company results may easily overstate or understate the effectiveness of the sales force. The major reasons for a good or poor year may have nothing to do with the sales force.

---

Measurement Spotlight: Sales per Person

Be careful when using only a single measure of sales force productivity.

Sales per salesperson is an example of a common productivity measure that combines results with activity measures to make an insightful ratio. Average sales per call is another common performance measure designed this way. Unfortunately, these types of productivity measures often make for good reading, but not for good management.

One may think that if sales per person are up, then productivity is up, but this ratio has a denominator as well as a numerator. A company can achieve tremendous sales per person if it fires all of the salespeople except one. Smart businesspeople disagree with the intuitive idea that high sales per person is good. If incremental sales per person are higher than the full cost of a salesperson, then adding salespeople both lowers the sales per person and increases the profits of the firm.

---

### Multiple Measures: Better than a Single Measure

Sales forces are complex organizations. It is impossible for a single measure to summarize their complexity. The five dimensions of the sales force productivity framework provide a conceptual framework and a comprehensive set of measures to capture the essential aspects of any selling organization.

Some dimensions are more important than others because they provide better insight into the true productivity of a selling organization. At the same time, some dimensions permit more reliable measures. Company results and call reporting data are two examples of reliable measures. However, qualitative measures such as those used for the measurement of people and culture and several of the sales force productivity drivers are also critical for a complete understanding of the sales force.

Figure 2-18 provides a rough gauge of the five dimensions of the sales force productivity framework in terms of measure importance and measure reliability. The final set of measures used in any sales force assessment process must balance the importance of the measures with their reliability.

The importance of the five sales force assessment dimensions parallels the order in which they appear in the sales force productivity framework. The sales force productivity drivers are the root of sales force productivity. Implementation of best practices for the drivers affects all of the other dimensions favorably. Recall that company results measures are affected by many variables in addition to the sales force.

Measure reliability increases as more accurate quantitative data become available. This is usually the case as one moves from left to right in the productivity framework.

## Sales Force Strategy: A Comprehensive Statement

A comprehensive statement of sales force strategy has three sections. The first section contains an assessment of the current sales force, the

**Figure 2-18.** Measure Importance and Measure Reliability for the Five Sales Force Assessment Dimensions.

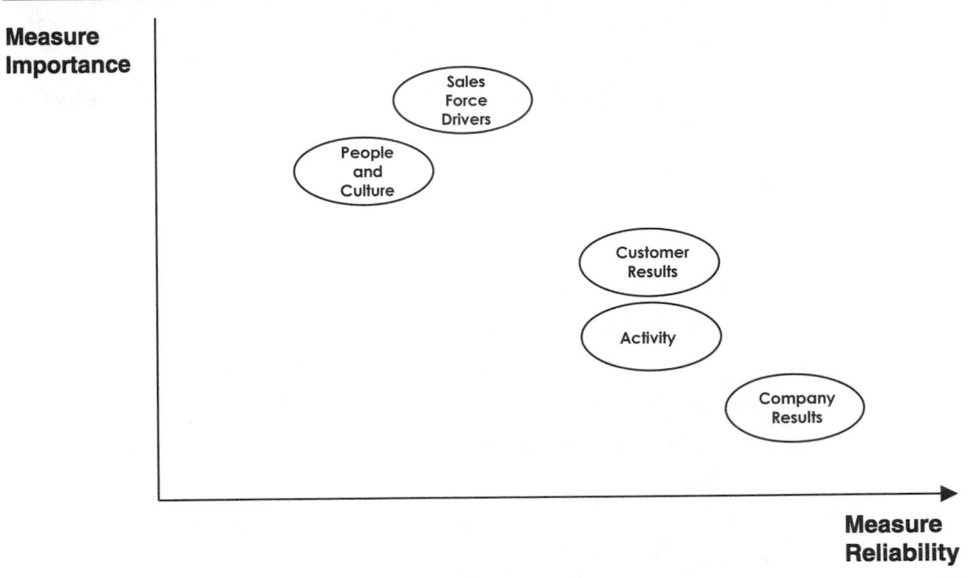


second provides a list of the goals and objectives the sales force would like to achieve in both the short and the long term, and the final section provides the changes that need to be made to the sales force productivity drivers to attain the stated goals and objectives.

## Section 1: The Sales Force Dashboard—An Assessment of the Current Sales Force

The five sales force components introduced earlier in this chapter provide practical dimensions for measurement and assessment. The measures can be presented on a sales force dashboard. Measuring all five components is too time-consuming and expensive for companies that are just beginning to engage in a comprehensive sales force assessment. Repeated measurement is considerably easier for sales forces that are already capturing the data. Figure 2-18 assesses the value of each component when only some of the components are measured. The assessment should focus on the most important sales force productivity dimensions.

## Section 2: Sales Force Goals and Objectives

The sales force assessment reveals sales force strengths, weaknesses, and opportunities. Opportunity gaps are the basis for the goals and objectives of a new sales force strategy. Viable goals can be stated in terms of all five sales force components. Several examples are presented in Figure 2-19.

## Section 3: Initiatives to Enhance the Sales Force Productivity Drivers

The sales force assessment process identifies problem areas. For example, the assessment may show that the company is not generating enough new business or that the sales force is not spending enough time selling. The ultimate solution to these problems resides in the sales force productivity drivers. Unfortunately, the best correction is not always obvious. For example, the problem of not generating enough new business can be addressed in several ways: The recruiting process can be changed to look for more assertive and enterprising people, sales-

**Figure 2-19.** Examples of Sales Force Strategy Goals and Objectives.

| *Sales Force Component* | *Examples of Goals and Objectives* |
|---|---|
| Sales force productivity drivers | • Revitalize the hiring process to expand the applicant pool using the Internet<br>• Upgrade the sales force automation system to incorporate new software options |
| People and culture | • Increase technological sophistication of the sales force so that salespeople are equipped for e-commerce<br>• Emphasize customer empathy, customer solutions, and customer service as cultural values |
| Activity | • Increase frequency of calls to high-volume customers by 25%<br>• Decrease overnights by 10%<br>• Reduce administrative time by 15%<br>• Spend more time with end users and less time with distributors |
| Customer results | • Achieve an overall customer satisfaction rating of 4.5 (out of 5.0)<br>• Reduce lost sales by 10% |
| Company results | • Increase sales by 15%, profitability by 20%<br>• Achieve next year's sales target<br>• Increase market share to 25% |

people can be trained to "hunt" more effectively, a well-crafted incentive program can be created to encourage salespeople to develop new accounts, or the sales force can be reorganized into "hunting" and "farming" teams.

An analysis may be required in order to determine which sales force productivity drivers address the problem areas that surface during a sales force assessment. However, there is a natural hierarchical sequence to follow if a sales force change is anticipated. Some productivity driver decisions naturally precede others. Sales force productivity driver decisions fall into two categories; they are the level 2 and level 3 decisions in Figure 2-20.

The level 1 decisions shown in Figure 2-20 are top management decisions that are typically handed down to the sales force. They are not within the sales force's control. The sales force does, however, have control over the level 2 and level 3 decisions. Level 2 decisions need to be consistent with level 1 strategies. If the sales force is undergoing change, it is best to articulate the corporate and go-to-market strategies before finalizing the customer attraction and retention process, the size

**Figure 2-20.** The Natural Sales Force Decision Sequence.

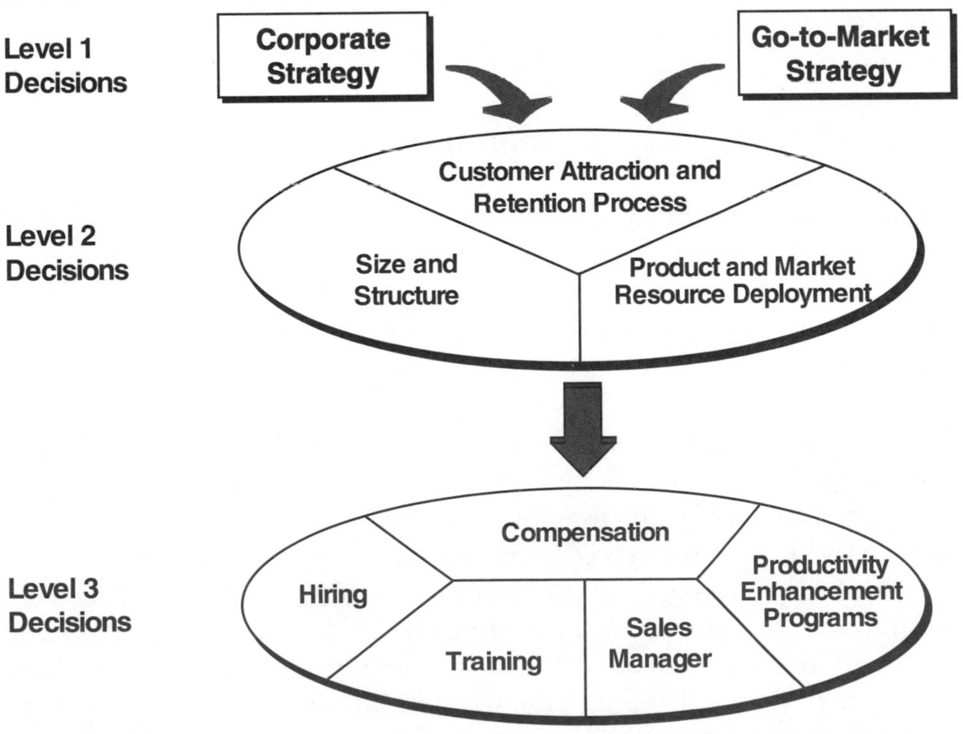

and structure of the selling organization, and the best allocation of sales force effort across the company's products and markets. Chapter 1 discussed how to determine the sales force's role in the company's go-to-market strategy.

Similarly, level 2 decisions need to precede level 3 decisions. As an illustration, if a major compensation overhaul is implemented, and then the sales force is reorganized to create a new team-selling environment, the compensation plan will have to be revised again after the reorganization. It is best to accelerate the reorganization or postpone the compensation overhaul so that a single compensation change is implemented. In addition, the recruiting profile, training requirements, and sales information systems may need to be updated because of the new team-selling environment.

The sales force productivity driver decisions in the sales force strategy must be in alignment, and they must be consistent. Inconsistent choices are difficult to implement effectively. For example, implementing a hiring process to find assertive, enterprising, and highly motivated people will be difficult if the compensation plan is a straight salary plan that pays at the median of the industry. Similarly, a straight commission plan paying from the first dollar combined with sales territories that are not balanced will never yield a pay-for-performance culture. Before finalizing the strategy, a consistency check is worth the effort.

## Summary

A sales force assessment identifies areas that need improvement. The sales force productivity drivers are the place to look for the appropriate changes, which are not always unique or obvious. The sales force driver hierarchy suggests that there is a dependency relationship among the sales force productivity decisions—that is, certain decisions need to precede others. However, one thing is clear: If the productivity driver decisions are made successfully, the sales force will be successful. The remaining chapters of this book present practice-based sales force insights that are useful for making wiser productivity driver decisions. Each of these areas is covered in a separate chapter in this book.

Sales force strategy cannot be static. Good sales force productivity cannot be achieved once and kept forever. Productivity fluctuates over time, and market, competitive, and other environmental changes affect the productivity of a selling organization. Markets shift as customers consolidate their buying processes and become more sophisticated.

New products, frequently inspired by new technologies, make existing selling approaches obsolete. Boundaryless supplier relationships require a revision of the traditional approach to selling. Companies look to their sales forces for productivity gains when they attempt to increase profitability through cost reduction programs. Alternative ways to go to market, such as the Internet, telemarketing, direct mail, part-time selling organizations, and rental selling organizations, are explored. Sales forces must also be mindful of competitive actions. They need to constantly adapt to competitive marketing strategies, product launches, and pricing changes. Finally, federal and local governments have an impact on markets and their sales forces. Even regulated utilities are reengineering their sales forces for the first time in decades because of imminent deregulation.

The successful selling organization is an evaluative organization—it is paranoid. "Only the paranoid survive," suggests Andrew Grove of Intel. The successful selling organization evaluates constantly, whether markets are changing dramatically or just simmering, and develops strategies accordingly.

Chapter 3

# Sizing the Sales Force for Strategic Advantage

This chapter discusses sales force size. A properly sized selling organization assures that customers and prospects receive appropriate coverage, company products get proper representation, the sales force is stretched but not overworked, and the company makes an appropriate investment in its sales resource.

The chapter is designed to help you:

- Understand the impact that sales force size has on sales, costs, and profits in both the short and the long term.
- Recognize the symptoms of a sales force that is not sized and/or structured appropriately.
- Get practical advice for sizing a sales force in different situations, such as expansion into new markets, new product launches, downsizing, and technological change.
- Understand five different methods that companies use to size their sales forces, and learn which of these methods are most appropriate in a given situation; specific examples that demonstrate how to implement each method are provided.

## Sales Force Size and Structure—Crucial Decisions

How can you determine if your sales force is sized correctly and structured properly?

Your sales force may be undersized if you are experiencing some of the following situations. Key customers wonder where your sales representative is. Your salespeople do not have enough time to take orders, let alone determine how customer needs might be changing or provide solutions to these needs. Current customers feel neglected and are considering switching suppliers. New business development is down. Your salespeople feel overworked; their territory goals seem like a considerable stretch. A number of your salespeople are circulating their résumés. However, company costs seem to be under control, and the company should still make its top-line results because of the increased efforts of the sales force.

On the other hand, your sales force may be too large if you can relate to some of the following descriptions. Your favorite customers are asking, "Didn't I just see you?" Overall, your customers seem to be getting plenty of attention. In fact, some of them are wondering about the size of your margins because your cost of sales must be quite high. Your salespeople have considerable free time and don't seem to be sufficiently stimulated. The financial staff has observed that the company's cost of sales is out of line with industry norms; perhaps you have even missed your profit objectives for several quarters.

Finally, your sales force may not be structured appropriately if you observe the following. Your customers complain that your sales force doesn't know its products well enough and doesn't understand their business very well. They are concerned that their needs are not being met. Your salespeople feel uncomfortable; their customers and competitors know more than they do. They feel ill-equipped to do their jobs. Alternatively, they may not be getting access to the decision makers; no one is "walking the carpeted floors." Product managers are not achieving their product growth and market penetration objectives.

A correctly structured sales force ensures that the appropriate selling process, whether individual or team, is implemented for every targeted market segment. It ensures that the selling and maintenance effort is as effective as possible while utilizing the selling resources most efficiently. A properly designed selling organization directs the company's selling effort appropriately across its product line and against its target markets.

With a properly sized selling organization, customers and prospects receive appropriate coverage, company products get proper representation, the sales force is stretched but not overworked, and the company is making an appropriate investment in its sales resource.

This chapter discusses sales force size, and Chapter 4 discusses sales force structure. Top management is justifiably concerned about the sales force size and structure decisions because these decisions directly affect company profitability. Sales force investment increases with the size of the sales force and the complexity of the sales force organization. Since cost containment and productivity enhancement are common organizational goals, top management finds size and structure decisions to be highly salient. At the same time, individual salespeople are also directly affected by these decisions. Sales force size and structure decisions dictate whom every salesperson calls on, what skill and knowledge are required, who is on the selling team, who each salesperson's manager is, and what each salesperson's overall income opportunity is. Size and structure decisions affect the entire sales organization.

This chapter has two sections. First, we present practical sales force design observations and insights. This discussion includes commentary on both sales force size and structure. In the second section of this chapter, we develop alternative approaches for sizing sales forces. Alternative approaches for structuring the sales force are presented in Chapter 4.

## Ten Insights for Better Sales Force Design

Acknowledging sales force and market dynamics helps management make better sales force design decisions. We have conducted several hundred sales force size and structure studies across various industries and in many countries. The following insights are based on the outcomes of these studies.

### Sales Force Effort Drives Sales

*The sales force creates sales.* Sales force effort has a dual impact. First, the sales force generates sales in the short term. In other words, *sales force effort this year results in sales this year.* Additionally, effort this year has a long-term impact. *There are residual, or carryover, sales in subsequent years that can be attributed to our sales force effort this year.*

The short-term impact is easily seen when territory-level data are analyzed. The graph in Figure 3-1 demonstrates the relationship between territory-level call effort and territory-level sales for one of several different products sold by a sales force. In this case, each salesperson determined individually how much time to spend on each product in the product line.

**Figure 3-1.** The Relationship Between Territory-Level Call Effort and Sales.

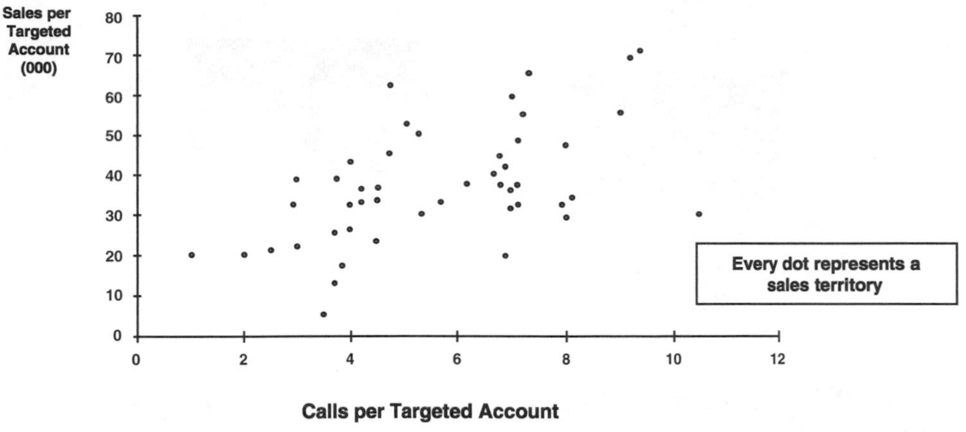


Some salespeople spent a lot of time on this product, while others allocated less time to it. Notice that high levels of selling effort generated more sales than lower levels of selling effort. In general, anywhere from 20 to 90 percent of the annual sales in any one sales territory is the result of the salesperson's effort in that year.

Extrapolating the result shown in the graph in Figure 3-1 suggests that larger sales forces have incrementally higher sales than smaller sales forces. Adding salespeople adds incremental sales for the company, and downsizing the selling organization produces lower sales.

## Carryover Exists

The territory-level graph in Figure 3-1 also shows a long-term impact. Observe that territory-level sales are expected to be nonzero when sales force effort is removed. In fact, in a few, rare instances, we have seen vacant territories lead their regions.

Where do these sales come from when sales force effort is eliminated? They are the result of customer relationships established through prior selling effort. Figure 3-2 shows how sales in any one year can be attributed to selling effort in prior years.

*Some selling environments are conducive to high short-term impact, while others have significant carryover.* For example, consider two product categories in the pharmaceutical industry: acute-care products and chronic-care products. Acute-care products, such as antibiotics and antihistamines, typically have high short-term impact and low carryover, because patients usually take these medications for a short pe-

**Figure 3-2.** An Illustration of Carryover.

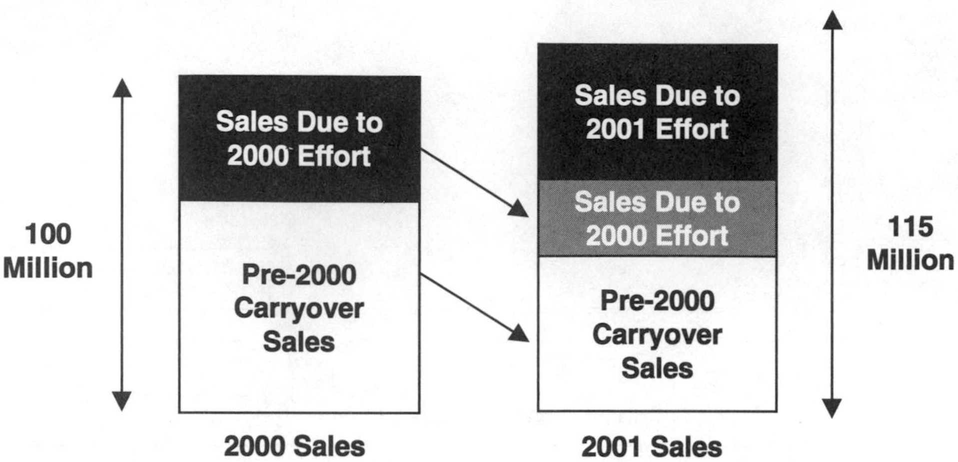


riod of time. Salespeople can often persuade physicians to try a new acute-care medication for their patients, particularly when the medication has very little risk associated with it. On the other hand, chronic-care products, such as a high-blood-pressure medication or a treatment for Alzheimer's disease, typically have lower short-term impact and high carryover. This is because once patients start on one of these medications, they are likely to stay on the medication for a long time. If the medication is effective, the physician is reluctant to switch the patient to a new medication, since there is typically some risk involved.

Figure 3-3 compares some of the conditions leading to high levels of short-term impact and high levels of carryover.

The following example demonstrates the long-term and short-term dynamics of the effect of sales force size on company sales. Consider a company with 100 salespeople who are forecast to sell $125 million this year. The average sales per salesperson is $1,250,000. This company is experiencing growth in its existing product lines and is anticipating several new product launches over the next two years. Figure 3-4 shows a reasonable three-year forecast.

The company has instituted several productivity enhancement programs and is considering reducing the sales force size to lower its personnel costs. It would like to lower its sales force size to 90 at the end of this year.

Given our assertion that sales force effort drives sales, Figure 3-5 provides an estimate of what is likely to happen incrementally if the company reduces its sales force next year.

**Figure 3-3.** Conditions That Affect Short-Term Impact and Carryover.

| *High Short-Term Impact and Low Carryover* | *Low Short-Term Impact and High Carryover* |
|---|---|
| Low switching costs | High switching costs |
| High levels of new incremental business | Low levels of new incremental business |
| Many new customers/small purchase volumes/short selling cycles | Few new customers/large purchase volumes/long selling cycles |
| No maintenance or service activity | High levels of maintenance or service activity |
| New products | Mature products |
| High levels of competitive noise | Low levels of competitive noise |
| Growing market | Flat or declining market |
| Products similar or nearly identical to competitors' products | Highly differentiated products |
| Weak brand and/or company loyalty or new brand and/or company | Strong brand and/or company loyalty |
| Sales force is the only promotion vehicle | Many promotion vehicles in addition to the sales force |

**Figure 3-4.** Three-Year Forecast with 100 Salespeople.

| | *Sales Force Size* | *Sales* | *% Increase vs. Last Year* |
|---|---|---|---|
| This year | 100 | $125 million | — |
| Next year | 100 | $150 million | 20% |
| Year after | 100 | $190 million | 27% |

**Figure 3-5.** Three-Year Forecast with 90 Salespeople.

| | *Sales Force Size* | *Sales* | *% Increase vs. Last Year* |
|---|---|---|---|
| This year | 100 | $125 million | — |
| Next year | 90 | $145 million | 16% |
| Year after | 90 | $175 million | 21% |

Notice that *the total incremental impact of a size change is not immediate*—it increases over time. Sales are just $5 million lower next year with the smaller sales force, but the gap grows to $15 million the year after. Also notice that sales next year increased by 16 percent over sales this year in spite of the reduction in the field force. This could lead to a sense of satisfaction and achievement, and also to the faulty conclusion that the sales force had been too large.

We have frequently heard the following argument: "We cut our sales force last year and sales went up. Therefore. . . ." This argument is easy to make, since it is impossible to know precisely what would have happened had we maintained the 100 salespeople. However, be assured that sales with 100 salespeople are going to be greater than sales with 90. The real question is, how much greater? Is it profitable to keep the extra 10 salespeople? In our example, the incremental $5 million in sales marginally pays for the extra salespeople next year, but the incremental $15 million in the subsequent year certainly pays for the additional head count and generates significant incremental profit.

## Sales Force Reduction Should Not Be Used to Justify Productivity Enhancement

Frequently, as in the example above, companies use productivity enhancement programs such as automation, targeting, time management, and more effective selling protocols to justify sales force reductions. A typical argument is: "Our productivity program will increase our sales force productivity by 10 percent. Therefore, our sales force can be reduced from 100 to 90. This head count reduction will actually pay for the program."

However, it is likely that the productivity enhancement program reduces the firm's selling costs. With a lower cost per call, the company can call profitably on more accounts and prospects. Calling directly on customers for whom a call was previously too expensive is now profitable. Hence, expanding the sales force upon the implementation of a productivity initiative may actually increase profitability.

*Sales force sizing and productivity enhancement are independent decisions and activities.* Sales force productivity should be increased regardless of the sales force size. Sales force reduction should not be used as a justification for productivity enhancement. Any sizing decision should assume that the sales force will be as productive as possible.

## The Sales Force Sizing Decision Affects Company Profitability

As we stated earlier, the sales force creates sales. The company's sales are dependent upon the size of its sales force, and so are its costs. Hence, sales force sizing affects company profitability.

A division president told us that he sized his sales force for profitability. When we asked how, he responded that he maintained his sales force costs at 14 percent of sales. Hence, profits were always maximized. Many corporations, like this president's division, use financial approaches such as the "ratio maintenance" approach or the "affordable" approach to size their selling organizations. They feel that they can manage their profits by using these approaches. However, these are cost containment approaches. Cost containment is not the same as profit maximization.

We continue with our example to illustrate the difference between cost containment and profit maximization. We will alter our original discussion slightly. Assume now that the company has decided to downsize to 90 salespeople for next year, with a sales projection of $145 million. Then:

- The sales force will generate a little over $1.6 million per territory ($145 million divided by 90 salespeople).
- Assume that fully loaded sales force costs will be $225,000 per territory, which represents a sales force cost ratio of about 14 percent. (Fully loaded sales force costs include salary, benefits, taxes, bonuses, car, travel, call reporting, administrative support, and field support.)

Suppose another salesperson is added, for a sales force of 91. To maintain the 14 percent ratio, the additional person must generate an incremental $1.6 million in sales. This happens only in rapidly growing markets or when the selling organization is woefully undersized. Usually, because of diminishing returns, additional salespeople will not be able to match the company's average sales per territory. In fact, we are forecasting only $5 million in incremental sales with the addition of 10 salespeople in our example. So, the additional head count will raise the sales force cost ratio. A company that is set on maintaining this ratio will increase its field force size only reluctantly.

Continuing the example, suppose our company has a 60 percent gross margin. (Gross margin is defined as 1 minus all variable product costs, i.e., the costs that vary with how much of a product is sold.) Then:

A sales force of 90 people averaging $1,600,000 in sales produces an average of $960,000 in gross margin per territory.

The average gross margin per territory is determined by multiplying $1,600,000 by 60 percent.

The break-even sales per territory is $375,000.

Break-even sales is calculated by dividing fully loaded sales force costs ($225,000) by the gross margin (60 percent).

Average sales per salesperson ($1,600,000) is nearly four and a half times the break-even sales ($375,000) per salesperson.

Ten additional salespeople generating $5,000,000 in incremental sales next year will increase the sales force cost ratio to 15 percent.

The sales force cost ratio is calculated by dividing the cost of the sales force (100 salespeople times the fully loaded cost of $225,000) by $150 million in sales.

At the same time, these additional 10 salespeople will add $750,000 to the bottom line.

Incremental profit is calculated by multiplying incremental sales ($5,000,000) by the gross margin (60 percent) and then subtracting the incremental cost of the additional people ($225,000 times 10).

In the subsequent year, 10 additional salespeople generating $15,000,000 in incremental sales will add $6,750,000 to the bottom line.

As you can see, the sales force sizing decision affects the company's sales, sales force cost ratio, and profitability. These measures (metrics) can be in conflict. Increased profits usually come at the expense of an increased sales force cost ratio. Management often needs to choose between profit maximization and cost containment. The example we have given illustrates the long-term impact of incremental sales force effort. If the long-term impact is acknowledged, larger sales force size and investments are preferred.

There is significant evidence to suggest that companies with a short-term perspective tend to undersize their selling organizations. We studied fifty companies that had analyzed and changed their sales force sizes, sales force structures, and sales effort deployment. Our goal was to assess the impact of alternative strategies on company results. The study, called the ZS Study, included sales forces from the United States and five European countries. Most of the sales forces were in the health care industry. The ZS Study evaluated the impact that sales force size has on company short- and long-term marketing contribution. The results are shown in Figure 3-6.

Each of the fifty sales forces in the study was of a different size. We indexed the strategy that maximized long-term contribution at 100 salespeople for comparability. Notice that across all of these sales forces, the sales force size for the best one-year strategy is approximately 18 percent less than the best long-term sales force size. It is actually between 9 and 27 percent smaller with 95 percent confidence. This confirms that companies with a short-term perspective tend to undersize their selling organizations.

**Figure 3-6.** The ZS Study: A Comparison of the Best Short-Term and Long-Term Sales Force Size.

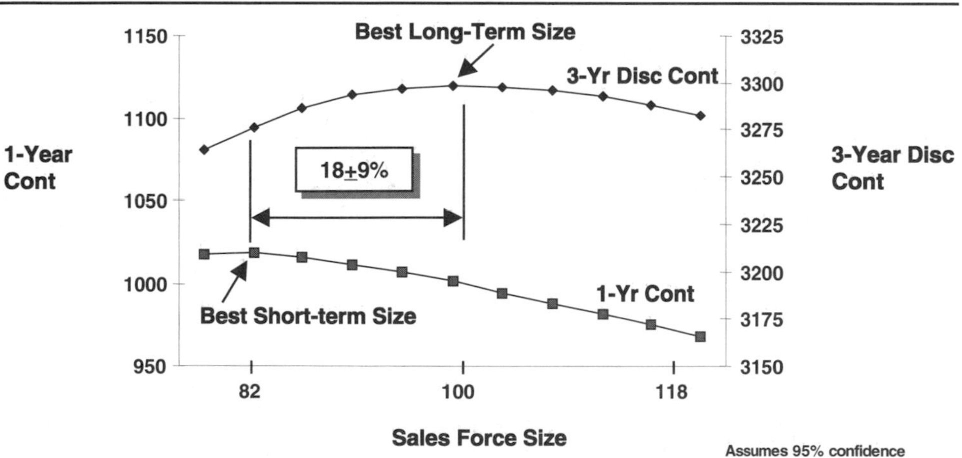


1-Year Cont is the one-year contribution and is defined as:
Net sales less consolidated variable product, less advertising and promotion cost, less field support cost, less sales force cost.

3-Year Disc Cont is the three-year discounted contribution and is defined as:
The present value of the next three years of contribution.

## Phased Growth Is Rarely Optimal

Too frequently, companies launching new products or expanding into new markets increase the field force size when the sales opportunity is *realized,* as opposed to *investing* in the *prospective* opportunity. Hundreds of millions of dollars have been left on the table by companies pursuing this risk-free strategy. Profits are usually maximized if all the required salespeople are hired at once—now. They will be fully trained when they are needed, morale will be higher, and there will be less disruption if they are all hired at once. Since sales force effort has a cumulative effect, the impact of the new salespeople's effort will be accumulating from the day of hire. Figure 3-7 shows three sales force scale-up strategies that were contemplated by a large pharmaceutical firm. A three-year forecast of the sales and profit consequences associated with each strategy is also presented.

The "quick build" strategy realizes sales of $120 million and profits of $50 million more across three years than the "earn-your-way" strategy. Notice, however, that the "earn-your-way" strategy provides $4 million more in year 1 contribution. This is the cost of investing in the future.

## Gradual Downsizing Seldom Works

Gradual downsizing results in significant, ongoing disruption to salesperson-customer relationships; therefore, it is seldom a good strategy. To illustrate the dynamics of a downsizing, consider a metropolitan sales district with six salespeople. The company chose to downsize gradually; it closed one territory immediately and another six months later. Consider the impact on customers and on the four salespeople that remained with the company after the downsizing. When the first territory was closed, the accounts and geography were divided among the three bordering territories. However, these three territories then had more work than the two nonbordering territories, and the company did another realignment to balance the workload across the five territories. When the second territory was closed, the accounts and geography that it had covered were again divided among the three bordering territories. However, the three territories again had more work than the fourth nonbordering territory, so a fourth realignment was needed to create four balanced territories.

The result of continuous realignment can be devastating for a sales organization. Salespeople become frustrated with the constant change

Figure 3-7. The Sales and Profit Consequences of Three Sales Force Scale-Up Strategies.

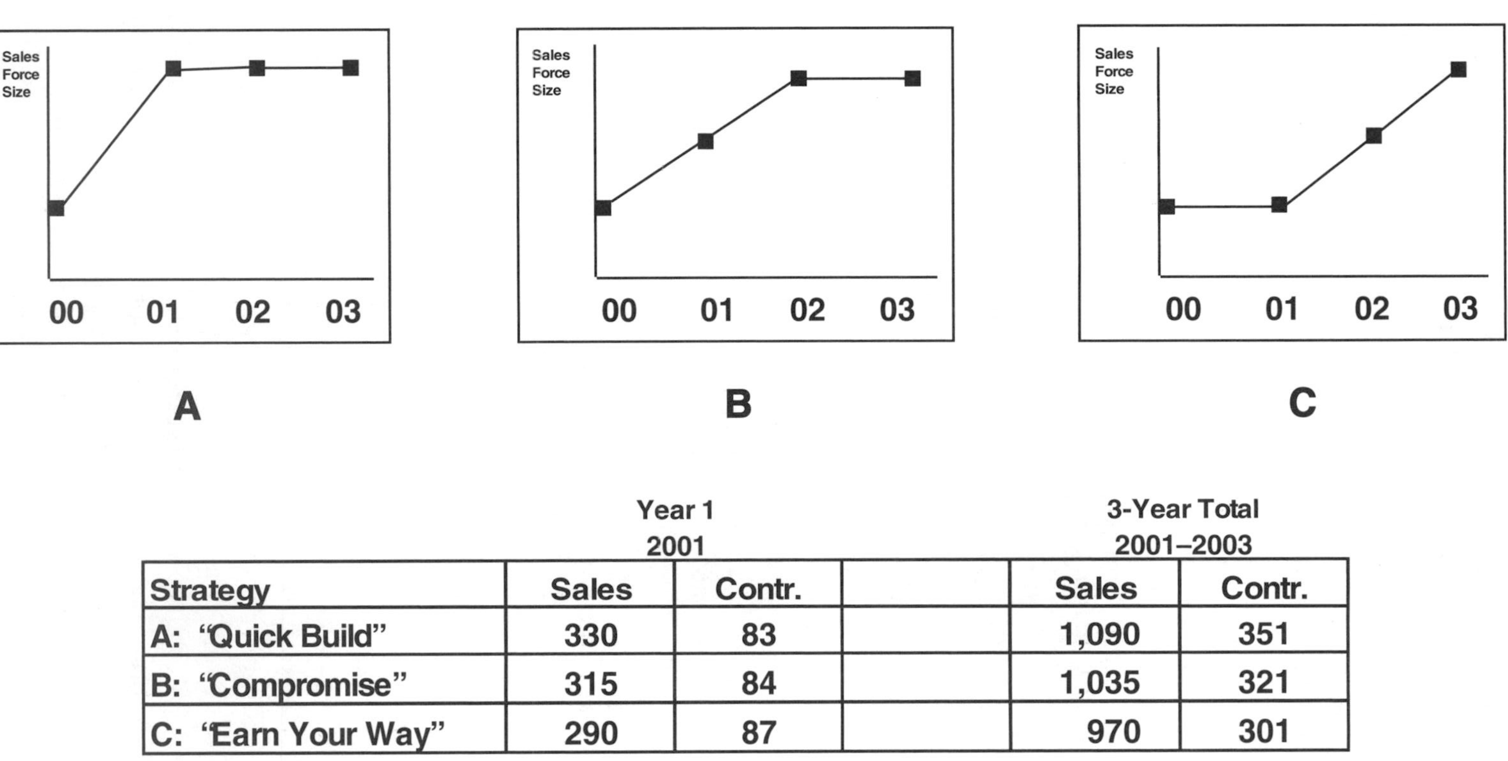


| | Year 1 2001 | | | 3-Year Total 2001–2003 | |
|---|---|---|---|---|---|
| Strategy | Sales | Contr. | | Sales | Contr. |
| A: "Quick Build" | 330 | 83 | | 1,090 | 351 |
| B: "Compromise" | 315 | 84 | | 1,035 | 321 |
| C: "Earn Your Way" | 290 | 87 | | 970 | 301 |

in their assignments, and top performers may leave the company. In addition, there is a significant risk of alienating customers. In this scenario, many customers saw three different salespeople in a period of just over six months. A few customers were even assigned to a new salesperson, only to be reassigned to their original salesperson six months later. The disruption multiplies with each additional phase of downsizing.

If a downsizing is required, do it all at once. Let the survivors know as soon as possible, since these are people you cannot afford to lose. Use sensitivity when informing the salespeople who are victims of the downsizing. A company should help people with career placement if they are being let go. Some of them may go to work for a customer.

### The Sales Force Is a Resource Allocator

The sales force is the "potential energy" of the firm. It is the sum total of all the personal interactions between the firm and its customers. The entire sales force makes daily decisions about whom to call on, what products to sell, and what activities are important. It is a resource allocator. The scope of these allocation decisions is illustrated in Figure 3-8. Marketing and sales managers try to influence the sales force allocation through organizational structure, product/customer marketing programs, goal setting, and incentive compensation.

### Resource Deployment to Customer Segments, Products, and Selling Activities Can Be More Important Than Resource Investment

A vice president of sales and marketing was given a huge sales goal for the coming year. His immediate and natural response was to go to his management to request an increase in sales force size. He knew that he had a better chance of making the goal with a larger sales force. Resizing the sales force is typically the first thing that sales executives think of when they are faced with aggressive sales objectives or declining sales opportunity. They often do not realize that the optimal deployment of the sales force has a bigger impact on sales and profits than optimal sizing. In other words, it is better to work smarter than to work harder. A sales force that allocates its time optimally among different customer segments, products, and selling activities will outperform a larger sales force with an average deployment of sales force effort.

The ZS Study, mentioned earlier, sheds light on the value of an appropriate deployment of sales force effort. The study included an

**Figure 3-8.** Sales Force Allocation Decisions.

**Sales Force Time and Effort**

**Customer Resource Allocation Decisions**

What industry to call on

What volume segments to call on:
- High volume vs. low volume
- National account vs. smaller accounts

What profitability segments to call on: highly profitable vs. less profitable

New vs. existing accounts

High-penetration vs. low-penetration accounts

What geography to focus on

Headquarters vs. field calls

**Production Resource Allocation Decisions**

New vs. existing products

High-volume vs. lower-volume products

Easy-to-sell vs. hard-to-sell products
- Familiar vs. unfamiliar products
- Products with high short-term impact and low carryover vs. products with low short-term impact and high carryover
- High-tech products vs. low-tech products
- Long selling cycle vs. short selling cycle
- Differentiated vs. nondifferentiated
- Highly competitive vs. noncompetitive

**Activity Resource Allocation Decisions**

Hunting vs. farming

Selling vs. servicing

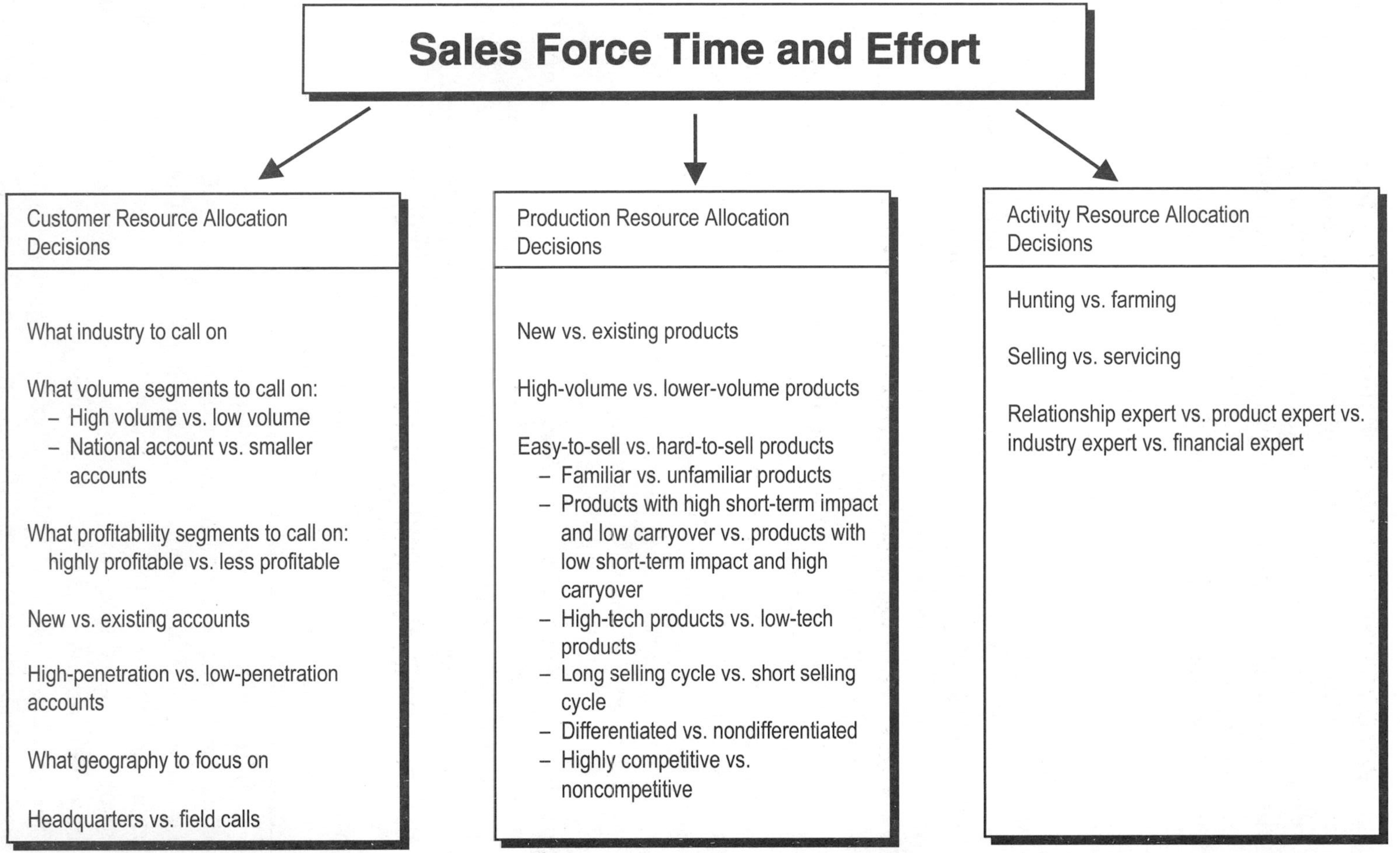

Relationship expert vs. product expert vs. industry expert vs. financial expert

analysis comparing the "current" three-year sales force size and sales resource allocation plan with an "improved" three-year size and sales resource allocation plan for each of the fifty selling organizations in the study. The improved plan increased three-year profitability by 4.5 percent on average across the fifty sales forces. Of this improvement, the change in size accounted for 1.3 percent of the gain, while the improved effort deployment contributed 3.2 percent.

To put it simply, most sales forces do not deploy their resources optimally. Compensation systems can reward short-term sales achievement at the expense of effort allocated to strategic products and markets. Salespeople go to the easy accounts and present products and services with which their comfort level is high. Aggressive product managers get disproportionate effort for their products. The selling organization may not know how responsive its various products and markets are to sales force effort and thus may encourage an inappropriate allocation of effort.

Optimal sales force effort deployment occurs when the incremental return from additional effort on all products and markets is equal and equals the incremental cost of the effort. This complicated rule is much easier to say than it is to accomplish. The analyst needs to measure incremental returns in order to determine the optimal resource deployment. Fortunately, in many industries, this can be done using some historical data and a lot of ingenuity.

Figure 3-9 shows the sales response to sales force effort for five products sold by a U.S. sales force selling medical instruments. Each product graph estimates what the sales will be for each level of sales force time spent on the product. The sales force effort is measured in terms of rep equivalents (REs). One rep equivalent allocated to a product is the same as one full-time salesperson spending all of his or her time selling that product. This is rarely the case for this sales force, since all the salespeople sell the entire product line. Consequently, each product's time allocation is the sum of fractions of REs accumulated across the entire sales force.

The dots on the curves represent the current planned allocation of time across the five products. For example, Product D is scheduled to get 31 REs, Product B will get 9 REs, and so forth. The numbers at the right of Figure 3-9 are the anticipated change in sales if one RE is added to or subtracted from the planned allocation. These numbers can also be called *product elasticities*. Notice that the incremental sales gain from adding one RE to Product C greatly exceeds the incremental sales loss associated with a one-RE reduction for Product B. For most sales

**Figure 3-9.** Sales Response to Sales Force Effort: A Comparision of Five Products.

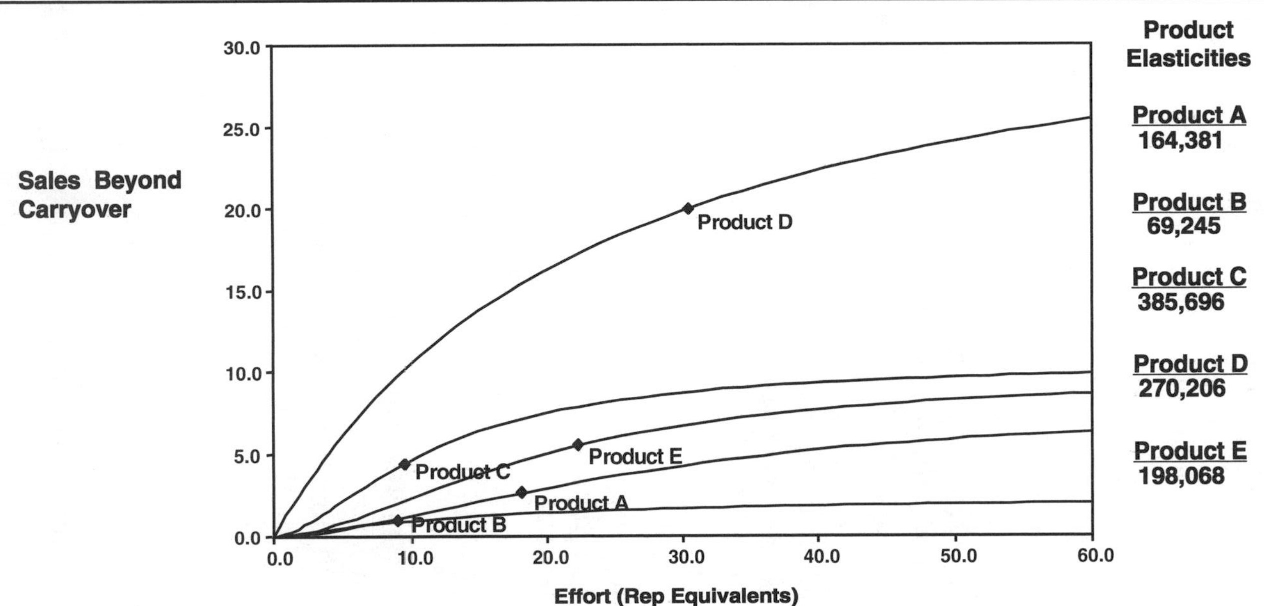

forces, elasticities differ widely across the targeted products and markets. For example, on average, the largest product elasticities were eight times the smallest product elasticities for the fifty selling organizations that participated in the ZS Study. When adjusted for product margins, these differences explain the earlier observation that sales forces, in general, do not deploy their effort optimally.

Based on the ZS Study and other sales force size and structure consulting projects, two resource allocation recommendations can be made. First, *companies with high-volume, highly differentiated products should call on a very large set of customers and prospects, while companies with low-volume products should target selectively.* With strong products, a sales force can afford to call on many customers and prospects. However, with weaker products, there is a lower chance of sales success, and the sales force can afford to call on only a few customers and prospects.

For example, consider a pharmaceutical sales force that sells two cardiovascular drugs. One of the drugs is a new, highly successful therapy that is different from any other drug on the market. The other drug is an older, more conventional therapy that is similar to several other drugs. Both drugs treat the same disease, so they could potentially be prescribed by the same group of doctors. Analysis shows that the sales force can make profitable sales calls to about 150,000 doctors for the new, highly differentiated drug. On the other hand, the best strategy for the older product is to focus on just 20,000 of these doctors, the ones who are most likely to prescribe the drug, and to ignore the rest of the market.

The second resource allocation recommendation emerging from the ZS Study is that *focused strategies dominate scattered strategies.* The familiar 80-20 rule, though seldom literally true, reflects the accurate belief that potential tends to be concentrated. Therefore, strategies that focus sales force effort on the right customers and prospects typically dominate those that spread this effort across all possible customers and prospects. A key consideration in determining sales force size is the degree to which sales are concentrated among customers.

## When Launching New Products, Launch Hard, but Protect Your Strengths

Frequently, companies are faced with launching several new products while at the same time wanting to continue to promote a strong existing product franchise.

A successful new product launch usually demands a sizable investment in selling. The sales force is a fixed resource in the short term, so any selling effort that is allocated to new opportunities must come at the expense of the current products and the existing markets. Strong existing products will suffer if the selling effort is reduced. Assuming that existing products will retain their sales without selling effort is dangerous. Sales may be maintained, but only for a short period. Almost every product will suffer in the long run if its selling effort is cut. New product launches and new market entries can capture as much as 50 to 60 percent of a sales force's selling effort. The allocation to existing products is usually halved. This explains why many existing products fail to make their sales goal.

Our experience suggests that the following strategy dominates: *Launch hard, but protect your strengths.* The only way to accomplish both successfully is by expanding the sales force. However, this strategy has a risk of its own. Specifically, what if the firm needs the expanded selling capability only for a short strategic window? In the worst case, attrition can be used to modulate the sales force size if the capacity is needed for only a short period of time. U.S. sales force turnover rates average about 20 percent. This implies that a firm can manage its new product/service opportunity by increasing the sales force size and then systematically using attrition to bring the field force size back to a steady-state level. Smart attrition management should enable the firm to launch hard, protect its strengths, and increase its profitability. However, it does require planning to ensure that the sales force maintains optimal geographic deployment and that disruption of the customer-salesperson relationship is kept to a minimum.

Outsourcing is another way of managing a temporary need for additional selling resources. Companies can obtain short-term sales force resources by borrowing or renting selling capacity. Other sales divisions or part-time sales forces can help out. Temporary or "rent-a-rep" forces are commonly used to help launch products. Outsourcing has several advantages. First, it turns fixed costs into variable costs that can be cut if necessary once the launch phase is complete. In addition, outsourcing frees up the management time required to recruit, screen, and hire new, permanent salespeople. Thus, management has more time to support product launch activities. Finally, if temporary salespeople are successful, they may want to stay with the company permanently. Thus, temporary salespeople can provide a good pool of potential candidates for permanent positions.

### Company Politics Can Encourage Undersized Sales Forces

Consider the following story: A product manager is asked for a sales forecast to help determine the appropriate level of sales support for a product. After careful analysis, the product manager comes up with a reasonable number. To be conservative, however, the product manager chooses to shave a little off his estimate before reporting it to the vice president of sales. ''After all,'' the product manager reasons, ''I'll look like a hero when sales come in ahead of forecast.''

When the vice president of sales hears the number, she also decides to reduce it before making a promise to the company president. ''I'm assured of looking good because we'll make our number,'' she thinks. Then the company president decides to add a little more ''cushion'' before making a promise to the board of directors. By the time a final number is agreed on, so much cushion has been added that the sales forecast is drastically lower than the product's true potential. Too little sales force support is allocated to the product, and considerable profit opportunity is forgone.

Be aware of the incentives that individuals at different levels of the company have when making product forecasts. Make sure that these incentives do not undermine your attempts to size your selling organization appropriately.

## Finding the Optimal Sales Force Size—Successful and Unsuccessful Methods

Several methods are commonly used for sizing sales forces.

### "Same as Last Year" Method

''We had a sales force of ninety last year and we made our numbers. Next year's goal is a stretch. Why change anything? It is working!'' If this sounds familiar, then you are sizing your sales force using the ''same as last year'' approach. Be aware that this is a decision. Even though you are not changing anything, you are *deciding* that this year's sales force size is best for next year.

In many cases, this may be the best strategy. It minimizes disruption and allows the sales force to maintain existing customer relationships, focus on satisfying customer needs, and achieve territory goals. Furthermore, changing the size of the sales force can be costly. Hiring or severance, training, relocation, and other administrative costs are incurred when size changes.

Alternatively, maintaining last year's size and structure can be a complacent strategy. Business and environmental change can make the current sales force strategy obsolete. Last year's size and structure may be inappropriate if market behavior has changed, if new and different products and services have entered the company's portfolio, or if competitors have implemented successful new selling strategies. Keep in mind that if competitors alter their sales force size, then your share of voice with customers will change unless you alter your size too. In competitive markets, sales may be more a function of your share of voice with customers than of the amount of time you spend with them.

"Fix it before it breaks" is good advice. Many U.S. companies reassess their sales force size and structure about every two to three years.

## Financial Methods

Two financial approaches are used to size sales forces: the affordable approach and the ratio maintenance approach. The affordable approach determines sales force investment by subtracting all variable product costs, fixed administrative costs, and desired profit from a sales revenue estimate. The remainder is what the company can afford to spend on the sales force and marketing. Then, the anticipated marketing expenditure is subtracted to determine the affordable sales force investment.

The ratio approach is similar to the affordable approach in that both methods focus on cost containment. The sales force cost ratio approach specifies the fraction of sales revenue that the firm is willing to invest in the sales force. If the company anticipates revenues of $145 million and the sales force cost ratio is 14 percent, then the company is willing to invest $20.3 million in the sales force. At a cost of $225,000 per territory, this translates into a field force size of ninety.

Many firms incorporate the sales force cost ratio into their sizing decisions. They feel that it is easy to calculate, easy to understand, and easy to use. They think that adhering to this ratio ensures a certain level of profitability. Ratios are established historically. The company tracks past ratios and decides on a ratio that is intuitively appropriate. Ratios vary across industries. They can be as high as 20 percent (educational services, chemicals, and real estate) or as low as 2 percent (petroleum, coal, agriculture, forestry and fishing, and lumber). Frequently companies will look at the ratio for their industry to help them decide on a reasonable ratio for their use.

Regrettably, financial approaches are backward approaches. They base the sales force investment on a sales revenue forecast. If revenues are high, then the company can afford a large field force. If revenues are low, then downsizing is prescribed. Sales determines the sales force investment in these approaches. However, markets operate in precisely the opposite direction: Sales force investment drives company sales. When a sales force of 90 for next year is compared with one of 100, the one with 100 will almost certainly generate higher sales than the one with 90. A decision rule that ignores this concept rarely arrives at a profit-maximizing size for the field force.

Compulsive use of financial approaches can lead to various sales force sizing errors. In certain cases a conservative financial approach is necessary; however, millions (sometimes hundreds of millions) of dollars of sales opportunity are left on the table when "earn-your-way" strategies are used excessively. Blockbuster products are underfunded during launch periods when a constant spending ratio is applied, and the underfunding dampens growth. Low investment levels depress carryover opportunity, sacrifice long-term profitability, and allow competitors to catch up. The management team basks in the success of the new product without realizing the extent of its opportunity loss. To restate an earlier point: Phased growth is rarely optimal.

In addition to lost upside opportunity, adhering to the sales force cost ratio can lead to premature downsizing. If the cost savings is less than the incremental profit decline resulting from the reduction in sales force size, downsizing is unwarranted. Expect that sales will suffer when there is a downsizing, and recall from the earlier example that the break-even on a salesperson can be quite low.

A sales force resource allocation error occurs when sales force cost ratios are applied to products to determine the best allocation of sales resources to those products. Products with high sales can absorb more resources than products with lower sales without exceeding a predetermined ratio. Consequently, products with high sales can obtain a disproportionate amount of sales force resources. Product managers usually do not discourage excessive allocation because their success is determined largely by the revenues their products achieve. Recall an earlier recommendation: Allocate resources using incremental returns.

Applying industry norms for the sales force cost ratio can hurt a firm with a small market share. If a firm with a small market share uses the industry ratio to size its sales force, then its share of sales force effort will mirror its market share. A low share of sales force effort translates into a low share of voice and hence a low mind share in the marketplace and reduced sales. Ultimately, a downward sales spiral sets in that can eliminate the firm with a small market share in the long run.

A sales and marketing executive facing a sales force sizing decision cannot overlook the sales force cost ratio, since the ratio helps gauge the anticipated profitability of the firm. However, locking into a ratio and ignoring the impact that sizing has on sales and profits is shortsighted and clearly nonoptimal.

## Competitive Parity Method

Most companies are aware of what their competitors are doing. Changes in competitors' sales forces are scrutinized to determine the competitors' strategy and see if it can lead to a sustainable advantage. Retaliatory measures are developed and implemented. Entire industries go through sales force expansions and reductions over time. Frequently, the other industry participants copy the market leader's strategy. Followers feel that the leader has more information or better analytical capabilities to develop a good strategy.

Matching a competitor's strategy makes sense when the strategy being matched is expected to produce higher sales and profits than the status quo strategy. However, plain mimicking assumes that the competitor knows what it is doing, and this is not a safe assumption. Respond to the leader's strategy, and improve upon it.

## Market-Based Methods

In this chapter we have stressed that sales force effort drives sales. Accurate sales force sizing can be achieved only if market behavior is taken into account in the sizing analysis. Figure 3-10 outlines a four-step market-based process. A general description follows; actual implementation requires much more detail.

**Step 1: Customer Understanding.** The first step is to identify the customer universe. For some companies, this is easy. For example, there are industries, such as pharmaceuticals and medical imaging, in which companies know the location of every customer and prospect. Companies may even know their market share at each customer site. In other industries, companies are unable to even list their set of prospects, let alone determine these prospects' potential. This is typical if the company's products can be purchased by a large number of buyers. A sales

**Figure 3-10.** A Four-Step Market-Based Process for Sizing a Sales Force.

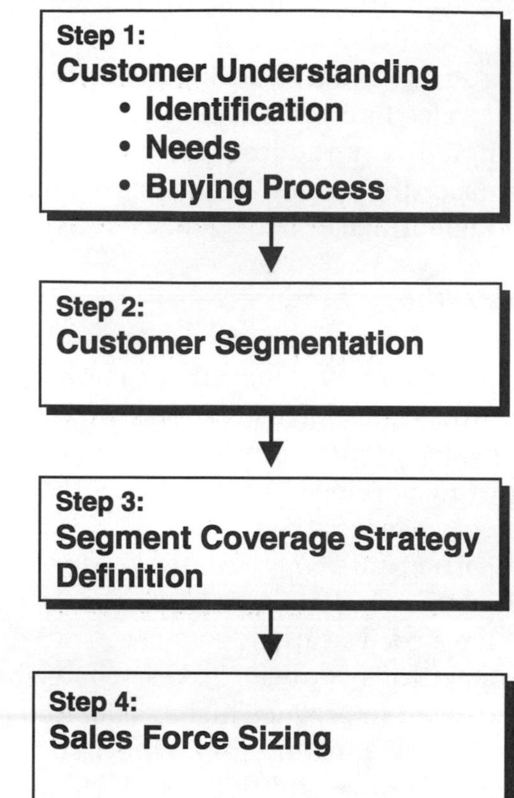


force for an industrial distributor for material replenishment or one selling newspaper advertising or insurance can sell to almost anyone. Consequently, the customer universe becomes difficult to define. Fortunately, advances in technology have made it possible for more companies to develop good customer and prospect lists. Data mining techniques make it easier for companies to match internal company data sources with market data sources, such as Dun & Bradstreet, so that salespeople can determine whom to sell to. In addition, for many companies, the Internet is a useful way to locate high-quality prospects. Some salespeople use the Internet as a worldwide electronic Yellow Pages, enabling them to create high-quality prospect lists with the click of a mouse.

Once customers and prospects have been identified, their requirements need to be determined. What are their product needs, service needs, and support needs? How do they prefer to buy? How can the sales force provide value? What is the best selling process? Needs and buying processes vary across different customers and prospects. It is worthwhile for headquarters to cluster customers with similar needs or buying processes into market segments so that the sales force can use its time most effectively.

**Step 2: Customer Segmentation.** Market segmentation is the second step. Typical sales force segmentation dimensions include industry or customer type, sales volume or sales opportunity, business solution or product requirements, number and type of buyers and influencers, maintenance versus new business, geography, and accessibility. Usually, the requisite selling activities differ across customers and prospects. However, most markets can be segmented so that customers and prospects who require about the same selling process are placed in the same segment.

Several illustrative sales force segmentation schemes appear in Figure 3-11.

Another way to segment customers is by the type of relationship with salespeople that they desire. For instance, relationship selling is a clear trend that has developed in recent years. Many firms are dismissing the hard-sell, short-term orientation of traditional personal selling in favor of a more customer-oriented, long-term approach. DuPont, however, has observed that while many of its customers prefer the new relationship selling model, some still prefer the traditional transaction-oriented approach. As a result, DuPont has developed different customer interface strategies for defined customer groups.

As Internet purchasing increases, defining customer segments according to the way companies like to buy may become more common. Customers who are technology savvy may prefer on-line purchasing to a direct sales call; others may desire the personal interaction and socialization that takes place during a face-to-face sales call. Customer preferences should be considered when segmenting markets so that members of each segment receive roughly the same selling process.

**Steps 3 and 4: Segment Coverage Strategy Definition and Sales Force Sizing.** A sales force coverage strategy should be developed for each market segment. The segment coverage strategy specifies the average workload required to cover each account in the segment. The word *average* is key. This is the average coverage across accounts in the market segment. Some accounts within the segment will have heavier workloads, while others will have lighter workloads. In the end, salespeople determine the most appropriate sales coverage strategy for each of their ac-

**Figure 3-11.** Examples of Customer Segmentation Schemes in Three Industries.

Consumer Products

| *Volume* | *Tobacco/ Candy* | *Grocery, Wholesale* | *Chain Grocery* | *Co-op Grocery* | *Wholesale Club* | *Discount/ Variety* | *Drug* | *Military* | *Vendors* | *All Others* |
|---|---|---|---|---|---|---|---|---|---|---|
| Very low | | | | | | | | | | |
| Low | | | | | | | | | | |
| Medium low | | | | | | | | | | |
| Medium | | | | | | | | | | |
| Medium high | | | | | | | | | | |
| High | | | | | | | | | | |
| Very high | | | | | | | | | | |

**Yellow Pages Advertising (Las Vegas) Top Markets**

| RANK | HEADSPL |
|---|---|
| 1 | Attorneys |
| 2 | Physicians & surgeons—M.D. |
| 3 | Insurance |
| 4 | Dentists |
| 5 | Chiropractic physicians |
| 6 | Restaurants |
| 7 | Entertainers—adult |
| 8 | Auto repairing & service |
| 9 | Air condtg contrs & sys |
| 10 | Plumbing contractors |
| 11 | Hotels |
| 12 | Real estate |
| 13 | Veterinarians |
| 14 | Storage—self service |
| 15 | Swimming pool contrs, dlrs, & designrs |
| 16 | Locks & locksmiths |
| 17 | Automobile renting & leasing |
| 18 | Florists—retail |
| 19 | Carpet, rug, & upholstery cleaners |
| 20 | Transmissions—automobile |
| 21 | Glass—auto, plate, window, etc. |
| 22 | Appliances—major |
| 23 | Automobile dealers—new cars |
| 24 | Schools—business & vocational |
| 25 | Optometrists, O.D. |
| 26 | Contractors—building, general |
| 27 | Beauty salons |
| 28 | Jewelers—retail |
| 29 | Pest control |
| 30 | Pawnbrokers |
| 31 | Janitor service |
| 32 | Travel agencies & bureaus |
| 33 | Printers |
| 34 | Optometrists |
| 35 | Automobile wrecking |
| 36 | Carpet & rug dealers—new |
| 37 | Clinics |
| 38 | Mortgages |
| 39 | Electric contractors |
| 40 | Furniture dealers—new |
| 41 | Roofing contractors |
| 42 | Hospitals |
| 43 | Pizza |
| 44 | Wedding chapels |
| 45 | Motels |

**Appliances**

- **Buying Group Members**
- **Independent Dealers and Other Buying Group Members**
  > $1.0 Million
  > $0.5–$1.0 Million
  > $0.25–$0.5 Million
  $0–$0.25 Million
- **Branch Stores of National Accounts**
  > $500,000 Stores
  $250,000–$500,000 Stores
  < $250,000 Stores
- **Retail Telesales Accounts**
  > $100,000
  > $50,000–$100,000
  > $25,000–$50,000
  $0–$25,000

counts. However, average workload is appropriate for sizing a sales force, since the accounts requiring heavier and lighter workloads tend to cancel out.

If segment strategy development is based on sound data analysis, it can be used to help guide the selling effort of the sales force. Specifically, it can help the individual salesperson with targeting, the training department with customer description materials and instruction, and the sales manager with coaching and territory alignment.

The first decision to make for each customer segment is whether the segment should receive any direct sales force coverage. If any of the following is the case, then the segment should not be covered by the company's sales force.

- The segment has low potential.
- The segment is unresponsive to sales force effort.
- Other marketing instruments (e.g., advertising, direct mail, or Internet selling) are more effective at creating sales.
- Distributors, manufacturers' agents, a contract sales force, a part-time sales force, or a telemarketing sales force can reduce the cost of customer contact to an acceptable level compared to their reduced effectiveness.

Three reasonable approaches for determining customer segment coverage have been developed. They are the activity-based approach, the target-return-per-call approach, and the sales-response approach. A description of each approach follows.

*The Activity-Based Approach.* This approach centers on the development of a list of "best" sales force activities required to cover the members of each customer segment. The activities are usually specified in one of two formats: an in-depth format or a modified format. In an in-depth format, the entire selling process for the average account in a segment is developed and specified. A generalized version of a selling process is presented in Figure 3-12.

Salespeople need to find prospective customers. They should understand their prospects and customers—know the buyers, know their business, and assess customer needs. Salespeople have to prioritize and target their opportunities. They must communicate with their customers and be good at listening, persuading, presenting, and negotiating. They need to be able to ask for the business. Finally, salespeople must service their customers in order to maintain and expand their business.

**Figure 3-12.** General Illustration of a Selling Process.

**Customer Attraction and Retention Process**

- **Find**
- **Understand/Assess Needs**
- **Prioritize/Target**
- **Analyze/Solve**
- **Communicate**
  - —**Listen**
  - —**Persuade**
  - —**Present**
  - —**Negotiate**
- **Close**
- **Maintain/Service**
- **Expand**

In a modified format, activities are specified in less detail. The modified format is most useful when the selling process is relatively consistent across calls, such as in retail merchandising or pharmaceutical detailing. The account call is the basic building block in this approach. Customer activities for each of the market segments are specified in terms of:

- *Reach*: The percentage of each market segment that needs to be covered
- *Frequency*: The average number of calls per year that should be made on the average account in the fraction of the segment that is reached
- *Duration*: The average number of hours that are required for a typical call

Segment workloads are computed by adding up the time required to cover all of the accounts in the segment using the most appropriate activity definition. The two examples shown in Figure 3-13 demonstrate an activity-based computation.

The data for developing activity-based size recommendations come from several sources. Salespeople and sales managers can articulate what has worked in the past and what they anticipate their customers will require in the future. Customers can tell the firm what they require from the selling organization. Other channel members, such as distributors and wholesalers, can supply yet another perspective. Finally, the

**Figure 3-13.** Two Examples of Activity-Based Computation of Sales Force Size.

In-Depth Format: Chemical Example

| *End-User Market Segments* | *Paint & Coatings* | *Paper* | *Carpet* | *Adhesives* | *Textiles* | *Nonwovens* |
|---|---|---|---|---|---|---|
| # of accounts | 1,600 | 900 | 330 | 650 | 850 | 100 |
| % reached | 20 | 18 | 12 | 35 | 10 | 65 |
| Task Groups: (Time in hrs./year required) | | | | | | |
| Precall planning | 5.8 | 11.5 | 30.3 | 7.6 | 5.4 | 6.9 |
| Calling: technical | 7.2 | 9.4 | 18.4 | 9.4 | 9.5 | 6.0 |
| Calling: nontechnical | 6.4 | 12.1 | 17.1 | 7.2 | 6.3 | 6.6 |
| Postcall activities | 6.6 | 11.0 | 36.9 | 6.8 | 5.7 | 6.3 |
| Special situations | 2.9 | 8.4 | 29.0 | 5.0 | 4.7 | 4.2 |
| Total hrs./year/account | 28.9 | 52.4 | 131.7 | 36.0 | 31.6 | 29.8 |
| Total hrs./year | 9,238 | 8,493 | 5,215 | 8,195 | 2,682 | 1,937 |
| Useful rep hrs./year | 1,490 | 1,490 | 1,490 | 1,490 | 1,490 | 1,490 |
| Reps required | 6.2 | 5.7 | 3.5 | 5.5 | 1.8 | 1.3 |
| Total field force | 24.0 | | | | | |

Salespeople needed = 24

Modified Format: Consumer Example

| *Account/Coverage Description* | *Number of Accounts* | *Calls per Year* | *Hours per Call* | *Total Hours* | *Salesperson Equivalents* | *% of Effort* |
|---|---|---|---|---|---|---|
| Service call—dept. store | 841 | 12 | 1.0 | 10,092 | 7.6 | 11.7% |
| Service call—other store | 1,279 | 4 | 1.0 | 5,116 | 3.9 | 5.9% |
| Group buyer | 99 | 12 | 1.5 | 1,782 | 1.4 | 2.1% |
| Direct retail—over $25K | 112 | 12 | 2.0 | 2,688 | 2.0 | 3.1% |
| Direct retail—$12–25K | 784 | 6 | 2.0 | 9,408 | 7.1 | 10.9% |
| Direct retail—$5–12K | 2,543 | 4 | 2.0 | 20,344 | 15.4 | 23.6% |
| Direct retail—under $5K | 6,559 | 3 | 1.0 | 19,677 | 14.9 | 22.8% |
| Headqtrs/warehouse—over $25K | 237 | 12 | 2.0 | 5,688 | 4.3 | 6.6% |
| Headqtrs/warehouse—$10–25K | 85 | 12 | 1.5 | 1,530 | 1.2 | 1.8% |
| Headqtrs/warehouse—under $10K | 128 | 12 | 1.0 | 1,536 | 1.2 | 1.8% |
| Key account—over $1,000K | 24 | 26 | 6.0 | 3,744 | 2.8 | 4.3% |
| Key account—$500–1,000K | 11 | 26 | 4.0 | 1,144 | 0.9 | 1.3% |
| Key account—$250–500K | 16 | 26 | 3.0 | 1,248 | 0.9 | 1.4% |
| Key account—under $250K | 31 | 26 | 2.0 | 1,612 | 1.2 | 1.9% |
| Telephone call | 373 | 3 | 0.5 | 560 | 0.4 | 0.6% |
| Total | 13,122 | | | 86,169 | 65 | 100.0% |

Note: Annual hours per salesperson = 1,320.

Salespeople needed = 65

firm can investigate how its competitors treat their customers and how sales forces in other industries organize their activities.

Companies can obtain activity information using personal interviews, telephone interviews, focus groups, mail questionnaires, or group-judgment consensus approaches (e.g., Delphi techniques) or by analyzing internal sources such as call reporting or performance reviews.

*The Target-Return-per-Call Approach.* This approach establishes the segment coverage strategy by determining the account call frequency that achieves a company's target rate of return per call. Calls will be added to a segment until the next call drops the average return per call below a specified norm. Like the modified activity-based approach, this approach is most appropriate when customer calls are reasonably similar within and across the segments. This approach can be seen more clearly with an example.

An eight-step approach is described in Figure 3-14. It is presented in two columns. The first column is a verbal presentation of the approach, and the second is an illustration of the process using an example from the pharmaceutical industry.

*The Sales-Response Approach.* The sales-response approach employs the "sales force drives sales" concept directly. If the relationship between sales force investment and company sales can be estimated, then alternative sales force sizing scenarios can be evaluated in terms of their impact on sales and profit. Profit-maximizing sales force size recommendations are derived after assessing a set of alternative scenarios.

Every sales force has variability in its call coverage. Some accounts get high call frequencies; others get low call frequencies. This may be due to something as subtle as misaligned sales territories (salespeople with large sales territories cannot possibly cover all of their accounts adequately), or something as simple as a territory's being vacant for part of a year. When accounts with similar sales potential have different call frequencies, it simulates the results of field forces with different sizes. This situation can provide data to estimate the sales-response relationship. A simple sales-response relationship is presented in Figure 3-15.

To determine the right sales force investment for each segment, compare the anticipated sales obtained with different call frequencies with the costs associated with these different call frequencies. In Figure 3-15, additional sales force effort directed toward the high-potential accounts generates incrementally more sales, and consequently profit,

**Figure 3-14.** An Eight-Step Approach to the Target-Return-per-Call Method of Sales Force Sizing.

| | The Target-Return-per-Call Calculation | The Target-Return-per-Call Illustration from the Pharmaceutical Industry | |
|---|---|---|---|
| Step 1: | **Gather data** | | |
| | • Product sales | $100,000,000 | |
| | • Average cost per call | $100 | |
| | • Target return goal | 50% | |
| | • Sales attributable to this year's sales force effort | 60% | |
| | • Carryover rate for future years | 80% | |
| | • Profit margin | 80% | |
| | • Number of accounts | 100,000 | |
| | • Maximum number of calls that can be made on any account | 8 | |
| Step 2: | **Segment the account universe into volume segments** | *Quintile* | *Number of Accounts* |
| | • Usually quintiles or deciles are used. | I (top) | 20,000 |
| | | II | 20,000 |
| | | III | 20,000 |
| | | IV | 20,000 |
| | | V (bottom) | 20,000 |

| Step 3: | **Calculate the value of each account in each volume segment** | |
|---|---|---|
| | • Calculate the total sales volume attributable to sales force effort this year:<br>*(Product sales)* * *(Percentage of sales attributable to this year's sales force effort)* * *(2-year carryover)* | $100,000,000 * (0.6) * (1 + 0.8 + 0.8 * 0.8) = $146,000,000 |
| | • Partition the sales volume into the volume segments:<br>*(Total sales volume)* * *(Percentage of volume attributable to the segment)* | see table below |
| | • Apply the profit margin:<br>*(Volume)* * *(Profit margin)* | see table below |

| *Quintile* | *% Volume* | *$ Volume* |
|---|---|---|
| I | 45% | 65.7 |
| II | 25% | 36.5 |
| III | 15% | 21.9 |
| IV | 10% | 14.6 |
| V | 5% | 7.3 |
| Total | 100% | 146.0 |

| *Quintile* | *% Profit* |
|---|---|
| I | 52.6 |
| II | 29.2 |
| III | 17.5 |
| IV | 11.7 |
| V | 5.8 |
| Total | 116.8 |

*(continues)*

**Figure 3-14.** Continued.

| | | Quintile | Number of Accounts | Profit per Account |
|---|---|---|---|---|
| | • *Divide profit by the number of accounts in each segment.* | I | 20,000 | $2,630 |
| | | II | 20,000 | $1,460 |
| | | III | 20,000 | $ 875 |
| | | IV | 20,000 | $ 585 |
| | | V | 20,000 | $ 290 |

| | | |
|---|---|---|
| Step 4: | **Calculate the target return per call**<br>*(Cost per call) * (1 + target return goal)* | $100 * (1 + 0.50) = $150 |

| | | Quintile | Target Number of Calls |
|---|---|---|---|
| Step 5: | **Calculate the target number of calls per account in each segment**<br>*(Profit per account) / (Target return per call)* | I | 2,630 / 150 = 17 |
| | | II | 1,460 / 150 = 9 |
| | | III | 875 / 150 = 5 |
| | | IV | 585 / 150 = 3 |
| | | V | 290 / 150 = 1 |

| Step 6: | **Compare the targeted number of calls with the maximum possible number of calls, considering customer accessibility. Choose the smaller of the two** | *Quintile* | *Targeted* | *Maximum* | *Choice* |
|---|---|---|---|---|---|
| | | I | 17 | 8 | 8 |
| | | II | 9 | 8 | 8 |
| | | III | 5 | 8 | 5 |
| | | IV | 3 | 8 | 3 |
| | | V | 1 | 8 | 1 |

| Step 7: | **Calculate calls for each segment. Add calls across segments** | *Quintile* | *Number of Accounts* | *Calls (Choice)* | *Total Calls* |
|---|---|---|---|---|---|
| | | I | 20,000 | 8 | 160,000 |
| | | II | 20,000 | 8 | 160,000 |
| | | III | 20,000 | 5 | 100,000 |
| | | IV | 20,000 | 3 | 60,000 |
| | | V | 20,000 | 1 | 20,000 |
| | | Total Number of Calls per Year | | | 500,000 |

| Step 8: | **Divide by the capacity of a rep to calculate the number of reps required** | Total Calls / Capacity = # Reps<br>The average number of calls per salesperson per year is 1,600.<br>500,000 / 1,600 = 313 |
|---|---|---|

Figure 3-15. A Simple Sales-Response Relationship.

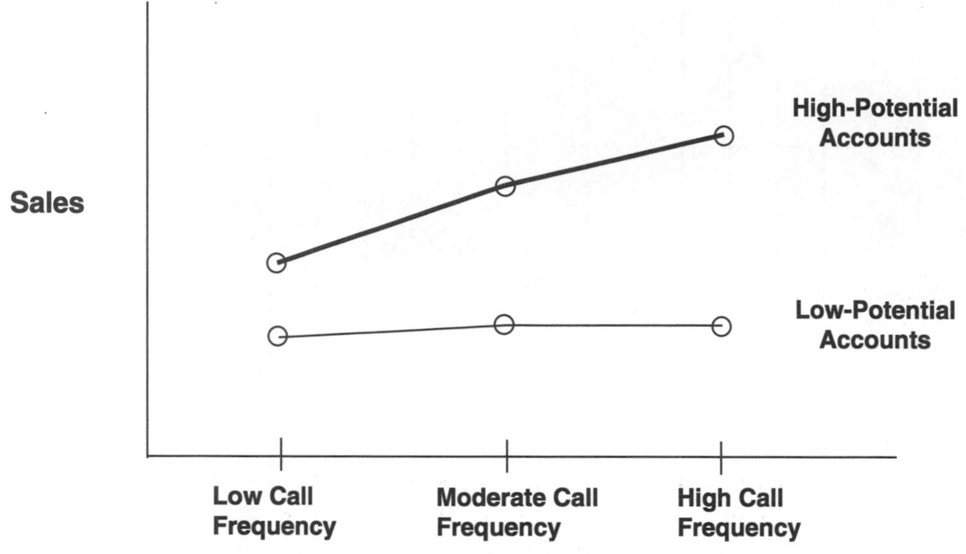


than a similar investment in low-potential accounts. The recommended investment in high- and low-potential accounts depends upon the sales force costs. For example, assume all accounts are currently covered with low frequency. To decide whether or not to increase the frequency of calling on each account segment, compare the cost of the additional salespeople needed to increase the coverage with the expected profit increase. For example, if the additional sales force costs exceed the profit increase for low-potential accounts but are less than the profit increase for high-potential accounts, the best sales force investment strategy is to increase to high call frequency on high-potential accounts and keep a low call frequency on low-potential accounts.

To derive a profit-maximizing sizing decision, management must evaluate the profit-maximizing strategies for each market segment. Using the carryover estimates for each segment to forecast the three-year sales and discounted contribution associated with each sales force investment strategy enriches the analysis. One-year sales, one-year contribution, and three-year discounted contribution curves can be established for each market segment using the sales-response approach. An example of these curves is shown in Figure 3-16.

Sizing of the entire sales force is accomplished by integrating the segment-level data for all of the segments. This financial analysis can be performed easily with spreadsheet software.

Data for developing sales-response relationships are usually of two

**Figure 3-16.** Sales and Contribution for Alternative Sales Force Sizes.

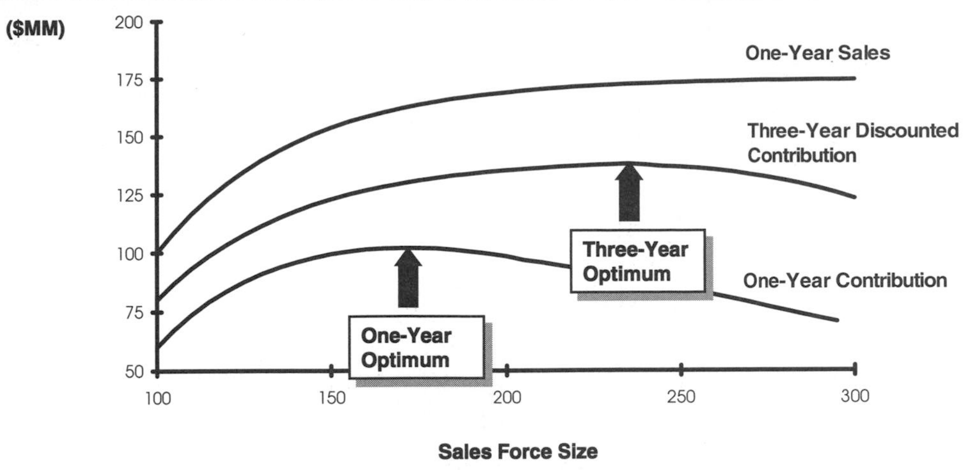


types: historical data and judgmental data. Cross-sectional and time-series historical data can be analyzed statistically. Examples of typical cross-sectional and time-series data linking market call and sales data are displayed in Figure 3-17.

Both data sets show variation in call frequency. The cross-sectional data set shows variation in call frequency at the territory level, and the time-series data show variation over time. This variation can be exploited to forecast how responsive a market is to sales force effort.

Judgmental data can be used to complement historical sales and call data by asking sales and marketing managers to forecast expected sales resulting from alternative investment strategies. Questions such as the one in Figure 3-18 can be used to develop sales-response estimates.

Judgmental data are captured best using an interactive, group-judgment consensus approach such as a Delphi forecasting exercise. Modern Delphi sessions use interactive computer networks to provide instantaneous feedback to participants, who can revise their opinions in light of information other participants share with the group. Subsequently, useful sales-response estimates are derived.

Academic research by the authors demonstrates that historical and judgmental sales-response forecasts are almost equally effective. However, it seems that forecasts based upon historical data perform better when markets or products are stable. Judgmental data are preferred when markets are dynamic and changing or when products are new or are competing in dynamic markets. The best forecasts incorporate both judgment and the statistical analysis of historical data.

Figure 3-17. Data for Developing Sales-Response Relationships.

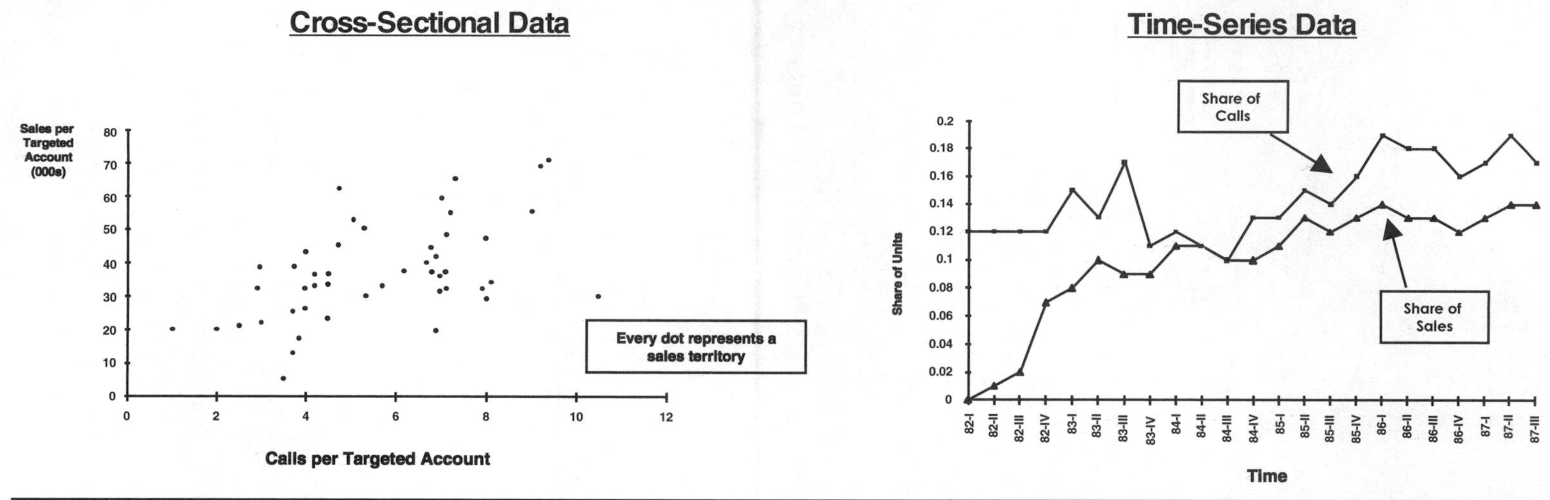

**Figure 3-18.** Sample Question for Gathering Judgmental Data for Sales-Response Estimation.

MARKET SEGMENT:

*Estimate the expected sales arising from different call frequencies.*

| | *Zero Effort* | *50% Current* | *Current Effort* | *150% Current* | *Twice Current* |
|---|---|---|---|---|---|
| Call frequency (calls/year) | 0 | 4 | 8 | 12 | 16 |
| Sales estimate ($ millions) | | | | | |

The sales-response approach was used with the fifty companies that participated in the ZS Study. It is useful to repeat two of the results from this study.

1. The best sales force size and sales resource deployment has about a 4.5 percent larger contribution than the current size and resource deployment.
2. The best sales force size is about 18 percent larger when long-term contribution is used for sizing than when sizes are based upon a myopic short-term objective.

*A Comparison of Approaches.* The three approaches to determining customer segment coverage are contrasted in terms of several important dimensions in Figure 3-19.

## The Impact of Technology on Sales Force Size

Rapid advances in technology are having an impact on the way business is conducted in every market. There is a concern about how these changes affect the size of the sales force. Some experts predict that as electronic sales channels become more important, sales force sizes will be reduced to half of today's levels, yet sales will double. Others argue that while technology can make sales processes more efficient, the need for socialization between buyers and sellers is so great that technology can never replace it to this extent. Some have argued that sales force sizes will increase initially as salespeople provide customers with the

**Figure 3-19.** A Comparison of Alternative Sales Force Sizing Approaches.

| *Approach* | *Understandability* | *Data* | *Analysis* | *Cost* | *Probability of Getting the Right Answer* |
|---|---|---|---|---|---|
| Activity-based | Simple, easy to explain | Relatively easy to obtain | Straightforward | Low to moderate | Moderate |
| Target return per call | Complicated | Easy to obtain | Straightforward | Low | Moderate |
| Sales-response | Complicated | Requires sales and activity data | Requires statistics | Moderate to high | Very high |

technical training and support required to start up new systems. Technology will replace routine tasks such as order taking and inventory management on an ongoing basis. However, new tasks such as providing customers with ongoing technical support will replace the old tasks.

Technological change is only one example of environmental change. Selling organizations need to develop change processes so that they can adjust their sales force investment faster than their competitors can. The sizing process developed earlier in the chapter serves as a framework for performing a sizing analysis in a changing world. The example in Figure 3-20 provides a simple illustration of how to implement the sizing process. It focuses on the decisions a company needs to make when integrating technology into its selling process.

Sales force size needs to be reexamined whenever there is a major technological change affecting the sales force.

## Final Sizing Recommendation

Better sales force sizing decisions are made when sales force and market dynamics are acknowledged. A good sales force sizing process has the following steps:

1. Use one of the market-based sizing approaches to derive a good initial sales force size.
2. Perform a financial check for the recommended size. Most companies track the sales force cost-to-sales ratio. A quick check to make sure this ratio is within historical and industry norms

**Figure 3-20.** An Illustration of the Sizing Process When Faced with Technological Change.

| *Process Step* | *Illustration* |
|---|---|
| Understanding markets | Study how technology affects the way our customers use our products and how they will choose to buy from us in the future. As an example, some will want to process all interactions over the Internet; others may choose to maintain a personal relationship with our salespeople. |
| Customer segmentation | A revised segmentation acknowledges the way technology is incorporated into customer interactions and reflects buyer interaction preferences. Internet buyers and non-Internet buyers would most likely fall into different market segments. |
| Coverage strategy definition | The best selling process for each market segment needs to reflect the new role of technology. As another example, technology has enabled some companies to streamline routine and time-consuming tasks. Companies like Xerox have automated most maintenance of their copy machines by linking the machines to the central office via telephone lines. Historically, the function of servicing customers after they purchased a Xerox product took up the greatest amount of sales force time. The new system drastically reduces the need for salespeople to perform maintenance tasks. |
| Sales force sizing | The best sales force size depends upon the activity required to service the targeted market segments. In the Xerox example, when salespeople are freed from their maintenance requirements, they can spend more time selling new products to existing and new customers. Because maintenance costs are reduced, it is now profitable to call on many customers who were not profitable to call on before. |

should be done. Managing this ratio helps to minimize executive anxiety.

3. Perform a competitive check. Compare the recommended sales force size to the competitors' sizes. This ensures that the sales force will not be outshouted and that the sales force obtains a desired share of voice.
4. Perform a customer check. Look at coverage. Will the sales force see the customers who need to be seen with the appropriate frequency?

A properly sized selling organization ensures that customers and prospects receive the appropriate coverage, company products get the proper representation, the sales force is stretched but not overworked, and the company makes the appropriate investment for its sales resource.

# Chapter 4

# Structuring the Sales Force for Strategic Advantage

This chapter discusses sales force structure. A sales force must be well organized if it is to meet customer needs efficiently and effectively and to sell the firm's products and services. Sales force structure decisions influence how customers see the firm. They also affect the selling skills and knowledge level required of salespeople, which in turn affect compensation, recruitment, training, and the role of the sales manager. The structure affects each salesperson and sales manager. Job descriptions, reporting relationships, and teaming decisions are all contingent upon the sales force structure.

The chapter is designed to help you:

- Evaluate the trade-off between efficiency and effectiveness, which is at the heart of the sales force structure decision
- Understand the four fundamental sales force structures companies use and learn which structure or combination of structures is most appropriate in a given situation
- Use a four-step process to develop an adaptive, efficient, and effective sales force structure

## Introduction

Any group performing a series of activities or tasks is most successful when it organizes to achieve its objectives. Sales forces, in particular, need to be well organized if they are to efficiently and effectively meet customer needs and sell the firm's products and services. Sales force organizational structures range from geographic, where each salesperson sells all products to all customers, to highly specialized, where teams of salespeople focus on specific products, markets, or selling activities.

Sales force structure decisions affect all members of the selling organization and consequently have a direct impact on the company's customers. From a customer perspective, sales force structure decisions determine the number of salespeople the customer sees, how responsive the salespeople can be to the customer's needs, and how knowledgeable the salespeople are about the products they sell and the customers they sell to. From a sales force perspective, the sales force structure defines the salesperson's job. It determines the type of customers a salesperson calls on, the product or service portfolio the salesperson sells, and the activities the salesperson engages in. Similarly, the sales force structure defines the sales manager's role and the reporting relationships.

Usually the senior managers in a company organize the sales force and make sales force structure decisions. Progressive managers reevaluate the sales force structure every two to three years. New products, new markets, environmental changes, mergers and acquisitions, divisional reorganizations, competitive moves, technology changes, sales force lethargy, and lack of motivation can all create the need for a structure change.

As shown in Figure 4-1, the sales force structure affects many other sales force decisions. Since the structure specifies the job description

**Figure 4-1.** Sales Force Structure Affects Many Sales Force Decisions.

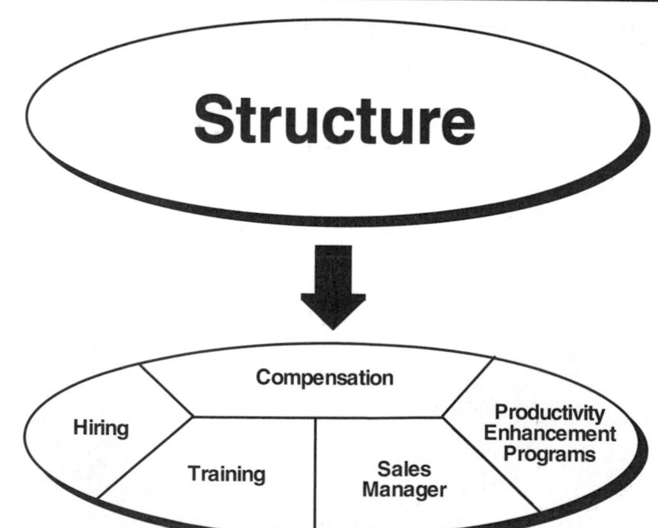

for each sales force job, it affects the type of people who need to be selected for sales and sales management positions. It also affects the training programs, performance evaluation systems, compensation plan, territory alignment, sales force database, and automation tools to be used.

## The Three Sales Force Structure Objectives: Adaptability, Efficiency, and Effectiveness

A good sales force structure is adaptive, efficient, and effective.

If the sales force structure is adaptive, the company can react quickly to product and market changes without a major structural overhaul. A structure is viewed as adaptive if a selling process change resulting from product or market fluctuations can be accommodated within the existing sales force structure.

Efficiency and effectiveness are also important sales force structure objectives. These concepts are illustrated in Figure 4-2.

The money a firm invests in its sales force is used to employ salespeople and managers who generate calls and interact face to face with customers and prospects. The sales calls are directed at a marketplace, and the marketplace responds to the calls by buying the products and services of the firm. *Efficiency* reflects the rate at which the sales force converts its money investment into calls. A highly efficient sales force has a high level of call activity for its investment. *Effectiveness* represents the buyer's response to the calling level of the selling organization. A highly effective sales force has high impact per call; it generates high levels of sales for the call investment.

### Encouraging Efficiency: The Geographic Structure

The geographic, or generalist, structure is a basic sales force structure. Companies using this structure assign their salespeople to sales territo-

**Figure 4-2.** Sales Force Efficiency and Effectiveness.

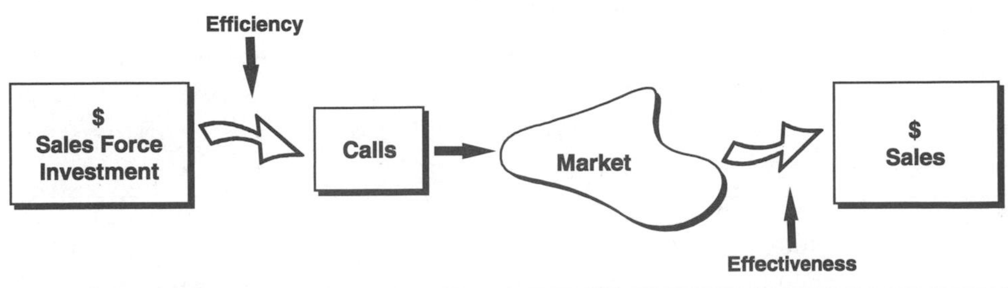

ries made up of a list of accounts or a group of contiguous geographic units, such as counties or zip codes. Each salesperson sells the firm's entire product line to all of the accounts and prospects in his or her territory. The salesperson is responsible for all selling activity in the territory. This is usually the most *efficient* structure available to the firm. Sales territories tend to be smallest and most compact in a geographic structure. Consequently, a sales force with a geographic structure usually generates higher call activity and more face-to-face selling effort than one with some other structure.

## Encouraging Effectiveness: Specialized Structures

Why aren't all sales forces structured geographically if this is the most efficient structure? Market, product, and activity heterogeneity and complexity provide an answer.

**Market Heterogeneity and Complexity.** A company's market typically has many participants. Some are customers; others are prospects. Some are large; others are small. It is unrealistic to expect them all to be similar. In fact, most markets are heterogeneous; the participants have different needs and requirements. Some customers are price-sensitive, while others desire customization. Some need immediate delivery; others need ninety-day dating. Some need vast amounts of information, while others just want expeditious order processing using the Internet. Some provide high sales and profit opportunity, while others provide marginal opportunity, perhaps not even enough to pay for the sales force effort. The nonuniformity of customer needs requires a sales force structure designed to accommodate heterogeneity.

Figure 4-3 lists some dimensions that create market-based heterogeneity.

In addition to being heterogeneous, some markets are very complicated. They may have many buyers with different needs. For example, when Boeing and Airbus approach a customer or prospect, they have to deal with several buyers and influencers. The financial people need low-cost financing; the operations people need easy maintenance, high reliability, and interchangeable parts; the marketing people want comfortable seating. Airline needs are also highly technical, requiring state-of-the-art engineering.

**Product Heterogeneity and Complexity.** A company's products can also introduce heterogeneity and/or complexity. Some companies, such

**Figure 4-3.** Dimensions That Create Market-Based Heterogeneity.

Industry
Geography
Account size (large/small)
Account potential (high/low)
New account/existing account
Multiple buyers at the account site
Different needs at the account site
Different needs across customers
Different buying processes across accounts
Product/service has high/low importance to the buyer
Prospects are aware/not aware of product/service offering
Accounts are happy/unhappy with current supplier
Different levels of technology usage across customers
Different attitudes toward Internet purchasing

as Lego, sell a limited product line. Other companies, such as W.W. Grainger and Baxter Corp., sell thousands of products. Some products may require the sales force to visit diverse buyers with various needs and ways of doing business. Companies with large numbers of products need salespeople with differing selling skills and an expanded product knowledge repertoire. The heterogeneity induced by a broad, diverse product line makes it difficult for a single salesperson to sell all the company's products successfully.

Products can be highly complex as well. Salespeople in some industries, such as medical imaging and specialty chemicals, require six- to eighteen-month training programs before they can represent their products effectively.

**Sales Force Activity Heterogeneity and Complexity.** Sales force activity is a final source of heterogeneity and/or complexity. The sales force needs to find customers, identify their needs, solve customer problems, sell, service, maintain, partner, and expand the business. Many firms find it particularly difficult to find salespeople who are skilled at both selling and technical problem solving. This dichotomy is often described by the question: "Do I hire an engineer or a fraternity/sorority president?"

Figure 4-4 lists some dimensions of activity-based heterogeneity.

Complexity can also be an issue with sales force activities. Complex products and markets translate into complex activities for the salesperson. Varied buying influences must be accommodated, each requiring salespeople with high levels of skill and knowledge.

**Figure 4-4.** Dimensions That Create Activity-Based Heterogeneity.

Lead generation/selling
Hunting/farming
- New sales/maintenance
- Prospecting/converting
- Selling/servicing

Headquarters/local
- Market analysis/strategic planning/contracting/pull-through/merchandising

Customer relationship/product expertise
Selling/financing/problem solving/distribution/logistics

**The Need for Specialization.** Excessive heterogeneity or complexity in any of these areas—market, product, and/or selling activity—can create a need for specialization if the firm wants to add value for its customers. Specialization allows a company to accommodate heterogeneity or complexity without losing effectiveness. In many cases, a company needs to focus on one of these three areas, and specialization provides that focus.

A geographically organized sales force that is promoting a complex product line or selling into a heterogeneous marketplace that requires diverse selling skills will incur effectiveness losses. It is impossible for one person to sell a broad product line in a heterogeneous marketplace without missing some business. Lack of skill or knowledge will result in ineffective sales calls. Of course, an alert salesperson in these environments makes good choices when allocating his or her time. Realizing that expertise and value creation are dominant customer strategies, the alert salesperson focuses his or her effort on those products and customers with which he or she is comfortable or can be the most successful. However, it should be noted that even the best salesperson cannot be good at everything, and effectiveness is lost.

Specialization is the mechanism that deals with heterogeneity. Salespeople who specialize in a market, product, or activity use their focus to increase their effectiveness. Because of their expertise and skill, they generate higher levels of sales per call. A sales force with a specialized structure manages heterogeneity by focusing its sales resources on the basis of the causes of the heterogeneity.

While they are highly effective, specialized sales forces tend to be geographically redundant. They often have overlapping sales territories, with different specialized salespeople covering the same geography but calling on different market segments, selling different products, or engaging in different activities. Consequently, specialized sales forces are rarely as efficient as geographic selling organizations.

To summarize, specialization increases effectiveness in a heterogeneous or complex environment. Effectiveness is increased in several ways:

- Knowledge
- Focus
- Problem-solving ability
- Ability to make recommendations quickly
- Persuasiveness
- Skill

However, specialization usually introduces efficiency losses. So, a good rule of thumb is: Specialize as long as the gains in effectiveness exceed the losses in efficiency. Don't specialize if an increase in effectiveness cannot be demonstrated. Companies contemplating multiple specialized field forces need to examine the incremental increases in effectiveness from each specialized field force.

## Five Sales Force Structures That Create Results

There are four fundamental sales force structures: generalist, market-based, product-based, and activity-based. These four structures are contrasted in the sales force structure cube shown in Figure 4-5. A fifth structure, the mixed organization, is a hybrid of two or more of the four fundamental types. Each structure is described below.

### Generalist Sales Force Structure

In a generalist structure, each salesperson sells the firm's entire product line to all accounts and prospects in a defined geographic area. A generalist structure is appropriate when the firm sells a manageable product line and the selling process is relatively homogeneous for all customers and prospects. Generalist structures are usually the most efficient. The example shown in Figure 4-6 illustrates the reason for this efficiency.

Generalist salespeople typically have smaller sales territories, less travel time, and the most face-to-face time with customers. They also have a greater opportunity to gain in-depth knowledge of economic, cultural, and competitive conditions in the territory.

Although generalist territories are efficient, their effectiveness can be low in highly heterogeneous environments. They also have low

**Figure 4-5.** Alternative Sales Force Structures.

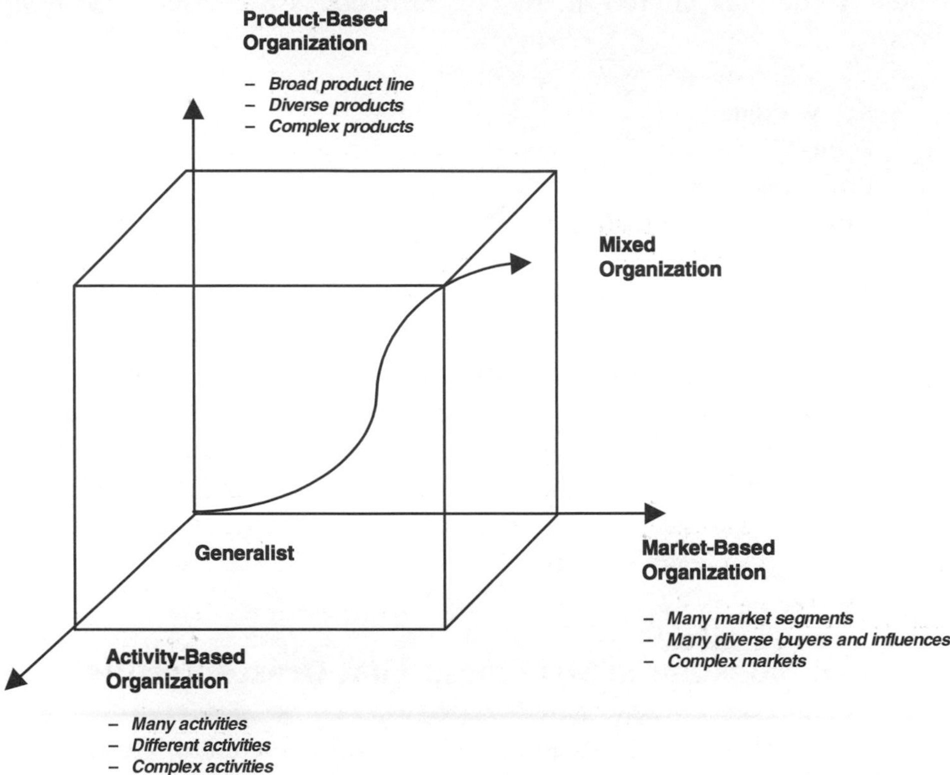


**Figure 4-6.** A Comparison of Efficiency in a Generalist Versus a Specialized Structure.

| | *Scenario I* | *Scenario II* |
|---|---|---|
| **Sales force organization** | A single generalist team | Two specialty teams |
| **Number of salespeople** | 100 | 70 and 30 |
| **Sales territory description** | Each sales territory has roughly 1% of the country. | Territories overlap.<br>The 70-person team has territories that are on average 43% larger in size than those of the generalist team.<br>The 30-person team has territories that are on average $3\frac{1}{3}$ times the size of those of the generalist team. |

adaptability when buying behavior changes and are unsuited to customer buying organizations that span several sales territories. For example, a chain retailer may have a regional headquarters that purchases products for all of its retail stores in a metropolitan area. If the chain headquarters and each of the individual stores are assigned to salespeople simply on the basis of geography, extensive coordination is required between the salesperson covering the headquarters and the salespeople who cover individual stores. Merchandising and pull-through activity is required in each of the stores, even if a promotional program is sold at headquarters. The time required to handle this coordination is likely to offset the travel-time savings of a geographic alignment. In this case, a market-based structure, as described in the next section, may be more appropriate.

## Market-Based Sales Force Structure

Market-based heterogeneity and complexity are probably the most important and most interesting forms of heterogeneity and complexity. They involve the sales force's most important asset: the customer. Customers and prospects may fall into many market segments, each with its own needs and buying behaviors. Within each segment there may be many decision makers. Typically, a market-based structure is a response to market heterogeneity and complexity.

A market-based organization improves sales force effectiveness through customer knowledge. Each of the market-based selling teams develops the most appropriate selling process for the segment it serves, and the organization is highly adaptive to changes in customer needs and buying behavior. Since it is focused, each market-based selling team can quickly adapt its selling process to respond to changing market conditions.

Market-specialized teams have an additional benefit—through team sizing, they ensure that each market receives the appropriate selling resources. A market-based sales team of 100 allocates 100 salesperson equivalents of sales force effort to its market segment. Generalist sales forces that split their effort among multiple markets cannot make the same guarantee.

The downside of a market-based structure is that it can lead to conflict with the marketing organization, which is usually organized around products. For example, a product manager may have to work with multiple sales organizations to implement a product's marketing strategy. This is much more difficult than working with a single product-based or geographically based sales force. In addition, with some forms of this structure, measuring sales force effectiveness becomes more difficult. For example, when sales forces specialize to accommodate different types of buyers, several salespeople can be assigned to different buyers at the same account. In this case, accountability and measurability blur because each of the salespeople synergistically contributes to the sales to the account. It may be impossible to separate individual contributions. In the worst case, this structure can allow "free riding" on the account team.

Several structuring options are illustrated in Figure 4-7.

## Product-Based Sales Force Structure

A product-based sales organization is appropriate when the firm has a large, complex, or diverse product line. The organization is more effective because of the product specialization and expertise of the sales force.

Several other situations also warrant the use of product specialization. Specialized product teams can help differentiate competing lines. It may be difficult for a single sales force to sell competing lines to a customer. Distributors that represent competing manufacturers can sell the competing products because they have different specialized field forces devoted to the competing brands. Liquor distributors and consumer product brokers are good examples of this type of specialization. Also, companies that sell in developing countries frequently find that there are only a few high-quality distributors. In this case, the distributors will sell competing brands with different sales forces. The authors have observed that two sales forces selling competing product lines independently will most likely have higher sales across the lines than a single sales force selling all the products.

Product lines may have positioning conflicts that preclude having them sold by the same sales force. For example, it might be difficult to ask a sales force to sell both Bibles and sex manuals.

The firm's corporate financial reporting structure can induce a product-based sales force structure. If product groups are accountable for their own profit and loss (P&L), they will probably want to control their own selling effort and sales resources. Consequently, each product group will have its own sales force.

Finally, the only way to ensure that a product or product line receives a specific level of selling effort is through organization. If a product needs a team of thirty people to sell it into a market effectively, the

**Figure 4-7.** Market-Based Structuring Options.

| *Source of Heterogeneity* | *Potential Sales Force Structure* |
|---|---|
| Industry<br>SIC codes | The sales force is organized around industries. |
| Geography<br>Regions of the country may be sufficiently different to warrant their own sales force | Regionalization structure: The sales force is organized by regions.<br>Each regional manager is responsible for all of the selling tasks in the region.<br>More advanced forms of this structure require that each region manage its own P&L, maintain its own marketing and sales support, and develop the most appropriate size and structure for the region. |
| Account size<br>High/low sales volume<br>High/low sales potential<br>High/low profitability | Large accounts are assigned to a major account team; smaller accounts are assigned to a generalist team. Telephone or Internet selling can be used for small accounts, especially those in remote locations. |
| Selling vs. maintenance<br>New accounts/existing accounts<br>Sales/servicing | The sales force is split into a selling team and a maintenance team, sometimes called "hunters" and "farmers." |
| Multiple buyers with different needs at the account site | Customer-focused selling teams service the accounts' needs. The teams include an account manager who manages the relationship and is assisted by product specialists, financial specialists, market analysts, and distribution/logistics specialists. |
| Very large accounts | Vertical selling teams can be employed to focus on an individual account, supplying its entire product and service needs. Manufacturer-supplier partnering may require special efforts. For example, major consumer product companies frequently assign dedicated selling teams to major retailers, such as Wal-Mart, as part of a partnering program aimed at maximizing sales to consumers. |

only way to make sure that this amount of effort is actually devoted to the product or product line is to establish a sales force of thirty dedicated salespeople. Managerial directives, training, coaching, and incentive compensation plans can be used to try to achieve this allocation of effort, but their success is not guaranteed.

**Independent and Integrated Structures.** There are two types of product-based organizational structures: independent and integrated. The two types differ in their management reporting structure. In an independent structure, product teams report to a common management structure only at the highest levels of the sales organization. In an integrated structure, product specialists report to a common manager at a lower level in the sales organization, frequently the first-level sales manager level.

An independent structure is usually simpler to manage. Each sales team has its own management team, calls on its own customers, sets its own goals, and rewards its members uniquely. However, when two or more product-based teams have a common customer, there can be customer confusion. Large customers may want special coordinated attention, one-stop shopping, and lower prices. In these situations, firms establish customer-focused selling teams. Each of these teams usually has an account manager who has responsibility and accountability for the account. Product specialists assist the account manager in selling and servicing the account. The product specialists may report to the product-based selling team, or, if the account is big enough, the team may be totally dedicated to a single account. Dedicated teams are often called vertical selling teams. Customer-focused selling teams and vertical selling teams are examples of mixed structures, which are discussed in more detail below.

Whenever two or more product-based teams call on the same accounts and considerable coordination is required at those accounts, it is best to integrate the product specialists at low levels in the organization. It is a good idea to have the various product specialists report to the same first-level sales manager. Integration and coordination benefit the customer; hence integration close to the customer is preferred. The preferred structure is illustrated in Figure 4-8.

A concern with low-level integration is that the first-level sales manager may not be able to manage the product line breadth completely. If the manager can do so, then integration is desirable. If not, the sales teams should be organized separately for at least one or two levels of management.

**Figure 4-8.** Alternative Ways to Organize Product-Based Structures.

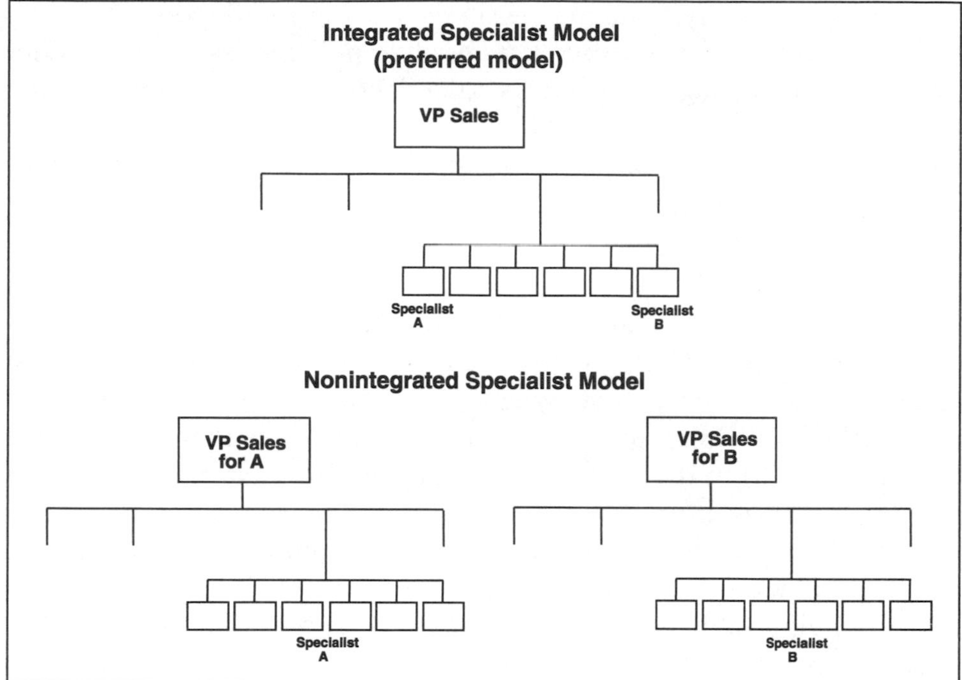


Unfortunately, product-based organizational structures have low geographic efficiency and low adaptability to changes in buying behavior. They can also create confusion on the part of customers and lead to excessive internal competition. Ultimately, the customer's best interests may bc compromised.

## Activity-Based Sales Force Structure

The best activity or selling process for a sales force is highly dependent on the firm's products and markets. Product and market heterogeneity require diverse skills and knowledge. Different customer needs over a buying cycle can also require different selling skills or servicing behaviors for the sales force. The sales force gains considerable efficiency by specializing on the basis of critical activity. Examples include:

- A team to sell new accounts and a team to maintain and expand business at existing accounts
- A national headquarters sales team and a geographic sales team to maintain a local presence
- Separate selling teams for account management, problem solving, and buy/lease decision making

- A selling team and a merchandising team that stocks shelves, sets up displays, and manages inventory at retail stores
- An end-user team to generate product pull-through and a reseller team to manage distributors, manufacturer's representatives, and value-added-resellers (VARs)
- A telephone selling team for small, hard-to-see, and geographically remote accounts and/or prospects and a direct selling team for all other accounts

Frequently, teams are established when activity-based specialization is required. Collectively, the team meets the needs of its customers. Teams work best when participants bring separate and nonoverlapping skills and competencies, and when there is a strong dependency within the team. Dependency implies that the overall sales and service tasks cannot be completed without the skills and competencies of each team member. Teams usually contain process, product, market, and leadership expertise harnessed together with a clear objective. A well-established team easily handles multiple buying influences, decision makers, and products, as well as sales service and account maintenance.

Usually team members' compensation is based on two sets of goals: the goals of the entire team and the goals associated with individual performance. Total group goals tend to be based on results, and individual objectives tend to be based on each participant's activities. Incentive compensation is usually based on a predetermined formula or allocated by the team leader.

Artificial teams do not work. Team members can become disgruntled when their individual contribution is lost because of an equal allocation of team-based incentive compensation.

## Mixed Sales Force Structures

Mixed sales force structures incorporate multiple forms of specialization. They may include product and market specialization (for example, product-based selling teams, each with a national account and generalist team), or they may be structured around markets and activities (for example, industry teams, each with its own hunters and farmers). The combinations are numerous. In fact, the possibilities grow multiplicatively and become overwhelming. The cube shown in Figure 4-9 represents the structure one U.S. sales force proposed. The sales force wanted to organize around four geographic regions, five market segments, and

**Figure 4-9.** A Mixed Cube Structure Proposed by a U.S. Sales Force.

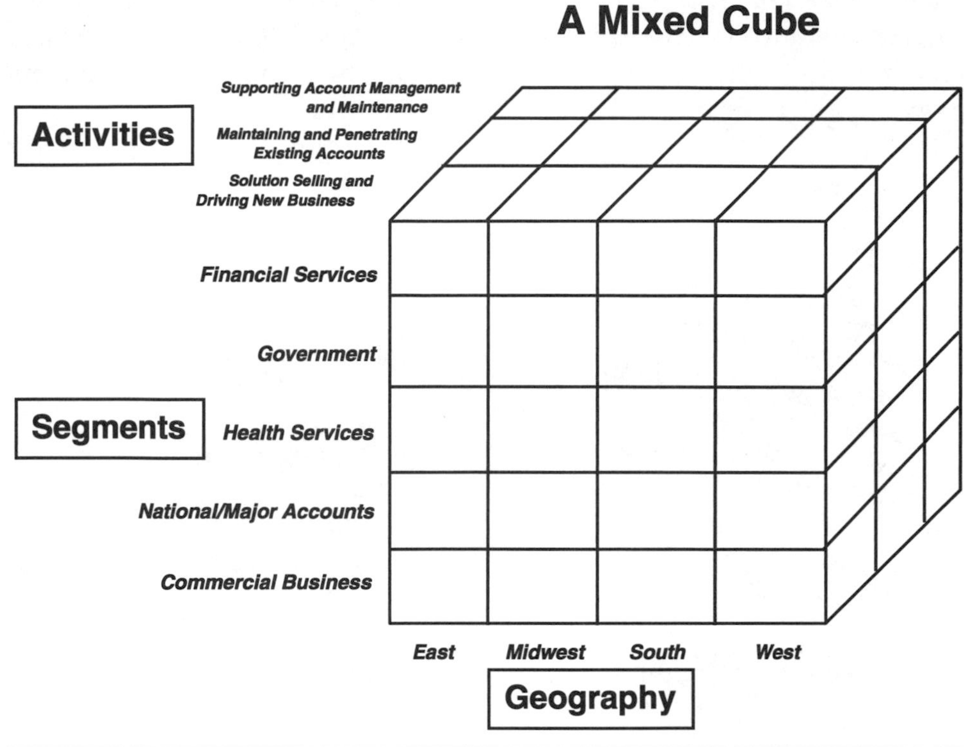


three activities. The total number of specialties was sixty (= 4 × 5 × 3). Clearly this is a lot of selling faces, even for a large sales force.

Specialization produces effectiveness gains. Overspecialization creates efficiency losses. The best organization structure obtains the right balance. It is good advice to have as few selling faces as possible while obtaining the greatest potential effectiveness gains.

Mixed organizations are a response to customer heterogeneity and product complexity, multiple and diverse buying influences, systems buying, or manufacturer-supplier partnering. These selling organizations are adaptive, are tailored to customer organizations, and gain effectiveness through product expertise and customer knowledge. However, they require more internal coordination and can suffer from low geographic efficiency.

## Developing an Efficient and Effective Sales Force Structure—A Four-Step Process

Sales force structuring is an art. Scientifically developed algorithms for optimal sales force structure selection do not exist. Individuals who understand their product lines, know their markets, have developed an effective selling process, and are not afraid to change the current structure are able to develop good structures. Frequently, firms perpetuate poor structures because they are afraid to change. Some reasons a company may be hesitant to change its structure are:

- Salespeople will leave because they like the old structure.
- Some people will lose power.
- The company is launching several new products and is afraid that disruption will jeopardize the launch.
- The company has an annual revenue goal that it must achieve.
- Everyone in the industry is doing it this way.

A four-step process for developing an efficient and effective structure is outlined in Figure 4-10. It has two phases: structure generation and structure evaluation. The first three steps make up the structure generation phase. They are designed to develop structure alternatives. Step 4 is the structure evaluation phase.

### Step 1: Study the Products, Markets, and Activity

The need for specialization is assessed in this step. How heterogeneous or complex are the products, markets, and sales force activities? Are there opportunities for effectiveness gains? Here are several questions to consider:

#### *Product Questions*

- Can one person sell all the products?
- Can significant effectiveness gains be obtained through product specialization?
- Will important products be ignored if a generalist sales force sells them?

#### *Market Questions*

- Can the market be segmented so that customers and prospects in each segment have similar selling processes? Is there customer synergy within the segments? Is there heterogeneity across these segments? Do the segments have significant market potential?
- Can significant effectiveness gains be obtained by specializing for these segments?

**Figure 4-10.** A Process for Developing Efficient and Effective Sales Force Structures.

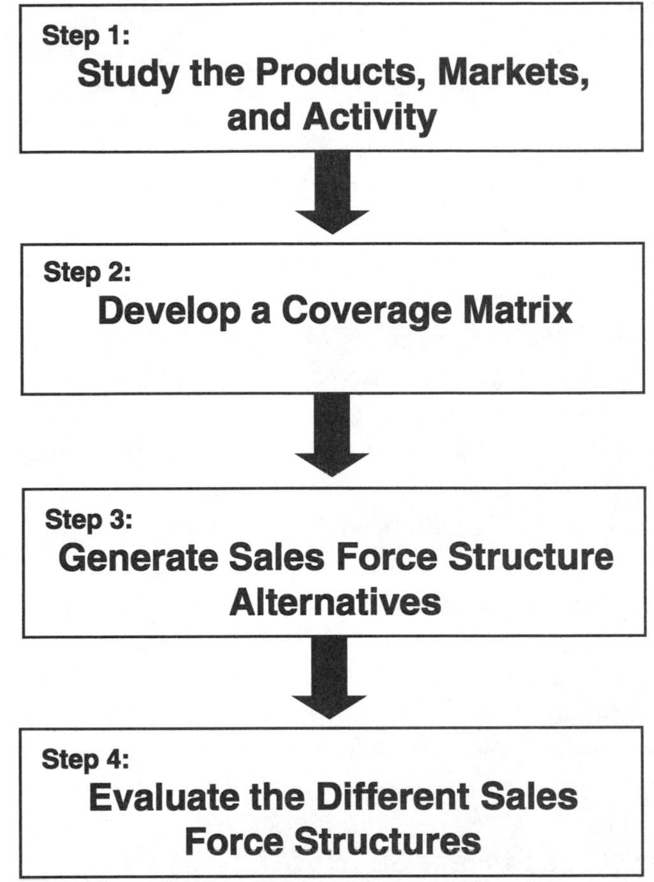


- Will important markets be ignored if a generalist selling organization sells to all of them?

### *Activity Questions*

- Can significant effectiveness gains be achieved if the sales force specializes by activity?
- Will a generalist sales force avoid essential selling activities when working with some customers and prospects?
- Will the Internet change the role of the sales force and create opportunities for activity specialization?

The answers to these questions help establish the opportunity for specialization. If the gains in potential effectiveness exceed the potential cost of inefficiency, then creativity can be used to generate structure options. In the next step, a coverage matrix is developed that identifies viable structures.

## Step 2: Develop a Coverage Matrix

A coverage matrix is a grid that displays any two of the three sources of heterogeneity—products, markets, or selling activities. The first step in developing the matrix is to decide which of the three sources of heterogeneity—markets, products, or activities—should be used for the rows and columns of the matrix. For example, the coverage matrix shown in Figure 4-11 displays the products and markets for a pharmaceutical sales force. It is best to pick the two dimensions that create the greatest heterogeneity. In our example, these are products and markets, although the analysis can be repeated with other pairs as well.

The products are listed in the rows, and the markets are listed in the columns. Every cell in the matrix represents a product/market opportunity for the sales force. Some cells require a lot of sales force attention, while others can be ignored. Some can be covered using methods other than the direct sales force, such as telesales and the Internet. Each cell is likely to have its own selling process. Cells with similar selling processes can be clustered into groups. Clusters of similar cells represent specialization opportunities for the sales force. Each set of clusters corresponds to a sales force structure.

## Step 3: Generate Sales Force Structure Alternatives

Once the matrix has been selected, it is possible to generate alternatives. Structure alternatives can be viewed as either partitions of the

**Figure 4-11.** Coverage Matrix for a Pharmaceutical Sales Force.

| | *Markets* | | | | | |
|---|---|---|---|---|---|---|
| *Products* | *Generalist* | *Allergist* | *Pediatrician* | *Psychiatrist* | *Cardiologist* | *Hospital* |
| Antibiotic—oral 1 | | | | | | |
| ACE | | | | | | |
| Antidepressant | | | | | | |
| Antibiotic—oral 2 | | | | | | |
| Antihistamine | | | | | | |
| Antibiotic—injectable | | | | | | |

matrix or clusters of cells. For clusters, the selling process for the cells within the cluster should be similar (intracluster similarity) and the selling processes for different clusters should be different (intercluster diversity). That is, the clusters are internally homogeneous and externally heterogeneous. Additionally, product/market combinations that require communication and coordination should be placed in the same cluster. The matrices shown in Figure 4-12 demonstrate several alternative organizational structures for our pharmaceutical example.

The first matrix represents a market-based structure. This structure includes two sales forces, one selling to physicians and another selling to hospitals. The second matrix represents a product-based structure. This structure also includes two selling teams, each selling a different product line. The third matrix is a mixed structure; there are five different selling teams, each with its own products and/or markets. The blank cells represent product/market combinations that will be uncovered or covered using a marketing instrument that is less expen-

**Figure 4-12.** Sales Force Structure Alternatives for a Pharmaceutical Sales Force.

| | Markets | | | | | |
|---|---|---|---|---|---|---|
| **Products** | Generalist | Allergist | Pediatrician | Psychiatrist | Cardiologist | Hospital |
| Antibiotic—oral 1 | | | | | | |
| ACE | | | | | | |
| Antidepressant | | | | | | |
| Antibiotic—oral 2 | | | | | | |
| Antihistamine | | | | | | |
| Antibiotic—injectable | | | | | | |

| | Markets | | | | | |
|---|---|---|---|---|---|---|
| **Products** | Generalist | Allergist | Pediatrician | Psychiatrist | Cardiologist | Hospital |
| Antibiotic—oral 1 | | | | | | |
| ACE | | | | | | |
| Antidepressant | | | | | | |
| Antibiotic—oral 2 | | | | | | |
| Antihistamine | | | | | | |
| Antibiotic—injectable | | | | | | |

| | Markets | | | | | |
|---|---|---|---|---|---|---|
| **Products** | Generalist | Allergist | Pediatrician | Psychiatrist | Cardiologist | Hospital |
| Antibiotic—oral 1 | | | | | | |
| ACE | | | | | | |
| Antidepressant | | | | | | |
| Antibiotic—oral 2 | | | | | | |
| Antihistamine | | | | | | |
| Antibiotic—injectable | | | | | | |

sive than the sales force. Overall, these matrices provide a framework for creating sales force structure alternatives.

### Step 4: Evaluate the Different Sales Force Structures

Once developed, the alternatives must be evaluated. The structure that is finally selected must be good for the firm's customers, good for the firm's employees, and good for the firm. A template for evaluating structures is summarized in Figure 4-13.

Overall, the final structure should provide the firm's customers with value, be responsive to their needs, and enhance a partnership in

**Figure 4-13.** Dimensions for Evaluating Sales Force Structures.

**Customers**

- Will the candidate structure add value for customers?
- Will the sales force be more responsive to customer needs?
- Will the candidate structure enhance trusted relationships?
- Is it easy for the customer to interact with the sales organization (one-stop shopping and coordinated effort)?

**Employees**

- Will the candidate structure provide rewarding work?
- Will the candidate structure provide growth opportunities?
- Will the candidate structure minimize transition disruption?
- Will the candidate structure enhance the earnings opportunity for the top performers?
- Are all of the roles and responsibilities manageable in the candidate structure?

**Firm**

- Does the candidate structure provide effectiveness gains?
- Does the candidate structure provide efficiency gains?
- Is the candidate structure adaptable?
- Does the candidate structure provide for the minimum number of selling faces without losing effectiveness?
- Does the candidate structure match resources with opportunities and provide for P&L control?
- Will the firm be able to implement the best sales strategy with the candidate structure?

which both the firm and its customers succeed. It should provide the firm's employees with rewarding work, growth opportunities, and income potential. Finally, it should provide the firm with consistent sales and earnings through gains in efficiency, effectiveness, and adaptivity.

Evaluate frequent or drastic changes in structure carefully, because structure changes can be difficult to implement. They can require major realignment of territories and management structure, significant reprogramming of sales systems, revamping of sales force compensation plans, and retraining of sales personnel. In many cases, structure changes create new job definitions with new hiring profiles. This may mean that many current salespeople are not suited for jobs in the new structure. For example, in response to changes in the health care environment, a pharmaceutical company decided to downsize its traditional physician detailing sales force and establish a new sales force to call on managed care administrators. Since the skills needed to call on administrators were different from those needed to call on physicians, few salespeople could transfer from one job to the other. This forced the company to lay off a number of existing salespeople and replace them with new people with new skills.

## Conclusion

Changing the sales force structure presents many challenges. However, sales managers should not be afraid to change a structure that is outdated. As stated earlier, progressive sales managers reevaluate the sales force structure every two to three years. Even three years may be too long given how quickly the Internet is changing the selling landscape.

The sales force structure is a critical decision. It affects how customers see the firm. Will they see generalists or specialists, place orders via the Internet, or receive phone calls? The structure determines the selling skills and level of knowledge required of the sales force. This in turn affects recruitment, training, and coaching. Finally, the structure affects each salesperson and sales manager. Job descriptions, reporting relationships, and teaming decisions are all contingent upon the sales force structure.

Good sales force structures are adaptive to ongoing change, while at the same time allowing salespeople to efficiently and effectively meet customer needs and sell the firm's products and services.

# Chapter 5

# Designing Sales Territories That Increase Sales

This chapter discusses sales territory alignment, or the assignment of customers to salespeople. Good sales territory alignment is important, as it enhances customer coverage, increases sales, fosters fair performance evaluation and reward systems, and lowers travel costs.

The chapter is designed to help you:

- Recognize the symptoms of poor sales territory alignment
- Understand the impact that territory alignment has on productivity, sales, and profits
- Recognize the conditions that create the need to realign sales territories
- Overcome the obstacles that prevent companies from maintaining good territory alignment
- Realign sales territories using an objective, data-based process that incorporates local sales management input

## The Story of Brian, Bruce, and Brenda

Brian, Bruce, and Brenda are salespeople working for a company that is a long-standing industry leader. Their manager, Bob, is concerned about his district's sales. Some of his salespeople are not performing up to his expectations, and he is formulating a plan of action to improve matters. Figure 5-1 shows how these four people perceive the current situation.

How can Bob help Brian, Bruce, and Brenda? He solicits opinions from some of the company's experts. Their advice is shown in Figure 5-2.

**Figure 5-1.** Alternative Perceptions of Salesperson Performance—Part 1.

| | What Brian Thinks: | What Bob (Brian's Manager) Thinks: | What Brian's Customers Say: |
|---|---|---|---|
| **Brian:** | *"My sales have led the region for years."* | *"Brian brings in good business."* | *"Brian doesn't expedite our orders. He's not around enough."* |
| **Bruce:** | **What Bruce Thinks:** | **What Bob (Bruce's Manager) Thinks:** | **What Bruce's Customers Say:** |
| | *"I'm on top of my accounts."* | *"Sales don't look good. Bruce has a problem finding new accounts."* | *"Bruce is a nuisance!"* |
| **Brenda:** | **What Brenda Thinks:** | **What Bob (Brenda's Manager) Thinks:** | **What Brenda's Customers Say:** |
| | *"I'm making more calls than anyone."* | *"Sales are low, and Brenda's expense account is high!"* | *"Who's Brenda?"* |

**Figure 5-2.** Alternative Perceptions of Salesperson Performance—Part 2.

| | What Cathy, the National Marketing Manager, Thinks: |
|---|---|
| **Cathy:** | *"Bruce and Brenda are not motivated enough. Let's pay more commission and lower the salary."* |
| **Colette:** | **What Colette, the Vice President of Human Resources, Thinks:** |
| | *"Bob has too many salespeople to manage. He does not have enough time to coach, motivate, train, and lead his people. The company needs a lower span of control and better training. Additionally, HR needs greater involvement in determining who gets hired in the field and who gets promoted to sales manager."* |
| **Charlie:** | **What Charlie, the National Sales Manager, Thinks:** |
| | *"Brian does not seem to need any help. We should give him a sales award and send him to Florida for the company sales award meeting. Bruce lacks prospecting skills. How did he get this job, anyway? He's not motivated to call on new accounts, and he seems to annoy his current customers. Let's give him a list of prospective accounts in his territory, train him in cold calling, and force him to get to work. Brenda is obviously ineffective. She's working hard, but she does not bring in sales. Send her to a refresher sales training course, give her six months to improve, document her performance, and then fire her if she cannot make quota."* |

### Another Solution

In addition to these compelling but contradictory opinions, there is yet another solution: Change the sales force alignment. As the map in Figure 5-3 shows, Brian has a dense urban territory with plenty of customers, Bruce has a territory that is too small, and Brenda has a large rural territory that requires too much work and travel. Making adjustments in account assignments is the best way to improve everyone's effectiveness.

Alignment problems often masquerade as other problems, particularly performance problems. Poor performance is sometimes attributed to the salesperson's abilities, when in reality it should be attributed to a poor territory. Similarly, managers often view salespeople as successful when their success is mainly due to working in a high-potential territory.

## What Is Territory Alignment?

Salespeople have an activity capacity. Customers and prospects have activity and coverage requirements. Allocating customer requirements across the sales force, or, equivalently, the assignment of customer requirements to the members of the sales force, is called a *sales territory alignment* (or *territory assignment*). *Geographic deployment* and *dis-*

**Figure 5-3.** Map of Brian, Bruce, and Brenda's Sales Territories.

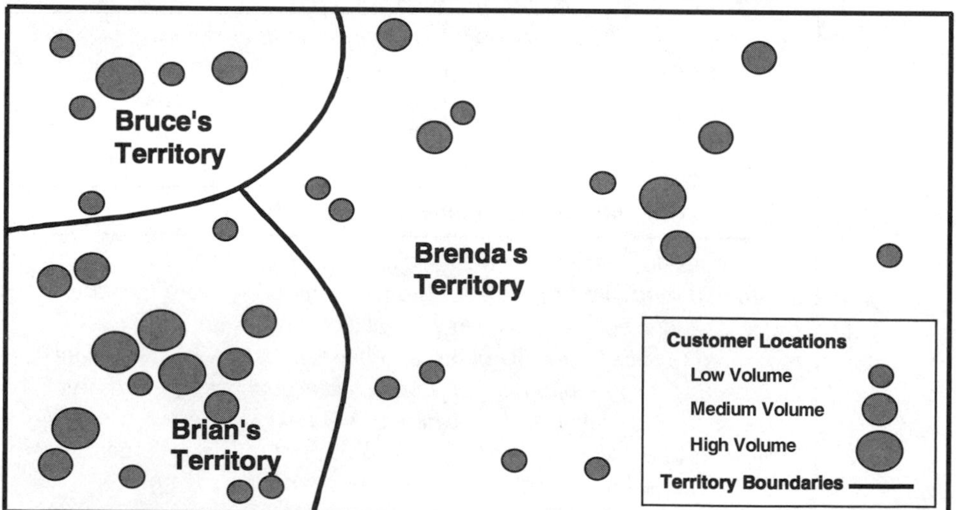

*tricting* are other terms that are used interchangeably with territory alignment. Often, the number of accounts and prospects a company services is very large, and the alignment task can be onerous and difficult. To design territories efficiently, it is often easiest to aggregate accounts and prospects into geographic units such as census tracts, zip codes, or counties. The territory alignment then becomes an assignment of geographic units to salespeople. Sometimes alignment decisions also include routing, as in bakery, beverage, or snack food sales organizations.

Some selling organizations do not have specified or exclusive alignments. Examples of these geographically overlapping alignments include organizations selling financial services, insurance, and in-home cosmetics. In these organizations, a salesperson develops his or her own alignment in the course of selling. Hence, there are geographically overlapping alignments, as the salesperson is not constrained within a geographical territory. However, a large majority of sales forces have some kind of exclusive territory alignment that specifies each salesperson's or sales team's accountability and activity mix. In an exclusive alignment, account responsibility is well defined, and customers see only a specific salesperson or sales team.

Part of the alignment decision is where to locate salespeople. The best locations are those that are close to customers and provide a high-quality standard of living for the salesperson.

## Three Reasons Why Sales Territory Alignment Is Important

There are *many* different ways to assign salespeople to accounts. In fact, there are more than 1,000 ways to assign ten accounts to two salespeople. Since the problem grows exponentially with additional accounts and salespeople, the number of alignment possibilities for any reasonably sized sales force is virtually endless. Not surprisingly, there are hundreds of potentially good alignments and an enormous number of bad ones. Not only is there a huge number of possibilities, but alignments can be extremely complex. Many companies have a number of specialized sales forces with different structures depending on whether they serve an urban or a rural setting. Consider, for example, a consumer product sales force. In an urban setting, there may be dozens of vertical (or specialized) sales forces focused on individual customers. There may be a dedicated Kroger sales force, a dedicated Safeway sales force, and so on. However, in a rural setting, Kroger, Safeway, and all other stores may be called on by a single salesperson. Often, these sales forces also have a mix of full-time and part-time salespeople.

Corporate account management structures can also lead to complicated alignments. For example, a corporate account manager may be assigned to lead each account team. Each account falls within a specified market segment, and there are segment salespeople who are assigned to the account as segment specialists. There are also product specialists who supplement the corporate account manager and the segment specialists. Each of these organizations has an alignment. The overall alignment should encourage effective teamwork across the various selling organizations. Companies such as Baxter and IBM have corporate account management structures and the consequent challenge of aligning their territories.

## Improving Workload Balance Can Increase Sales 2 to 7 Percent

Well-designed territories increase sales because total customer coverage is increased, and incremental sales are generated because the sales force sees more good customers. Balanced sales territories keep every salesperson equally busy and are good for the business. Balancing the workload shifts work among salespeople so that all customers receive appropriate coverage. For example, a salesperson who has additional call capacity can provide coverage on an account that is currently managed by a salesperson who is too busy. A neglected account in a high-workload sales territory may turn out to be one of the best accounts in a low-workload sales territory. It is likely that salespeople with too much time are seeing unprofitable accounts and salespeople with too little time are missing key accounts. Workload balance enhances sales force responsiveness. Our research shows that rectifying a workload imbalance can improve sales by between 2 and 7 percent.

If the activities of the sales force are tightly controlled, then unbalanced alignments are inherently unfair. If each salesperson must spend one hour in each store zoning merchandise (restocking and rearranging shelves), then all the salespeople should have approximately the same number of stores.

Figure 5-4 is an example from the cosmetics industry that illustrates the degree of workload imbalance that exists in many sales

**Figure 5-4.** Territory Workload Imbalance for a Cosmetics Sales Force.

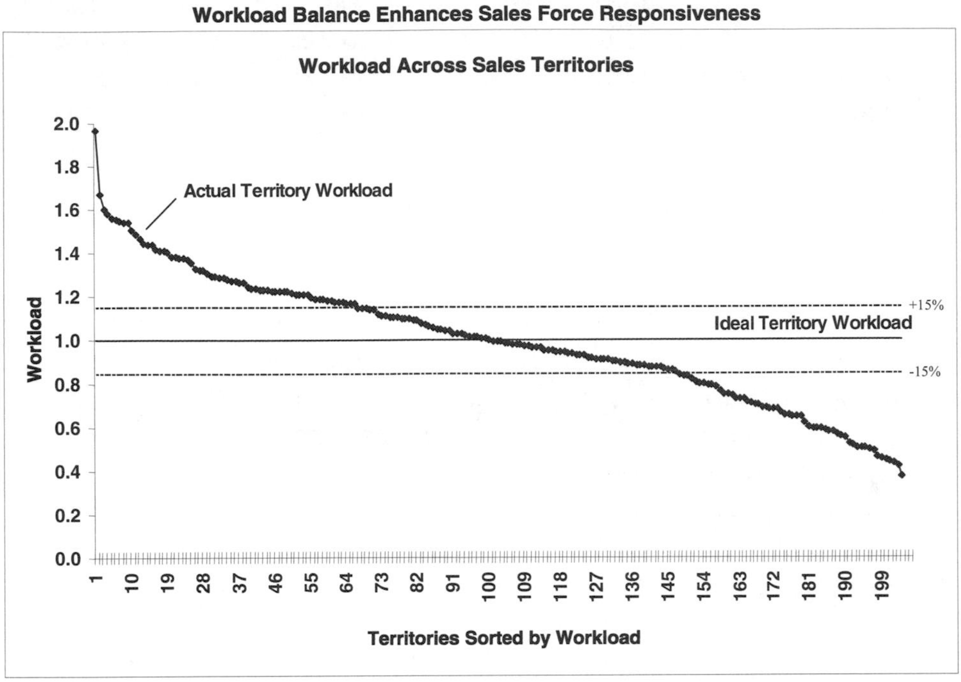

**Workload Balance Enhances Sales Force Responsiveness**

**Workload Across Sales Territories**

Actual Territory Workload

+15%

Ideal Territory Workload

-15%

Workload

Territories Sorted by Workload

forces. The account workload for each of the 200 territories in the sales force is indexed on the vertical axis. The territories are sorted from highest to lowest workload, and each territory is plotted as a point along the curved line. The ideal territory workload line represents the annual workload capacity of one salesperson. Territories with indices significantly above 1.0 have too much work for one salesperson, while territories with indices significantly below 1.0 have insufficient work. By comparing the points along the curved line (actual territory workload) with the horizontal line (ideal territory workload), it is possible to see the extent of workload imbalance. As the +15 percent and −15 percent lines show, approximately 60 percent of the territories have workloads that deviate from the ideal by more than 15 percent. Thus, many accounts in the high-workload territories are getting inadequate coverage, while at the same time some salespeople have insufficient work.

Workload imbalances like this are very common. In fact, sales managers are frequently surprised to learn how out of balance their sales territories really are. A study based on a representative sample of over 4,800 sales territories from eighteen companies in four industries found that well over half of the territories in the sample were not the right size. Approximately 25 percent of these territories were too large to be covered effectively by a salesperson. At the same time, approximately 31 percent of the territories were too small to keep a salesperson sufficiently busy with productive work. By assigning some accounts from high-workload territories to salespeople who have insufficient work, sales can be increased.

## Realignment Can Reduce Salesperson Travel

Realigning territories can also reduce travel time. Territory alignments that do not acknowledge roadways and airline routes increase travel time and therefore reduce productivity. Figure 5-5 shows how alignments that do not acknowledge road networks lead to travel time inefficiencies. Notice how the Before alignment requires Salesperson A to travel extensively through Salesperson B's sales territory to reach some of his accounts. The After alignment remedies this situation.

Reducing travel time has several benefits. For example, a large industrial distributor with over a thousand salespeople reduced salesperson travel time 13.7 percent by realigning. This translated into almost $1 million in savings in annual travel expenses. In addition, the reduced travel time enabled the sales force to increase selling time by 2.7 percent. The company estimated that this increase in coverage would result in over $15 million in additional sales and over $3 million in additional profits. Other benefits of reduced travel included more nights at home for salespeople and higher sales force morale.

**Figure 5-5.** A Comparison of Salesperson Travel—Before and After Alignment.

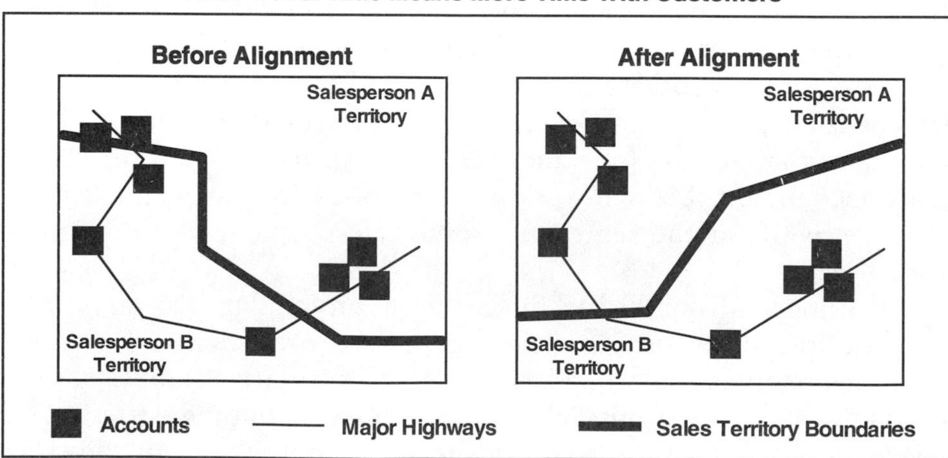

In another example demonstrating travel time reduction, a consumer products company decided *not* to cover some customers located in remote areas with its field sales force. Instead, the company decided to use telemarketing, direct mail, and Internet selling to reach low-potential, remotely located accounts. While these approaches were not as effective as face-to-face selling, the benefits of reduced travel time more than compensated for any lost sales. As a result of the realignment, the company reduced the amount of geography the direct sales force was responsible for covering by 75 percent and still retained customers representing more than 80 percent of the company's total sales volume.

## Poor Alignment Can Lead to Low Morale and High Turnover

A sales manager looking at the graph in Figure 5-6 would probably guess that the horizontal axis measures some characteristic of the salesperson, such as experience, ability, or effort. In fact, the measure on the horizontal axis has nothing at all to do with the salesperson; it is territory sales potential. Studies across industries and firms indicate that territory sales potential is a much better predictor of territory sales than any factor related to the salesperson. Territories with high market potential have high sales, regardless of sales force effort. Similarly, in territories with low potential, the firm tends to have high market share.

**Figure 5-6.** A Good Predictor of Territory Sales.

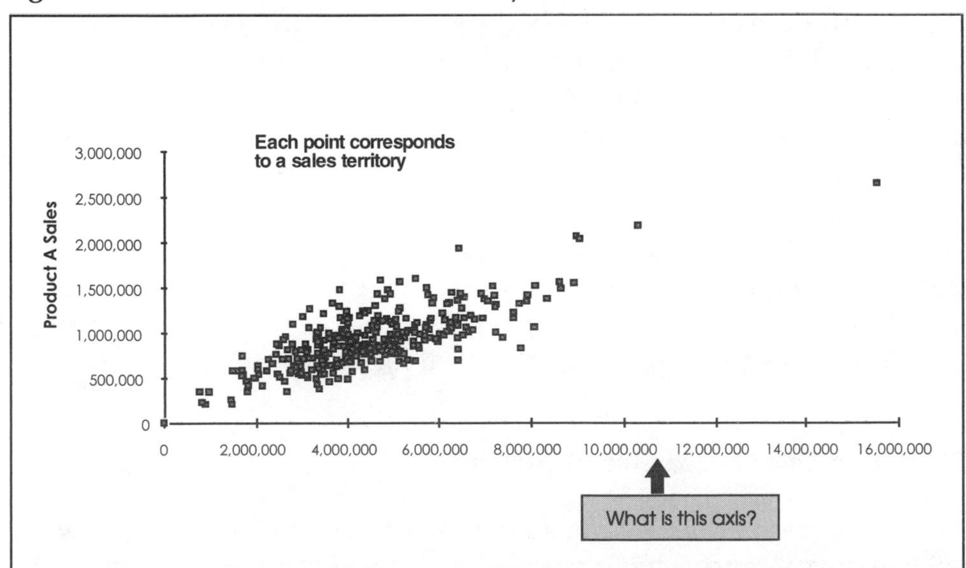

The following situation at a consumer product company illustrates this point. The territory ranked fourth highest out of 250 territories in sales for a full year had been vacant for most of the year. Analysis revealed that the territory had huge potential, which led to high sales despite the lack of sales force effort.

Management must be careful to reward the salesperson and not the sales territory. Poor alignments lead to inequitable rewards. Consequently, some very good salespeople have low job satisfaction and are unmotivated. They may leave the company if other opportunities arise. On the other hand, the salesperson who has been sent on reward trips for the last ten years may not really deserve the trips. Balancing the alignment improves morale and gives every salesperson a fair chance at success.

The effect of a poor alignment is accentuated when a highly leveraged compensation plan is in effect. Inequities in territory potential lead to inequities in sales force compensation, and the smart salesperson will try hard to obtain a high-potential sales territory.

Regrettably, compensation and recognition are affected by territory factors. This leads to low job satisfaction and low morale for salespeople in low-potential territories. Performance evaluation is often unfair to those with below-average sales territories.

## Seven Events That Create a Need to Realign

A number of events can require minor alterations to a sales territory alignment. For example, major accounts may relocate, requiring a reassignment. Or a new account may shift from a hunter (a person who prospects for customers) to a maintenance salesperson (a person who maintains customer relationships). Occasionally, a temporary realignment may occur. For example, a sales manager may ask other salespeople to cover accounts when a salesperson leaves the company.

Major realignments usually occur every few years at many U.S. companies. Typically, major alignments are the result of an important sales force change or restructuring.

Conditions that can create the need for realignment are described below.

### Change in Sales Force Size or Structure

Any company that is creating a new sales force, restructuring its sales force, or significantly changing sales force size must create a new alignment. Restructuring and upsizing both require reassignment of accounts and prospects. However, downsizing requires more than rearrangement of accounts. Decisions need to be made about who is to be retained, who is to be asked to relocate, and who is to be asked to leave the company. These are very serious decisions that cannot be made indiscriminately.

Sales force size and structure decisions cannot be completely separated from the geographic deployment (or alignment) decision. For example, specialized sales forces are less suited for markets (or accounts) that are geographically dispersed. A case in point: A health care company was considering developing a vertical selling organization to service reference labs. The decision focused on whether the geographically dispersed reference labs could support a focused selling organization. The company decided that reference labs were important and should be covered by a specialized field force. However, the inefficiencies resulting from the geographic dispersion of these sites required an incremental head count increase as well.

Frequently the amount of change, whether it is relocation or territory adjustment, is not equally distributed across the sales force. Some salespeople are unaffected, while others may see major changes. Some managers go to great lengths to protect their favorite salespeople; others use alignment data objectively. Arbitrary decisions lead to poor workload balance.

## Mergers and Acquisitions

Mergers and acquisitions, both of divisions and across companies, require the corresponding integration of selling organizations. This integration results in a redesigned selling organization. Any change in size or structure creates a need to realign the sales force. These realignments can be particularly troublesome if the two selling organizations that are merging have disparate cultures, customers, product lines, and/or job requirements.

## Unbalanced Territories

Some companies have not adjusted their sales territories in the last five, ten, or more years. Is it reasonable to believe that markets and product opportunities have not shifted geographically over time? The following are some examples to consider.

**Signals from Customers.** Customers in territories that are too large may say, "No salesperson ever calls on me" or "What is the name of your company?" On the other hand, customers in territories that are too small may say, "Is all this attention I'm getting showing up in my price?" or "Didn't I just see you?"

**Signals from Salespeople.** Companies should consider realigning when complaints from salespeople are heard, such as, "I'm paid too little" or "Other reps are overpaid" or "These territories aren't fair" or "I have to drive through other territories to get to my accounts."

A company that has not realigned in years is not aware of the increased sales opportunity, improved morale, and reduced turnover that a good alignment provides. Improved alignment opportunities are available every year. Sales force turnover is typically between 0 and 50 percent; the U.S. average is about 20 percent. On a positive note, this represents a 20 percent opportunity to fine-tune a sales territory alignment.

## Market Shifts

An adaptive selling organization moves to take advantage of market opportunities. The best sales territory alignments position company resources where market opportunities are greatest. Hence, geographic market shifts usually require realignments. Since markets and coverage needs change over time, alignments should be modified to meet these needs.

## Demographic Shifts

Every day, the center of the U.S. population moves a few feet to the west and a few feet to the south. Each year, the population of the western part of the United States is expected to grow by one million people. The Northeast, in comparison, is expected to have limited growth. Demographic shifts also manifest themselves in other ways. For example, in the next fifteen years, the southern part of the country will see an increase of 2.3 percent per year in the population over forty-five years of age. For firms whose end-user market segment is mainly in this age group (e.g., health care and leisure travel), this population increase will have a dramatic impact on the geographic deployment of the sales force. Failure to react to demographic shifts like these can result in missed opportunities.

Frequently, population and demographic shifts do not affect the balance of sales territories within a district. But when comparisons are made across districts and regions, a firm that has not effectively reacted to these shifts will find that emerging geographic areas are not properly covered.

### New Products

New product launches shift market opportunity and hence require re-alignment. New products are a particularly crucial reason to realign.

### The Need to Shake Things Up Occasionally

Finally, it is useful to consider realignment for its own sake. Give different customers to different salespeople. Bringing a new salesperson with a fresh perspective into a territory can have a positive impact. The new salesperson learns the customer's needs afresh and, as a result, may discover ways to increase sales that were overlooked by the old salesperson. Also, a new salesperson can often make a difference with reluctant prospects and can eliminate some of the "no see" accounts. Finally, realignment provides a new challenge for salespeople and extends a salesperson's experience set.

## The Forces against Change

There are several reasons why companies find it hard to maintain an up-to-date alignment.

### Realignment Disrupts People's Lives

A national review and redesign of sales territories may result in the relocation of salespeople. Salespeople do not always welcome relocation. The uprooting leads to a new social environment, possibly new schools for children, and a new job for the spouse. Even without a relocation, a realignment requires a salesperson to call on new and unfamiliar customers and prospects. Rapport must be established with the buyers for these accounts. Moving a single account between territories can be seen by one salesperson as losing the best account and by the other salesperson as gaining the worst. Also, territory redesign often leads to new reporting relationships. These sources of dissonance, for both salespeople and their managers, make territory realignments unattractive.

## Realignment Disrupts Customer Relationships

In many industries, salespeople need in-depth customer knowledge in order to be effective. As a result, management must take great care to ensure that this knowledge is not lost when a realignment takes place. A good relationship transition program addresses this concern. For example, each customer who is transferred should be introduced to the new salesperson by the departing salesperson. Together, the salespeople coordinate the transition. A compensation plan that rewards smooth transitions also helps in maintaining customer-company relationships.

The following evidence from an industrial distribution sales force supports the need for a good relationship transition program following realignment. After a realignment, the sales force implemented a transition program at the largest accounts. As a result, there was no loss in sales at these accounts. However, no transition program was used for the next lower segment of accounts. These accounts were not transferred effectively to the new salesperson, and the company experienced a 20 percent sales loss. As this case illustrates, careful planning for relationship transition is often an important part of a successful realignment.

## The Sales Force Compensation Plan Can Discourage Change

The sales force incentive compensation plan influences sales force behavior. This behavior is not always consistent with what is best for the organization as a whole. For example, incentive plans based on sales volume encourage salespeople to want more accounts than they can cover effectively. More accounts mean more opportunities to build sales. In contrast, incentive plans based on market share encourage salespeople to want fewer accounts than they could manage. With fewer accounts, a salesperson can penetrate the accounts more deeply and drive out the competition. Finally, growth-oriented incentive plans encourage salespeople to want territories with large numbers of accounts with untapped potential.

Salespeople with good territories do not want to give up income. A salesperson whose territory is targeted for reduction in size or loss of accounts may fight to keep the existing territory with the following argument: "I have done a good job for you. It is unfair that my 'reward' is to have my territory split." If management receives complaints from the best performers, it may relent in the realignment effort.

The resistance to realigning sales territories often increases as the proportion of pay based on incentive (as opposed to salary) increases. This is because the higher the incentive component of compensation, the more likely it is that a change in territory boundaries will affect a salesperson's income.

In some cases, the sales force compensation plan should be modified at the same time as a realignment occurs. Certainly territory goals need to change.

### Realignment Is Cumbersome

A manual sales force realignment is time-consuming and unrewarding. Moreover, manual realignment may take anywhere from three to six months for the largest sales forces. District managers and sales force analysts who perform manual realignments must pore over maps and account-level reports. The difficulty of the task can lead to answers that are far from optimal.

Computerized technologies, such as the MAPS system pioneered by ZS Associates, have helped to reduce the complexity of the alignment process. In fact, with today's technology, it is hard to imagine anyone completing a manual alignment.

### Realignment Is Costly

When relocation costs are included, companies often spend from $10,000 to $1,000,000 on a realignment.

### Data Are Limited

Some firms are unwilling to commit significant resources to realignment because they do not believe they have the right data. For example, a company entering a new product category will require an entirely new database. Another company may lack confidence in its current customer database. Yet another company may have an exceptionally large database, with tens of thousands of products and/or customers. Regardless of the scenario, a company may hesitate to make a large investment in a realignment if it is uncertain of its data.

Other companies feel that they cannot measure particular customers' sales because of complex distribution systems. For example, sales may get lost somewhere in the channel. When products are shipped first to a distributor's warehouse and then to individual accounts, credit cannot be assigned to individual territories if the second shipment is not tracked.

Finally, some companies are not able to define precisely who their potential customers or prospects are. For example, for companies selling Yellow Pages advertising, newspaper advertising, or business forms, almost anyone can be a potential customer.

Fortunately, as technology advances, the accuracy and availability of data are increasing. Typically, surrogate measures for territory business value can be developed. The sales force can help create a database or can enhance an existing database to be used for alignment. The authors have helped realign over 200,000 sales territories in the United States and, with help from the company, have identified useful data each time.

## Maintaining an Effective Alignment—A Three-Step Process

It is important for sales forces to maintain a good alignment, despite the many forces discouraging alignment change. There are three steps to a good alignment:

1. Defining appropriate alignment criteria
2. Auditing alignments annually
3. Using a combination of centralized planning and local expertise when faced with a major realignment

The following is a detailed description of each step.

### Alignment Criteria

What do the customer, the salesperson, and the company want from the alignment? Figure 5-7 provides some answers to this question.

**Alignment Goal.** There are five main alignment goals: balance the workload, balance sales potential, minimize disruption, develop compact territories, and equalize marginal returns. Figure 5-8 shows how each of these alignment goals affects what each of the different stakeholders want.

**Figure 5-7.** What Different Stakeholders Want From the Alignment.

| *Customers Want* | *Salespeople Want* | *Firm Wants* | *Economist Wants* |
|---|---|---|---|
| Salespeople who are competent and empathetic | High opportunity | A motivated sales force | Equal marginal returns across sales territories |
| Salespeople who understand their needs and are responsive | Manageable workload | Sales results | |
| Continuity of salespeople | Little change and low risk | Cost control | |
| | Control of overnights | Effort control | |

**Figure 5-8.** The Impact of Each of the Alignment Goals.

| | | *Balance the Workload* | *Balance Sales Potential* | *Minimize Disruption* | *Develop Compact Territories* | *Equalize Marginal Returns* |
|---|---|---|---|---|---|---|
| **Customers** | Responsiveness | X | | | X | |
| | Relationships | | | X | | |
| **Salespeople** | Earnings opportunity | | X | | | |
| | Manageable workload | X | | | X | |
| | Reduced uncertainty | | | X | | |
| | Control of overnights | | | | X | |
| **Firm** | Sales results | X | X | X | | |
| | Effort control | X | | | | |
| | Motivation | X | X | X | X | |
| | Travel cost control | | | | X | |
| **Economist** | Equal marginal returns | | | | | X |

*Balancing the workload* maximizes sales force coverage and improves responsiveness to customers. It also improves sales results and is critical if sales force activities are tightly controlled.

*Balancing sales potential* gives salespeople equal earning opportunity and also improves sales results.

*Minimizing disruption* of the current alignment preserves relationships, eliminates uncertainty for salespeople, and increases motivation.

*Developing compact territories* improves responsiveness to customer needs, gives salespeople fewer overnight trips, and keeps travel costs down.

*Equalizing marginal returns across territories* is a goal preferred by economists. Unfortunately, this is an impractical measure to obtain. Measuring marginal returns at the account and territory level with any accuracy is very expensive and frequently impossible.

**Importance of Alignment Goals.** Although alignment goals vary by company and industry, balancing workload and balancing sales potential are usually selected as key alignment goals. Since some disruption is an inevitable outcome of a realignment, an effective alignment process considers such dimensions as trade areas and key customer relationships. Finally, when developing compact territories, road networks and travel times should be taken into account. In cases where salespeople fly to cover their territory, airline routes and fares should be considered as well.

The alignment goals must focus on what the sales force does. For example:

- For a highly commissioned sales force, emphasize sales potential balance in order to equalize earnings opportunities for salespeople.
- When relationship selling and in-depth customer knowledge are important, emphasize minimizing disruption.
- When workloads can be estimated accurately at the account level, emphasize workload balance. For example, sales forces that perform a set of well-defined tasks for their customers should have territories with balanced workloads to encourage optimal customer coverage. An example would be in-store merchandisers in the consumer products industry.
- When controlling the number of hours worked is important, as with part-time salespeople, emphasize balanced workloads and minimal travel.

It is important to note that balancing company sales is not the same as balancing sales potential. Sales reflect where the sales force is currently spending its time. Sales potential and workload suggest where it should be spending its time. Territories that are balanced in terms of sales can become inherently unfair and remiss in covering untapped potential.

**Measuring Alignment Criteria.** Having a good measure of the alignment criteria is critical to a successful realignment. A company should plan to spend a significant amount of time creating, evaluating, and verifying any data that drive alignment decisions. While alignment measures vary by company and industry, some ideas for measuring different alignment criteria are provided in Figure 5-9.

Creating good measures of workload and potential often requires effort. The accuracy and detail of the data used for these measures are critical for field acceptance. In some industries, data vendors supply fairly complete data. For example, health care companies know where hospitals, surgicenters, and physicians are located. They also know the

**Figure 5-9.** Measures of Different Alignment Criteria.

| *Workload* |
| --- |
| Number of accounts<br>Number of accounts by segment<br>Number of prospects<br>Number of hours required to cover accounts or prospects<br>Time expended<br>. . . |
| *Potential* |
| Total industry sales<br>Buying power index<br>SIC information<br>Demographic information (population by age, etc.)<br>. . . |
| *Compactness* |
| Square miles<br>Average travel time<br>. . . |
| *Disruption* |
| Percentage of accounts that have been reassigned<br>Percentage of dollar sales that have been reassigned<br>. . . |

number of hospital beds, hospital procedures, and patients, and sometimes even the sales volumes associated with these customers. Consumer product firms know their customers' store locations and have all commodity volume estimates.

In other cases, companies can use surrogate measures obtained from statistics gathered by the Census Department. Data such as buying power index measures and SIC information may be appropriate in some situations. Frequently, external data are complemented by account and prospect statistics compiled by the salespeople or the company. Salespeople can list possible customers and make an assessment of their value. The best potential data incorporate not only historical market sales, but a prediction of future market sales as well.

Keep in mind that the alignment decision does not go away just because perfect data are not available. Often, companies must seek creative ways to build new or improve upon existing databases. If the data are good, the alignment will be fair to the salespeople, enable the company to serve its customers better, and generate higher sales volume.

## Annual Audit

Every alignment should be examined annually. The following questions need to be answered:

- Has the market changed?
- Is the alignment consistent with the new product priorities specified in the marketing plan?
- Are there better data sources available for consumer and market information?

Figure 5-10 is an example of the type of information that can be developed to evaluate (and possibly validate) an existing alignment. The map shows how population density varies over the entire United States. This type of data can be used to locate salespeople geographically.

The audit analysis of the alignment also helps sales organizations manage territory vacancies. Salesperson turnover creates opportunities to redeploy sales effort without relocating salespeople. A vacant territory in a low-potential area can be closed down, and a new person can be hired in another location where there is greater opportunity.

One national sales manager keeps a sales force location map in his desk drawer. The map is the future blueprint for his sales organization. On the map, each territory is represented with a dot in one of three

**Figure 5-10.** Analysis Useful for Auditing an Alignment.

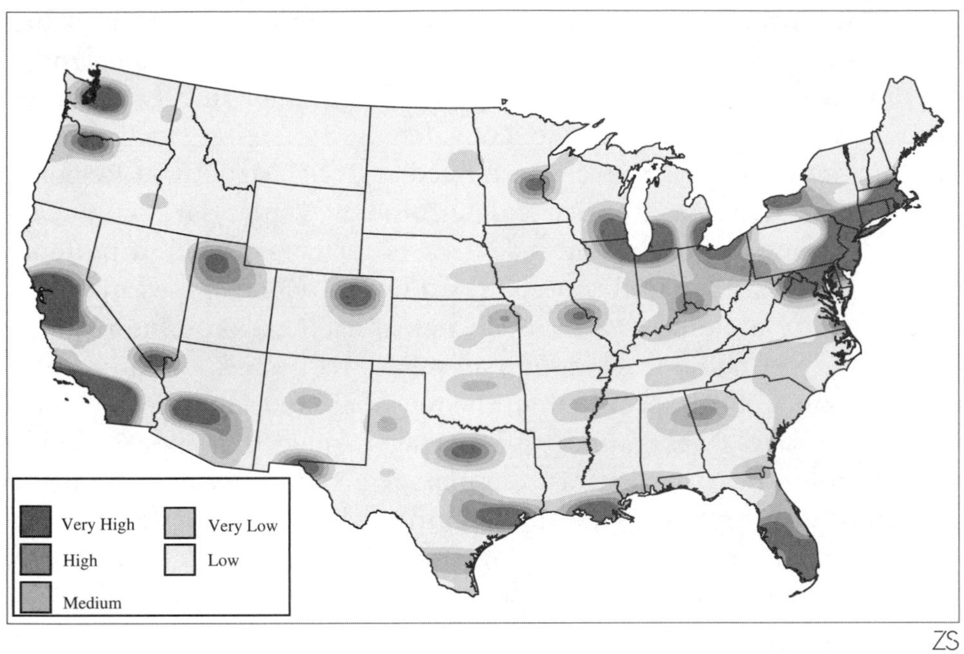


colors. Green dots are existing territories with good future potential, black dots are existing territories with poor future potential, and yellow dots are proposed new territories. Each time a territory becomes vacant, the manager checks the map. If a vacancy occurs in a black dot territory, the territory is closed and a new territory is opened up in a yellow dot location. Through proactive attrition management, this sales organization maintains a good alignment without relocating salespeople.

## Implementing a Major Realignment

Many companies delegate alignment decisions to their first-line sales managers. There are several important reasons for this. First, a centrally developed alignment may miss many local conditions. Local factors include customer relationships, salesperson preferences, and local trade patterns. Moreover, most area sales managers will challenge a centrally developed alignment. Second, first-line sales managers must take ownership of the alignment. If they do not, it will be difficult to manage any dissonance from salespeople whose account responsibility has changed. A changed alignment affects people's lives; therefore, it must be supported and accepted by the sales organization. Finally, alignment is a difficult problem, and delegating part of this work to sales managers helps get the work done more quickly.

While local delegation of alignment has some advantages, it has one major disadvantage: Even if first-line managers develop a balanced alignment within their area of responsibility, major imbalances may exist across areas. For example, consider the following story about a sales organization with a decentralized regional structure. Regional managers were given authority to determine the appropriate sales headcount for their region. To provide a basis for comparison, a national model was created that allocated headcount to regions based upon the percentage of national market potential in each region. One regional manager, who had a background in sales, requested a significantly larger number of salespeople than the national model suggested. Coming from a sales background, this manager knew that "more people means more sales." In contrast, another regional manager, who had a background in finance, requested significantly fewer people than the national model suggested. Coming from a finance background, this manager knew that "more people implies higher costs." In addition, more people means more management and more work, which some managers want to avoid. Because of the different experiences, personalities, and viewpoints of field sales managers, cross-regional personnel allocations are usually suboptimal when regional managers have a significant input into their headcount allocation. Suboptimal regional headcount allocations contribute to a national territory misalignment even in cases where local sales managers develop ideal local alignments.

One company rewarded its sales managers using a "sales per person" measure. What incentive does this sales management team have for adding salespeople?

The following quote from a sales vice president further illustrates the shortcoming of complete delegation: "My sales manager in St. Louis says he doesn't need any more salespeople. Currently, he says, he does not have enough accounts to call on, and I believe him." Meanwhile, St. Louis has 35 percent more potential than the average sales area. The St. Louis manager is not wrong in his perception of his sales area; he has just decided to target a small list of accounts and prospects. He may also be myopic; he may not be aware of his sales area's potential compared to other sales areas.

A major realignment requires central benchmarking because cross-regional personnel allocations are usually suboptimal when alignment decisions are delegated locally.

**A Process That Works: Central Alignments with Local Adjustment.** The best solution for a realignment usually involves centrally derived alignments with local adjustments by first-line sales managers. An acceptable alignment must take into account global factors such as personnel balance, as well as the local conditions that are of importance to the sales management team. The process illustrated in Figure 5-11 accomplishes both objectives.

First, alignment criteria, such as "minimize disruption and balance workload," are selected. Second, a database is developed for the alignment, including customer and prospect locations, estimated workload, sales potential, and travel time. Then, salesperson locations or territory centers are developed centrally, based on business needs. With any alignment, it is imperative to determine salesperson locations first. It is impossible to have a good alignment if people are located in the wrong places. In conjunction with regional managers, the territory centers are audited and finalized. Next, optimal alignments are developed centrally. Last, alignment recommendations are finalized with the help of first-line sales managers.

The process illustrated in Figure 5-11 facilitates successful imple-

**Figure 5-11.** An Effective Alignment Process.

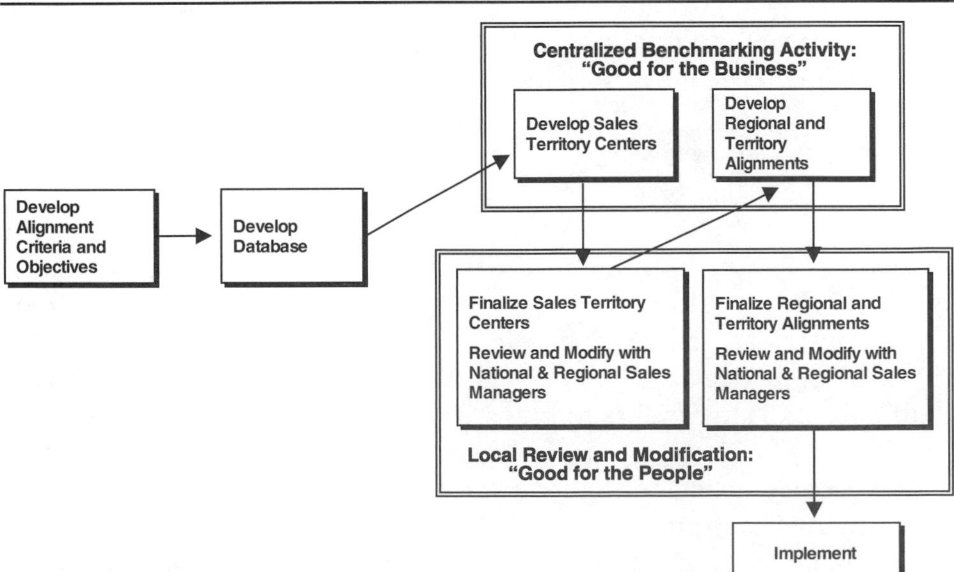

mentation of alignment changes. The process builds an alignment that is good for the business because the central benchmarking activity defines consistent, objective alignment criteria that support the sales force's strategic goals. A central benchmark also ensures that salesperson resources are distributed appropriately across the country. At the same time, the process builds an alignment that is good for the people because the input of local management is a fundamental part of the process.

The following quote from a human resources director at a large pharmaceutical firm summarizes the value of sales force buy-in during an alignment: "A lot of people don't realize this, but after an alignment, most of the dirty work ends up in my office. After we aligned poorly five years ago, I received almost a thousand complaints from the field force. We did it right two years ago. I received only two complaints. We had a minimum of disruption, relocations, and turnover."

Another quotation from a district sales manager: "My input was taken into account. Management didn't just give me an alignment and say 'go work it.' "

**Alignment Tools.** Two types of software are available to enhance the territory realignment process. Territory optimization software enables managers to develop optimal regional and territory alignments quickly. Territory manipulation software improves the regional and territory alignment by enabling field managers to explore the consequences of fine-tuning an alignment before making it final. Both types of software are available on personal computers. In the future, territory manipulation capabilities will be available via the Internet as well.

*Territory Optimization Software.* As stated before, there are countless ways to align sales territories, even for the simplest selling organizations. It would take a long time to manually generate and evaluate all of them. However, the search capabilities of computers can be harnessed to help with this task. The authors have developed algorithms for finding optimal sales territory alignments and are using them in their consulting practice at ZS Associates. These algorithms search the space of all potential alignments to find alignments that:

- Have compact contiguous sales territories relative to the U.S. highway system
- Are balanced in terms of workload and sales potential
- Minimize disruption

- Minimize travel time
- Recognize trade areas

Territory optimization software has been used to develop multiyear alignments, which are required when a sales force is experiencing a multiyear expansion or contraction. Sales territories added in the first year of an expansion are selected so that they will be appropriately located for subsequent years of the expansion.

Alignment optimization is not enough. For a successful implementation, it is critical to obtain input directly from the sales force, since virtually everyone in the sales force is affected by a territory alignment. It is impossible for a computer to represent the full complexity of a sales environment. The only time when an optimal alignment has been implemented without changes, in our experience, is when a sales force has been created from scratch.

*Territory Manipulation Software.* Territory manipulation software, typified by ZS Associates' MAPS software, applies computer power to a data-intensive and complicated task. A typical MAPS application combines a computerized map of territories with market and sales data for the geographic units that make up the territories. A first-line manager can adjust territories to see how sales and potential would be redistributed in the revised alignment.

Using MAPS for a typical U.S. alignment greatly simplifies the alignment task. For example, every zip code area is shown on the screen with the correct shape and relative size. Each zip code area is colored to indicate which salesperson it "belongs to." It is also possible to see any numerical data that are kept by zip code, such as sales of a particular product. Account-level data can also be shown. With one click of a mouse, a zip code or account can be changed from one salesperson to another. A report listing zip codes or accounts by territory, including totals of any data kept in the database, is instantly available.

Territory manipulation software usually has the following features:

- It is interactive, easy to use, and menu-driven.
- It integrates all alignment data with the geographic database.
- On-screen maps show roads, geographic boundaries, and individual account locations.
- Reports compare individual salespeople and give territory, district, and region totals.
- Several alignment scenarios can be saved and compared.

For large alignments, this type of software saves a great deal of time and money.

*Territory Alignment Over the Internet.* The Internet can play a significant role in territory alignment for many companies. An effective territory alignment process, which includes central alignment with local adjustments, requires ongoing communication between the central office and salespeople across the country. Since the Internet provides a very powerful and efficient means of communication, Internet alignment applications can streamline the entire realignment process.

First, the Internet can help streamline the process of building an alignment database. Salespeople can visit a Web site where they can see a map of their territory and a preliminary list of accounts. On this site, they can "clean up" the data for their territory by adding or deleting accounts, modifying the size or potential of an account, or inserting the accurate location for an account. The information they provide is stored in a central database. This interactive process involves the salespeople, who know the accounts best, in developing an accurate database. As a result, sales force buy-in to the realignment is enhanced.

Second, Internet applications can help sales forces audit their current alignments. A sales manager can visit a Web site, answer questions describing the sales organization, and use the site to determine whether or not territories are well balanced. The site can give the sales manager the ability to optimize territories that are out of balance.

Third, the Internet can provide an easy means of communicating alignment changes to the field. Maps and reports reflecting alignment changes can be distributed in a secure manner on a Web site or via bulk e-mail. This eliminates the costly and time-consuming process of printing and collating maps and reports and shipping them to salespeople.

Finally, the Internet can provide sales forces with a means of making alignment changes from the field. First-line sales managers can visit a Web site and make predetermined territory alignment changes. Once these changes have been approved, they are automatically registered in a central database. Full Web-enabled territory manipulation allows first-line sales managers to visit a Web site where a computerized map of their territories showing the latest market, sales, and account workload data is accessible. They can experiment with territory changes online and immediately see the impact that these changes have on territory geography as well as the redistribution of sales, market potential, and workload across territories. In turn, sales managers can e-mail new territory maps to their sales force so that salespeople can become productive immediately.

The Internet has become a major worldwide sales channel for many goods and services. Companies will need to redesign their selling processes more frequently as the capabilities and usage of the Internet expand. These changes in selling processes will affect the size and structure of sales forces and individual sales territories.

On-line territory alignment can help reduce the anxiety that frequent realignment can cause. It allows decisions to be made and communicated to the field quickly, so that uncertainty is reduced. In addition, on-line territory alignment allows the sales force to participate in realignments more easily, thereby enhancing buy-in.

## Final Territory Alignment Insights

### Look at the Territory: Do the Right Thing

A territory is a separate entity. It can be customized slightly to fit a specific salesperson's strengths. However, it should not be customized too much because territory alignments typically outlast a specific salesperson's assignment to the territory. When considering a change for a territory, it is important to consider the following questions:

- Is this the right thing to do regardless of who the salesperson is?
- Is this the right thing to do for the geography and the set of accounts?

A territory is built to serve the customer—consider how customers perceive coverage. Alignments are developed for sales potential, not for salespeople. Do not design territories around individual skills. The alignment will prove to be suboptimal if a territory is designed for a particular salesperson and then that salesperson leaves the company.

### Balance Workload to Maximize Sales Force Coverage

Accounts in every territory will receive balanced service if every salesperson has the same workload. Coverage will be balanced because all important customers will have access to the appropriate share of their salesperson's time. Of course, customers may be seen too frequently or too little if the sales force is not sized appropriately.

## Reward and Recognize Individual Performance, Not Territory Performance

In many cases, average salespeople with great territories receive recognition, promotions, and compensation that they don't deserve. This inequity can cause significant motivation problems in a good sales force. Balanced sales territories help give recognition for individual performance.

## Consider How Alignment Affects Compensation and Other Systems

Realignment affects human resources, compensation, mailings, and numerous other systems throughout the company. It's critical to think through all the possible ramifications of an alignment change. For instance, a change in customer assignment might require the salesperson to send orders to a different warehouse for processing. Also, systems may need to change to reflect new sales credits.

Compensation plans and territory goals also need to be considered when implementing realignments. A new set of customers can require new territory goals and may even create the need for a reevaluation of the compensation plan.

## Manage Vacancies to Create Opportunity for Change in Territory Locations, While Avoiding Relocation Costs

Vacancies can create opportunity. Redundant or low-potential territories can be closed, and new salespeople can be hired in high-opportunity areas. Conscious territory management enables a sales force to meet a future blueprint.

## Avoid the Local Knowledge Trap

First-line sales managers and salespeople undoubtedly have a great deal of knowledge about local conditions in their area of responsibility. However, they lack the broader perspective of how their area compares to other sales areas. This broad perspective is essential to achieving good alignment. An effective approach for a successful realignment typically involves developing a centrally derived alignment to act as a benchmark, followed by local adjustments by first-line sales managers.

### Manage the Transition to a New Alignment

Realignments are a source of dissonance for salespeople, managers, and customers. It is possible to manage this dissonance, however, by minimizing disruption where possible and by implementing a well-planned relationship transition plan.

## Conclusion

Alignment is an overlooked sales force productivity tool. There are many obstacles that prevent companies from creating and maintaining good alignments. However, the benefits of good alignment are significant. Alignment deserves more attention and consideration from management than it often gets. Keep striving for good alignments, and watch out for the possible alignment blockades listed in Figure 5-12.

**Figure 5-12.** Potential Alignment Blockades.

| *Potential Alignment Blockade* | *Favorite Quotation* |
|---|---|
| President's Cup Paula | "How am I going to win the salesperson of the year award after you steal my accounts?" |
| Mel the Mellow Manager | "If it ain't broke, don't fix it." |
| Peter the Pessimist | "We can't realign—our account data are no good. Besides, there's no way to measure potential for our markets." |
| High-Commission Harry | "You're not touching any account I earn a 20 percent commission on." |
| Chatty Charlie | "This is a relationship sell. We can't change accounts around." |

## Chapter 6

# Recruiting the Best Salespeople

This chapter explores the sales force recruiting and hiring process. A sales force cannot be successful if it does not attract and retain the best people: People who meet customer expectations, sell well, become successful sales managers, establish and reinforce a successful culture, and make the best decisions for each sales force productivity driver.

The chapter is designed to help you:

- Know when it is best to hire an experienced salesperson and when to hire an inexperienced one
- Develop a recruiting process that attracts good people and at the same time is objective and thorough, fast and cost-effective, legally defensible, and consistent with organizational goals
- Execute the six steps of the recruiting process—job definition, candidate profile, applicant pool, selection, attraction, and evaluation/improvement—effectively, giving practical suggestions for each step
- Learn why interviewing alone is a poor predictor of sales success
- Develop a job profile by combining experience with job analysis and statistical profiling
- Identify and utilize the best sources of good candidates
- Increase the odds of success in recruiting by using referrals, behavioral interviews, tests, simulations, reference and background checks, and other proven techniques
- Use the Internet effectively to enhance the recruiting process

## Introduction

Sales managers from a variety of industries agree: Hiring is the most important decision a sales manager makes. For over ten years, we have polled participants in the sales force productivity programs at Northwestern University's Kellogg Executive Development Center. According to this poll, sales managers agree that of all the decisions they make, hiring decisions have the greatest impact on sales success. Hiring, training, and the sales manager are consistently ranked as the three most important factors, with hiring generally regarded as the most important.

Successful companies everywhere echo this sentiment:

- *"Recruiting is the number 1 priority with us—finding quality people who can analyze data, see things through the customers' eyes, and interface with marketing people." (RJR Nabisco)*
- *"It's hard to separate recruiting top people and keeping top people. It doesn't matter how good your training or products are—if you don't have good people to begin with, you're nowhere." (Procter & Gamble)*
- *"Recruiting and holding top people—salespeople are the single most important factor in our success." (Times Mirror)*
- *"Recruiting and keeping top people is most important to us. If you can keep your best people, that means you'll be opening new accounts and keeping them, and you're also assured of a good reputation among your customers." (Communications Satellite Corp.)*

## The Hiring/Training Tradeoff

Selling organizations such as Procter & Gamble, Johnson & Johnson, Coca-Cola, and Xerox mainly hire recent college graduates for their sales positions and train them thoroughly to be successful. These companies view their training programs as a corporate asset that generates a differential competitive advantage. In contrast, some other companies hire only people with sales experience; they expect the new hires to integrate quickly and contribute to the selling effort.

The labor market has an impact on which of these hiring strategies a company chooses. In tight labor markets, it's typical for companies to seek inexperienced hires. Economic recessions, on the other hand, result in corporate downsizing initiatives that force many experienced people into the job market. Thus, companies have an opportunity to hire experienced people. However, companies rarely lay off their best people when downsizing, so careful screening of applicants is recommended in this economic environment.

Is it better to hire people with experience or without experience? This recruiting decision is evaluated from eight perspectives in Figure 6-1.

Over the years, hundreds of district, regional, and national sales managers have helped resolve the hiring/training controversy for their own companies. Many of these managers were participants in executive development courses taught by the authors at the Kellogg Graduate School of Management and were asked to define the characteristics of the successful salesperson. The essence of their extensive list is shown in Figure 6-2.

Researchers have also worked at determining the skills that lead to sales success. In a recent study, James O'Hara identifies six traits of the best salespeople. They are:

- Innate desire to serve
- Strong work ethic
- Integrity
- Ability to put others at ease
- Effective communication skills
- Willingness to listen

A fundamental question that should come to mind as these lists are reviewed is which of these characteristics can be developed through training and which are innate? Notice that almost all the characteristics in both lists are inherent in the candidate. Only skills and knowledge can be taught. As a sales executive once said, "You can't send a duck to eagle school."

Nordstrom is a department store chain in the United States that is known for its impeccable customer service. We once asked a Nordstrom manager, "How does Nordstrom train its salespeople to be so customer-oriented?" "Nordstrom doesn't train—the salesperson's family does" was the answer. In other words, the hiring process is critical for Nordstrom's sales success.

Every organization wants the members of its sales force to have most of the characteristics listed above. No single individual has all of these characteristics. Hiring and training both contribute to the development of a high-performance selling organization, but their roles are different. The role of hiring is to locate individuals with the core characteristics and values that lead to success in sales. The role of training is

**Figure 6-1.** A Comparison of Recruiting Experienced Versus Inexperienced Salespeople.

| *Perspective* | *Experienced Hire* | *Inexperienced Hire* |
|---|---|---|
| **Financial** | Experienced people are productive more quickly. They have selling skills, they may know the products and markets, and they have established customer relationships. They may actually retain some of their current customers. They contribute immediately to helping the company achieve its sales targets.<br><br>Experienced people cost more. Good people need to be paid more than they are earning at their current company, or they need to see more upside opportunity if they move at the same salary. Also, if a search firm finds the experienced person, as is often the case, the search firm's fee must be paid. | Inexperienced salespeople cost less overall.<br><br>Training and coaching costs are higher with inexperienced salespeople.<br><br>Inexperienced salespeople tend to be less effective initially. |
| **Culture** | Hiring inexperienced people fosters parochialism. Experienced people bring diverse ideas and approaches. However, they may be set in their ways and find it difficult to conform. | Hiring inexperienced people and growing them builds loyalty. Inexperienced hires are eager to learn and succeed in their first sales job. Over time, they learn the market, learn the company's preferred selling process, and fit into the culture of the organization. Young people adapt to an existing corporate culture quickly and more thoroughly. |
| **The Candidate** | Experienced people usually bring desirable selling skills to their new organization.<br><br>Experienced people know the workplace. They are not naïve about working, and they have more realistic expectations for their jobs. | Inexperienced hires are unencumbered. They have few biases and few bad habits.<br><br>College graduates are just starting out in their careers. They may be "trying out" sales to see if they like it, or they may view the sales job as a stepping- |

*(continues)*

**Figure 6-1.** Continued.

| *Perspective* | *Experienced Hire* | *Inexperienced Hire* |
|---|---|---|
| **The Candidate (cont.)** | Experienced people around thirty years of age are likely to be in the establishment phase of their careers. Because of this, five to seven years of strong performance is likely.<br><br>Occasionally experienced people bring baggage with them. Their selling skills may not meet the expectations of the recruiting sales force, they may lack loyalty, or they may be wedded to an incompatible sales culture. | stone to bigger and better things. As a result, the turnover rate among inexperienced hires can be high.<br><br>Academic studies have shown that hiring at the entry level and promoting from within increases salespeople's trust in the organization and reduces sales force turnover and opportunistic behavior. |
| **Customer** | Prior sales experience is a liability if it is incongruent with the needs of the new customers and the new selling process. | Some customers may be unhappy with an inexperienced salesperson. They may resent having to "train" someone in their ways of doing business. |
| **Selling process** | An organization can grow very quickly by hiring experienced salespeople who have a good grasp of the company's products and markets and can engage in the company's selling process immediately. | It is beneficial to hire inexperienced people if the job requires a high degree of job-specific selling or account management skill, or a high level of product and market knowledge that cannot be gained outside. |
| **Management** | Experienced people can be challenging to manage. Rigid individuals who bring incompatible skills may never adapt to the needs of management.<br><br>Experienced people do not want to be treated like inexperienced people. Management needs processes that integrate them into the organization in a compassionate manner. | Inexperienced people are less threatening to manage; they can be molded. |
| **Co-workers, peers** | Peers may suspect that new salespeople are entering the company at pay levels higher | Coworkers may feel more comfortable with young, inexperienced people. They can guide |

*(continues)*

**Figure 6-1.** Continued.

| *Perspective* | *Experienced Hire* | *Inexperienced Hire* |
|---|---|---|
| **Co-workers, peers (cont.)** | than their own. "Why else would someone leave her or his current company?" | them and serve as their mentors. |
| **Probability of hiring the right person** | Experienced people are more practiced interviewees. They tend to be more convincing and better able to mask their foibles. Recruiting mistakes are more severe with experienced people. Severance costs are higher, and their exit can be more disruptive.<br><br>It may be difficult to find high-quality experienced candidates. Successful people tend to stay in their current jobs because they feel successful. | It is difficult to assess candidates for jobs that they have never done before. |

to give these individuals every opportunity to succeed by providing them with the knowledge and skills that will allow them to meet customer needs.

High-performance selling organizations try to get the best possible salespeople, experienced or inexperienced. These organizations then ensure that their new hires are equipped to succeed by providing excellent training. The first-line sales manager is critical to this equation, because his or her job includes selecting and building the team. Consequently, he or she is involved in both the hiring and training aspects. The first-line manager is usually the key decision maker in the hiring decision. Since every salesperson will report to, work closely with, and contribute to the success of his or her manager, the firm usually hires people who are recommended by the sales managers. Sales managers are also critical participants in the training process. They provide instruction, feedback, evaluation, and coaching. This chapter and the two that follow describe these important sales force drivers in more detail. This chapter discusses hiring, Chapter 7 discusses training, and Chapter 8 focuses on the first-line sales manager.

## The Impact of Hiring Decisions

Hiring is a critical activity because it affects company results, management effectiveness, and company culture. A report by the Harvard Busi-

**Figure 6-2.** A Cross-Industry and Worldwide View of the Characteristics Associated With Successful Salespeople.

| | | |
|---|---|---|
| Ambitious | Self-confident | Likable |
| Motivated | Secure | Sociable |
| Go-getter | Assertive | Empathic |
| Takes initiative | Persistent | Responsive |
| Hard-working | Thick-skinned | Outgoing |
| Ego-driven | Decisive | Personable |
| Goal-oriented | Adaptive | Has integrity |
| Competitive | Flexible | Trustworthy |
| Enthusiastic | Spontaneous | Good listener |
| Disciplined | Knowledgeable | Articulate |
| Follows through | Experienced | Perceptive |
| Independent | Educated | Persuasive |
| Customer-oriented | Problem solver | Creative |
| Organized | Techno-capable | Intuitive |
| Diligent | Analytical | Leader |

ness School estimates that a bad hiring decision can cost a company three times the salesperson's annual compensation, including expenses, training costs, benefits, and incentive pay.

## Hiring Directly Affects Company Results

An unsuccessful recruiting effort can result in the hiring of a disproportionate number of salespeople who are either average or poor performers. What happens to these new salespeople? Some will continue to be salespeople, and some will not. In the better outcome, the poor performers will leave, either of their own accord or because of management action. However, when a salesperson leaves, the expense of hiring and training a new employee is incurred again. Furthermore, turnover leads to a sales force that is low on the learning and productivity curves. High turnover results in a company with a perennially inexperienced sales team, vulnerable to customer defection because it is not serving its customers well. High turnover also contributes to low morale among the salespeople who stay, as they may be required to pick up the slack caused by the departure of their colleagues.

The other possibility, of course, is that the weaker performers stay. This leads to low customer satisfaction, inferior territory management, and subsequent market share losses to a competitor with a better sales force. Only the best salespeople can adapt and take full advantage of product, market, or environmental opportunities. Moreover, weak salespeople absorb company resources at a high rate. They consume management time for coaching, training, and appraising and are inefficient in terms of company travel and expense budgets.

Hiring too many poor performers also damages the morale of the better performers, since the best people like to surround themselves with other successful people. This increases the turnover of good salespeople and contributes to the decline in sales force quality.

The value of the sales lost by a single ineffective salesperson could be as much as $300,000 to several million dollars per year depending upon the industry. This opportunity cost is the result of customer mishandling, such as poor needs assessment, inappropriate "solutions" or product recommendations, slow delivery, or inadequate service. A good relationship between a customer and a company can disintegrate quickly if the salesperson is below average. Every salesperson affects her or his company's performance, either positively or negatively.

The corollary to this bad news is that good hiring leads to success. One study we did for a pharmaceutical company indicated that bringing the bottom half of the sales force up to average would result in a 9 percent increase in sales.

The Japanese policy is to assume that when you hire, you are hiring for life. Everyone should attempt to be as careful and thorough in their recruitment of salespeople.

### Hiring Directly Affects Managers

Effective first-line sales management is crucial to sales success. A sales manager has many responsibilities, including setting individual goals, coaching, evaluating, leading, motivating, analyzing, deploying resources, hiring, training, resolving conflicts, traveling with salespeople, researching the market, selling, and firing. Everything the sales manager does is easier if good people are hired.

### Hiring Affects Culture

New recruits bring their own values to the company. Successful people can become heroes for the company, and the company develops legends from successful "war stories." New hires affect the current culture and create the future culture.

## Key Insights That Will Improve Your Hiring

Successful hiring is easy to describe: Identify the kind of salespeople required, find people who fit the profile, and attract them to the company. However, successful hiring is hard to do. This section describes a number of key insights that can enhance the recruitment of salespeople, and the following section presents a process for effective hiring.

## Ad Hoc Interviewing Is Unreliable as a Hiring Tool

Some companies rely mainly on two ad hoc interviews, one with the first-line sales manager and the second with the regional or national sales manager. This hiring process can be improved.

Studies (across many job categories) show only a 14 percent correlation between interview predictions and job success. Interviewing alone is not a good method of evaluating prospective employees.

Regrettably, many companies believe that interviewing is very effective. A decision made by a single interviewer is about as good as a guess. One way to understand this is to think about marriage. Almost 100 percent of newlyweds think they will stay married to their new spouse for the rest of their lives. However, in the United States, 50 percent of marriages end in divorce. You can have faith in your interviewing abilities and faith in your marriage, but the odds are against you.

How bad are the odds? Take a look at the meta-analysis done by John E. Hunter and Ronda F. Hunter, shown in Figure 6-3. In this figure,

**Figure 6-3.** Results from the Hunter and Hunter Meta-Analysis of Job Success Predictors.

| *Predictive Technique* | *Validity* |
|---|---|
| Ability composite (tests) | .53 |
| Tryout | .44 |
| Biographics (data on résumé and application) | .37 |
| Reference check | .26 |
| Experience | .18 |
| Interview | .14 |
| Training/experience ratings | .13 |
| Academic achievement | .11 |
| Education | .10 |
| Interest | .10 |
| Age | −.01 |

*Source:* John E. Hunter and R. F. Hunter, "Validity and Utility of Alternative Predictors of Job Performance," *Psychological Bulletin* 96 (1984), pp. 72–98. © 1984 by the American Psychological Association. Reprinted with permission.

the predictive technique is an assessment tool used to determine whether a person will be successful at a job. The validity is a percentage indicating the correlation between the predictive technique and ultimate job success. A 0 in validity would indicate no predictive power for the technique. Age, for instance, is virtually useless as a predictor of job success. A 1.0 in validity would indicate that the predictive technique is completely accurate. This meta-analysis is a summary across many jobs and many research studies. We believe that these results are appropriate for sales jobs in particular.

Since hiring is one of the most important management decisions, a process that involves only ad hoc interviews is not sufficient. Tests, in addition to the interviews, can close some of the gap. The best tests examine the behaviors that lead to job success.

### The Best Results Occur When the Recruiter Can Observe the Behaviors Important to the Job

It is necessary to identify desirable salesperson behaviors before it is possible to test for these behaviors. A list of success characteristics for salespeople might be drawn from the list in Figure 6-2. Methods for identifying attributes that form a "success profile" are described in detail in the section of this chapter on the hiring process ("Step 2: Candidate Profile").

It might seem difficult to test for "success" behaviors during the recruiting process, but recruiters do it all the time. The recruiter notices if the candidate is late to the interview, if the candidate's résumé contains typos and grammatical errors, and if the candidate fails to send a thank-you note. However, these are simply indications of the candidate's professionalism, and while this is important, a job generally requires more specific abilities.

The best results occur when the recruiter can observe behaviors the candidate needs in order to do the job well. This is supported by the meta-analysis in Figure 6-3. Methods that enable the recruiter to observe the potential recruit's behavior include temporary job tryouts, simulations, tests, and behavioral interviewing. Referrals, reference checks, and background checks rely on others who may have observed a candidate's sales ability. These methods are discussed further in the section of this chapter on the hiring process ("Step 4: Selection").

### Companies Must Train Their Recruiters Well

Sales managers have many roles, and time spent on recruiting reduces the amount of time they have available to handle other job functions.

Since hiring is important to the company, it is an activity that the sales manager, often a key recruiter, needs to do efficiently and effectively. All recruiters must be trained well.

Interviewing skills and testing skills are two areas that often require training. Because of their strong people skills, sales managers are likely to be good ad hoc interviewers, but they probably need training and practice in advanced techniques such as structured and behavioral interviewing.

Large companies may consider using a regional recruiter. A person assigned specifically to recruiting develops expertise in hiring because it is his or her only job. Also, a regional recruiter provides the same quality of recruiting throughout the region and is more objective and effective at screening than the individual sales managers. Using a regional recruiter increases the traveling cost for recruiting but cuts down on the expense of training first-line managers in recruiting. However, while the first-line managers do not have so many interviews when there is a regional recruiter, they still should interview the most promising candidates.

Regional recruiters, as well as others who recruit, can be evaluated and given bonuses based on how well their recruits perform. This is especially effective with national recruiters. Since district sales managers are usually compensated on the basis of district sales results, they are indirectly evaluated on their ability to recruit well. The evaluation becomes more immediate when experienced people are hired, as their effectiveness is more quickly apparent. Success is more difficult to determine for positions that require long training periods.

Companies with a large span of control (many salespeople reporting to one manager) may also benefit from having a specialized regional recruiter. The first-line manager should not be spending all of his or her time recruiting.

### Use the "Ramsey Principle"

Figure 6-4 demonstrates a common observation: People tend to hire people with whom they are comfortable. Successful people will not be intimidated by successful job applicants—in fact, they will look for people who they think will be successful. If a company wants excellent salespeople, it must have excellent sales managers.

### Avoid "Warm Body" Hiring

Salespeople can always find work selling something. They tend to be both self-directed and confident enough to try something new. For man-

**Figure 6-4.** The Ramsey Principle.

*"I like your looks, Ramsey. You're hired."*



agement, this means that dealing with turnover can be a regular event. Vacant territories can create panic—customers are not being served, new accounts are not being opened, the district's or region's quota is in jeopardy. Consequently, some managers rush to fill vacancies. This is a mistake. Rush to hire a star candidate; never rush to fill a position. The habit of hiring someone just to replace the vacant spot with a "warm body" eventually leads to all the salespeople in the district being warm bodies. The short-term problem has been turned into a long-term problem—a district full of warm bodies who might just as well be cold and dead for all the sales they are generating.

If the product is selling itself, hire a temporary worker to help with the paperwork, or ask the sales manager to call on the key accounts temporarily. Another way to alleviate the need for "warm body" hiring is to recruit constantly.

### Recruit Constantly

The time to assuage the empty position panic is before the position becomes empty. An empty position should be filled right away—with an excellent salesperson. Effective sales managers have a list of worthy candidates, so that when a territory becomes vacant, they can check their list, make several calls, and hopefully fill the vacancy quickly. The "time to hire" is too long for many companies, but a good manager cuts it down quickly by being ready to hire from a list in his or her desk drawer.

Candidate lists can be made up of employee referrals, candidates who rejected offers in the past, customers' employees, former employees, employees in other functions, and people met in various social settings. Keep a list; you never know when it may come in handy.

Companies whose salespeople require a large amount of training before becoming effective should consider a "bench." The bench would consist of current employees who are in training or serving in staff positions until a vacancy becomes available in the sales force. As territories become available, the bench is utilized. This way, vacant territories are rapidly staffed with trained salespeople.

### Not Every Hire Will Be Perfect

Some of the people who are hired should not have been hired. It is crucial to have evaluation systems that identify successful salespeople and deal with the average or below-average performer quickly and fairly.

Effective selling organizations develop processes that give everyone a chance to succeed. They give new hires credible and useful feedback, train them, coach them, and ensure that those who are good stay. The hiring process is the first step in employee life-cycle management. It is recommended that new hires be evaluated quickly and losses cut fast if the new hires are not working out.

At McKinsey Consulting, only one out of every ten to fifteen people succeeds. This does not appear to be a very good hiring ratio, but the good people stay at the company. There is a process in place for training the new employees, giving them opportunities to succeed, and evaluating their progress. The company has observed the behaviors of new employees and identified the successful ones over a period of years. Those that do not succeed at McKinsey often benefit from their experience and succeed at other companies. Most companies have higher retention rates than McKinsey, but everyone can take a lesson from McKinsey's posthiring process.

### Too Many Sales Managers Think They Hire Well

Most sales managers think they recruit well, when in fact they only do an average job. Too many sales managers rely primarily on one or two interviews. Too many sales managers think their salespeople are better because their sales went up last year. Why, then, are there other explanations when sales go down?

There are two reasons managers think their hiring process is excellent:

1. They were hired.
2. They are in charge of the hiring.

A 1980 study indicated that if the U.S. government had used ability tests for all its employees, the productivity improvement would have been equal to the federal budget. This is just one example of how inefficient our systems for matching people to jobs are. A good hiring process will match people to jobs at which they will succeed, and success goes a long way toward work satisfaction.

## The Hiring Process—Six Steps to Success

A six-step hiring process is presented in Figure 6-5. Each step is important for locating and attracting the best job candidates. Omitting any of these steps compromises the quality of incoming employees.

### Step 1: Job Definition

The first step in hiring is to develop job requirements. Companies in different industries have different requirements for salespeople. Consumer route salespeople perform different activities from industrial sales engineers. Also, job requirements change over time. Companies should continuously reevaluate job objectives and activity priorities as

**Figure 6-5.** A Hiring Process.

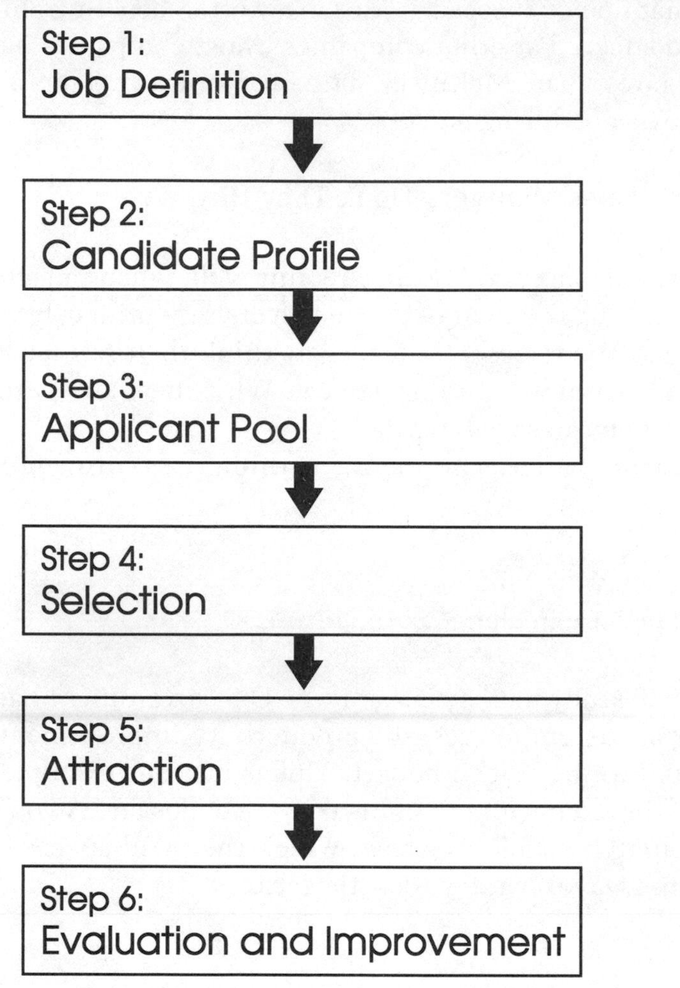


competitive and market conditions change. Job definitions are specified in terms of several dimensions:

***What Are the Goals and Objectives of the Sales Job?***

- Sales
- Profits
- Market share
- Orders
- Customer value creation
- Customer satisfaction

### *What Activities Are Required to Achieve These Goals?*

- Prospecting for new accounts
- Account maintenance and penetration
- Servicing
- Reporting (administration)
- Market condition evaluation and competitive intelligence reporting
- Product, market, and customer knowledge
- Solution selling
- Order taking
- Partnering and alliance development
- Territory management

### *How Will Achievement Be Measured?*

- Quantitative measurements
- Qualitative evaluations
- Management by objective

## Step 2: Candidate Profile

The "success profile" is closely connected with the job definition. The specific job requirements suggest the type of person that is likely to succeed. The characteristics listed in Figure 6-2 describe what it takes to be successful at sales, and they can be used to define the desired candidate profile.

**Success Profiles Guide the Search.** No one can be superior on every attribute listed in Figure 6-2. Even superiority on every attribute in an abbreviated success profile is unlikely. Sales success is a gestalt, and it can best be recognized by trained recruiters. Profiles provide concrete ways to evaluate candidates.

Profiles are useful because what makes a candidate "good" has to be specified before good candidates can be identified. Unfortunately, it is difficult to predict what drives sales success. It is impossible to identify a few truly discriminating attributes or characteristics that will accurately predict success every time. There are bright people who are average salespeople and people with average intelligence who are great salespeople. There are experienced people who are good salespeople and experienced people who are poor salespeople. There are extroverted people who are good salespeople and introverted people who are good salespeople. However, a significant lack of an important attribute leads to sales failure. Individuals who cannot communicate, totally lack empathy, or have no motivation are highly unlikely to be successful at sales. A candidate needs a minimum level of competence on the most important attributes if she or he is to succeed. Profile dimensions should be used to eliminate candidates, not to select them.

Each individual selling organization has unique success characteristics. The attributes and abilities that lead to customer satisfaction and sales success depend on the product line, the target market segments and their needs, the competitive landscape, and the desired sales force culture. Of course, it is useful to hire outside the profile occasionally to gain other value-added experience and to avoid inbreeding. The profile is a guideline, not a requirement.

---

Profiling for Technical Sales

A common problem in technical sales is whether to hire the technically competent person or the socially adroit person. It may be difficult to get people who are both. There is no solution to this quandary, except to consider which aspect is easier to train for and which aspect the customer values more. Look for both abilities and try to maximize the training of new hires on the weaker dimension.

---

Numerous articles by academics and practitioners suggest attributes that predict recruiting success. But, how can attributes be identified for any specific success profile?

**How to Determine the Profile.** A good starting point is to examine the current sales force and determine what is required in order to be successful. Companies have used three approaches: experience, job analysis, and statistical analysis.

*Experience.* Salespeople sell every day. Managers have sales experience and are intimately involved in the current selling process. The process of performance appraisal makes managers reflect on salespeople's success and compare their performance. This experience can be tapped to develop a candidate profile.

A job specification inventory is useful to focus the sales manager's experience. The inventory is a long questionnaire that provides a comprehensive list of all possible attributes that could be part of the final profile. For example, a job attribute like "relating to others" includes a spectrum of possible dimensions from team leader to silent participant. A sample of salespeople and sales managers would rate the importance of each dimension in performing the sales job effectively. A profile of important dimensions is developed by observing what survey participants deem to be important.

*Job Analysis.* Companies can easily become myopic. Occasionally, an external view provides a level of objectivity that cannot be obtained internally. A job analysis produces an external view of the most appropriate candidate profile. Outside consultants, usually industrial psychologists, interview salespeople and travel with them to catalog and observe successful behaviors. Then the field observations are matched with internal company performance measures to determine the attributes and activities that differentiate good performers from average performers.

Job analysis can be an excellent tool for determining a success profile. It tends to be objective and can lead to some surprising conclusions. For example, one might think that the best salespeople would be compulsive planners, but the job analysis might indicate that the best performers plan only one day in advance. One obstacle to good job analysis is the tendency of people to behave differently when someone is watching them. If a salesperson will carefully vacuum out his or her car before a manager's visit, what behavior can be expected when an outside observer is present? Also, the objectivity of an outside observer comes at the cost of inside knowledge.

*Statistical Analysis.* The final way to identify success attributes is with statistics. A statistical approach determines the strength of the relationship between sales force attributes and measures of sales success. Work of this kind has produced useful results. The analysis presented in Figure 6-6 is the basis of what is called the statistical profiling approach (SPA). The SPA model attempts to answer two questions:

How is performance related to salesperson characteristics and behaviors?

How should the observed relationship affect the hiring program?

SPA employs the following five-step procedure:

1. Managers use their judgment to establish characteristics or behaviors that are believed to lead to sales success. Assertiveness,

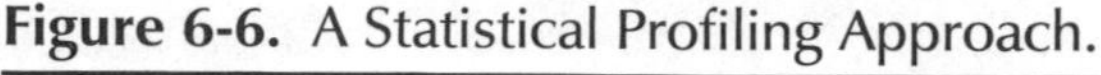

**Figure 6-6.** A Statistical Profiling Approach.

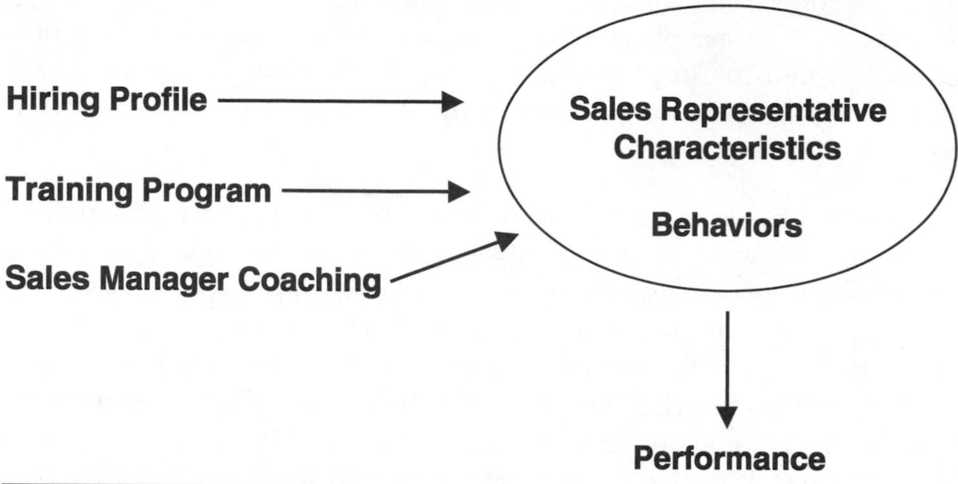


precall planning, effective listening, and technical knowledge are examples of attributes that have been included.

2. Each member of the sales force is rated on these attributes. Typically, the evaluation is stated in terms of the salesperson's rating relative to other members of the sales force. For example, a questionnaire might include the following question:

   *In comparison to all of the other salespeople you have managed or encountered, where does this salesperson fall in terms of planning and organization skills?*
   *The top 5 percent?*
   *The top 25 percent?*
   *The top half?*
   *The bottom half?*
   *The bottom 25 percent?*

   Results of social-style tests (e.g., Myers-Briggs) and psychological tests can also serve as predictor variables. Finally, self-assessment, where salespeople rate themselves on key characteristics or behaviors, has also been used.

3. Measures of sales success are identified. Examples include sales, market share, salesperson ranking, or percent of quota achieved.
4. Data for each salesperson are accumulated for both the characteristic and territory output measures. Whenever "hard" output measures are unavailable, judgmental measures of success can be substituted.

5. The link between the attributes and the results is examined statistically. This analysis can vary in levels of sophistication, and a good statistician usually can draw interesting conclusions.

Following is an example from a health care company that performed a statistical analysis. The company used a Myers-Briggs social-style evaluation as part of its personnel evaluation. The social-style evaluation provided ratings for each salesperson on assertiveness, responsiveness, and versatility. These were used along with information on precall planning, territory knowledge, and some other behaviors as a set of dimensions to develop a candidate hiring profile. All of the salespeople were assessed. Territory sales and share were the performance measures that were used.

The company sold several products; one was a commodity, and one was a highly differentiated niche product. Some of the results of the analysis appear in Figure 6-7.

The people scoring above average on assertiveness had 18 percent higher sales for the commodity product than those scoring below average on assertiveness. This product required high levels of exposure to get marketplace attention.

The groups with greater territory knowledge and better planning, organization, and administrative skills had 22 percent higher niche product sales per territory than the groups with lesser ability in these areas. This type of product requires territory knowledge and planning; the right customers had to be located.

These results are compelling. They provide powerful insights into the kind of people who should be hired.

*A Recommendation.* Companies use experience frequently, job analysis occasionally, and statistics rarely in developing their profiles. It would usually be possible for companies to maintain profiles in a more scientific way. The authors recommend the following:

- Make sure an up-to-date job profile is available.
- Use experience to update the profile regularly.
- For large sales forces, perform a job analysis or a statistical analysis at least every three to five years.

**Profiles Can Differ by Product or Market.** As the statistical study in Figure 6-7 shows, different products can require different selling skills. Salespeople selling products in a highly competitive category, such as a

Figure 6-7. An Illustration of a Statistical Analysis for a Health Care Company.

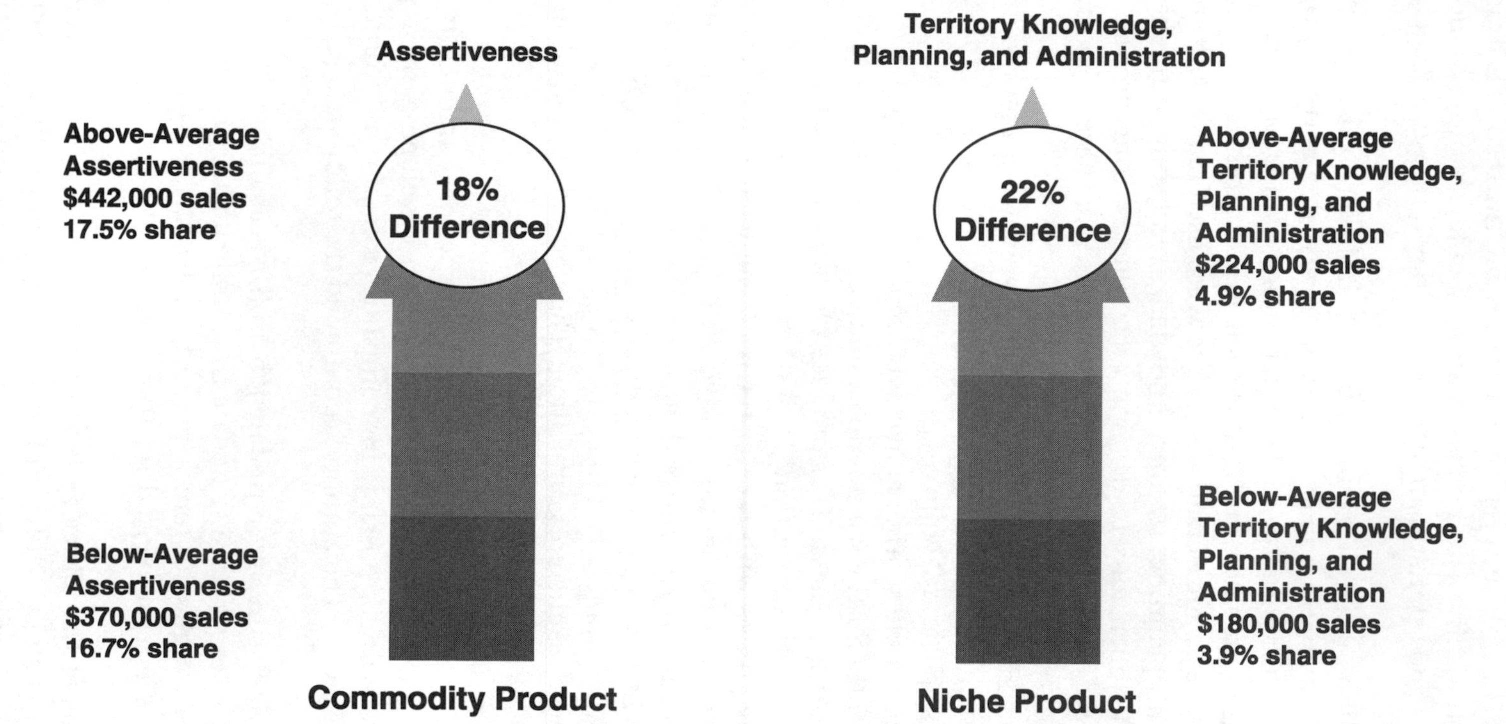

low-tech commodity, require different abilities from salespeople touting a highly differentiated, highly technical product. Some situations require assertiveness, aggressive communication, and a competitive spirit ("hunters"), while other situations require customer service and careful planning ("skinners"). These different product and market environments need different selling personalities. The final candidate profile must acknowledge these differences.

**The Success Profile Can Change over Time.** Obviously a company's products and markets change over time. Therefore, the requirements of the sales force also change, and the success profile evolves. By working with the natural 10 to 20 percent turnover in most sales forces, management can use new hires to slowly change the profile of the sales force over time.

Some financially driven companies reduce sales force headcount at every opportunity; they hope for productivity gains from their reduced sales force. These reductions may require that the profile change. As one vice president of sales for an appliance manufacturer recently put it: "Now I need to find high-energy individuals with high work capacity and a high tolerance for frustration." Companies that downsize frequently use telephone sales to achieve productivity gains. This requires a different profile. Finally, most sales force restructuring results in a work redefinition and a consequent change in the salesperson profile.

### Step 3: Applicant Pool

The quality of the candidates who are given job offers depends upon the quality of the applicant pool. Good candidates cannot emerge from a weak applicant pool. There are a number of sources of applicants:

- Referrals
- Campus recruiting
- Internal placements
- Agencies
- Company recruiting Web site
- Headhunter Web site
- Internet job boards
- Unsolicited write-ins
- Job fairs
- Former employees
- Customers

- Competitors
- Advertisements
- Trade shows

*Sales and Marketing Management* magazine surveyed its readers to determine the most successful sources of candidates. The percentages in Figure 6-8 represent how respondents answered the question, "Where do you find the best sales candidates?"

The authors have also conducted a similar survey. The respondents were sales managers and vice presidents attending the sales force productivity courses at Northwestern University's Kellogg Executive Center. The survey participants identified referrals, current employees, and customers as the best sources of new salespeople.

Another study, based on data from a pharmaceutical company, revealed that employees who were in nonselling positions within the company, and were therefore familiar with the company and its selling environment, were the best salesperson candidates.

As these studies show, recruiters have the most success when they have reliable information from trusted sources about a candidate and his or her likelihood of success. The Lutheran Brotherhood Insurance Company uses pastor referrals to help staff its sales force. The pastor may have known the candidate all his or her life.

## Step 4: Selection

Selection is the process of developing a candidate database and sifting through all the information in that database to determine which candidate would be best. Selection boils down to two questions:

1. Can the candidate do the job well?
2. Would the candidate fit well with the company?

**Figure 6-8.** A *Sales & Marketing Management* Magazine Survey on Sources of Applicants for the Sales Job.

| Where do you find the best candidates? | |
|---|---|
| Referrals | 48% |
| Recruiters | 31% |
| Competitors | 10% |
| College placement offices | 9% |
| Newspaper ads | 9% |

*Source: Sales & Marketing Management magazine.*

There are various ways to answer these two questions.

**Interviews.** Interviewing is always a part of the hiring process. A variety of people can conduct the interviews:

- District manager
- Regional manager
- Human Resources or Recruiting Department
- Regional recruiter
- Current salespeople
- Hiring agency

Interviewing can be done in several ways:

- Individual interviews
- Panel (several-to-one) interviews
- Day in the life or sample job day

Multiple interviews allow the best evaluation of the candidate, since hiring risk is shared and more interviewers provide more input into the hiring decision. A fourth interviewer can catch something the first three missed. Panel interviews (many-on-one) work well. A good strategy is to keep the same panel for all candidates and interview the candidates within the same few days. In panel interviews, one interviewer is usually responsible for leading and asking questions, with the other members interacting intermittently but primarily observing.

If the sales position requires the salesperson to interact with internal groups such as marketing, operations, or finance, consider having the candidate interview with someone from these functional areas as well.

Many hiring processes are structured, with each candidate being asked identical questions. This helps to increase the reliability of the process when there are different interviewers. Although the interviewers are different, the questions are the same. The big challenge with interviewing is validity: Does the interview predict job success? According to the meta-analysis by Hunter and Hunter (Figure 6-3), ad hoc interviews are mediocre in this regard. An interview is not really a sample of the work that the employee will do. Interviewing skills are important for salespeople to have, but interviews do not constitute typical sales work.

Following are some ideas beyond standard interviews to help with the hiring decision.

**Behavioral Interviews.** The validity of interviewing improves significantly when behavioral interviewing is used to assess a candidate's past behavior. In this technique, the interviewer asks candidates to recall experiences that demonstrate the desired characteristics defined in the profile. Past behavior is a good predictor of future behavior when the requisite behavior cannot be observed. For example, to assess motivation, the interviewer might say to the candidate, "Tell me about a project you completed with little direction," or "Tell me about a tough sale you made and how you made it." To assess persuasiveness, the interviewer might say, "Tell me about a situation in which you had to convince others that your position was right." Satisfactory responses indicate that the candidate may have the desired attribute. Probing is necessary when using this technique, because candidates can be superficial or even misrepresent their experience, especially if they are aware of the interviewer's objectives.

---

Improving Your Interviewing Skills

- Talk to other interviewers before and after the interviews to see how your expectations and evaluations compare. Are you more critical than other people? Are you more swayed by expertise in particular areas? Become aware of your own biases.
- Try not to form an opinion of the candidate before the interview. Prejudice (prejudging) is possible when you learn about the candidate from somewhere other than the interview itself—even from the résumé!
- Know the law about illegal interview questions. It can be easy to ask an illegal question in an attempt to be friendly. The law presumes that any questions asked will be used for hiring. Avoid questions that are not essential to evaluate the candidate's qualifications for the job.

---

**Test for Behaviors in the Interviews.** There are many types of written tests to evaluate candidates. However, the best test for a successful salesperson is a demonstration of the behaviors that will be needed if he or she is to succeed on the job. Depending on the type of sales job, this might be prospect identification, call planning, overcoming objections, or closing the sale. While an interview is a sales call of sorts, it is not a sales call for the company's product. However, it can be turned into a simulation of a real selling situation.

The use of a case study is an attempt to approximate selling behaviors. Certain divisions at Abbott Laboratories, Procter & Gamble, MetLife, and AT&T have used this approach. Several days before the interview, the candidates receive a thick case study (fifteen to fifty pages). The case contains a description of a selling situation, including the industry, products, and customers. The assignment is to plan a day, plan a month, select the target customers, and develop a plan to sell to one of the target customers. On the day of the interview, the candidate is asked to defend the plan and then to role-play a sale to the "customer." The "customer" presents objections and has questions about the products.

What does this scenario test?

- *Motivation* and *organizational skills*, because of the large amount of work needed to prepare for the interview
- *Planning skills*, by preparing and presenting the plan for the day and month
- *Motivation, resiliency and persistence, empathy*, and *listening skills*, by the selling role-play

The "in-basket" test is also commonly used. In this test, a candidate is given a full in-basket and asked to prioritize and develop an action plan for the work in the basket. This exercise tests planning and organizing, prioritizing, managing interrelated items, written and oral communication, human relations, and creativity.

The possibilities for creative selling tests are endless. For example, interviewers for one large metropolitan newspaper ask candidates to sell them a "corner of a room." An electronics company asks its candidates to prepare and deliver a thirty-minute presentation in which they "sell themselves."

As technology advances, it will become possible to put prospective employees into virtual video environments to see their reactions to situations they will encounter on the job.

Japanese automobile manufacturers in the United States have used three-day interviews/tests for production workers. Candidates are required to build something to test their manual dexterity skills. Additionally, candidates work together on teams to demonstrate their team skills. After three days of observing the candidates' behavior, the employers feel that they know the candidates well. Companies in Europe have assessment centers that test their candidates, and successful candidates are hired on a temporary basis. They give three-, six-, twelve-, and eighteen-month employment contracts. Candidate evaluation continues on the job. One European sales manager recently commented, "You use too much blah, blah, blah in the U.S. interviewing process." European companies need to be careful when they hire because labor laws and union contracts make it very expensive to dismiss people after several years on the job.

Behavior observation is the best predictor of success. However, running a case scenario or extensive testing requires significant preparation and well-trained interviewers. Furthermore, these testing procedures should be validated to show that they are good at predicting sales success. Demonstrating the link between success and the screening method is not just good practice, it is the law.

The 1964 civil rights act requires that selection criteria be "job related." Any information that is used in hiring is a "test," and only tests that are connected to job performance can be used to hire. The Hunter and Hunter meta-analysis reveals that testing is superior to interviews as far as candidate evaluation is concerned.

---

Many French companies demand handwritten letters from prospective employees so that graphologists can analyze the handwriting and make recommendations!

---

**Other Testing.** Other written or skill tests, while usually not "live action" like a simulation, can also mimic job requirements. Many retail companies have replaced paper applications and in-person interviews with computer kiosks for the initial screening of applicants. The computer programs query prospective employees on their employment history and work habits. They typically include psychological tests that help match job skills and personalities with openings.

**Referrals.** Referrals, usually friends or acquaintances of a company employee, are an excellent way to find candidates who are a good fit for the company. There are several reasons for this. Typically, the person making the referral has observed the candidate's behavior firsthand. Furthermore, since the employee making the referral is familiar with both the company and the candidate, presumably he or she has predetermined the candidate's fit with the organization. Finally, the employee has some career risk when recommending an acquaintance. As one thirty-year veteran told us, "I recommended two people who were hired. I was sweating bullets. Luckily they were both successful."

An incentive program can be used to reward employees for referrals. Typically the program awards cash, usually about $1,000 to $5,000, or prizes, such as dinner for two, for recommending a candidate who is subsequently hired.

**References.** It is wise to check references. In this litigious age, previous employers may not reveal much, but it is useful to ask anyway. References provided by the candidate may need to be discounted somewhat because of their positive bias.

**Background Checks.** In a 1998 survey by the Society of Human Resource Management, 90 percent of human resource professionals said that they had encountered candidates who had falsified the lengths of time that they had held previous jobs and the salaries they had earned. Also, 78 percent of those surveyed said that they had come across applicants who had lied about their college degrees. A quick background check reveals a great deal about a candidate's integrity. Web-based search tools allow firms to investigate an applicant's job history, credit rating, and criminal record within forty-eight hours at a very reasonable cost.

**Consultants.** Screening and selecting candidates, checking references, and other such tasks can be handled by firms that specialize in this type of work. Some consultants have developed special questionnaires to rate job applicants. The questionnaires can be administered over the phone or in person. However, when using consultants, be careful not to get a "canned" approach. Every company's success profile is unique.

**Temporary Contracts.** As mentioned earlier, temporary contracts to assess candidates' ability and fit with the company are common in Europe. Although these short-term contracts can be disruptive, and training may be a problem, they allow management to observe the candidates' behavior on the job. They also allow candidates to evaluate the company. Be aware that good candidates may not want to leave the safety of their current job for a "trial" position. Also, in sales, the employee interacts with the customer, and this relationship should not be jeopardized.

Clever prospects sometimes suggest that a company "try them out" for free for a short time. They are convinced that the company will be amazed by their abilities and will hire them.

**Informal Settings.** Assessing a candidate's fit with the company is often difficult. Company cultures and values are often not explicit, so ensuring that the candidate's values are similar to the company's may be difficult. Informal settings often provide the best place for both parties to learn more about each other.

Invite the candidate and his or her significant other, if appropriate, to a casual dinner. Hold a candidate barbecue with some of the company's salespeople to allow the candidate to assess the company culture. Ask the candidate to dress informally. Wearing a suit frequently leads the candidate to put on a "formal face."

**Provide Opportunity for an "Informed Reverse Selection."** Be sure that the candidate is exposed to people who have the job he or she will be doing and to the people he or she will be working for. The candidate must receive enough information about the company to reject the job offer if appropriate. Candidates have more information than the company does, since they know themselves very well. Therefore, each candidate needs to be able to decide "I'm not quite comfortable" or "I think I would love this company." The candidate is interviewing the company as well. This is why "a day in the field" is effective. It is better not to hire a qualified person who would be unhappy with the company. Not every rejection of a job offer is a failure. An honest job preview will yield less subsequent turnover.

Some major retailers use simulations to give applicants a clear idea of what the job demands. In traditional face-to-face interviews, managers are often eager to hire employees and may understate the stresses of the job. Simulation provides more accurate, consistent information so that candidates who are not well suited to a job are more likely to turn down a job offer, thus reducing the turnover rate among new employees.

**Two Final Thoughts.** An effective approach used by some companies is to have candidates experience a very rigorous interview process. Those who get selected feel a sense of accomplishment and consequently are more likely to accept an offer.

Yet, keep in mind that the candidate bases his or her decision largely on the interviewing experience. Do not make it unpleasant; rather, use it as an opportunity to sell the company. This is critical for candidates who ultimately get offers. Even those who get rejected should feel that the company was polite and had integrity; some of them may be customers in the future.

### Step 5: Attraction

Once the candidate has passed the hurdles for employment, the next step is to try to attract him or her to the company. Attraction consists of two closely related parts: the offer and the follow-up. The offer consists of the job itself and the characteristics that make the job attractive:

- Career opportunities
- Compensation package
- Benefits
- Company and culture
- Colleagues
- Products

The follow-up is how the offer is communicated and managed. Obviously, an attractive offer will increase the proportion of those accepting the offer. But good follow-up does not cost much and makes a big difference.

Here are some ideas for improving the follow-up.

*Let the candidate know you want him.* Tell the candidate over the phone. Tell her with a formal letter. Tell him in person. Woo the candidate with flowers, wine, and candy if appropriate.

*Do not forget about the candidate after you give the offer.* Ask how the offer looks. Suggest another tour of headquarters. Have several people call to show interest.

*Put a nonpersonnel person in charge of the candidate's application.* It is important to make the offer as personal as possible. Have the boss-to-be make the job offer. It gives a more personal feel and will encourage a sense of belonging to the sales organization.

*Follow up on rejections.* Sell the company even if the offer is refused. Find out why the offer was not attractive enough, and remind the candidate to contact the company if the job he or she chose instead does not work out. However, keep self-selection issues in mind. Some well-qualified candidates will have realized that they would not fit in and turned down the job for this reason.

### Step 6: Evaluation and Improvement

The final step in the recruitment process is evaluation and improvement. A good company continuously improves its process by gathering feedback and using that feedback. Here are two suggestions for evaluating and improving the hiring process.

**Collect Statistics Annually to Describe the Success of the Process.** Hiring statistics can be as simple as counts and lists. Count the number of applicants and hires, and derive ratios if that is helpful. Figure 6-9 shows some useful statistics.

**Examine the Winners.** Determine the sources of the best candidates. What are the sources of the candidates who get job offers? Of those that accept job offers? Contrast the successful and the average salespeople who stay in the sales force for more than three years. What was known about these people when they were hired? How did they perform in the hiring process? Who interviewed them? What kind of training did they receive? What kinds of offers were made? What recruiting factors resulted in good people being hired? Answers to these questions can reveal ways to improve the recruiting process.

## How the Internet Is Changing the Way Companies Recruit and Hire

The Internet increases the availability of information and decreases search costs. This affects both companies and job candidates. Companies can advertise open positions more easily and increase the number of applicants for each position by posting information on their own Web

**Figure 6-9.** Statistics for Evaluating a Hiring Process.

| *Data* | *Diagnosis* |
|---|---|
| Number of vacancies | This number indicates company turnover. |
| Number of applicants<br>or<br>Applicants per vacancy | A low number suggests poor company image or low awareness of the position. A high number suggests good advertising or poor communication of job requirements. |
| Number of offers<br>or<br>Percentage getting offers | A low number of offers implies poor prescreening or a low number of applicants. |
| Number of acceptances<br>or<br>Percentage of offers accepted | A low number of acceptances implies poor compensation or a poor opinion of the company after interviewing. |

site or on an Internet job board. Candidates can identify available positions and can gain information about the company and the position without interfacing with human resources personnel.

It is unlikely that companies will be able to make hiring decisions using only the Internet and electronic communication techniques. However, the Internet gives companies an opportunity to allocate their human resource expenditures more efficiently. Efficiency gains are possible at several steps of the recruiting process.

## Applicant Pool

Recruiters agree: Online recruiting is an efficient way to generate a large applicant pool. For this reason, many companies have already shifted large portions of their recruiting budget to online advertising, primarily at the expense of newspaper advertising and search agency fees. One recruiter estimated that a shift from print ads to the Internet saved his company $16 million over two years. In addition to providing broader exposure at lower cost, the Internet also allows richer ads with more information than a traditional newspaper classified ad.

While online advertising of job openings has these advantages, many recruiters find that the widespread availability of information and the reduced cost of submitting résumés to multiple employers via the Internet leads to an abundance of unqualified candidates in the applicant pool. This means that companies need to spend more money and resources screening the résumés they receive online.

Technology addresses the issue of overdelivery of résumés in several ways. First, by including search mechanisms on their Web sites, companies make it easier for candidates to identify specific positions. Many companies have Web sites that let candidates search by functional discipline, office location, and business unit. After searching via one of these methods, a detailed job description is provided. With detailed company and job information available, candidates can self-select more easily.

Standardized submission forms for electronic résumés are another way in which technology helps employers deal with the overabundance of online résumés. The forms make it easier for employers to electronically screen out candidates with inappropriate or unsatisfactory credentials. They also enable the creation of candidate databases.

Finally, Internet Web sites are becoming more sophisticated in their ability to match candidates with jobs. Some Web sites use advanced semantic recognition programs that filter information about a candidate even when the information is not submitted in a standard electronic form. For example, a résumé submitted in a word processor file could be interpreted and rejected or prioritized based on the information it contains. Some career network Web sites also have the ability to learn a company's preferences. For example, recruiters who reject candidates with a certain profile will not be shown similar candidates in the future.

### Selection

Improved communication and information transfer affect the selection process as well. If candidates provide specific information during the application process, they can be automatically routed to the appropriate internal resource. One recruiter reports that online résumé processing allows him to receive a résumé, process it, and deliver it to the appropriate manager within one day.

In addition to efficiency gains, the Web offers employers the opportunity to get more, richer information about a candidate before meeting him or her. For example, the use of real-time or prerecorded video online can give employers an initial glimpse of the potential candidate's presentation.

Finally, companies that use written tests may reduce their costs by administering the test via the Internet. This allows company personnel to limit their interaction with candidates until they pass the test. This results in significant savings of human resource effort and reimbursement of candidate travel.

Many companies have traditionally relied on employment agencies or headhunters to generate high-quality applicant pools. Therefore, a company that eliminates the use of headhunters in favor of using the Internet must improve its internal selection techniques in order to maintain standards.

### Attraction

As mentioned above, a well-designed Web site provides candidates with information about a company and the various positions available, an important feature that is lacking in traditional print ads.

### Evaluation and Improvement

The Internet gives a company an opportunity to solicit anonymous feedback from those who have experienced the recruiting process.

Companies can send applicants a request for information, directions to a Web site, and a password when they receive an offer. Given an anonymous forum, candidates with offers can provide valuable input that will help the company to further improve the recruiting process.

### You Can't Replace the Face-to-Face Interview

As stated earlier, companies should not rely upon the Internet alone in making hiring decisions. However, companies may be able to realize significant cost savings by generating applicants more efficiently, communicating with candidates electronically, and eliminating poorly suited candidates before they interact with company personnel.

## Conclusion

How many salespeople are above average in the IBM sales force? The Merck sales force? The GE sales force? Is it 90, 80, or 75 percent? The statistician says it is 50 percent, and the statistician is right. In every sales force, 50 percent of the people are performing below average compared to the sales force as a whole. Some of these people may be hiring errors. There is a big labor pool out there. Every firm could do better. Every hiring process has room for improvement. Hiring is the most critical activity sales management performs, so improvement is worth the effort.

A good hiring process is systematic, objective, and thorough. It is fast, it is cost-effective, and it meets organizational goals. Finally, it is legally defensible and attracts good people. All of these goals are important, but at any stage in recruiting, some goals are easier to affect than others. For instance, cost-effectiveness is most easily achieved by focusing on the applicant pool and the selection process. Profile development, though a critical recruiting step, does not usually require a large investment of time or money, whereas interviewing uses costly resources. Figure 6-10 describes how various steps in the recruiting process affect recruiting goals.

**Figure 6-10.** How the Recruiting Process Affects Recruiting Goals.

<table>
<tr><th></th><th colspan="6">Recruiting Goals</th></tr>
<tr><th>Steps in the Hiring Process</th><th>Objective</th><th>Cost-Effective</th><th>Fast</th><th>Meets Organization Goals</th><th>Attracts Good People</th><th>Defensible</th></tr>
<tr><td>Job definition</td><td rowspan="4">Need to be objective in each of these stages.</td><td colspan="2" rowspan="2"></td><td rowspan="2">Get the right people.</td><td rowspan="5">Make sure the right people are selected and join the company.</td><td rowspan="5">Process objectivity and implementation integrity lead to legal defensibility and a documentation trail.</td></tr>
<tr><td>Candidate profile</td></tr>
<tr><td>Applicant pool</td><td rowspan="2">Emphasize effectiveness and efficiency.</td><td rowspan="3">Emphasize efficiency; get it done quickly.</td><td rowspan="2"></td></tr>
<tr><td>Selection</td></tr>
<tr><td>Attraction</td><td colspan="2"></td><td>Hire them.</td></tr>
<tr><td>Evaluation/implementation</td><td>Are we objective?</td><td>Are we spending too much?</td><td>Are we fast enough?</td><td>Are we meeting our objectives?</td><td>Are we attracting good people?</td><td>Is the process defensible?</td></tr>
</table>

# Chapter 7

# Training the Sales Force

The purpose of sales training is to make salespeople successful—continuously successful. A good selling organization provides its salespeople with the opportunity to develop the competencies they need if they are to succeed.

This chapter will help you:

- Recognize environmental changes that can threaten salesperson competency and create capability gaps
- Design better training programs by providing numerous sales training insights and specific, practical ideas for enhancing a sales training program
- Conduct a four-step review of your sales training program, including the use of the Capabilities/Effectiveness (C/E) Matrix, which helps determine the extent to which your current training program is producing the desired outcomes

## Introduction

The conversations described in Figure 7-1 have been overheard frequently when sales managers travel with their salespeople.

The salesperson in each of these six situations lacked either the knowledge or the skill to do his or her job effectively. Companies design training and educational programs so that their salespeople can be as effective and efficient as possible.

This chapter has three sections. The role of training in preparing the sales force for success is described first. This is followed by several sales force training insights that are intended to help companies design better training programs. Finally, a process for evaluating and enhancing an existing training program is developed.

**Figure 7-1.** Several Conversations Between a Salesperson and His or Her Manager.

| *The Sales Manager Says:* | *The Salesperson Says:* | *The Sales Manager Thinks:* |
|---|---|---|
| "You explained our product's *features* very well." | "Thank you." | "But how about assessing the *customer's needs* and describing how our product *adds value* for the customer?" |
| "Do you think that the prospect will buy from us? What are the *next steps*?" | "I don't know." | "Why did you leave without at least scheduling a follow-up call?" |
| "Did you realize that the customer hardly said a word?" | "He was very interested in what I had to say." | "*Empathy* and *listening* are important in sales. You should be *asking questions*." |
| "You are a very hard negotiator." | "I got the deal, didn't I?" | "It may be the last one you get with this customer. What happened to *win-win*?" |
| "Do you think that there may have been a better answer to the customer's question on where we see the industry going in the next few years?" | "No one ever knows where this industry is going. Anything I might say would be pure speculation." | "We can add value through our expertise. We owe it to the customer to *be informed*?" |
| "I notice that 20 percent of your calls are on 'D' accounts." | "I am in the neighborhood; they like to see me; so I call on them." | "You need to *target* better. The sales that are generated by these calls do not pay for the calls." |

## The High-Performance Selling Organization Is a Good Training Organization

*Sales training exists to make salespeople successful—continuously successful.* The successful selling organization gives its salespeople the opportunity to develop the competencies they need in order to succeed in every selling situation. There is a clear difference between highly trained salespeople and those whose training has been deficient, regardless of their level of competence. Figure 7-2 lists ways in which successful training has a favorable impact on the customer, the sales force, and the company.

**Figure 7-2.** The Impact That Successful Sales Training Has on the Customer, the Sales Force, and the Company.

**Customer Impact**

- Customers' product and service needs are understood and met.
- Customers feel that their salesperson adds value and can be trusted.
- Customers feel that their salesperson is not wasting their time.
- Customers like to work with the company's salespeople.
- Changing customer needs are incorporated into an adaptive selling process.

**Sales Force Impact**

- New salespeople become productive quickly.
- Salespeople enter every selling situation confident that they are equipped to succeed.
- Salespeople are aware of technological, environmental, market, customer, industry, and product trends.

**Company Impact**

- Salesperson retention and sales force morale are high.
- Products and services are differentiated; price competition is minimized.
- The company culture is understood, supported, and embraced by the sales force.

It is in every firm's interest to equip its people for success. Regrettably, many firms maintain their equipment better than they develop their people. In France, there is a law that requires every company to commit 5 percent of its payroll to professional development and training. People gain self-esteem and provide more value to the firm when they grow professionally and develop competencies that enable them to perform their jobs more efficiently and effectively. They are also less likely to look for another job when their firm invests in their professional development.

Successful salespeople possess many of the competencies listed in Figure 7-3.

The role of sales force training is to provide salespeople with an opportunity to overcome deficiencies wherever they exist. *Capability gaps* arise when the sales force does not have the knowledge, skills, or capabilities to implement the most appropriate customer attraction and retention process for the company's marketplace and business model. The ideal customer attraction and retention process, in turn, depends upon responding most appropriately to the company's selling environment. Selling environments are made up of factors that are both external and internal to the company. Different competitive environments require different selling processes. Insurance is sold differently from

**Figure 7-3.** Sales Force Competencies.

***Knowledge***
- Product
- Customer
- Technology—database, information management, and tools
- Company policy, values, and culture

***Ability/Capability***
- Customer and industry research
- Customer and account profitability maximization
- Development of best selling process
- Quantitative analysis
- Problem solving

***Skills***
- Prospecting
- Needs identification
- Time and territory management
- Listening
- Persuasion
- Presentation
- Negotiation
- Closing
- Account maintenance and expansion

pharmaceuticals, which are sold differently from power plants. Similarly, the selling process is usually different for broad and narrow product lines, and for environments that demand account maintenance and those that demand new account development. The basic linkages are illustrated in Figure 7-4.

New salespeople face a capability gap the moment that they join the firm. They have much to learn about their new job. Inexperienced hires have the most to learn. They need to become acquainted with the selling environment facing the firm and with the most effective selling process for each of the firm's target markets. They have a significant need for training, and the firm's initial training program can be quite extensive. New hires with prior sales experience usually participate in abbreviated training sessions that focus on company-specific competencies and product knowledge. Ongoing training in static selling environments usually consists of new product updates, a presentation of new marketing initiatives, and selling skill refreshers.

Change in the selling environment is a second factor that threatens salespeople's competence and can create gaps. There are numerous sources of change in today's environment. Several are listed in Figure 7-5.

**Figure 7-4.** Factors Affecting Salesperson Development Needs.

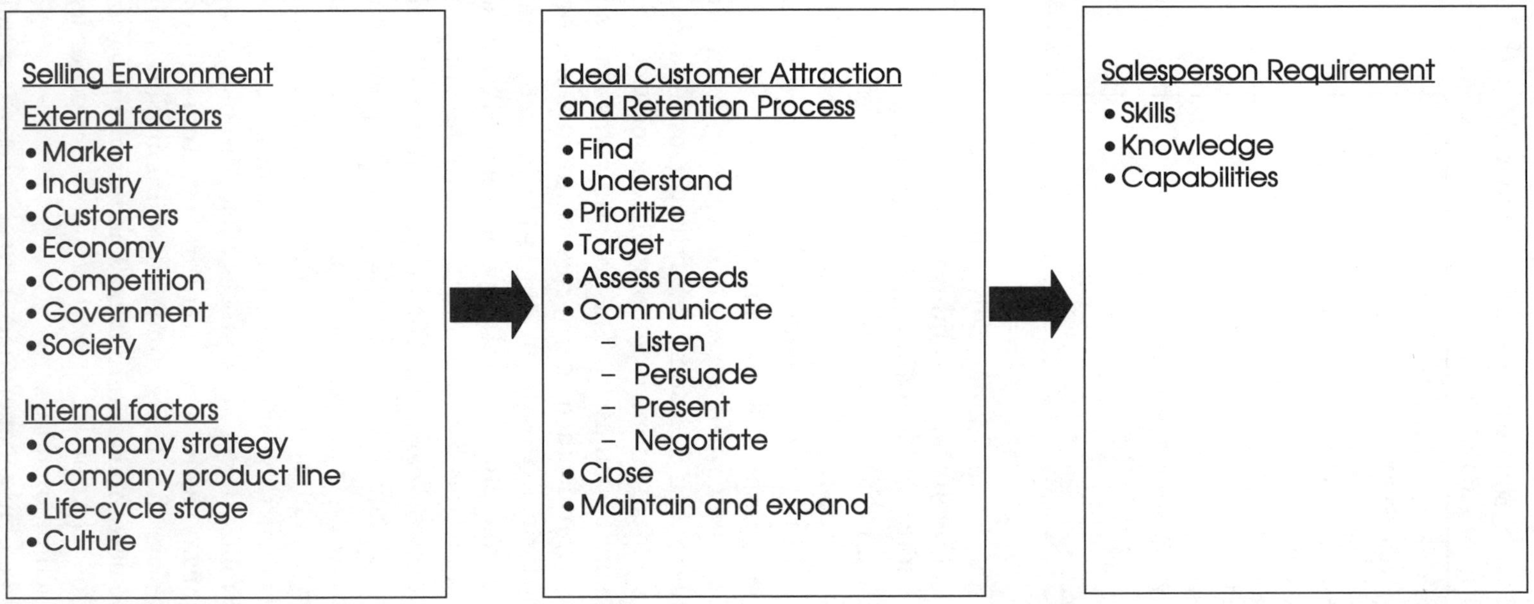

**Figure 7-5.** Several Sources of Change That May Require Salesperson Renewal.

- Increased buyer sophistication
- More demanding customers
- Buyer consolidation
- Deregulation
- Increased competition
- Commodification of products and services
- Mergers and acquisitions
- New products
- Broader, more diversified product lines
- Technological breakthroughs
- Internet commerce
- Selling process redesign

Each of these can dramatically affect the company's selling environment, redefine its ideal selling process, and alter the skills and knowledge that the salesperson will need in order to be successful. Each salesperson will need to retool to become more effective and efficient. Effective sales force training in times of change guarantees that the capability gap does not get too wide and ensures that the sales force sustains its success in the new environment.

Several examples can serve to illustrate how training programs have been adapted to overcome capability gaps induced by a dynamic environment. One insurance company had a focused product line that it offered to small businesses. The company was very successful in its niche. However, it decided that it needed to do something different to sustain its historical growth rate, and so it decided to broaden its product line by introducing several new products. The products served a different customer need and were currently offered by other insurance companies. The company reasoned that customers would like to have all of their insurance needs met by a single insurance company. It also felt that it knew its customers well and had developed strong relationships with them, and so it could be the company of choice. A company sales force visited the targeted small businesses. With the enhanced product portfolio, the selling process had to change significantly. In fact, the company decided to enter into a partnership with another insurance company that better understood the underwriting risk associated with the new product offerings. The training program was updated to include product knowledge, revised customer needs assessment, and partnership selling modules.

A major U.S. newspaper made two changes to its training program.

For years, the newspaper had been paying incentives to its advertising sales force based upon sales results. Then it started a profitability initiative. The sales force's incentive plan had to be changed to reflect this objective. Profitability was hard to measure, and its calculation was complex. To implement the new compensation program, the company needed to train its sales force to calculate territory profitability and train it in the new behaviors that would lead to higher profitability. In a second initiative, this newspaper developed software that enabled customers to develop newspaper advertising copy online. The training program was adapted to show the sales force how the new software could provide value to customers.

Training leaders are going to have significant challenges as segments of their company's customers begin to buy over the Internet. The role of the sales force will change. Salespeople will need to identify customers in the Internet segments and teach them how to order from the company's Web page. Otherwise, they will lose these customers to competitors. Are today's salespeople ready for the Internet challenge? Are today's training programs equipped to meet the challenge? Figure 7-6 describes a process for adapting a company's training requirements to an environmental change.

## Four Insights to Improve Sales Training

### The Firm's Level of Emphasis on Sales Training Is a Reflection of Its Culture

Every sales force culture makes a statement about what the sales force values and what it sees as important. Cultures that value professional development and individual growth will have effective training initiatives. Sales forces that place excessive emphasis on short-term revenue generation may actually discourage salespeople from seeking development opportunities. "What is there to learn?" and "I lose money every day that I am not in the field" are comments from the field that are typical of a low-development culture.

Training initiatives designed to remedy capability gaps affect both short-term and long-term revenues. Short-term revenues decline incrementally because salespeople are not in the field generating revenues. However, during the training, the salespeople are developing capabilities that will make them more effective in the long run. They are postponing their sales into the future. The challenge is coming up with the

**Figure 7-6.** Effective Training Programs Respond to a Dynamic Environment.

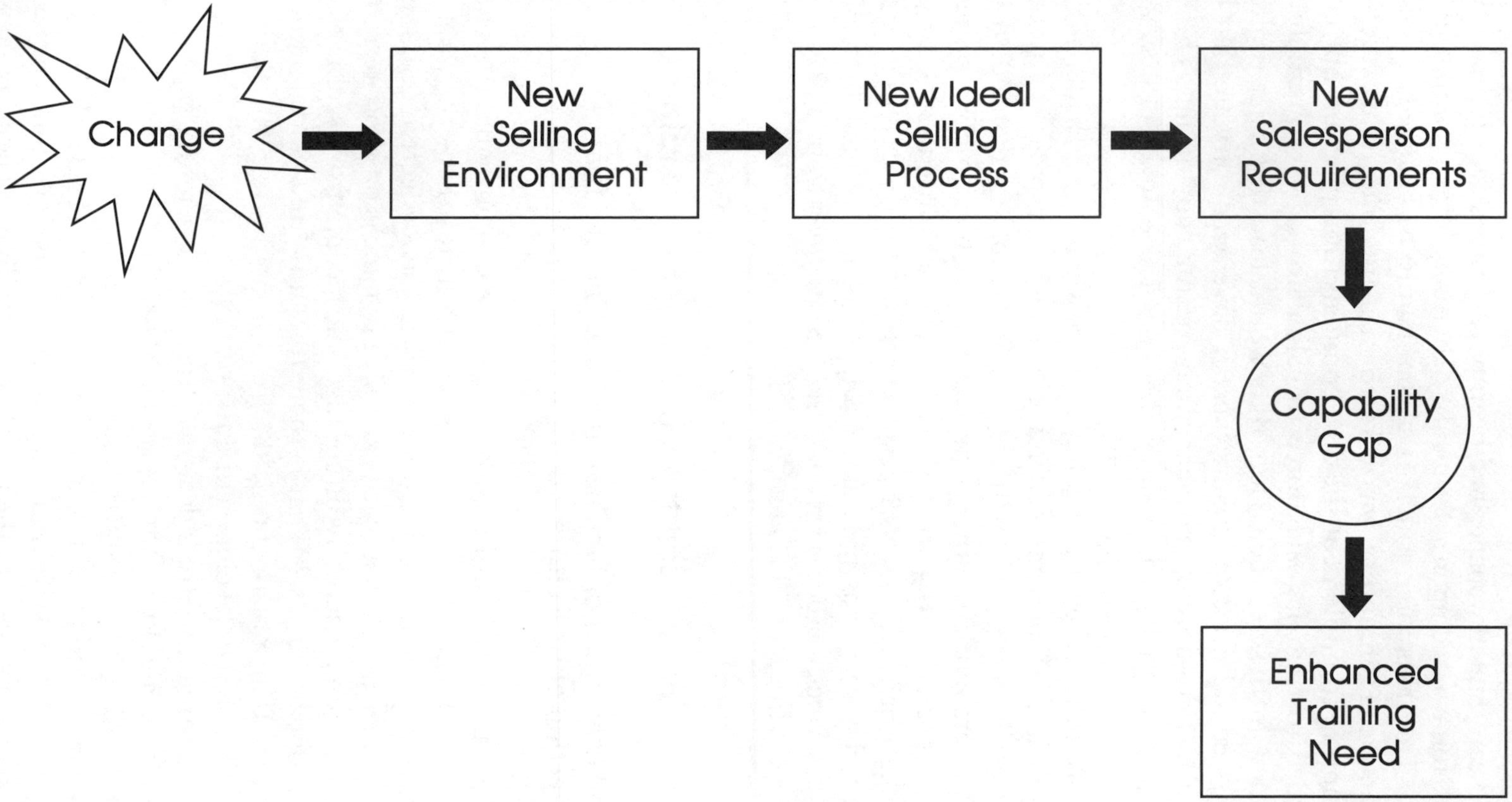

Change

New Selling Environment

New Ideal Selling Process

New Salesperson Requirements

Capability Gap

Enhanced Training Need

right training decisions that will balance short-term revenue losses and short-term training costs with long-term sales force effectiveness. Figure 7-7 conceptualizes this trade-off.

Several conditions may lead to a low-development culture. They include the following:

- Salesperson goals have a heavy financial orientation.
- All performance metrics are stated in terms of sales and/or profits.
- Only experienced salespeople get hired.
- The training budget depends upon company performance.
- Sales managers are the primary trainers, but they also carry a significant individual sales goal.
- The incentive compensation plan has a high variable (incentive) component.

Selling organizations that are learning organizations take a different approach to training. They usually hold the salesperson accountable for his or her own development. However, they act as an enabler. The learning organization begins by helping individuals to recognize their capability gaps and then develops individualized programs to overcome these gaps. Specifically, the learning organization helps individuals diagnose needs, develop objectives, design learning experiences, find resources, and evaluate learning outcomes. Some companies, like Motorola, require each salesperson to attend class for a specific number of

**Figure 7-7.** The Training Trade-off.

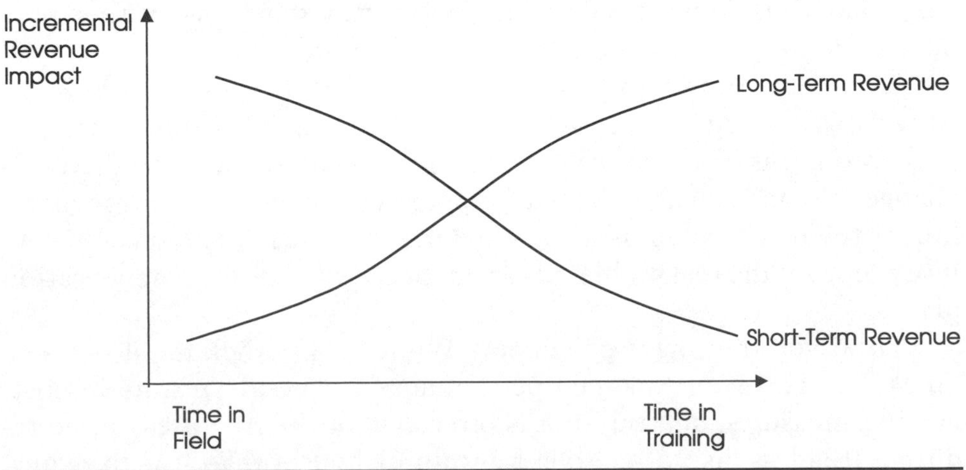

hours (e.g., forty) each year. Other organizations establish individual learning accounts, consisting of money and time, which are at the discretion of the sales manager for the purpose of developing salespeople. Learning is part of the culture. It is not optional.

## Training Is Frequently Viewed as the Easy Fix

Selling organizations constantly face challenges. Some of the more common ones that we hear are:

- Sales force turnover is too high.
- The sales force is generating sales, but not profitable sales.
- New business development needs to be improved.
- The sales force is calling on "friends and family" too frequently.
- The market has shifted and the sales force keeps selling in the old way.

Very often sales management looks to training for the solution to these challenges. Training is the easy remedy when management thinks that there is a productivity problem. Training is a quick fix. All the company needs to do is find some money and hire trainers—of which there are many.

Training has quick impact. Its influence is quicker than that of other sales force drivers. Seeing the impact of automation, hiring, resizing, and restructuring requires more time.

Training is less disruptive than other sales force driver changes. Selling roles do not change much, and sales territories are unaffected. Sales managers do not need to accept less important jobs, as they may have to do in a restructuring.

Expanding training is a positive statement. It says that the company cares about its people. Everyone will grow and become better.

Training is also the least risky sales force productivity driver to change. No one is being blamed for poor performance. Feelings will be hurt if the real problem is a weak management team. Salespeople may lose money if the real problem is an ineffective incentive compensation plan.

However, training is ephemeral. While it is a quick fix, it is also a quick "unfix." Poor financial performance frequently results in cost-cutting measures, and training is often one of the first areas to be reduced. It is less disruptive to cut a training budget than it is to reduce head count, restructure the sales force, or terminate an automation program.

## Ideas That Can Enhance Any Training Program

The following ideas can enhance any sales force training program:

- *Rapid prototyping works.* It is more cost-effective to implement a training program quickly and modify it as wrinkles appear than to wait until the "perfect" program has been developed before launching it. The "perfect" program will take too long to develop, incremental sales will be missed, and the program may be out of date before the sales force sees it.
- *Individualized training has advantages over group training.* Capability gaps differ across individuals. An individualized program is more effective but less efficient than a group program. The effectiveness gains from individualized instruction frequently exceed the efficiency gains that result from group programs. It is important for the selling organization to get fully effective salespeople in the field as quickly as possible.
- *Active learning is more effective than passive learning.* People learn more by doing than by listening. Studies confirm this—see Figure 7-8.
- *Training modules that are structured around actual business problems are very effective.* They are interesting. They get people involved. They stimulate learning. They allow salespeople to anticipate what it will be like in the field. Salespeople who have

**Figure 7-8.** What People Remember.

**People generally remember:**

**10% of what they *READ***

**20% of what they *HEAR***

**30% of what they *SEE***

**50% of what they *HEAR* and *SEE***

**70% of what they *SAY*, and**

**90% of what they *SAY* as they *DO* a thing**

*Source:* William Scholz, *Communication in the Business Organization*, © 1962, p. 86. Reprinted by permission of Pearson Education, Inc., Upper Saddle River, NJ, 07458.

received such training are more effective when they encounter the same or a similar business problem for the first time in actual practice. Many types of skills and knowledge can be integrated in these training modules. For example, a training module can incorporate both product knowledge and selling skill development.

- *Stretch experiences can enhance a salesperson's development.* Research is beginning to show that really high performers in many fields have had more stretch experiences in their background. Applying this concept to sales suggests that ongoing coaching and training initiatives that include stretch experiences would produce a larger group of really high performers.
- *The Internet has opened wide possibilities for delivering information-based training.* Training documents can be accessed from a local server. They are available day or night. They can include text or video. The software customizes the instruction to address each individual's capability gap. Web-based training metamediaries are likely to be the portals for large amounts of sales force training in the future.

## The Sales Manager Has a Significant Role in Professional Development

Chapter 8 describes the role of the sales manager as being made up of the following five activities: select the team, build the team, lead the team, manage the team, and reward the team. The manager is an essential participant in building the team. Anyone who has tried to acquire an athletic skill by just reading about it knows that reading alone is not enough. It is the coach who translates knowledge and theory into performance.

The sales manager implements several of the sales training ideas listed in the previous section. Specifically, he or she individualizes the instruction to the specific needs of the participant and also creates an environment for positive action learning. He or she is a coach and a counselor, providing constructive feedback to facilitate the learning process.

New training initiatives should be pilot-tested with the sales management team first. Salespeople who return from training need to have their newly acquired skills reinforced in the field. A manager who is not in touch with the new concepts and new vocabulary will not be a valuable coach and team builder.

The sales manager has a difficult and important job. Consequently, he or she needs training as much as or more than the salespeople. Regrettably, most organizations underinvest in the development of their sales managers.

## Updating Training and Development for Success—A Four-Step Process

Every training program should undergo a review at least once every three or four years. The knowledge and skill capabilities of the sales force may need to be updated to meet revised customer needs and a revised selling process as selling environments change. The four-step process in Figure 7-9 can be used to guide the review and revision of the sales training program.

### Step 1: Training Outcome Assessment

In the first step, training program outcomes are evaluated. This step requires four activities. These activities parallel the flow in Figure 7-6.

1. Scan the selling environment for significant changes.
2. Revitalize the selling process to incorporate improvements that will increase the competitiveness of the sales force.
3. Specify the salesperson requirements that are needed to support the new selling process.
4. Define training outcomes that will ensure that the sales force will be able to implement the new selling process.

Figure 7-10 illustrates the kinds of training outcomes that can be developed in step 1. A newspaper assessed its market and observed that its advertising sales force was experiencing significant competition from other media companies. Radio, magazines, local TV, cable TV, the Internet, and direct mail were all eroding its market share. The newspaper assessed its training program and listed those skill and knowledge outcomes that it deemed essential if it wanted to compete successfully in the future.

### Step 2: Training Program Evaluation

The current training program is evaluated in step 2 of the process. The Capabilities/Effectiveness (C/E) Matrix is a valuable tool for determin-

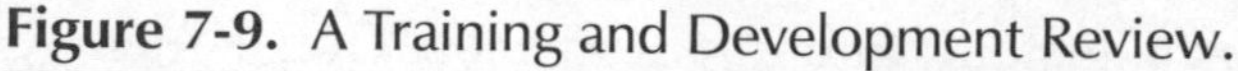
**Figure 7-9.** A Training and Development Review.

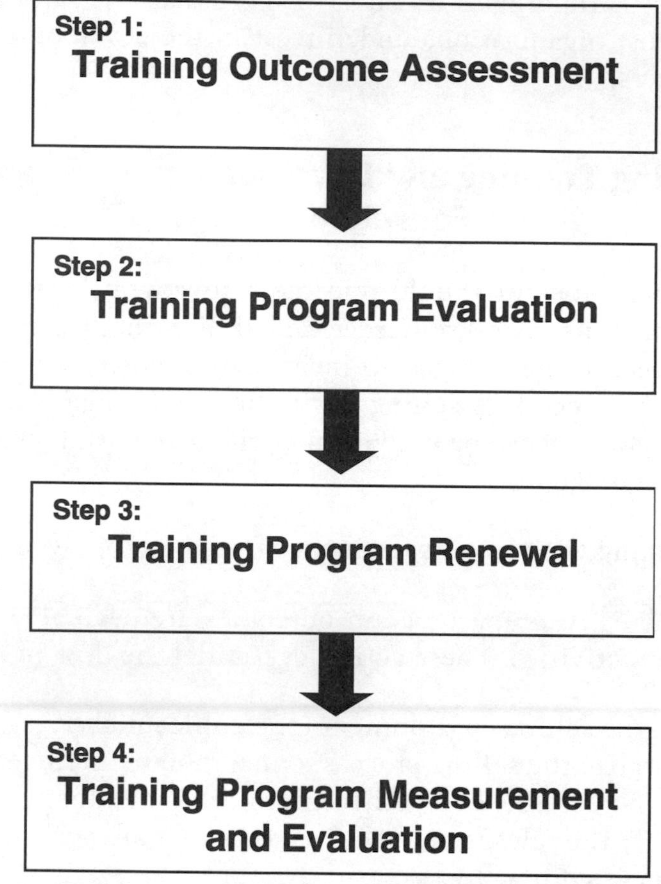


ing the extent to which the current training program is producing the outcomes specified in step 1. The C/E matrix has two dimensions. The horizontal dimension represents how effectively the current training program produces a desired training outcome or capability. The vertical dimension specifies how important the training outcome or capability is in determining the success of the sales force. Each training outcome is rated on a scale of 1 to 5 on each dimension. Figure 7-11 illustrates the training assessment for the newspaper advertising sales force mentioned in step 1.

Notice that the training outcomes that appear in the northwest quadrant are the most problematic. They represent outcomes that are important for sales success but are not being developed very effectively by the current training program. Virtually all of the training outcomes for the newspaper advertising sales force appear in this quadrant. A significant redesign of the training program for this sales force is necessary.

**Figure 7-10.** An Illustration of Training Outcomes for a Newspaper Advertising Sales Force.

| Training Outputs |
|---|
| Communications |
| Advertiser needs |
| Selling against the competition |
| Competitive products |
| New products |
| Negotiation |
| Existing products |
| Billing error resolution |
| Industry trends |
| Production process capabilities |
| Insertion order completion |
| Credit guidelines |
| Computer applications |

The situation of other training environments is not nearly as serious. Figure 7-12 shows a similar analysis for a sales force selling paper products. The training process for this company has a better balance than that for the newspaper company. Training in several important areas is delivered effectively. A few areas fall into the southwest quadrant. This is the low effectiveness/low importance quadrant. These competency areas probably have only a trivial impact on sales force effectiveness and can be reduced or dropped.

## Step 3: Training Program Renewal

The third step in the review process is the renewal step. The training program needs to be updated to reflect any improvement opportunities identified in step 2. The renewal has the three stages depicted in Figure 7-13.

Training content is determined first. Content falls into three categories: knowledge, skills, and culture. A representative list of content topics appears in Figure 7-14. The actual topics selected by any company would follow from the needs that are identified in step 2.

**Figure 7-11.** An Illustration of the C/E Matrix for a Newspaper Advertising Sales Force.

| | Management Assessment | | |
|---|---|---|---|
| | Effectiveness | Importance | Training Outputs |
| A | 2.64 | 4.35 | Communications |
| B | 2.67 | 4.32 | Advertiser needs |
| C | 2.38 | 4.31 | Selling against the competition |
| D | 1.88 | 4.26 | Competitive products |
| E | 2.84 | 4.23 | New products |
| F | 2.46 | 4.18 | Negotiation |
| G | 2.72 | 4.18 | Existing products |
| H | 1.87 | 4.02 | Billing error resolution |
| I | 2.15 | 4.02 | Industry trends |
| J | 2.16 | 3.91 | Production process capabilities |
| K | 3.09 | 3.87 | Insertion order completion |
| L | 2.33 | 3.80 | Credit guidelines |
| M | 2.30 | 3.73 | Computer applications |

**Definition of Effectiveness:**
Rating of the formal training reps received during the last year in the specified area

**Definition of Importance:**
Rating of the importance of training in the specified area

| | Response Value | | | | |
|---|---|---|---|---|---|
| | 1 | 2 | 3 | 4 | 5 |
| Effectiveness | Very Poor | Poor | Good | Very Good | Excellent |
| Importance | Not Important | Somewhat Important | Important | Quite Important | Extremely Important |

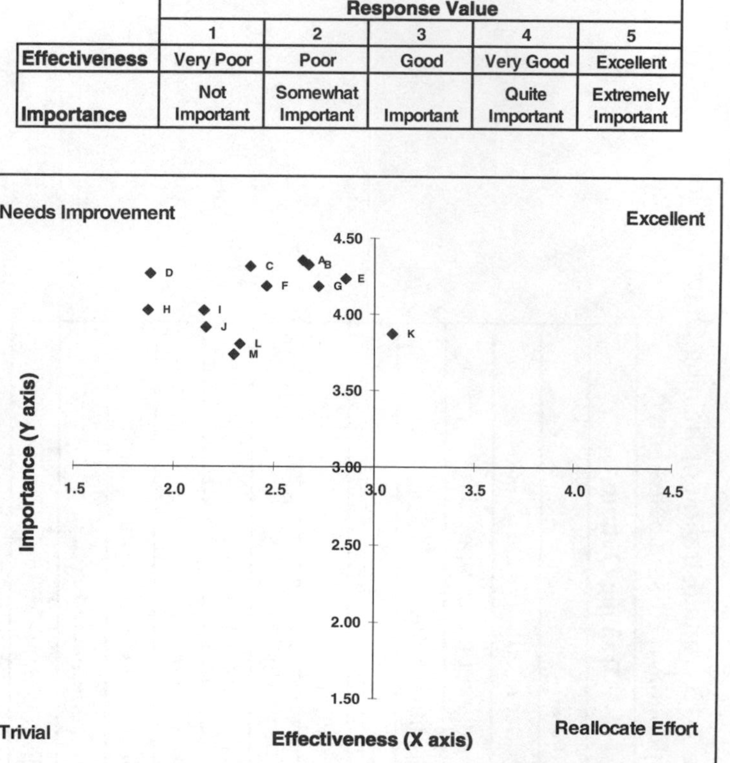

**Figure 7-12.** An Illustration of the C/E Matrix for a Paper Products Sales Force.

| | Response Value | | | | | |
|---|---|---|---|---|---|---|
| | 0 | 1 | 2 | 3 | 4 | 5 |
| **Effectiveness** | None Received | Very Poor | Poor | Good | Very Good | Excellent |
| **Importance** | | No Impact | Little Impact | Average Impact | Medium Impact | High Impact |

| Training Outputs | Management Assessment: Effectiveness | Management Assessment: Importance |
|---|---|---|
| **Selling Skills** | | |
| Transactional | 2.9 | 3.7 |
| Relationship | 3.1 | 4.0 |
| Consultative | 3.1 | 4.1 |
| **Business Knowledge** | | |
| Products, markets | 3.2 | 4.1 |
| Company capabilities | 3.1 | 4.2 |
| Competition | 2.5 | 3.8 |
| **Supporting Courses** | | |
| Quality | 2.8 | 3.3 |
| Legal | 3.0 | 2.5 |
| Finance | 2.7 | 2.5 |
| Others | 2.8 | 2.5 |

**Definition of Effectiveness:** Rating of the formal training the reps received during the past 12 months. Responses of "None Received" not incorporated into averages above.

**Definition of Importance:** Rating of the importance of training in the specified area

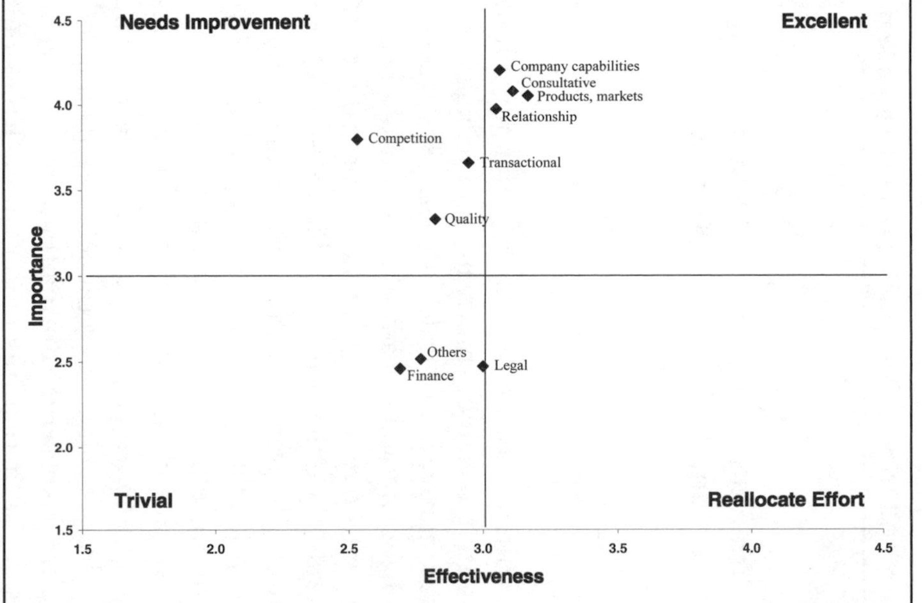

**Figure 7-13.** Three Stages of Training Program Renewal.

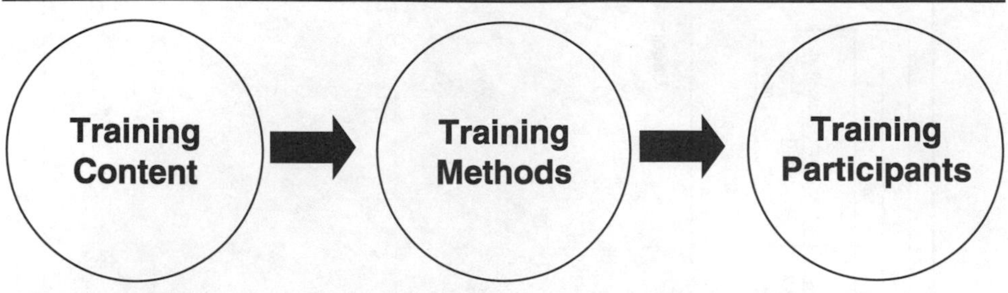


Different content requires different training methods to educate, enlighten, convince, motivate, and reengineer sales force personnel. A representative list of training methods appears in Figure 7-15.

Each method has advantages and disadvantages. Some methods are more effective, while others are more efficient. The appropriate choice depends upon the time available to complete the training, the amount of money budgeted for the training, the sales force culture, and the preconceptions of the training manager. Figure 7-16 places training methods on the efficiency/effectiveness continuum.

On-the-job training is clearly the most effective method of training sales personnel. It produces the highest retention rate for skills and knowledge applicable to the job, and its impact on individual performance can be observed during training. However, this method can be expensive, as it requires closer, more hands-on supervision than does

**Figure 7-14.** Training Program Content.

*Knowledge*

- **Product**
- **Market**
- **Customers**
- **Technical**
- **Economy**
- **Competitors**

*Others*

- **Internal customer management**
- **Customer service interface**
- **Team building**
- **Pricing**
- **Goal setting**

*Skills*

- **Selling**
- **Account strategizing**
- **Targeting**
- **Time/territory**
- **Analytical thinking**
- **Presentation**
- **Writing**
- **Negotiations**
- **Relationship development**

*Culture*

- **Corporate philosophy**
- **Values**
- **Work style expectations**
- **Heroes, legends, stories**

**Figure 7-15.** Training Methods.

*Classroom*

- Lectures
- Role-playing
- Case studies

*Participant and Observation Training*

- Plant tours
- Listening to customer service phone calls
- Observing company buyer
- Mentoring

*Self-Study*

- Optional courses
- Books, articles
- CD-ROM
- Videoconferencing
- Videotapes
- Internet/intranet
- On-line

*On-the-Job Training*

- Coaching
- Instructional guidelines
- Customer feedback

*External Seminars*

- Time management
- Negotiations
- Selling skills

classroom training. Self-study is the least costly solution, but it requires a level of motivation that not every salesperson possesses. Classroom training is a compromise between these two methods, but it doesn't necessarily reside exactly between the two in terms of efficiency and effectiveness. Some knowledge may be assimilated nearly as easily through self-study as via classroom instruction. In contrast, certain skills taught in the classroom may require role-playing or other active techniques that approximate on-the-job training to be effective.

Finally, someone needs to take responsibility and accountability for training the sales force. The sales training leader is usually the vice president of sales, the national sales manager, or the training manager. Members of the training team can include the individuals listed in Fig-

**Figure 7-16.** Efficiency/Effectiveness Trade-offs Among Training Methods.

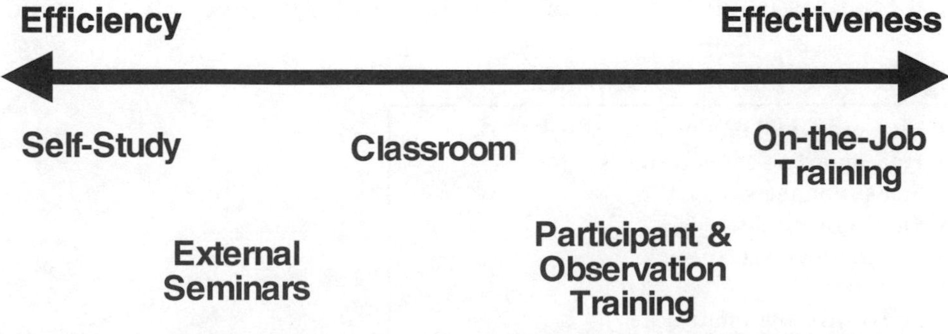

ure 7-17. Remember that the first-line sales manager is possibly the most critical participant in the training process. The sales manager works closely with the salesperson to overcome the salesperson's capability gaps. He or she coaches, provides feedback, and celebrates the salesperson's success. Frequently the sales manager is held accountable for the development of his or her people.

These three steps in training program renewal need to be integrated. The choices of content, method, and trainer need to be coordinated. Figure 7-18 diagrams combinations that are likely to be compatible.

Training program initiatives can usually be placed into two categories: "quick wins" and long-term initiatives. Quick wins have a quick payoff and build momentum and excitement that will guarantee the implementation of longer-term training change initiatives. Long-term initiatives usually require a larger investment in time and money but have a significant long-term payback. A company president giving a motivating speech on company values at the new employee orientation is an example of a quick win, whereas the design and implementation of an interactive intranet training module would take place over a longer period of time.

## Step 4: Training Program Measurement and Evaluation

The final step is measurement and evaluation. Years ago, one of the authors was asked by a sales executive how to measure the effectiveness of a proposed training program. "Why are you worried about measuring the training program? Shouldn't training be in your genes?" was the author's naïve reply. To which the sales executive responded, "I am spending a lot of money to switch to a new training paradigm, and I need to know if it is working before I commit even larger sums of money."

Training is hard to measure. It is hard to know precisely how well

**Figure 7-17.** Training Participants.

- **Vice president of sales**
- **Headquarters sales trainers**
- **Sales managers**
- **Field sales trainers**
- **Experienced salespeople**
- **Mentors**
- **Self-study administrators**

Figure 7-18. A Guide for Training Program Integration and Implementation.

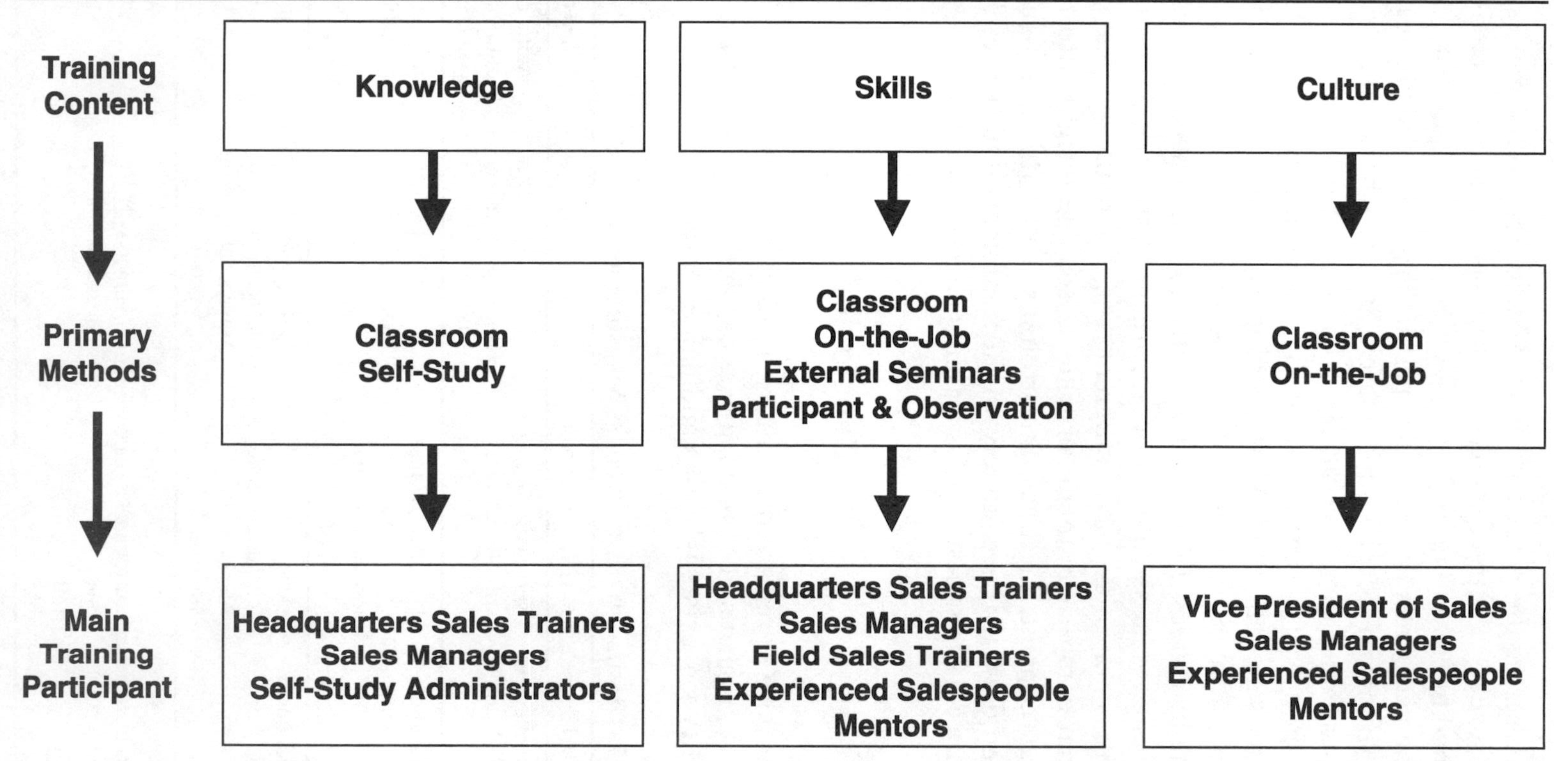

it is increasing the productivity of the sales force. Companies that try to measure its effectiveness use four types of measures. Each of these is explained briefly in Figure 7-19.

The use of results measures, particularly sales and profit increases due to training, is ideal. Unfortunately, it is very hard to disentangle all of the variables that have an effect on sales. Sales force experiments are the best way to separate all of the factors affecting sales. However, companies are reluctant to run training experiments because it is hard to justify training a subset of salespeople while the rest go without training just to see if training is effective. What is needed is a scientifically designed cross-company comparison of training programs. Since different companies have different training philosophies, a cross-sectional comparison might provide reasonable insight into the most effective content, methods, and trainers. Until this meta-analysis is completed, we will need to rely on the nonfinancial measures described in Figure 7-19 to measure sales training effectiveness.

## Conclusion

The purpose of sales force training is to make salespeople successful. Training programs need to change as capability gaps arise. A significant capability gap exists when a candidate is hired, and so most organiza-

**Figure 7-19.** Training Effectiveness Measurement.

| *Ways to Measure* | *What to Measure* | *How to Measure* | *When to Measure* |
|---|---|---|---|
| Cognitive effect—<br>"What do learners know?" | Knowledge of course content | Exams<br>Self-assessment<br>Interview | At the completion of training and at points in the future |
| Attitudinal effect—<br>"How do learners feel?" | Perceptions of training<br>Course evaluation<br>Instructor evaluation<br>Organization climate | Survey<br>Interview | At the completion of training |
| Behavioral effect—<br>"What do learners do?" | Skills<br>Job performance<br>Absenteeism<br>Turnover | Performance indicators<br>Observation<br>Managerial assessment<br>Self-assessment | Over the first year |
| Results—<br>"How do learner changes affect the organization?" | Job satisfaction<br>Customer satisfaction<br>Sales<br>Profits<br>ROI | Survey<br>Experiments<br>Managerial judgment | After a year |

tions have training programs for new salespeople. Changes in selling environments frequently induce capability gaps that require that a company modify its selling strategy and selling process. Too many companies are slow to make this adjustment. The training and development review process developed in this chapter can diagnose when and what training program change initiatives are necessary for enhanced sales force effectiveness.

# Chapter 8

# The Critical Role of the First-Line Sales Manager

This chapter explores the pivotal role of the first-line sales manager. A good sales manager selects, builds, leads, manages, and rewards the team. The manager succeeds when all of his or her people succeed.

The chapter is designed to help you:

- Learn how to excel at selecting, building, leading, managing, and rewarding the team. These activities are explored in the context of a case study that uses concrete examples of successful management practices.
- Understand and identify the characteristics of good sales managers.
- Put into place a five-part program for establishing and sustaining a strong first-line sales management team.
- Gain practical advice on how to make a number of important sales management decisions, including how to determine the right management span of control, select the best sales management candidates (internal and/or external), implement an opinion survey that asks salespeople to evaluate their managers, and appropriately reward the sales management team.

## Introduction

A consumer electronics manufacturer's Great Lakes Sales District has eight salespeople who call on retail outlets. This district is one of four that report to the Midwest Sales Region. The Midwest Sales Region is one of three regions into which the country is divided. Recently, a new Great Lakes District manager was appointed. The new manager is reviewing the regional manager's assessment of each of the eight salespeople in the Great Lakes District:

*Jack Aaron:* Jack is in his mid-twenties with one year of sales experience in the food services industry prior to joining the company a year ago. Jack's territory was a problem before his arrival. Jack is a friendly guy who seems eager to learn and works hard, but he is not exceptionally bright. He may not be the best person to turn around the territory because he does not have an aggressive sales approach.

*William Anderson:* William is an average performer who refuses to try new things with his customers. He attends all the training sessions but is unwilling to believe that anything other than personality closes sales. William is the stereotypical salesperson; he is fun to be around and is considered the unofficial social leader at sales meetings. He is in his early forties and has had the same accounts for the past five years. William's sales performance is likely to continue to be average.

*Frank Cady:* Frank is in his early thirties and joined the company two years ago. His preemployment tests suggest that he is very intelligent and has the general characteristics of a successful salesperson. However, his lackadaisical attitude and lazy work style are a problem. Several of his larger accounts are complaining about poor customer service, and it is possible that we are about to lose one or two of them. Frank is a real challenge for us.

*Renee Darby:* Renee is in her early forties and has been with the company for five years. She is a bright spot and a solid performer. Renee tends to be very active with her small accounts and not active enough with her large accounts.

*Patricia Ginsberg:* Patricia is in her early fifties and has been with the company for twenty years. She continually leads the district in sales and has the best sales territory in terms of opportunity. Unfortunately, she is in poor health, and her ability to sustain high levels of activity is questionable. When asked recently about taking a reduced assignment, Patricia became visibly upset, stating that she can handle as much work now as she has in the past. She is very territorial and definitely will not surrender any of her assigned accounts without a significant fight. She is quite popular with the salespeople in the district.

*Jason Hadley:* Jason is in his early thirties and has six years of experience with the company. At one time he was a top performer, with one of the highest penetration rates in the sales force. However, he is currently experiencing severe personal problems that are hindering his performance—his sales are only 60 percent of what they were two years ago. Some of the members of the sales force have observed that he has a serious drinking problem. Jason's customers appear to be impatient with him, and one recently complained that Jason missed two appointments in the past month. When asked about these meetings, Jason confided that he was having some trouble at home and needed some time to get focused on work again.

*Mark Jackson:* Mark has been with the company for ten years. He is in his late forties and has been a good performer, but his results are sliding and his interest in the company is fading. He has had fantastic success in a side business and is no longer concerned about the income he generates through his sales job. The other salespeople envy Mark because he lives in a large house in a fashionable suburb, takes expensive vacations, and works his assignment only three days each week. Mark was recently overheard telling another salesperson that "maintenance of existing accounts is all that I need to be happy. I've got better things to do than call on prospects and nonaccounts."

*Bob Lowell:* Bob is a "plugger"—an average guy with an average performance. He is in his late thirties and has been with the company for fifteen years. Bob is good at managing his accounts and planning his time but lacks flair when trying to sell big orders.

The new manager concludes that the sales district is performing poorly, and the quantitative results confirm this. Here is a district performance summary:

- Average sales per salesperson are 60 percent of the regional average and 65 percent of the national average.
- Gross profit margins are 85 percent of the national average.
- The district has 7 percent of the company's national market potential and 8 percent of the company's national sales force investment, but only 4 percent of the company's national sales revenues.

Why is the district not performing well? The fundamental reason is that the district had a nonperforming sales manager for too many years. The manager did not hire the right people, he did not develop them so that they could succeed, he did not coach or direct them effectively, he did not set aggressive goals and hold the salespeople accountable for their achievement, and he had a totally undisciplined approach to management. It is no wonder that the people in the district profile so poorly. The manager created a low-achievement culture that can be improved only with dramatic action. The new Great Lakes District manager must determine what that action should be.

For many years the authors have asked hundreds of sales vice presidents, national sales managers, and regional sales managers the question in Figure 8-1.

The vote is nearly evenly divided. There is a slight preference, however, for excellent salespeople.

In the short term, a team of great salespeople easily outsells a team of average salespeople. But great salespeople are promoted, retire, or quit because their average manager holds them back. When they leave, an average manager will probably replace them with average salespeople. Average managers rarely surround themselves with excellent salespeople. They may be unable to recognize talent, or they may be intimidated by excellence. In the long run, the average manager brings all the territories in the district down to his or her level.

On the other hand, an excellent manager brings excellence to all the territories in the district. Often people ask, "If that person is a great manager, why are his or her salespeople only average?" Well, the manager inherited them. But in the long run, he or she will counsel, coach, train, and replace them until the team is excellent.

The manager's job is important because of this long-term effect—the manager selects and builds a team.

**Figure 8-1.** Which Situation Do Sales Managers Prefer?

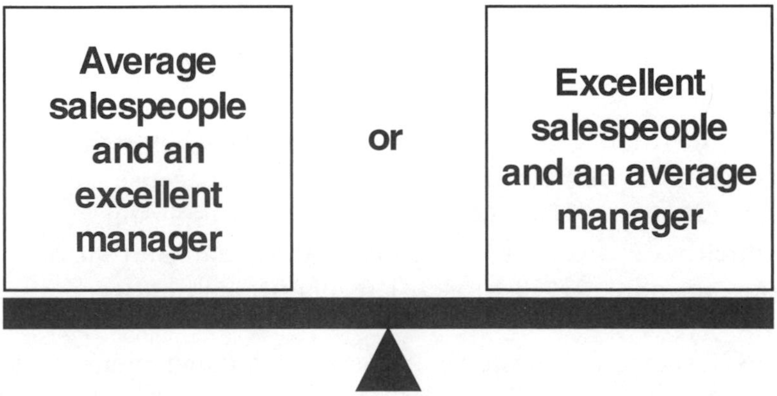

The job of first-line sales manager is the most important position in the entire sales force. Top management determines the direction for the organization, but the first-line sales managers ensure that the strategy is executed. A great sales manager turns average salespeople into high performers and achieves good results with an average marketing strategy. An average sales manager maintains average salespeople and produces average results with a good marketing strategy. A below-average manager can turn a highly effective group of people into low performers and produces results similar to those at the Great Lakes Sales District.

> *"In any sales force, you can get along without the vice president of sales, the regional sales directors, and the training manager, but you cannot get along without the district (first-line) sales manager."*
>
> *Andy Anderson*
> *Former Sales Representative,*
> *District Sales Manager,*
> *Regional Sales Manager,*
> *Vice President of Sales,*
> *and President, Searle U.S. Operations*

How can a sales organization ensure that first-line sales managers succeed in their pivotal role? How can fast-rising comets and steady warhorses be shaped into a successful sales management team leading a motivated and well-directed sales force? In this chapter, the role of the first-line sales manager is examined. The chapter also explores how the sales organization can establish and sustain a vigorous sales management team.

## The Sales Manager's Role

Typically, sales managers are former salespeople. They are familiar with the sales job, and their reports feel comfortable because their manager has "carried the bag." However, a promoted salesperson benefits if he or she quickly discovers the significant role changes that occur with promotion to manager. It is useful to distinguish between these two jobs.

The salesperson's mission is to serve two constituencies: the customer and the company. First, he or she must understand and meet the customer's needs. Second, he or she must make sure the company achieves its sales and profit objectives and must provide vital market information to the marketing and product development groups.

The sales manager's mission is to serve the customer, the company, and a third constituency: the salesperson. Like the salesperson's, the manager's responsibility includes meeting customer needs and achieving company results. The manager has overall responsibility for all of the customers his or her reports serve and all the sales they generate. But the sales manager does not achieve these objectives entirely through his or her own initiative and activity. The manager is not the "hunter," the "playmaker," or the center of action. Managers achieve customer and company success when their people are successful. Consequently, the existence of the third constituency—the salespeople—strongly differentiates the two roles. Managers are coaches, not players; they achieve their objectives through others. The missions of the sales manager and the salesperson are compared and contrasted in Figure 8-2.

The sales manager's role is made up of the following five activities:

- Selecting the team
- Building the team
- Leading the team

**Figure 8-2.** The Roles of the Salesperson and the Sales Manager.

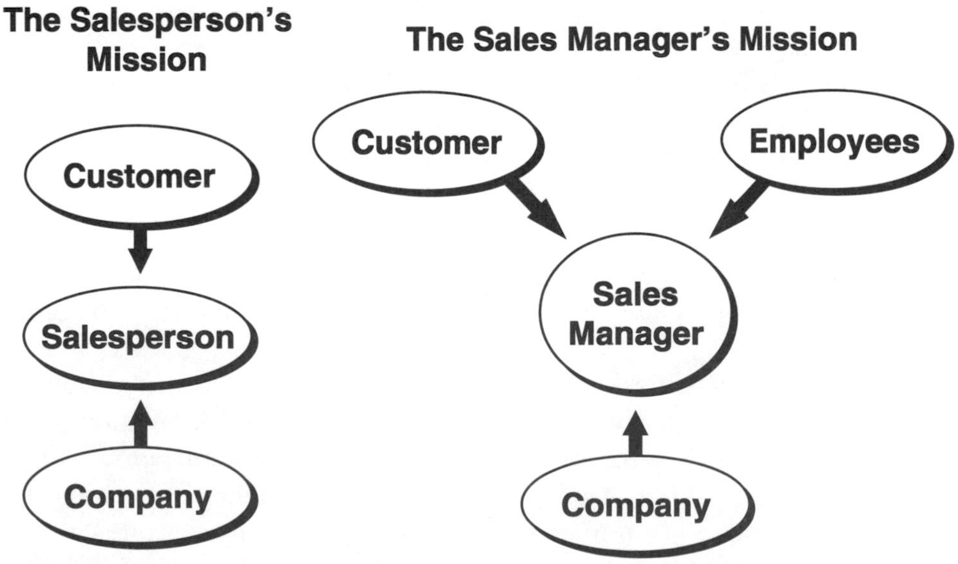

- Managing the team
- Rewarding the team

Each of these will be discussed in turn.

## Selecting the Team

As stated earlier, the sales manager succeeds when his or her people succeed. Consequently, the manager must create a team of winners. This starts with selection. Typically, first-line sales managers have the greatest input into who gets hired. They conduct the initial screening of the applicant pool and submit their choices to the regional manager for final approval. Since the first-line manager will have to live with the final choice, regional sales managers frequently accept the first-line manager's recommendation.

Consider the two recent hires in the Great Lakes Sales District. Both Aaron and Cady are hiring mistakes. It is unlikely that Aaron will become more assertive and smarter or that Cady will shed his lackadaisical attitude and laziness. These two hiring errors have significant consequences for the Great Lakes Sales District. First, 25 percent of the district's sales territories are not as productive as they could have been had the district hired competent and successful salespeople. Second, these two territories create a serious challenge for the manager.

The manager must take several steps to improve such a situation. Initially, the manager should diagnose and evaluate the situation, determining the problem and its causes. Is it the salesperson or the territory? If it is the salesperson, the manager needs to decide if the problem is remediable—is improvement possible? If it is remediable, the manager must establish developmental strategies for the salesperson. The manager should then provide feedback and monitor the salesperson's behavior changes and territory results. Finally, the manager needs to acknowledge the salesperson's success and provide further encouragement. If at any point the manager decides that the improvement process is unsuccessful, he or she should counsel the individual out of the organization.

A hiring error is hard to recover from. Good training and coaching may never be enough to overcome a poor selection. A manager can maintain mediocrity with coaching effort or find a replacement. If a salesperson such as Aaron or Cady leaves, a new salesperson must be recruited. The average replacement time in the United States is six months, and it may take several years for a territory to regain a high performance level. The difficulties that are created by a bad hire make hiring an extremely important part of the sales manager's job.

Chapter 6 describes an effective process for identifying and attracting good sales candidates. The sales manager needs to find people who have the right values and the right competencies. His or her selection also provides a signal to current team members concerning the skills and personal attributes that they should cultivate. Hiring is a chance to "walk the talk." Each new hire should demonstrate the values and competencies that management wishes to engender. Claiming that computer skills are important while hiring computer novices confuses the team.

Chapter 6 also demonstrates how difficult it is to select the most qualified candidates. Interviews have only a 14 percent predictive correlation. Even composite tests of ability have only a 53 percent predictive correlation. As a result, hiring mistakes are inevitable.

One of the hardest parts of a district manager's job is deciding what to do with an earnest salesperson who has wonderful intentions, but is ineffectual and has low productivity. Equally difficult for the manager are people like Hadley and Jackson in the Great Lakes Sales District. Hadley is struggling with personal issues, and Jackson has established several long-standing customer relationships, but now has other interests that are destroying the value system within the sales district. These individuals create an inherent unfairness for the other members of the district.

Since the Great Lakes Sales District has four underperforming salespeople, the other four have to work significantly harder to carry the district. The effective sales manager needs a process or a program for dealing with nonperforming salespeople. Deselection is an important part of creating a successful selling team. Perhaps some of the salespeople in the district would be better off selling other products or even in a different career.

Team selection is an ongoing process. Salespeople are regularly being evaluated, coached, counseled, and, on occasion, fired. Effective sales managers recruit continuously. They anticipate territory vacancies and have an active folder in their files labeled "potential applicants." They never get caught in a "warm body" hiring situation—they look toward filling a future spot rather than an open spot. Half of all recruiting can be done before the job is posted.

### Building the Team

Once the team has been selected, the first-line sales manager's attention should focus on how to build the team and develop it for success.

Managers succeed when their people succeed. A highly skilled, highly talented team with a good product to sell is bound to exceed expectations.

Salespeople usually do not arrive highly skilled and talented. Further, their talent will tarnish if it is not continually polished. It is the sales manager's job to develop the skills, knowledge, and competencies of the salespeople. For example, in the Great Lakes Sales District, Darby is not generating adequate sales revenue from the large accounts in her territory. A good sales manager would work with her to identify important target accounts and develop the most appropriate selling process for these accounts, help her with account planning, and coach her through the process. The district succeeds when Darby succeeds.

The salesperson is out in the field every day executing a selling process. The most appropriate selling process varies by market segment, but it usually has the components shown in Figure 8-3.

The successful sales manager ensures that each salesperson in the district has the knowledge, skill, and capabilities to use the most appropriate selling process with each customer and prospect. The manager accomplishes this objective by engaging in the following activities:

- Identifying weaknesses and areas of improvement for the salespeople
- Developing improvement plans with challenging goals

**Figure 8-3.** Components of a Selling Process.

**Sales Force Activity**

The sales force engages in a selling process:

—Find<br>
—Understand<br>
—Prioritize<br>
—Target<br>
—Assess needs<br>
—Communicate<br>
    —Listen<br>
    —Persuade<br>
    —Present<br>
    —Negotiate<br>
—Close<br>
—Maintain and expand

- Encouraging self-development
- Participating actively in action learning by training, coaching, and counseling
- Keeping salespeople on task
- Providing feedback
- Measuring progress
- Supporting and celebrating the achievements of the salespeople

The most appropriate selling process changes over time, especially when markets are in transition. The successful manager detects the essential modifications in the process, identifies the best practices, and then shares this information with the entire sales team.

The sales manager is an important training partner—a personal trainer. Action learning occurs when after the manager and salesperson finish a call, the manager asks the salesperson what he was trying to achieve and then tells the salesperson what she saw. Learning takes place when what the manager saw and what the salesperson was trying to achieve are different. The best training for salespeople takes place in real-life situations when feedback is given immediately. First-line sales managers are best suited to provide this kind of training. Good managers train and evaluate with no surprises, and feedback is prompt and regular. A good first-line sales manager has the biggest impact on a salesperson's development.

For many salespeople, the time they are spending on the job today is part of their broader professional development. Many have ambitions beyond their current selling position. In these cases, the sales manager's role should expand to include career counseling and development. The manager must always ensure the success of his or her people, even if this means that they get promoted or leave for other positions.

The successful manager is a professional development facilitator and team builder. He or she converts the two lies in the following joke into truths:

> *What are the two great sales force lies?*
>
> *When greeting a salesperson on his quarterly visit to the field, the sales manager says: "I am from headquarters, and I am here to help you."*
>
> *To which the salesperson replies: "I am glad to see you."*

### Lead the Team

The first-line sales manager leads the team. A leader gains trust and commitment from subordinates. He or she has their best interests in mind. Salespeople know that their manager will not let them down—that promises will be kept.

A good leader has a vision of what the team should accomplish in both the short and the long term. A leader has a vision for both individual accomplishment and group achievement. This vision is shared with and adopted by the team. A good leader persuades the group to have a common purpose.

Since a large proportion of the manager's time is spent with people, he or she must be a good listener and communicator. The manager must hear and understand the concerns and views of the salespeople. A good leader expresses strategy, expectations, and values very clearly and objectively.

A good leader is very knowledgeable. The leader knows his people—their strengths and weaknesses. The leader also understands the dynamics of the industry, the needs of customers, current economic trends, the competition, the current state of technological advances, and innovative business practices. She is aware of the firm's core competencies and the key company business processes. The leader can navigate the system efficiently, and has the skill to absorb, distill, and integrate the signals that arrive from the team, the company, the customers, and the environment.

Leadership is honed in crisis. The manager who is an effective leader usually builds commitment and loyalty from the way recurring district crises are handled.

## Managing the Team

It is Monday morning. The newly appointed manager of the Great Lakes Sales District looks at his "to do" list to determine how best to spend his time. The list has the following items:

- An account realignment is required. Ginsberg is unable to cover her territory completely, and Darby could use a few more accounts.
- Determine what to do about Jackson's latest vacation request. Ginsberg has left a voice-mail message complaining about having to carry too much of the district goal.
- Two of Cady's accounts are vulnerable. Call them to try to patch things up. Also, call Cady to develop an account plan for these accounts.

- Audit expense reports. Check Hadley's carefully—his expenses have been quite high lately.
- Schedule a meeting with Hadley to see how his personal life is going. We may need to ask him to join an employee assistance program.
- Return Anderson's call. He is challenging the call targets that we set in our last meeting. He doesn't seem to be making his activity goals. Listen to his arguments and decide whether to reevaluate the targets. Backing off would send a message to the rest of the district.
- Go through the proposal for the new training program and give feedback to the training department.
- The vice president of sales wants tighter controls and is insisting on an automated call-reporting system. The different system options must be evaluated.
- File last month's incoming résumés—we might need them if one of our nonperforming territories goes vacant.
- Decide on the site and agenda for the next district sales meeting.
- Schedule a meeting with the regional manager to address her concerns and to show how the district has improved since our last meeting. She also wants a forecast of next year's sales.

These are examples of the tasks sales managers face daily. A good sales manager makes sure everything goes smoothly and gets done without interfering with the selling process. Customers' needs are met, and salespeople go about their work with as few obstructions as possible.

*A good first-line sales manager is a good human resources manager.* She selects and develops a highly productive team and acknowledges and rewards its successes. Each of these important activities is described in detail in other sections of this chapter.

A good manager knows when to delegate and empower, and when to provide direction and advice. Delegation and direction are both part of the management equation. Salespeople need and frequently look for direction when they do not have the knowledge, skills, or capabilities to accomplish a task or to achieve an objective. Areas where it is common for managers to give direction include targeting, time and territory management, account planning, selling process redesign, and career planning. Too much direction, on the other hand, can decrease motivation. People are more productive and have higher job satisfaction when they are in control of their work content and work style. Managers who inspect every detail and "micromanage" are not well liked by their salespeople. Micromanagement fosters doubt; people feel better and work better when they believe that they are trusted and respected. A good sales manager determines when direction is necessary and when delegation is appropriate.

A successful manager performs his or her work seamlessly, with minimum confrontation. The district functions smoothly, and work is rarely interrupted. The team focuses externally on serving the customer and outperforming competitors. Little energy is expended internally on trying to extract concessions from one another.

Following are survey results characterizing the behaviors that salespeople ascribe to poor managers:

"My manager is inconsistent."
"My manager is indecisive; abdicates."
"My manager is thoughtless."
"My manager is unfair; exhibits favoritism."
"My manager takes undue credit; hogs the glory."
"My manager plays political games; I was 'politicized.' "
"My manager is dishonest; untrustworthy; unethical."
"My manager is a poor listener; a poor communicator."
"My manager dictates; controls; is closed-minded."
"My manager overworks the team."
"My manager is lazy; moody; always negative."
"My manager is a constant negotiator; I have to be willing to quit at all times if I want any resources."

A good manager avoids these pitfalls.

*A good first-line sales manager manages company assets effectively.* There are numerous company assets at the sales manager's disposal. The list may include:

- Cars
- Computers
- Telephones
- Faxes
- Demonstrator equipment
- Office space

A good manager utilizes these assets in the most productive way and does not abuse or squander them. New assets are added in a cost-effective manner when they are needed.

*A good first-line sales manager manages operating expenses effectively.* Each sales district has ongoing expenses. These expenses can get out of hand if they are not managed regularly and conscientiously. District expense items may include:

| | |
|---|---|
| Salaries | Samples |
| Relocation | Sales aids |
| Auto expense | Office supplies |
| Entertainment | Recruiting fees |
| Regional overhead | Travel |
| Telephone | Training |
| Meetings and exhibits | Postage and freight |

Historically, managers were heavy-hitting salespeople and sales management was an extension of the sales job. Today, sales managers are adding general management skills to their skill set. *A good first-line sales manager is a good general manager.* The world of sales is now complex, sophisticated, diverse, and fast-paced. The sales manager's role must adapt to the changing environment. The effective manager must be good at:

- Analyzing market opportunities
- Making sure customer needs are met
- Developing a district selling strategy
- Managing district profitability
- Developing a success culture
- Developing human capital
- Ensuring sales force quality
- Communicating with other parts of the organization, such as marketing, finance, and operations
- Organizing, planning, and reporting

A sales district should be viewed as a small business that the sales manager is responsible and accountable for.

## Rewarding the Team

Rewards are a source of direction and motivation for a sales force. A company rewards its people for their commitment, work, and results. Rewards can effectively align a salesperson's own motivators with the needs of the sales district.

The new Great Lakes District sales manager has begun to think about establishing a short-term reward plan. Since the district is not having a good year, the manager is having difficulty preparing a highly positive list. The following items are beginning to crystallize in the manager's mind:

- Call Darby and congratulate her on converting a very large account in Chicago. Also ask her if she could present a best-practice seminar on how to maintain accounts at the next district sales meeting.
- Ask Ginsberg if she would be willing to mentor Aaron. Ginsberg is very popular with the salespeople in the district and has lots of experience that would be useful to Aaron. She is likely to view the mentoring as recognition for her many years of service to the company, and she is probably entering that stage in her career where she would like to teach others how to be successful. Mentoring may also reduce her territorial inclinations.
- Talk to Jackson about the poor precedent he is setting with his lax work style.
- Recommend minimal salary increases for Aaron, Anderson, Cady, Hadley, and Jackson.

Notice that rewards can be extrinsic or intrinsic and positive or negative. The table in Figure 8-4 provides examples of rewards.

Salespeople are motivated by both opportunity and fear. Negative rewards are appropriate when performance is poor, but opportunity and recognition are usually better motivators. A personal story supports

**Figure 8-4.** Sales Force Rewards.

| | *Extrinsic* | *Intrinsic* |
|---|---|---|
| *Positive* | Money<br>Bonuses<br>Perks<br>Trips<br>Special events<br>Salary increase<br>Recommendation for promotion<br>Support for special projects or initiatives | Appreciation<br>Recognition<br>Security<br>Sense of belonging<br>Encouragement |
| *Negative* | Minimal salary and incentive pay increases | Constructive negative performance feedback |

this point of view. Recently one of the authors brought a puppy home. The puppy went to Puppy College and graduated with a degree in good behavior, and it then joined all the other dogs at the park on a routine basis. Watching a dozen dogs interact with their owners was an education in incentives. On one occasion, an owner who needed to go home called his dog. Of course, the dog was having a great time and had no interest in leaving the party so soon. The owner called again, and the dog again ignored him. He called again—no dog. By this time the owner had become aware that all the other owners were watching his interaction with his dog. The owner became embarrassed, and his voice became louder and angrier. When the dog finally arrived, he whacked it. What incentive does his dog have to obey when it knows that it will be whacked when the owner calls? The dog remembers only the whacking.

The managing director of a consulting firm recently told his recruiting manager that she had done a great job recruiting for his firm. Her response still rings in his ears: "Thanks. You made my day. No one *ever* tells me that we are doing OK." Appreciative, consistent, and credible intangible rewards frequently have a greater impact on people than tangible rewards.

Knowing what and when to reward is not always easy. Rewards should be deserved— rewards "for breathing" have little impact. Rewards should not be casual. They should be associated with significant, tangible outcomes, such as increased sales, outstanding customer satisfaction, and increased prospecting. Rewards should be sincere. "My boss always tells me I am great" lacks credibility after a while. Rewards should be salient. A reward is a reward only if it has value to the recipient. Receiving another toaster is not very motivating. Rewards should have a random component; entitlement can be deadly. Many of us have heard the following logic: "Two years ago they took us to Key Largo, last year it was Hawaii, next year it will probably be Fiji."

## Five Steps to Establishing and Sustaining a Vigorous Sales Management Team

The sales management team is one of the critical sales force productivity drivers defined in our sales force productivity framework in Chapter 2. It is a unique driver in that it is a collection of people rather than a process. In most organizations, it is a group of well-liked people who have been in the sales force for a long time. Therefore, any change in the sales manager driver may be difficult to implement. However, as the Great Lakes Sales District aptly demonstrates, the level of sales force success hinges on the abilities of this group. There are five things the selling organization can do regularly to ensure that the sales management team is highly effective:

- Evaluate the performance of the first-line sales management team.
- Enhance the skills, knowledge, and capabilities of the sales management team.
- Redefine the job description when different activities are required.
- Select the best candidates for the job.
- Reward the team appropriately.

Each of these will be described in more detail below.

## Performance Evaluation

Three dimensions for evaluating the sales management team are described in this section: team organization, team activity, and team results.

**Team Organization.** The most frequently asked organizational question is, "What is the proper span of control for my sales force?" That is, how many direct reports should each manager have? In sales, this is usually between four and thirty people. Too many managers are too expensive, but the sales force is ineffective when there are too few managers.

There are several approaches for determining the proper span of control. Some industries collect survey data and develop a benchmark span of control for the industry. Then each company decides how the span of control for its sales force should compare to industry norms. Another approach is for the vice president of sales to use the span of control that worked for him when he was a district sales manager. Alternatively, finance people may recommend cost-based approaches: How many managers can we afford and still keep costs in line with the sales projection? The final result can depend upon the outcome of a negotiation between these two parties.

The workload buildup approach is a useful process for determining an appropriate span of control. Stated simply, in this approach, the specific activities that an effective sales manager should perform for each of his or her salespeople are determined, and the average amount of time these activities require is estimated. To determine how much time the manager has available for people management, administration time is subtracted from total work time. To determine the span of control, the time the manager has available for people management is divided by the average time required to manage each salesperson. The data required to implement this approach are based upon both field input and external benchmarks. A simplified illustration of this approach is shown in Figure 8-5.

**Team Activity.** As stated earlier, a first-line sales manager is successful when his or her people are successful. The manager's activities need to focus on making the salespeople successful. To do this, the manager needs to select, build, lead, manage, and reward the team. The manager's direct reports can provide the best information about his or her abilities at achieving these objectives.

An annual employee opinion survey asking salespeople to evaluate

**Figure 8-5.** A Span of Control Workload Buildup Illustration.

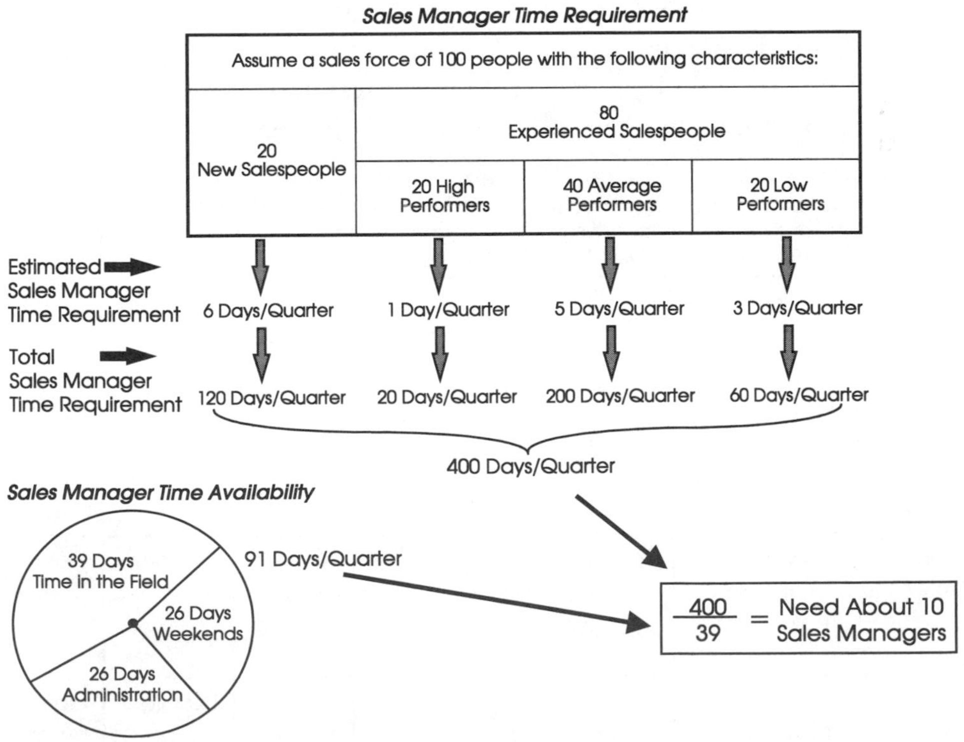

their manager provides a good view of the manager's activity. The survey provides individual feedback, although that is not the primary intention. The intention is to aggregate survey responses across all salespeople to derive a summary measure for the entire sales management team. The summary team measure provides a diagnostic for the sales manager productivity driver. It also masks the responses of individual salespeople and deters retribution, and hence is a more reliable measure of sales manager activity. Sample survey questions are shown in Figure 8-6.

In a recent implementation, sixty-six salespeople rated their managers using this instrument. Their average responses appear in the table in Figure 8-7.

The responses in Figure 8-7 tell a story. They say that the salespeople do not feel that the district sales management team meets their needs on these important dimensions. The district managers scored below average on four of the seven dimensions in the survey and only slightly above average on the remaining three.

Equally revealing are the histograms showing how the salespeople responded to the individual questions. The histogram in Figure 8-8 shows how the sixty-six salespeople answered the leadership question.

Notice that the responses in Figure 8-8 are bimodal. This may mean that each manager is liked by some salespeople and disliked by others. It is more likely, however, that the responses for each manager are consistent and that the salespeople feel that half of the managers

**Figure 8-6.** Evaluating the District Sales Manager: Field Questionnaire.

| *(Sample questions)* | *1* | *2* | *3* | *4* | *5* | |
|---|---|---|---|---|---|---|
| How good is your sales manager at motivating you? | Poor | Below Average | Average | Above Average | Excellent | Don't Know |
| How good is your sales manager at providing quick, accurate, and useful feedback? | Poor | Below Average | Average | Above Average | Excellent | Don't Know |
| How good is your sales manager at communication? (Are you well informed?) | Poor | Below Average | Average | Above Average | Excellent | Don't Know |
| How good is your sales manager at training? | Poor | Below Average | Average | Above Average | Excellent | Don't Know |

**Figure 8-7.** Results of a Field Survey to Evaluate District Managers.

**Figure 8-8.** How Salespeople Rated Their Sales Managers' Leadership.

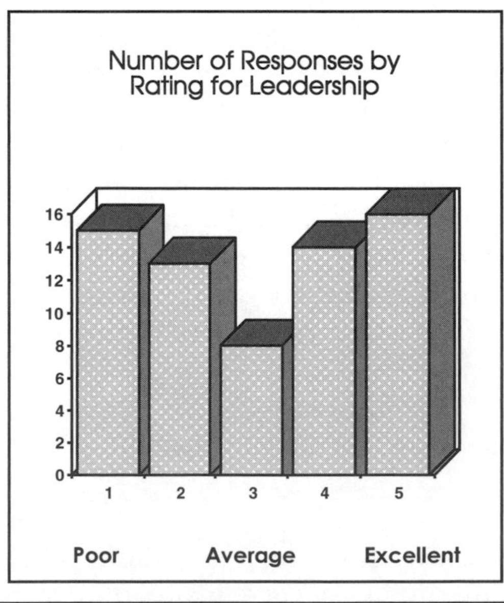

are good or excellent and the other half are incompetent. This information poses a challenge for the management of this selling organization.

**Team Results.** The sales manager is asked to select, build, lead, manage, and reward the team. Yet managers are not usually paid for these activities. They are recognized, rewarded, and remunerated for results. Luckily, results are the long- and short-term outcomes of the manager's investment in people selection and development. Company results, such as sales, profits, market share, and customer satisfaction, help the company assess the vitality of the first-line sales managers. These metrics are typically compared over time, against the competition, and cross-sectionally across all of the sales districts. Low performers such as the Great Lakes Sales District are very obvious. The regional management team is in trouble if there are too many low-performing sales districts in the region.

The manager's handiwork also shows up in the people and culture of the district. If there are too many low-performing salespeople, if the performance of the salespeople is inconsistent, or if the salespeople are not growing professionally, then the district manager is not doing his or her job very well. The first-line sales manager is also responsible for the district culture. Cultures are evaluated by observing the district values, hearing the district legends, and observing the district heroes. If Jackson, the salesperson with the successful side business, is the hero among the salespeople in the Great Lakes Sales District, then the district will struggle for years. An effective manager develops his people, celebrates their success, lobbies to promote their careers within the organization, and makes heroes out of the star performers. Alternatively, poor managers see the good salespeople retire or leave the firm.

**A Sales Management Team Diagnostic.** Periodic activity audits of sales managers provide the selling organization with a diagnostic scorecard as well as a record of improvement. Areas of deficiency may signal a need for job redefinition, redesign of the manager selection process, or enhanced training and development. Improvement over time should be celebrated and rewarded.

## Enhance the Skills, Knowledge, and Capabilities of the Sales Management Team

Change is the one thing that is certain. Markets change—they grow; they decline; they mature; they consolidate; they fragment; they deregulate; they become more competitive. Additionally, customers become more sophisticated. Each change requires a modification in the selling process that necessitates that sales managers acquire new capabilities.

Product lines also change—they broaden; they shrink; new products emerge and old products become obsolete. Product differentiation is transitory—competitors move in quickly. Companies constantly search for a differential advantage. They look to the sales force to participate through an enhanced service orientation. Sales managers must improve their capabilities as their product lines shift.

Finally, people change. Management demands more control or decides to increase empowerment. Teamwork becomes a popular concept. New salespeople are added—they require development. Some people plateau—they stop striving. Some people work for money; some work for plaques. People's risk profile changes. Sales managers need to enhance their capabilities as the people they manage change.

Professional growth needs to be part of the sales force culture rather than a reaction to an unanticipated change in market, product, or people. Managers become obsolete and atrophy if they do not take the initiative in growing professionally.

Companies traditionally underinvest in the development of their first-line sales managers. The salespeople receive initial training courses and periodic refresher courses, but the managers are expected to grow on their own. This works for the highly motivated manager, but the average manager may plateau prematurely. Recent employee surveys suggest that making career and professional development programs available to employees enhances the attractiveness of an employer. Providing ongoing professional development opportunities for the sales management team, especially in tight labor markets, is a wise strategy.

## Redefine the Job Description When Different Activities Are Required

Significant shifts in markets, products, people, or selling processes require changes in the first-line sales manager's job description. Other emerging trends also require modification of the sales manager's job description. Some of the more significant ones are listed below.

- The sales manager's job is moving toward more general business management. Many sales managers manage the entire P&L instead of just the revenue line.

- Spans of control are increasing. The manager must manage more people as companies continually try to reduce costs.
- More and more managers are working out of their homes. Companies are closing regional offices and asking their managers to establish virtual offices in their homes.
- Technology is changing the way sales forces work. Managers must be fluent with e-mail, voice mail, spreadsheet software, and the Internet.
- Companies are integrating sales, service, technical support, and/or telemarketing at lower levels within the organization. First-line sales managers need to manage a more diverse group of people.

### Select the Best Candidates for the Job

A successful first-line sales management team begins with sales manager selection. Too frequently, sales management teams suffer from the Peter Principle: Many managers rise to their level of incompetence and retire in this position. Good selection avoids this problem.

The steps in the recruiting process for a first-line sales manager are similar to those for recruiting salespeople, discussed in Chapter 6. The four steps in the manager selection process are outlined in Figure 8-9. The discussion here focuses on the features of each step that are unique to manager selection.

Selection errors are very expensive. It can take a district years to recover from the selection of a poor manager. First, the company must recognize that the manager is incompetent. Frequently, this awareness is obscured by product success, marketing success, or just plain market growth. Next, more time is required to convince the company that the incompetence is real. The manager needs to be given time and an opportunity to remedy a poor performance appraisal. Finally, dismissal is typ-

**Figure 8-9.** The Manager Selection Process.

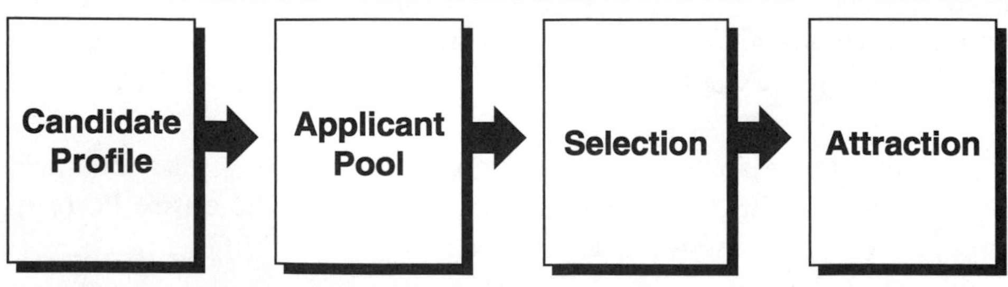

ically painful; it can entail denial and anger. Ultimately the selection process begins again. Until the manager is replaced, the hiring error is compounded: Weak salespeople are hired, salespeople remain undeveloped, and sales suffer.

**Candidate Profile.** Many of the characteristics that lead to sales success, such as ego drive, empathy, motivation, integrity, communication skills, and versatility, also lead to success as a manager. However, the sales manager's role is different from the salesperson's role. The manager needs to select, build, lead, manage, and reward a sales team. For these activities, an additional characteristic must be added to the profile: TATATO—the ability to achieve through others.

Good sales managers help others to be successful. They understand the needs of others and work through others to achieve success. Usually sales managers have been successful salespeople, and they can teach these selling skills to others. They are able to select the right people to build a team. Good sales managers usually have referent power because their philosophy and values draw others to them.

A salesperson deals with the customer and creates business results directly. A manager deals with salespeople and contributes to sales creation indirectly, though this can vary by company. While the sales goal is to bring customer and company interests together, managers must bring customer and company interests together while monitoring salespeople's desires. A salesperson can focus on the customer's needs, but a sales manager must let the salesperson make the sale in a way that is comfortable for the salesperson. Obviously, the manager will try to develop a salesperson's selling skills in conformity with the corporate culture, but this is done to increase the salesperson's natural abilities and tendencies, not to change them. A manager does more than sell; thus, a manager's profile is different from that of a salesperson. However, sales managers are hired for the same reason that salespeople are hired: to increase sales within the constraints of company culture.

Sometimes good salespeople make bad managers. A player-star is different from a teacher-coach. Good coaches make winning teams, but they themselves do not score any points. Nor do they demand that everyone on the team play the same way that they played or even as well as they played when they competed. Each member of the team does best using his or her own natural skills.

Highly successful salespeople are often individualists who bask in the glory of their own results—they enjoy seeing their name at the top of the list. Great first-line sales managers must be willing to give up credit and achieve their objectives through other people. While they can get credit for having the best district, their individual glory may be diminished.

Salespeople who work carefully to maintain accounts and develop relationships with customers are likely to be better managers than salespeople who hunt down new accounts and convert them. The manager needs to develop working relationships with the salespeople, and this is similar to fully developing a relationship with a customer.

Figure 8-10 summarizes some of the significant differences between salespeople and their managers.

**Candidate Pool.** There are two important questions to consider when defining the applicant pool for the first-line sales manager position:

1. Should an internal candidate be selected, or should the search focus on external candidates?
2. Should the candidate have selling experience?

To answer the first question, a company must determine whether qualified internal candidates exist. If there are no internal candidates that have the necessary qualifications (the candidates are too young or too inexperienced, or they lack the capabilities needed to succeed in the job), then the company has no choice but to look outside. If qualified internal candidates do exist, then the company must consider the consequences of choosing an external or an internal candidate, as shown in Figure 8-11.

With regard to the second question, many successful sales managers do come from other functions, such as finance or operations. However, these people usually enter the selling organization at a high level—vice president of sales, national sales manager, or regional sales

**Figure 8-10.** Differences Between Salespeople and Their Managers.

| *Good Salespeople* | *Good Sales Managers* |
|---|---|
| Listen to customers | Listen to salespeople |
| Do it themselves | Allow others to step up |
| Fight for the sale today | Fight for the sale someday |
| Control | Motivate |
| Strive for personal success | Strive for team success |
| Focus on customer needs | Focus on customer needs |

**Figure 8-11.** Consequences of Choosing an Internal or External Sales Management Candidate.

| *When Internal Candidates Are Chosen* | *When External Candidates Are Chosen* |
|---|---|
| A strong company identity and culture is developed. | The company gets a fresh perspective. In addition, it may acquire new skills or knowledge that are needed to deal with a rapidly changing marketplace. |
| The candidates know the company, along with its products, customers, culture, politics, policies, procedures, and people. | The candidates must learn the company. |
| The candidates have a proven track record. The company has a performance history that enables an accurate prediction of managerial capability. | The company must rely on a strong recruiting process to identify qualified candidates. |

director. Rarely do they succeed as first-line sales managers. The reason is simple: It is hard to get the respect of salespeople without having been one yourself. The successful candidate:

"Has carried the bag"
"Is in the club"
"Has been in the pit"
"Has carried the ball"
"Has been there"

Look for the most qualified person with sales experience.

**Selection.** In most companies, there are several positions that a salesperson can move into. A position in marketing, product management, national account management, training, or sales analysis could be a salesperson's next job. Among these positions, sales management is unique. Sales management is a transition to management, with all of its unselfishness and separation from the buzz of the sale. The selection process identifies people who want to be managers and can be successful in the job.

Most of the recruiting insights described in Chapter 6 apply equally well to the selection of first-line sales managers. The more important insights are as follows:

- A job performance history is available for all internal candidates. Since past performance is a good predictor of future performance, this information should not be overlooked. While behavioral interviewing is useful for external candidates, past job performance is more useful for internal candidates.

- Avoid selecting a sales manager based upon sales results alone. The best salesperson is not necessarily the best sales manager. Remember: The jobs are different.
- Often successful salespeople can participate in manager preparation activities to demonstrate their capabilities, assess whether they would like the manager's job, and gain some initial on-the-job training. Some common manager preparation activities include:

  *Local trainer:* Assisting in the development of newly hired salespeople

  *Mentor:* Helping newly hired salespeople navigate their way through the system

  *Interviewer:* Interviewing prospective candidates, assessing their capabilities, and recommending whether they should get a job offer

  *Special projects:* Working with marketing or product development on product strategy
- Tests are a good assessment tool. In a business case simulation such as the Great Lakes Sales District, candidates are asked to articulate what they would do if they became the new sales manager for this district. The candidate is asked to develop a personnel strategy, to select among several résumés from prospective salespeople, and to role-play interactions with Hadley, Jackson, and some of the other salespeople in the district. The candidate is measured on the ability to select, build, lead, manage, and reward within the Great Lakes Sales District.
- Avoid "warm body" hiring. An effective national sales manager constantly assesses potential manager candidates. He or she should have a "bench" ready in case a manager position opens up.

**Attraction.** It is usually easy to attract salespeople to the first-line sales manager's job. For many, this is their first career promotion, and they greet it with excitement. There are many intrinsic rewards associated with the new job. For example, new sales managers may feel that they are being "recognized for their achievements," that they are "successful," that they are "the boss," or that they are "moving toward the top."

There are extrinsic rewards as well. Sales managers usually make more money than their salespeople and begin to accumulate management perks. This is not universally true, however. In some industries, salespeople outearn their managers. In these industries, the best management candidates frequently opt to stay in sales, and companies can struggle to develop competent sales and marketing managers.

Two more reasons why salespeople may refuse a promotion to manager are a desire not to relocate and a reluctance to manage others. These are legitimate reasons that require offering the position to someone else.

Another issue is what to do when someone wants the job but is not the most appropriate candidate. Often salespeople seek a promotion to a manager's job. Some salespeople are just not suited to be managers. However, it is sometimes necessary to give a good salesperson a shot at management in order to keep that salesperson, even if the job does not seem right for him or her. Good salespeople have often earned the opportunity to try a manager's job. A company may be pleasantly surprised by such a salesperson's success, but it can lose a good salesperson if the placement does not work out. Sales force cultures that appreciate managers and salespeople equally are likely to place the right people into the sales management position.

## Reward the Team Appropriately

High-performing sales managers deserve to be rewarded. The rewards can be extrinsic or intrinsic. Money, acknowledgement, and recognition keep managers motivated and the sales team hustling.

The most common monetary reward is a bonus or commission payment that is tied to district sales performance. Many companies compute the district sales manager's performance as the average performance of all of the salespeople that report to that manager. As an example, if the eight salespeople in a sales district perform at −10 percent, +5 percent, +5 percent, +10 percent, +15 percent, +15 percent, +20 percent, and +20 percent relative to the goal, then the district manager is performing at the average of these eight numbers, or 10 percent above goal. A subtle observation with big financial impact for the sales manager can be made at this point: District averaging compresses the performance measure for the sales manager. That is, it is much harder for the sales manager to perform at 10 percent above goal than it is for any of his or her salespeople to perform at that level. Low performance cancels high performance for the manager. The performance range is much smaller for the manager than for any of the salespeople. Consequently, incentive payouts for managers need to be higher than incentive payouts for salespeople for the same level of goal attainment. Figure 8-12 shows a reasonable payout table.

Once again, the sales job and the sales manager's job are different. The salesperson generates business for the company; the sales manager selects, develops, leads, manages, and rewards the sales team. Consequently, managers need rewards beyond those that are linked to sales and profits.

Measures for selection, development, leadership, management, and rewarding are difficult to obtain. Some measures are possible, however. For instance, the performance of new salespeople (first- and second-year salespeople) can be used as a measure of salesperson selection and development. Good selection and development would be expected to lead to good rookie performance. Financial measures such as expense and asset management can also be observed and tracked. Assessments of leadership and general management need to be qualitative and come from a higher level of sales management.

The first-line sales manager needs to receive feedback on all of these broader measures. Sales districts regularly exceed expectations and have long-term growth and viability when reward structures acknowledge those managers who take the job beyond just making the sales goal.

## Conclusion

Sales managers tend to hear the same stories over and over again: A new salesperson is happy to call at 9:30 at night to tell about a big sale. It is tough to respond with equal enthusiasm when a manager has heard

**Figure 8-12.** Incentive Payout Table for Salespeople and Sales Managers.

| *Goal Attainment* | *Salesperson Incentive Payout (% of Salary)* | *Goal Attainment* | *Sales Manager Incentive Payout (% of Salary)* |
|---|---|---|---|
| 90% | 5% | 96% | 5% |
| 100% | 20% | 100% | 20% |
| 110% | 30% | 104% | 30% |
| 120% | 50% | 108% | 50% |

this same scenario a dozen times before. Even if a manager thinks that he or she has seen it all, he or she must show surprise, amazement, and appreciation. The next day the new salesperson will be on the road before the sun rises. A top-performing salesperson has high achievement in one sales territory, while a top-performing sales manager generates success in ten sales territories.

The first-line sales manager is a pivotal position in the sales force. Recall the quotation from Andy Anderson: "In any sales force, you can get along without the vice president of sales, regional sales directors, and the training manager, but you cannot get along without the district (first-line) sales manager."

The sales manager and the salesperson play different roles. Successful salespeople are energized by successful customer relationships. Successful sales managers are energized by the success of their people. Both are successful when the manager selects, develops, leads, manages, and rewards the sales team effectively.

# Chapter 9

# Motivating the Sales Force

This chapter explores sales force motivation, the fuel that moves salespeople to act. Motivation is a major factor in a salesperson's performance.

This chapter is designed to help you:

- Understand the five universal motivators: achievement, social affiliation, power, ego gratification, and survival
- Understand special features of the sales job that affect motivation
- Develop programs and management strategies that appeal to each of these five universal motivators to improve sales force performance

## Introduction

"How do I motivate my sales force?" is one of the most common sales force questions asked by sales managers and executives. The good news is that management efforts to improve motivation can clearly accelerate sales force performance. This chapter describes various ways in which management can energize individual salespeople and the sales force as a whole.

People differ; they have various capabilities, experiences, and financial needs. Motivating salespeople requires attention to individual characteristics. Good managers empathize with their people and support them by giving attention to their individual needs. However, designing comprehensive programs for motivating salespeople must move beyond the individual level. A general understanding of personal motivation will help managers design programs that will support everyone in an organization.

What appear to be motivational problems facing a sales force may actually be capability problems. Capabilities and motivation together determine sales force performance, as shown in Figure 9-1.

Three related questions are helpful in understanding sales force motivation:

- What are people like?
- What makes the sales job special?
- What programs will influence salespeople?

Salespeople have individual characteristics that influence their motivations. While different theories of motivation and categorizations of motivators have been proposed, this chapter focuses on the universal motivators that are most relevant for salespeople: achievement, social affiliation, power, ego gratification, and survival.

The sales job is unique, and each person responds differently to the unique challenges of selling. The sales job can be stressful; salespeople often work alone and experience frequent rejection. However, they have control of their time and effort. Management places high expectations on their performance. These characteristics of the sales job influence motivation and are a factor in designing motivation programs.

The sales force productivity drivers (size, structure, compensation, hiring, territory alignment, etc.) are the tools that management can use to improve motivation. Sometimes a motivational effect is a by-product of one of the productivity drivers. An unbalanced territory that is too difficult for a salesperson to cover effectively has a demotivating effect. Sometimes motivation is at the heart of a productivity driver, like the incentive compensation plan. A carefully designed compensation plan encourages salespeople to sell more effectively because of promised rewards.

Individual motivators, the characteristics of the sales job, and the

**Figure 9-1.** Sales Force Outcomes—A Function of Capability and Motivation.

| Motivation | Can't Do | Can Do |
|---|---|---|
| Will Do | Tries Hard | Highly Successful |
| Won't Do | Serious Hiring Error | Disappointment |

Capabilities

sales force productivity drivers are all important aspects of motivation. This chapter discusses these issues, then describes various motivational programs. The chapter concludes with useful insights regarding sales force motivation.

## Individual Motivators: What Are People Like?

### A Tale of Five Salespeople

Martha, a district sales manager, attended a motivation seminar and felt reenergized. After the seminar, her regional manager asked her to write a workshop summary, including recommendations for motivating her sales force. For the write-up, Martha used the approach she had learned at the seminar. Her notes about her salespeople, including their national standing in year-to-date sales, appear below.

*Ann, ranked fourth in the nation.* Ann ignores our quota and sets her own goals much higher. She has gone on the big incentive trip every year since she joined the company. She talks to me only if she has a concern about the sales materials. She told me that the selling tips page is her favorite part of the newsletter.

*Beth, ranked forty-eighth in the nation.* Beth solidly makes quota, but she was sweating it out until the fourth quarter last year. She enjoys playing golf with me and seems to know people everywhere she goes. Beth looks forward to the annual sales meeting, and she submits lots of items to the newsletter.

*Chris, ranked fifty-eighth in the nation.* Chris always makes quota, but at any given point in the year she might be far ahead or far behind. She resists my offers of extra assistance on the tough sales calls. She liked the last sales meeting but complained that the salespeople did not have any input into its location. The newsletter keeps her informed, since she rarely stops by the district office.

*Donna, ranked tenth in the nation.* Donna takes reaching quota as a given. She seems much more concerned with her ranking. The fact that Ann is ahead of her is a thorn in her side. She loves my compliments on her performance and the awards she gets at the sales meetings. Donna has a wall in her home office displaying her awards and a page of the newsletter on which she was the featured star.

*Ellen, ranked ninety-first in the nation.* Ellen is in her second year. She is having a problem making quota, and her future in sales is uncertain. She likes my coaching, but she is worried about the performance warnings I've given her. Ellen even jokes that the sales meetings take up too much of her customer selling time.

Looking at her list, Martha became more concerned. The current motivation programs were inconsistent; they worked for only some of the people some of the time. Some salespeople were almost indifferent to the motivation programs and incentive techniques.

Even though salespeople differ, companies need to find a common set of programs that will motivate all of them. These five salespeople have the same job and the same manager, but their prime motivations are very different. Ann is motivated by *achievement.* She wants to succeed, and her desire gets her through the tough times. Beth is motivated by *social affiliation.* She enjoys being part of the group, and her social skills can go a long way in sales. Chris is motivated by *power.* She wants to run her own life, and a sales job allows her to do that as long as she delivers. Donna is motivated by *ego gratification.* She wants to be the best, and her ego keeps her bouncing back after every rejection. Ellen is motivated by *survival.* She's working hard to make it in the company.

It is difficult to test and validate motivating factors. Behavior is observable, but needs and feelings are not. The universal motivators—achievement, social affiliation, power, ego gratification, and survival—are most directly relevant for understanding salespeople.

- *Achievement:* I'm succeeding.
- *Social affiliation:* I have friends.
- *Power:* I run things.
- *Ego gratification:* I'm the best.
- *Survival:* I don't want to fail.

While all people share these universal motivators, they manifest themselves differently in each person. Martha's district is an extreme case of this. One common way in which people differ is by stage of career development. Newer salespeople are trying out the sales job; they are likely to be sensitive to the achievement and survival motivators. They are trying to determine if they can succeed in the sales profession. More established, go-getter salespeople are looking for promotions and ego gratification. Entrenched salespeople are harvesting the benefits of their previous hard work. They are more likely to enjoy their power than to try to be the very best. Disengaging salespeople are coasting to the end of their careers. Social affiliation may be their strongest motivator.

One important factor that must be taken into account when considering motivation is the difference between internal and external motivators. The five motivators in the preceding list are internal; they are part of people's innate makeup. These motivators push people to act. Job characteristics and management programs are external motivators; they pull salespeople to act in certain ways. The sales job affects motivation, and the company develops programs to trigger salespeople's internal desires so that they will act in concert with the company's goals.

## Theories of Individual Motivation

Each of the five salespeople discussed earlier has a main motivating factor in her personality, but a person's emotional makeup can seldom be determined with such clarity. If it could be, motivating salespeople would be simple; however, each person's internal life is hidden, and everyone has multiple motivators that surface at different times. To determine how to motivate people, it is necessary to make assumptions about what people are like. The natural human impulse is to assume that everyone is like us, but this is not the case. Fortunately, there are several frameworks for understanding human motivation that help us to understand salespeople's motivations. This section explores four popular frameworks and describes how the five universal motivators fit into each framework.

**Maslow's Hierarchy of Needs.** Maslow's hierarchy of needs is the classic motivational structure. Maslow felt that people had two kinds of needs, deficiency needs and growth needs. The deficiency needs are physiological needs, safety needs, and social needs. The growth needs are ego needs and self-actualization needs. These needs are arranged in a hierarchy from lowest to highest in Figure 9-2.

As humans grow, the needs they try to fulfill are more likely to be higher-level needs, but all needs are active at any one time.

The five universal motivators can be fit into Maslow's hierarchy. The survival and social affiliation motivators are deficiency needs. Salespeople worry about earning enough money and about fitting in. Power, ego gratification, and achievement are all growth needs and fit into the ego needs category in Maslow's hierarchy. In the sales profes-

**Figure 9-2.** Maslow's Hierarchy of Needs.

**Deficiency needs:**
1. Physiological needs (food, water, sleep, clothing, shelter, and sex)
2. Safety needs (security from danger, threats, and deprivations)
3. Social needs (belonging, acceptance, love, and kinship)

**Growth needs:**
4. Ego needs (achievement, recognition, autonomy, and status)
5. Self-actualization needs (fulfilling one's potential)

sion, there is potential for great ego rewards, and many motivation programs help to provide those rewards. A sales career can be part of self-actualization, but this is likely to be created internally by the salesperson rather than influenced by management actions.

**Herzberg's Motivator-Hygiene Theory.** Herzberg's motivator-hygiene theory suggests that needs can have either a positive or negative influence. Hygiene factors are dissatisfying elements that affect a person's happiness, but that do not motivate positively by themselves. Correcting them is necessary for happiness but not sufficient. These include supervisory style, coworker relations, and sometimes salary. Motivators are items like achievement, recognition, the work itself, responsibility, advancement, and growth.

The five universal motivators can also be located within the Herzberg framework. The survival motivator is a hygiene motivator; it spurs action to avoid worry. Social affiliation can be either a hygiene factor or a motivator for salespeople. Power, ego gratification, and achievement are all Herzberg motivators.

Herzberg's theories are controversial but are popular with managers.

**McGregor's Theory X and Theory Y.** McGregor's Theory X and Theory Y specify how our assumptions about what people are like influence our choice of motivational style. McGregor's theories are summarized in Figure 9-3.

Theory X managers are controlling and bullying; Theory Y managers are empowering. Theory X managers appeal mainly to the survival motivator; Theory Y managers appeal to the other motivators. The way people are treated influences their behavior. If you trust them, they turn out to be more trustworthy than if you do not trust them. McGregor's theory is salient for managers. A company is asking for failure and high turnover if it recruits for maturity and self-direction but manages by

**Figure 9-3.** McGregor's Theory X and Theory Y.

**Theory X**

1. Average human adults are by nature indolent—they work as little as possible.
2. They lack ambition, dislike responsibility, and prefer to be led by other people.
3. They are inherently selfish and indifferent to organizational needs and goals.
4. They are resistant to change, by their very nature.
5. Finally, they are gullible, not very intelligent, and easily duped by manipulators.

**Theory Y**

1. People are not passive by nature. They have become so as a consequence of the way they are usually treated in organizations.
2. People possess, by nature, the potential to develop, assume responsibility, and behave in accordance with organizational goals. Management's responsibility is to recognize these potentials and to make it possible for employees to develop them themselves.
3. To do this, management should structure organization policies so that human beings can achieve their own goals while pursuing the goals of the organization.

Theory X. Instead, it is necessary to empower employees through training, access to information, authority to use real resources, and accountability.

**Expectancy Theory.** Motivationally, success begets success. When a person succeeds, the success acts as a positive reinforcement. Closing the sale becomes first possible, then easy. If the salesperson attributes the success to his or her own efforts rather than to chance or the environment, the result is improved confidence and competence. If the person believes that he or she is learning and growing, the comfort zone will expand and the salesperson will improve. If a salesperson believes that his or her talents have stabilized, he or she will not put forth increased effort. Expectancy theory models this motivation process. The cycle of performance and motivation is shown in Figure 9-4.

Capability and motivation affect effort. Effort results in a performance (a sale), and the performance results in rewards (acknowledgement or financial reward). If the rewards are satisfying, the salesperson is more motivated and sets higher goals. In this model, there are three links that keep the cycle strong:

- *Expectancy:* Does effort cause performance?
- *Instrumentality:* Does performance create rewards?
- *Valence for rewards:* Do the rewards motivate the salesperson?

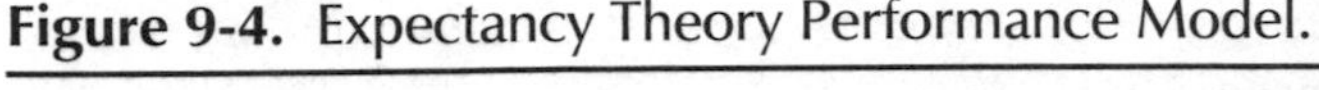

**Figure 9-4.** Expectancy Theory Performance Model.

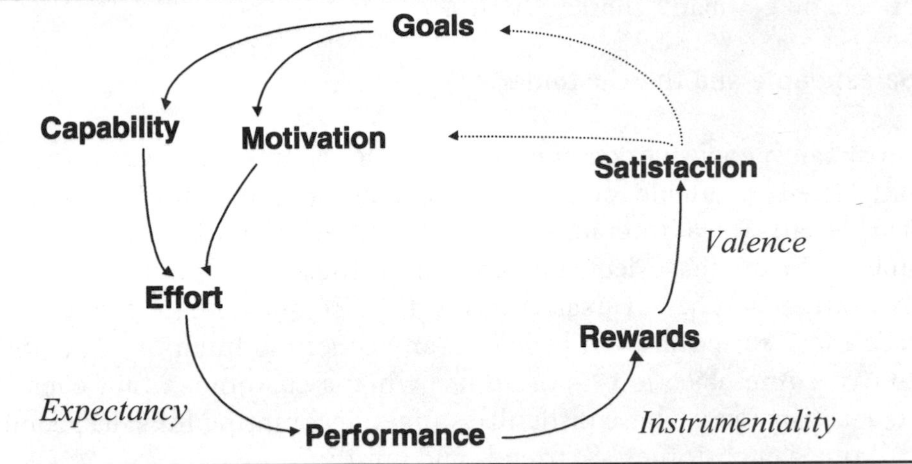


In each case, the salesperson's perception is important. If the salesperson feels that "working harder doesn't close any more sales," that "others get credit for my efforts," or that "this bonus isn't worth getting," then the virtuous cycle breaks down, and motivation is diminished.

Careful job design, a good incentive compensation strategy, and good performance management keep the motivation cycle functioning properly. However, many aspects of the job environment affect salespeople's motivation. Each salesperson is immersed in an environment created by management's decisions regarding the productivity drivers. The most confident, sales-loving, bonus-enjoying salesperson will quit the job if the manager is incompetent.

The five universal motivators—achievement, social affiliation, power, ego gratification, and survival—help explain what drives people. Motivation relies on an appeal to the personal needs of individual salespeople.

## Job Characteristics: What Makes the Sales Job Special?

The sales job interacts with and influences a salesperson's individual motivators. The types of sales jobs that exist in a company help determine the most effective motivational strategies.

Even though sales positions vary depending on the company's product, markets, and objectives, there are some general principles that apply to most sales jobs. These can be divided into customer, performance, and company characteristics.

## Salespeople and the Customer

Most salespeople work alone in a customer-centered job. Coworkers are not usually available for debriefing, celebration, or commiseration after a sales call. Social interaction can be infrequent, and the customer, who makes the purchase decision, often holds the power. Relationships with customers can be adversarial rather than cooperative, and salespeople face more rejection than people in any other job function. The ability to overcome objections is of no use when a customer won't even talk to a salesperson. These difficulties make it tempting for salespeople to call on easy customers—"friends and family."

## Salespeople and the Company

Salespeople are empowered; they usually control their time and activity. However, while they serve as a primary point of customer contact, they are not in control of every part of the interaction between the company and the customer. Conflicts can occur with marketing, advertising, customer service, delivery, or billing. Salespeople are responsible only for their own efforts, but they are accountable for the company's efforts.

The company often provides training in selling skills, product knowledge, and time and territory management, which is important to the salesperson. Lack of knowledge in any of these areas can significantly affect performance. Training is especially important for inexperienced employees.

Turnover in the sales job can be high, depending on the economy, the job market, and company performance. Selling skills are valuable to many organizations, so changing jobs can be easy. Sales forces are frequently perceived as a cost item by top management, so sales force layoffs can occur when the company is not achieving its financial objectives.

## Salespeople and Performance

Selling can be a high-risk job. Frequently, success runs in hot and cold streaks. There are high and low points, and success is not always dependent on the salesperson's actions. The product, customer service, team selling, and territory alignment all affect the effectiveness of the sales force. The variability implicit in selling puts more stress on salespeople's egos.

Typically, success is easily measurable by actual sales. There is no hiding from good or poor performance. Salespeople usually know when they are performing well and when they are not. Poor performers may be new people, or they may be long-time salespeople who have plateaued or become stale. Compensation is often tied directly to results via bonuses and commissions, so performance variability means pay variability.

Competitive people who like to win are attracted to the sales job because it is a job that can provide significant ego gratification. Even though success is uncertain, individual efforts clearly can pay off.

## Sales Force Productivity Drivers: What Programs Motivate Salespeople?

Innate motivators and the peculiarities of the sales job contribute to sales force motivation. The third variable in the motivation mix is the programs that management uses for motivation. Management influences motivation both directly and indirectly. All of the sales force productivity drivers discussed in this book influence motivation to some degree. However, the drivers that affect it most directly are discussed in this section. Because individual personalities vary, the real challenge of motivation is to set up systems that address all or nearly all of the various personal needs residing in the sales force.

Following is a summary of the managerial programs that most directly affect sales force motivation.

### Sales Territory Design and Sales Support

Salespeople will excel in a well-directed organization that is economically sound. Motivation is high when the sales force knows that it offers the best products and services and that it is well supported. An ideal environment for a motivated sales force can include many kinds of support. Marketing provides appropriate materials that enhance the sales force's ability to add value for the customer. Customer service ensures that all customer inquiries are responded to quickly, delivery is timely, and billing is correct. Sales administration sets appropriate goals and tracks sales accurately. The lead generation system provides good leads.

Finally, sales territories are sized correctly and provide the right amount of opportunity.

## Recruiting and Promotions

Hiring intrinsically motivated people is the easiest way to have a motivated sales force. It is difficult to change or dislodge people's deep motivators, so it's best to use intrinsic motivation to the firm's advantage. If the motivators that a person has are the right ones for the firm's culture, then that person is a good candidate. For example, highly ego-driven candidates do not belong in a salaried sales force, and salespeople who are motivated by social affiliation will be attracted to a team-selling organization.

Careful recruiting and culture development can produce a unified and more motivated sales force. When people with the right skills for the job are hired, their power and achievement motivations are engaged. If they can perform, they are empowered. People with insufficient skills become demotivated and give up. However, not all underperformers lack skills; they may just be selling the wrong product for the wrong company. Good recruiting yields more "can do" and "will do" candidates.

An established career track is also an important motivational tool. Promotions appeal to the ego and achievement motivators. The possibility of career advancement provides another way to "win." National accounts or senior salesperson positions can be made available as part of the design of the sales force.

## Training

Good training is especially important because it enhances the social affiliation, power, ego, and achievement drives and reduces survival fear. Training gives salespeople a larger comfort zone and a feeling of control. Salespeople who are well trained understand that rejection is part of the job. The loss of a sale, rather than being seen as a personal failure, becomes part of doing business. Good training also makes salespeople more successful, improving the power, ego, and achievement motivators.

Training has other motivational potential as well. Salespeople who train together or who have been through the same regimen have enhanced social affiliation and have a tendency to be more tightly knit. Nontraditional training can also be motivational—special training programs that are unusual in the industry or selective within the company can certainly boost the ego.

### Compensation

There is unanimous agreement that compensation affects motivation. Of course people work for money, but money has other, more indirect effects on motivation. Good pay strokes the ego, and money can serve as a measure of success for achievement-oriented salespeople. Lack of sufficient pay can have negative effects. Some people slack off to make their compensation "fair" if they feel underpaid. The survival motivation kicks in when there is fear of low pay, and salespeople can contemplate leaving. The base pay or a draw should provide at least sustenance pay to protect the company from this danger.

A variable compensation plan can serve as both carrot and stick. With such a plan, the salesperson's performance determines his or her pay. A large "at-risk" component can be very motivating for the achievement-minded salesperson.

### Recognition Programs and Contests

Realistic goals that a majority of the salespeople can achieve allow many egos to be gratified. Many companies would like to see at least 70 percent of the sales force achieve their goal. Other companies set stretch goals that only a small fraction of the sales force is likely to achieve. If the aim is to have a motivated sales force, consider setting realistic goals that many salespeople can achieve.

Contests and special incentive programs bring ego and achievement motivations into play. President's clubs or special roundtables can provide a goal for high achievers. Trips and noncash awards are a special and unusual type of reward. They feel like gifts—unlike money, which is earned. Salespeople may feel shortchanged if they miss a money goal, but a trip is a memorable reward that will not be categorized mentally as "livelihood." Contests allow some achievement victories and boost effort in the short term.

Careful design of a recognition program is important. The program should incorporate subtle motivation strategies:

- Reward over periods of time that are long enough to overcome the irregular nature of sales and to make salespeople feel more responsible for their own results.

- Use territory potential measures to ensure fairness.
- Give rewards for the success of a group, such as a district or region, so that more people feel the sense of achievement.

Special perks such as special treatment, titles, and training are also useful recognition programs. Promotions to new positions are a form of recognition and can help salespeople feel accomplished. Occasionally, powerful recognition can be inexpensive. Abbott Laboratories puts a star on the business cards of its top sales performers. This company also sends its star salespeople to a one-week course entitled "Strategic Sales and Marketing in the Healthcare Industry of the Future" at a prestigious business school. Carefully selected benefits can boost the ego or increase social affiliation. For example, membership in a special club, such as the President's Club, is a flattering prize and a chance to socialize at the same time.

### Coaching and Supervision

One-on-one interaction with the manager is crucial for motivation. Managerial attention provides recognition and may also put fear into a lagging performer. Managers provide social affiliation and can act like an ally. In addition, managers can provide coaching, which helps improve ability and performance. Performance evaluation is important for feedback and motivation.

Managers must maintain a fine balance between criticism and reassurance. Too much anxiety is bad for performance, especially in difficult jobs; however, straightforward jobs are done better when the salesperson is energetic and excited. The manager must remember that the same job can be terribly taxing for a new salesperson and simple for an experienced hand. The new salesperson needs calming and coaching, and the competent performer needs a little more encouragement. Too much attention can be perceived as micromanaging and can threaten the salesperson's autonomy. There is a motivational cost in selling environments where the salesperson's message needs to be carefully controlled by management.

Managers rely strongly on good interpersonal skills in motivating their salespeople. Here, it is especially important to understand what drives the individual. Yelling and backslapping work for some people, while others need only subtle reminders. Good managers create a sense of urgency. They give salespeople credit for success in front of other people and let other salespeople tell them they are doing well. Often the best manager is the one that the salespeople like best, tough but fair.

### Communication

Sales meetings and newsletters are a medium for communicating success. They are an integral part of recognition programs, and they encourage healthy ego and achievement motivations. They also foster connection to the company and to other salespeople in the company. When these programs are used frivolously, they can be shallow, "rah-rah" motivators rather than appealing to deep motivations. A serious, professional look and feel for the communications programs provides the best motivation.

### Culture

Culture is reflected in norms, values, and work style. Most salespeople find it motivating if the work culture is consistent with the salesperson's beliefs, values, and attitudes. This encourages a sense of belonging and an understanding of the company mission. Good cultures embody the positive aspects of the innate motivators.

The sales force culture determines how to motivate. For a shark culture, chum the waters. For a squirrel culture, throw acorns. Sales force culture is discussed in depth in Chapter 15.

### Other Company Factors

Nonsales areas often affect sales force motivation. Salespeople are more successful if all areas of the company are focused on customer service. Good products, good service, and good value all energize the people who sell the offering. It's tough to feel like a sales winner if the product is bad or if good customer service is lacking. Difficulties with nonsales functions can be improved if salespeople have a process for venting frustrations and a way to provide information about products and customers to other parts of the company.

## Motivation Strategies

Figures 9-5 through 9-9 illustrate how the characteristics of the sales job favor various motivation strategies. The motivation strategies are

**Figure 9-5.** Appealing to the Achievement Motivator.

| *The Sales Job* | *Program Strategies* | *Manager Strategies* |
|---|---|---|
| Success is usually measurable: sales, orders, profit, market share. | Measure sales and other performance metrics when they are available. Look for good surrogates and approximations when it is difficult to measure sales and/or profit. What gets measured gets recognized. | Communicate successes formally and informally to others.<br>Communicate appreciation to the salesperson when he or she is successful. |
| Success can have significant variance: high and low points. | Use occasional small contests.<br>Reward for longer time periods to overcome variance. "We're making our year-to-date plan." | Reward for group success: district or region. "We are all winners." |
| Success is not always dependent on the salesperson. The product, customer service, team selling, or territory alignment can all affect sales force effectiveness. | Fix product, customer service, alignment, and compensation problems. | Monitor conditions for unfairness and lobby top management for change.<br>Let the salesperson know that management is aware of the problem and what steps will be taken to correct it. |
| Some salespeople may have plateaued or are underperforming. | Make varied career paths available for salespeople. Sometimes the new job can be inside the company, in a different sales force or in a more technical role. | Assess whether underperformers are selling the wrong product for the wrong company; work with them to revitalize their career path. |

divided into two types: program strategies and manager strategies. Program strategies are motivational programs that result from changing some of the sales force productivity drivers. Manager strategies are those that are used directly by sales managers. Manager strategies are valuable for motivation because they affect results rapidly. They can create a quick change, whereas program changes usually take longer.

## Five Key Insights for Better Sales Force Motivation

### Provide Something for Everyone

Even in the most carefully selected sales force in a company with a strong culture and uniform policies, salespeople differ. Their natural

**Figure 9-6.** Appealing to the Social Affiliation Motivator.

| *The Sales Job* | *Program Strategies* | *Manager Strategies* |
|---|---|---|
| Salespeople often work alone. | Foster connection to the company with sales meetings: district, regional, and national.<br>Reduce paperwork so salespeople can spend more time with customers.<br>Publish newsletters that promote connection to others. | Act as an ally.<br>Converse with each salesperson on a regular basis. |
| Rejection occurs frequently on the job. | Provide training to make salespeople more successful. | Coach salespeople that rejection is part of the job. "It is part of doing business. It is not about you." |
| The job is customer-centered. | Hire empathetic people who like people. | Teach partnership with the customer. If we are win-win, we all fit in. |
| There can be destructive competition with peers. | Promote healthy competition:<br>• No poaching<br>• Equitable territories<br>• Fair compensation<br>• Appropriate rewards and recognition | Use best practice sharing in a success culture. "*We* are the best." |

makeup varies, and their desires and motivators change as they age and as their career matures. In order to keep the entire sales force motivated, management must have a varied program that covers all five motivators: achievement, social affiliation, power, ego gratification, and survival. Neglecting any motivator means that some salespeople are not fully engaged. The motivation program must have something for everyone.

## Avoid Conflicts in Programs

For maximum effect, motivational programs need to be consistent. Motivation suffers when go-getters are hired for a salaried position. Managers will be unhappy if they have too much selling responsibility when coaching is their most important job function. Training and hiring programs need to dovetail so that new salespeople are not thrust into a job with insufficient preparation. Motivational policy needs to be aligned in a logical, commonsense way.

**Figure 9-7.** Appealing to the Power Motivator.

| *The Sales Job* | *Program Strategies* | *Manager Strategies* |
|---|---|---|
| The sales job is empowered.<br>Salespeople usually control their time and activity. | Provide training so that salespeople utilize time effectively and succeed in their customer interactions.<br>Provide customer data to enhance targeting and customer effectiveness. | Avoid micromanagement. |
| Salespeople may feel helpless in tough situations if they are underequipped in the areas of selling skills, product knowledge, or time and territory management. | Diagnose the areas of inadequacy.<br>Provide training to help people feel more in control.<br>Hire the right people for the job. | Be available to assist new hires.<br>Provide feedback and field training to salespeople who feel underequipped. |
| It is tempting for salespeople to call on easy customers: "friends and family." | Give stricter guidelines for targeting customers.<br>Demonstrate how wasted calls affect income negatively.<br>Provide incentives for new customer development. | Train and coach the salesperson into a larger comfort zone. |
| Power often rests with the customer, who makes the purchase decision. | Develop good products, good service, and good value.<br>Create a win-win partnership of equals. | Participate with the salesperson in difficult situations. |
| The salesperson is not in control of all interactions with the customer. Problems could occur in customer service, delivery, or billing. | Keep all areas of the company focused on servicing the customer.<br>Provide salespeople with an avenue to vent frustrations, as well as a way to provide information to other parts of the company about products and customer needs. | Keep all areas of the company focused on servicing the customer. |

**Figure 9-8.** Appealing to the Ego Gratification Motivator.

| *The Sales Job* | *Program Strategies* | *Manager Strategies* |
|---|---|---|
| Competitive people who like to win are attracted to the sales job. It is a job that gives significant ego gratification. | Compensate well. Pay for performance.<br><br>Provide special treatment:<br>• Special training<br>• Sales assistants<br><br>Give promotions and special titles:<br>• Senior salesperson<br>• National accounts<br><br>Communicate successes:<br>• Newsletters<br>• President's club<br>• "We work for money, we strive for plaques"<br><br>Give special assignments:<br>• Mentor for new salespeople<br>• Recruiter<br>• Regional trainer<br><br>Provide sales perks:<br>• Pink Cadillac<br>• Golf shirts<br>• Sales meetings at luxury resorts. | Interact one-on-one with the top performers and let them know they are doing well.<br><br>Occasionally ask top performers to substitute for the manager.<br><br>Ask leading sellers to manage and/or present best practices at district and regional sales meetings. |
| Salespeople face frequent rejection. | Set goals realistically so at least 70 percent of the people achieve the goal. | Show interest in employees. Coach, support, listen, and counsel. |
| Selling success runs in hot and cold streaks. | Use year-to-date quotas. | Provide coaching through the rough spots.<br><br>Appeal to a higher cause:<br>• We are the best sales force, or<br>• We have the best product, or<br>• We work for the best company. |

**Figure 9-9.** Appealing to the Survival Motivator.

| *The Sales Job* | *Program Strategies* | *Manager Strategies* |
|---|---|---|
| Salespeople can be poor at the job. | Hire and train properly. | Create fear in under-performers.<br>People on the edge should know where they stand. |
| Results are usually very measurable. There is no hiding from poor performance. | Develop an accurate and equitable performance evaluation system. | Coach the poor performers so that the achievement motivator replaces the survival motivator. |
| Compensation can have a high variable component. | Ensure that salespeople will earn at least subsistance pay. The survival motivator might urge salespeople to quit if pay is too low. | Teach persistence. Sales and personal income follow from sustained effort. |
| Selling is a high-risk job. | Pay a salary if the market is too unpredictable, or if a significant level of sales is not determined by the salesperson's competence and effort. | Understand that fear will keep the survivors afloat during the tough times. Coach them through the fear. |
| Turnover can be high. It is often hard to keep good people in good job markets.<br>Tight job markets eliminate other opportunities. | Provide good compensation plans and good recognition programs to keep motivation high and to retain the good people. | Be aware that good managers retain their good people. |

## Distinguish Between Can't Do and Won't Do

What appears to be a motivational problem (a "won't do") may in fact be a competency problem (a "can't do"). Most people won't want to do activities that they can't do. This is why appropriate training and hiring are essential for motivation. Properly prepared salespeople expect their efforts to pay off. They remain motivated even in difficult selling situations.

## Avoid Unfairness

Unfair territories, compensation plans, quotas, contests, and managers are a roadblock to motivation. Unfair conditions strike at the ego, power, and achievement motivators. It is hard to feel special if you have been cheated. It is difficult to be empowered if you do not get a fair shake. Only the strongest achievers can shake off biased conditions and do their best.

### Know That Too Much "Rah-Rah" Is Blah

"Rah-rah" pep talks and speeches wear thin fast. They provide only a short-term boost and should be used infrequently.

## Conclusion

People are hired for their intrinsic motivations, but each company needs to have extrinsic motivational programs as well. Appealing to achievement, social affiliation, power, ego gratification, and survival through motivation programs and the sales force drivers accelerates sales force performance.

Chapter 10

# Compensating for Results

The vast majority of U.S. sales forces use incentive compensation plans to motivate and encourage salespeople. Incentive plans have a major impact on organizations because they affect the type of person who is attracted to the sales job and they influence the activities and behaviors of salespeople. This chapter presents a framework for understanding the impact of a sales force compensation plan. The chapter provides specific, practical advice on how to make four key decisions regarding sales force compensation:

- *Level of pay:* How do labor market forces, company profitability, and job-related factors affect compensation levels?
- *Salary versus incentive:* What factors determine the right mix?
- *Performance measures:* Should salespeople be paid on the basis of results or activity? Should they be paid when the order is taken or when money is collected? Should they be paid for high customer satisfaction?
- *Performance-payout relationships:* How should payment vary with measured performance? Should the plan include goals? Bonuses? Commissions? Should the plan be capped? Should the plan use multiple measures? Should it be based on individual or team performance? How frequently should payment occur?

The chapter concludes with practical advice on how to implement incentive plans in several situations, including changing from one plan to another, dealing with windfalls, and administering successful contests.

## Introduction

Three corporate financial analysts were discussing the sales forces at their companies. "Our salespeople make lots of money; they are among the highest paid people in the company,'' said one. ''Fortunately, they are not yet paid as much as our officers, although I hear that is the case for some of our competitors. Our salespeople receive cars and incredible trips. One was to Hawaii—with just a few meetings sprinkled between golf rounds. Some of our salespeople took three trips this year—two new-product launch meetings, a few sales contests, and the President's Club trip. Who else in the company gets these perks?'' The second analyst reflected on the compensation plan for his company's sales force. ''Our incentive plan gives a bonus for education—take a few courses and get 10 percent of your bonus payout. We also pay the salespeople for making calls—$25 per call for our new product. Isn't this part of the job? What is salary for?'' He continued, ''Then the new product did incredibly well, the annual goal was achieved in the third quarter, and they all made lots of money. Did they make the product big? Wasn't the product a winner anyway? Now the problem is more serious. The salespeople feel that they're entitled to make even more money next year.''

''Our plan keeps changing,'' said the third analyst. ''Two years ago we wanted to increase sales quickly. So, we paid a significant commission on all sales above the prior year's level. Last year we launched a new product targeted toward an entirely new market, and we instituted a plan rewarding growth on the new product, as well as goal attainment on our core strategic products. This year we are merging with another company that has a more leveraged plan, which means big changes to one of our plans. Why do we keep constantly changing our pay plans? Do we really need to worry so much about pleasing our salespeople?''

Compensation is the money and other benefits that a company provides to its workers in exchange for their efforts. Salespeople typically have unique compensation plans. Their plans are designed to motivate and encourage them to strive for high levels of success. Hundreds of plan variations have been developed. As a motivating factor, many plans include a large incentive component, such as bonuses, commissions, trips, cars, stock options, or other awards. The average incentive income for salespeople in the United States is 40 percent of total income.

Some quality experts, such as Deming, feel that individual incentives can do more harm than good. They feel that the work itself should be motivating enough and that incentives can lead to undesirable behavior. So, why is it that about 85 percent of the sales forces in the United States use some kind of incentive plan? What is unique about the job that demands the use of incentives?

There are three aspects of a sales job that make it desirable to use incentives. First, the sales force drives the top line; its efforts generate sales. A highly motivated sales force will have higher sales than a less motivated sales force. Since the top line is critical, the sales force is important to the success of the management team. Usually, company sales goals are sales force sales goals. A management team that is concerned about achieving its sales targets frequently uses incentives to motivate the sales force to achieve the company goal. The sales force also affects the profitability of the company by increasing sales, controlling expenses, and maintaining prices. Frequently, company profit goals are transferred to the sales force as well.

Second, the output of individual salespeople is usually measurable and comparable. Most companies track sales, costs, and other results-oriented metrics at the territory level. Territory results can be benchmarked against last year's results, market potential, the territory goal, the region's performance, and sometimes even against the competition. Thus, management can objectively evaluate a salesperson's performance, compare that salesperson's performance with the performance of others, and identify who is doing well.

Finally, many sales jobs are devoid of supportive social interaction and involve considerable rejection. Other company employees interact with their supervisors and peers on a regular basis. They receive regular feedback and recognition. Salespeople spend most of their days unsupervised and often call on people who see them as intrusive. They may spend six months doing a customer needs analysis, configuring a customer solution, developing a proposal, and negotiating a price, only to be rejected in the end. An incentive payout is a reward and a measure of the salesperson's success. A high payout acknowledges that the salesperson is successful. It provides motivation to go forth and get the next hit. The sales job attracts risk takers and individuals who are receptive to significant incentives to achieve high levels of performance. Most sales jobs in the United States would go unfilled if compensation consisted of only salary.

A sales force incentive plan can have a significant impact, although the impact is frequently subtle and nonobservable. Incentive plans have an immediate impact on the sales force. The effects can be felt in two ways. First, the plan influences the type of person who is attracted to the organization. Second, the plan affects the sales force's activities and behaviors. The sales force can be enthusiastic and motivated, or it can feel discouraged and let down by the plan. The salespeople's attitude affects their activities and behavior, which subsequently affect their interaction with customers and, ultimately, the company's performance. Figure 10-1 presents several potential consequences of an effective plan and an inappropriate plan.

## A Sales Force Incentive Compensation Framework

Since the impact of a sales force incentive plan is significant and the forces at work can be subtle, it is helpful to think about sales force compensation dynamics in terms of the framework pictured in Figure 10-2.

The framework describes three constituents affected by the compensation plan: the company, the salesperson, and the customer. These three constituents make decisions and see results. The *company* decides on a compensation plan. The *sales force* decides how it will spend its time. Although numerous factors affect the salesperson's choice of activity, the compensation plan has a very significant influence. The *customer* decides whether it wants the company's products or services

**Figure 10-1.** The Impact of the Sales Force Incentive Plan.

| *An Effective Incentive Compensation Plan . . .* | *An Inappropriate Incentive Compensation Plan . . .* |
|---|---|
| Attracts and retains the best people | Attracts and retains average people |
| Pays the market rate | Overpays or underpays |
| Pays for performance | Pays the wrong people |
| Encourages sales force activities that are consistent with corporate strategy | Encourages sales force activities that are inconsistent with corporate strategy |
| Allocates sales force effort to the right products | Allocates sales force effort to the wrong products |
| Allocates sales force effort to the right markets | Allocates sales force effort to the wrong markets |
| Encourages an appropriate balance between new business development and account maintenance | Encourages salespeople to call on friends and family |
| Encourages the sales force to meet customer needs | Encourages overselling |
| Helps the company exceed its sales and profit expectations | Prevents the company from meeting its sales and profit targets |

**Figure 10-2.** Compensation Framework.

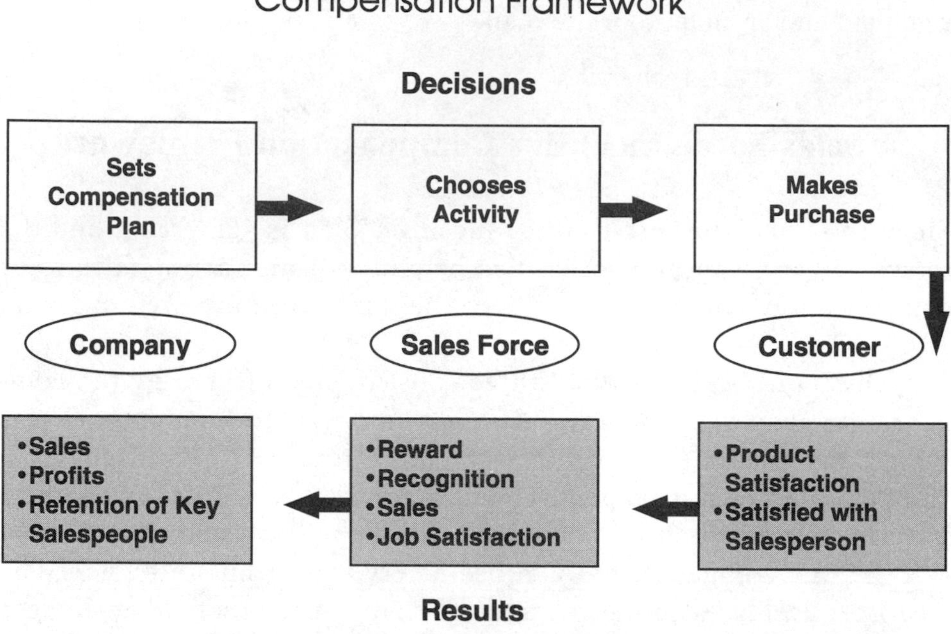


and defines the boundaries of its relationship with the company's selling organization.

The company can decide on only the plan. The other two decisions are not under its direct control, although they are influenced by the choice of the plan.

Anticipated results shape the decisions the three constituents make. Customer results include satisfaction with the product and satisfaction with their relationship with the company's selling organization. People will not buy from people that they do not like or people who do not meet their needs.

Satisfied customers generate sales. High sales volume and profitability for a territory lead to increased income, recognition, and rewards for the salesperson. Plans that provide income and recognition motivate the salesperson and enhance her or his energy and commitment.

Successful salespeople generate excellent company results. Sales and profits exceed expectations, and good performers stay with the company. By affecting sales force activity and behavior, the compensation plan affects customer results, salesperson results, and, ultimately, the company's results.

More detailed observations regarding these three decisions are presented in the following sections.

## The Company Decision

The company decides on the sales force compensation plan. There are hundreds of plans to choose from; however, most companies want a motivating plan that helps them achieve their strategic objectives, attract and retain the best people, establish and maintain a successful culture, and attain their sales and profit targets.

The compensation plan influences the type of person who is attracted to the company. Consider the two plans shown in Figure 10-3 and think about the type of people who would be attracted by each plan.

Plan A might be appropriate for a high-tech start-up. Such a firm needs salespeople who are risk takers and who want the opportunity to earn a high income as a reward for hard work and sales success. Plan B might be appropriate for a mature business that values loyalty, professional development, customer satisfaction, and steady sales and profit growth.

All sales force compensation plans communicate what is important. As a result, they need to be consistent with corporate strategy. For example, if a company promotes sales over the Internet but does not reward the sales force for introducing customers to electronic ordering, the goals are at odds. The incentive plan needs to align the salespeople's activities with the firm's objectives. Contrast the two plans shown in Figure 10-4.

Notice that the intent of each plan in Figure 10-4 is different. Each plan elicits different activity from the sales force. The activity in an effective plan is consistent with management's desires.

The company needs to articulate what it wants before it designs its plan. What type of people does it want to attract? What results need to be measured and rewarded: sales, margin, more sales of specific product

**Figure 10-3.** A Comparison of Two Incentive Plans: What Type of Person Would Each Plan Attract?

| *Plan A* | *Plan B* |
|---|---|
| • 100% commission from the first dollar<br>• No cap<br>• No draw<br>• On-the-job training | • 100% salary, reviewed annually<br>• Company car<br>• Generous health and insurance benefits<br>• Promotions into marketing and sales management are encouraged<br>• Professional development is valued |

**Figure 10-4.** A Comparison of Two Incentive Plans: What Type of Activity Is Rewarded by Each Plan?

| *Plan A* | *Plan B* |
|---|---|
| • 2.5% commission on all sales up to last year's sales<br>• 7.5% commission on sales exceeding last year's sales | • Salary plus a 20% bonus opportunity<br>• Bonus is paid in the following proportions:<br>—Customer satisfaction—20%<br>—Profitability—60%<br>—Educational and service objectives—20% |

lines, more sales from certain customer segments, or customer satisfaction? A compensation plan's power is enhanced by simplicity, which adds to the challenge of designing it. The firm must distill everything it wants to communicate through the compensation plan into a few clear and dominant elements.

Figure 10-5 illustrates the link between corporate strategy and sales force activity. The compensation plan is an important part of this link.

## The Sales Force Decision

Each salesperson decides how hard he or she will work and how he or she will spend the available time. These choices are influenced by many factors—the personality of the salesperson, other nonwork activities competing for the salesperson's time, the utility for money for the salesperson, manager or peer pressure, and the corporate culture. The compensation plan also exerts an influence on how a salesperson decides to spend his or her time. For example, which of the two plans in Figure 10-6 encourages salespeople to work harder?

The sales force constantly allocates its time while on the job. Time allocation decisions fall into three categories: What products do I spend my time on? What customer segments do I spend my time on? What activities do I engage in? The diagram in Figure 10-7 illustrates these choices.

The plans in Figure 10-8 have features that encourage salespeople to use their time in specific ways.

Salespeople usually set goals or choose a focus to guide their activities. They may emphasize their customers, focus on achieving sales and profit results, or invest in their own professional development. The compensation plan communicates which of these are most important to the company. Plans that pay on sales results elevate the importance

Figure 10-5. The Compensation Plan Is an Important Part of the Link Between Corporate Strategy and Sales Force Activity.

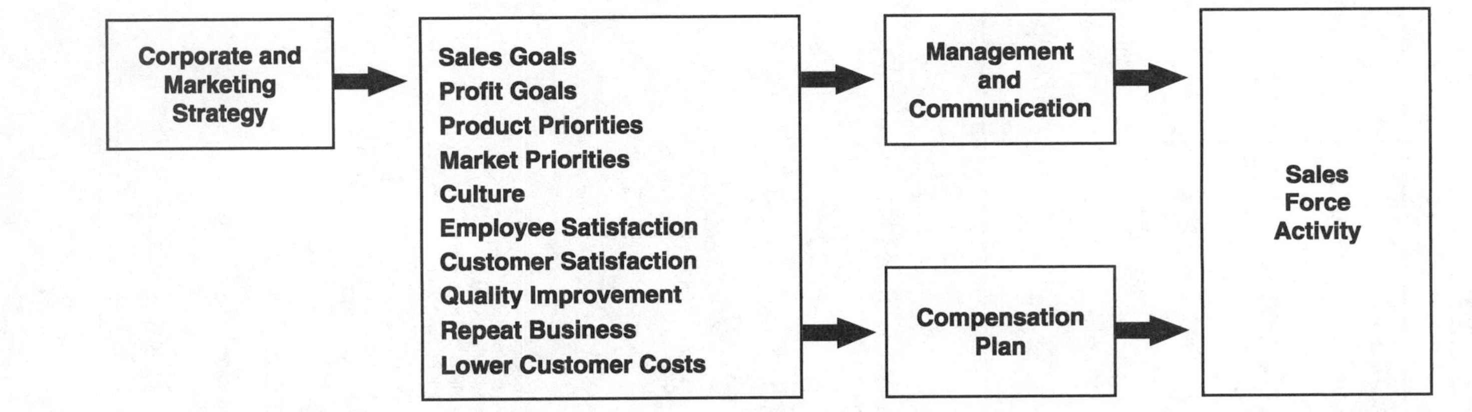

**Figure 10-6.** A Comparison of Two Incentive Plans: Which Encourages Salespeople to Work Harder?

| *Plan A* | *Plan B* |
|---|---|
| • Salary up to 95% of goal<br>• 2% commission from 95 to 100% of goal<br>• 3% commission from 100 to 110% of goal<br>• Income is capped when 110% is achieved<br>• Annual incentive payments | • Salary up to 90% of goal<br>• 2% commission from 90 to 95% of goal<br>• 3% commission from 95 to 100% of goal<br>• 4% commission from 100 to 110% of goal<br>• 6% commission on all sales above 110% of goal<br>• No caps<br>• Quarterly incentive payments |

**Figure 10-7.** Time Allocation Choices for Salespeople.

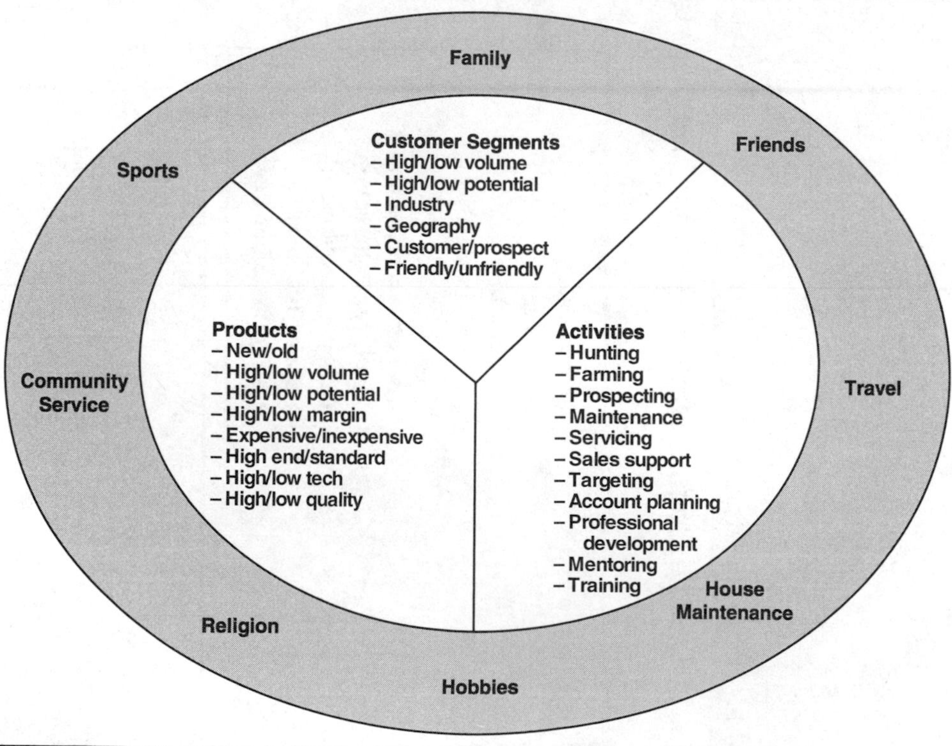

**Figure 10-8.** Incentive Plans That Influence the Way Salespeople Spend Their Time.

| *Product Allocation* | *Customer Allocation* |
|---|---|
| • 2% commission on sales of Product A<br>• 3% commission on sales of Product B | • 2% commission on business from existing accounts<br>• 3% commission on business from new accounts |

of "getting the sale." Those that pay on customer satisfaction or customer retention raise the importance of the customer. Incorporating professional objectives into the incentive plan shows that the company values the personal development of its people.

Salespeople have various needs, which are satisfied on the job in different ways—for example, through skill acquisition or by winning over a tough prospect. Individual needs often compete, such as safety versus adventure. Compensation plans can help meet these desires too. Safety needs are met by a plan with high salary and low incentive pay. Ego and social needs are met by reaching quotas and receiving sales awards, or by being named to the President's Club. Recognition can take many forms besides simple compensation. For example, Wall Data, Inc., has rewarded top sellers by donating money to the charity of a salesperson's choice or by starting a scholarship in the salesperson's hometown. Often, personal, special, and unique rewards are more motivating than cash alone.

All sales forces are heterogeneous, including risk takers and risk avoiders, techies and nontechies, expressives and analyticals, and amiables and drivers. It's impossible to have a single incentive plan that will satisfy everyone's needs. Each individual will react to the company's plan in a different way. Some will be highly motivated, while others will cut back. It is important for the firm to anticipate sales force behavior before implementing any new plan.

## The Customer Decision

The customer decides whether or not to purchase the firm's products or services. Customer needs vary across industries, across companies in the same industry, and even across buyers within the same company. There are economic buyers, user buyers, and technical buyers. Some buyers merely want product information; others are looking for integrated business solutions. Some customers seek servicing or merchandising; others want a good price, online ordering, and quick delivery.

Some customers make a few large purchases, while others make small, frequent automatic purchases. Some customers have high switching costs; others can switch suppliers easily. Some customers are responsive to sales force effort, while increasing call frequency has no effect on others.

Customers' needs influence their purchase decision. If the compensation plan entices salespeople to act in a way that is contrary to their customers' needs, sales will suffer. A commission plan might discourage building a relationship with a relationship-oriented customer. A salary plan might encourage relationship building when the customer is concerned with nothing other than timely delivery. To craft the appropriate incentive plan, it's critical to consider customer needs.

## Four Key Decisions for Effective Incentive Compensation Plan Design

Designing an effective incentive compensation plan requires the company to make four key decisions, shown in Figure 10-9. Each of these decisions is discussed in detail in this section.

### Level: How Much Should a Salesperson Be Paid?

The annual income level for full-time salespeople varies significantly. It can be as low as $25,000, and in some cases it can exceed $1,000,000. Income differences exist between industries, within the same industry, and even within the same company.

Interindustry income differences are usually due to the need for different types of salespeople. Customers differ across industries. They

**Figure 10-9.** Four Key Decisions for Compensation Plan Design.

| *Decision* | *Description* |
|---|---|
| Level | How much should the salespeople be paid? |
| Mix | What proportion of a salesperson's compensation should be incentive (variable, at-risk) pay? |
| Measures of performance | What measures should be used to determine the incentive component of the salesperson's compensation? |
| Performance-payout relationships | How should the incentive payment vary with measured performance? |

have various needs and buying processes. Meeting these needs requires different selling processes, selling skills, and capabilities. Figure 10-10 shows statistics from a recent Dartnell survey that illustrate interindustry differences.

Intraindustry differences tend to be smaller than interindustry differences. Profitable companies are inclined to pay more, while cost-conscious companies typically pay less.

Intercompany pay differences also exist. Usually, large pay differences are due to large differences in the incentive portion of the payout. Highly leveraged plans (those with a high incentive component) tend to have the highest variance in total salesperson income. In some companies the highest incentive payout is several times the average incentive payout. Large intercompany differences are not bad, as long as they are warranted by differences in performance.

Sales force income levels can be explained by a combination of external, internal, and job-related factors.

**External Factors: Supply and Demand.** The labor market affects most sales forces. Pay levels escalate when the supply of a particular type of salesperson is tight and demand is high. The supply/demand balance

**Figure 10-10.** A Comparison of Salesperson Income by Industry.

**Average Pay of Intermediate Salespeople (1999)**

| | *Average Pay ($000)* |
|---|---|
| Chemicals | 50.7 |
| Communications | 42.4 |
| Electronics | 60.8 |
| Fabricated metals | 59.5 |
| Hotel/lodging | 40.2 |
| Insurance | 51.3 |
| Manufacturing | 55.0 |
| Office equipment | 60.4 |
| Printing/publishing | 37.1 |
| Retail | 45.2 |
| Wholesale | 34.5 |

Reprinted with permission from *Dartnell's 30th Sales Force Compensation Survey,* copyright 1999 by Dartnell Corporation, 360 Hiatt Drive, Palm Beach Gardens, FL 33418. All rights reserved.

varies across industries. Demand usually exceeds supply in high-growth industries that need skilled salespeople. The medical device industry experienced this in the 1980s, although pay levels have moderated in recent years. The data communications industry experienced it in the 1990s, and the business-to-business e-commerce companies saw it in the late 1990s. There is major competition for people in high-employment economies. The United States in the late 1990s is an example. In such an economy, workers have numerous job opportunities and diverse career choices. Sales forces need to pay more to attract and retain the best people.

**Internal Factors: Industry and Company Profitability.** Another factor driving pay levels is industry profitability. High-margin industries can afford to pay more. Low-margin industries pay less. When an industry leader sets a certain pay scale, followers or less competitive participants tend to emulate the leader's behavior. Over time, industry pay norms develop.

When evaluating pay levels for salespeople, firms should be competitive, while setting pay levels that the firm can afford. In some industries, this leads to internal parity problems. For example, a typical salesperson may earn more than a product manager or sales manager. While this is not inherently a problem, it does lead to lower levels of career advancement and cultural isolation for the sales organization. In other cases, companies with weak products pay less than the industry norm simply because they cannot afford to pay more.

**Job-Related Factors.** Sales jobs differ widely. Some are difficult to do well, requiring high levels of knowledge, skill, and stress management (e.g., selling power plants or commercial airplanes), while others are relatively easy (e.g., consumer product merchandising). Sometimes maintaining accounts means simply taking orders; sometimes it requires diplomacy of the highest order. Finding new customers can be nearly impossible, or it can be as easy as looking in the phone book. Income levels tend to be higher for the more difficult sales jobs. Figure 10-11 examines several dimensions of why some salespeople earn more money than others do.

Most companies benchmark once a year to see if their sales force pay levels are appropriate. Nearly every company tries to have its sales force incomes fall within the upper half, if not the upper quarter, of the industry. It is not easy for a vice president of sales to tell the sales force that the company's strategy is to pay in the lower half or lower quartile

**Figure 10-11.** Dimensions That Determine a Salesperson's Income.

| Low Income | High Income |
|---|---|
| The selling process is easy to learn and execute. | The selling process is hard, requiring high levels of competence to learn and execute. |
| The sales force is not very prominent in the sale. Sales are due primarily to a strong brand, advertising and promotion, or long-term contracts negotiated by others. | The sales force is prominent in the sale. Sales are due primarily to the skill, effort, and motivation of the individual salesperson. |
| Selling is effort-based. | Selling is skill- and knowledge-based. |
| The salesperson is primarily a "farmer"; activities include servicing, stocking, and customer maintenance. | The salesperson is primarily a "hunter"; activities include lead generation, prospecting, and new customer development. |
| The salesperson adds some value for customers. | The salesperson adds considerable value for customers. |
| The salesperson is responsible for accounts in a local area. | The salesperson is responsible for national or other major accounts. |
| Most purchases are simple, minor. | Most purchases are complex, major. |
| The company has a monopoly position—high switching costs for the customer, high product differentiation. | The company sells in a competitive market—low switching costs, no product differentiation. |

within the industry. Expanding the benchmarking to include an analysis of the future labor supply/demand balance, the forecasted profitability of the company, and any anticipated job-related changes will enhance the firm's ability to set the right pay levels.

Finally, companies usually specify a targeted income for the sales force. The *income range* may be a more useful concept than a single number. The income range specifies what people can earn, depending on their performance and the company's performance. For example, rather than designating an average target income of $85,000, the firm identifies an average payout range of $80,000 to $90,000, depending on sales force and hence company performance.

## Mix: What Proportion of a Salesperson's Compensation Should Be Incentive Pay?

**Salary Versus Incentive: The Controversy.** There is a great deal of debate about the need for incentives for salespeople. Some argue that salespeople should get salary just like everyone else. A typical argument is:

> Why should salespeople be treated differently? They should be expected to do their jobs like everyone else, with salary

> plus a year-end bonus if the company has a good year. The rest of the professional world gets paid this way, so why can't salespeople? Commissions inspire mercenary, greedy behavior that is often at odds with long-term company success. At best, salespeople should have an anchored pay rate, say from $50,000 to $60,000. If the company has a good year, they will earn at the top part of their range. If the year is bad, they earn the lower figure. The best reward is to have pride in your work; this higher reward is corrupted for salespeople by incentive compensation.

Opponents of this view argue that salespeople need incentive compensation because their job is unlike any other job. They argue:

> Salespeople affect sales directly and measurably. They work alone, with significant rejection, and crave recognition. Salespeople need powerful motivators like incentive kicks and uncapped plans to keep going. Salaried salespeople will avoid the tough work of closing the sales and company results will suffer. Salespeople make sales happen, and they deserve to share the rewards directly.

The incentive component of the compensation plan can vary from 0 percent (total salary) to 100 percent (total incentive). As Figure 10-12 shows, there are significant differences across industries.

Notable differences can also arise within industries. In the 1980s, IBM's salespeople had 30 to 40 percent of their cash compensation at risk, whereas Digital's had 0 percent. Many companies in markets with comparable sales processes and environmental conditions have pay plans that are quite different.

Differences in the salary/incentive mix exist across sales positions as well. For example, salespeople in the telecommunications industry sell long distance, Internet access, and other communications services. National account salespeople within the industry are paid an average of $112,000, including 20 percent bonus. Large account representatives are paid an average of $91,000 and have 35 percent incentive pay (both bonus and commission). Geographic salespeople are paid an average of $82,000, with 50 percent of pay as bonus and commission.

As another example, one medical device and supplies manufacturer uses independent representatives and account managers. Both types of salespeople call on hospitals, surgicenters, and distributors—the jobs

**Figure 10-12.** The Salary/Incentive Mix by Industry.

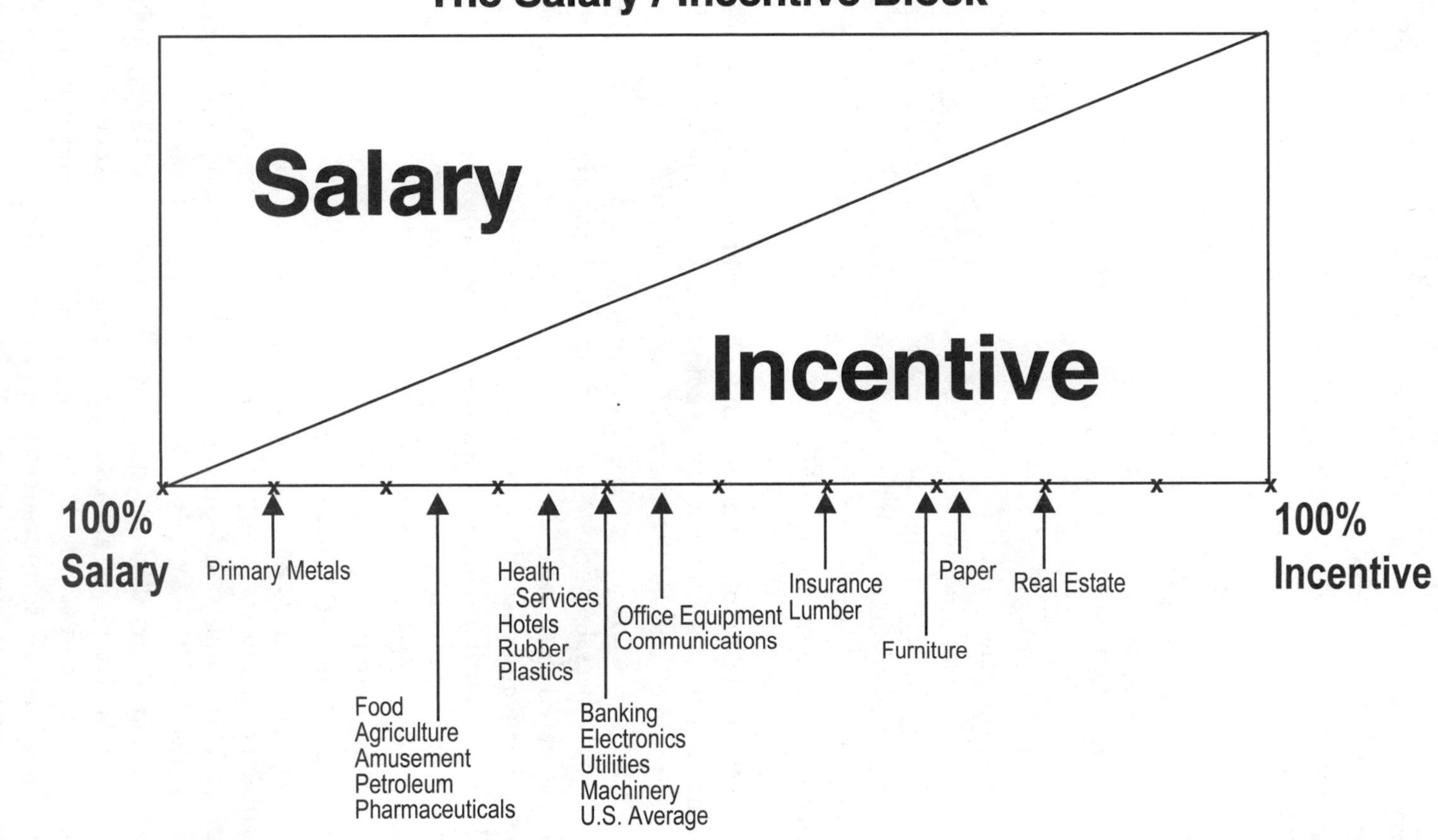


Reprinted with permission from *Dartnell's 29th Sales Force Compensation Survey,* copyright 1996 by Dartnell Corporation, 360 Hiatt Drive, Palm Beach Gardens, FL 33418. 

differ only in compensation. In 1996, the independent representatives received 100 percent commission and paid for their own benefits and expenses. The pay range for the independents was $123,000 to $147,000. In the same year, account managers received 40 percent of their earnings in salary and 60 percent in commission, and the company paid for their benefits and expenses. The pay range for account managers was $43,000 to $167,000.

How does one determine the best mix of salary and incentives from among all of the available options? Four dimensions are important:

- Measurability of company and customer results
- Sales force causality
- Selling process
- People and culture

Since the level of incentive pay affects the company, salesperson, and customer decisions and results, it is useful to refer to the compensation framework shown in Figure 10-2 to discuss the optimal mix of incentive pay and salary.

**Measurability of Company and Customer Results.** Compensation plans that have a high incentive component assume a strong "pay for performance" and "share the risk" sales force culture. Performance is usually assessed in terms of one or more performance criteria, and pay is tied to the salesperson's success on these criteria. Measurability of the selected criteria is critical to the success of any incentive-based plan. If it is not possible to measure sales accurately, then it is impossible to pay fairly on those sales. The weaker the measurement is, the less desirable it is to reward salespeople with incentive pay. *Incentives do not work if the performance criteria cannot be measured.*

Most performance criteria for salespeople can be organized around company results and customer results within the compensation framework in Figure 10-2. Sales, contribution, and market share are common company measures. Customer satisfaction, customer retention, customer complaints, and message measurability are typical customer measures.

Measurability depends upon data availability, accuracy, and timeliness. Incentive plans are effective when performance data for every sales territory are available, accurate, and timely. Unfortunately, there are many threats to measurability, and the sales force will surely find them. Several examples appear in Figure 10-13.

**Figure 10-13.** Threats to Measurability of Performance.

| | |
|---|---|
| **Data availability** | Territory sales get lost in a complex distribution system. Sales to resellers are tracked, but sales to end users are lost. Hence, salespeople do not get credit for their work with end users.<br>The company does not know how much the customer is buying. For example, pharmaceutical firms may not be aware of how much of their product is prescribed by physicians.<br>Sales cannot be attributed to an individual salesperson in a team-selling environment.<br>Sales tracking systems may not capture all of the sales transactions. |
| **Data accuracy** | Performance measures are estimated from a sample when a census is not available, and estimates can have sampling error. How well does a salesperson understand sampling error?<br>Customer satisfaction surveys are subject to data accuracy issues when the salesperson focuses inappropriately on getting good survey results.<br>The information technology group can have errors in its processing procedures. |
| **Data timeliness** | Data that are months late because of collection delays and processing errors are not very motivational. |

**Sales Force Causality.** Sales force causality, or the extent to which the sales force creates sales, is another factor to consider when deciding on the appropriate salary/incentive mix. Sales force causality is illustrated in the following example.

Dan Peterson sells home mortgage loans for a large New York bank. He calls on realtors and lawyers, hoping to persuade them to use his services when they advise new homebuyers on how to finance their new home. Dan's income depends mostly on commission earnings from the loan volume that he produces. Dan's marketplace is very competitive because home mortgage loans are a commodity offered by numerous lenders. He begins each day at sea level, not knowing how much he will sell or earn.

Sally Lorimer sells medical diagnostic instruments and the necessary reagents for the tests done with these instruments. Sally calls on hospitals and large reference laboratories. Her company is the market leader with a family of highly differentiated products. Since most of her sales and profits come from the reagent trail that commences after instrument adoption, she hopes to sell her units at a competitive price.

Sally begins every day knowing that there will be orders arising from her established relationships. Since she has reached her territory goals for the last three years, she is confident that she will again get an attractive bonus to supplement her competitive salary.

Sales force causality can be explained by decomposing a firm's sales in any period, say a year, into three parts. *Carryover sales*, introduced in Chapter 3, is the portion of this year's sales that is the result of prior years' sales force effort. *Franchise sales* is the portion of this year's sales that is due to non-sales force factors, such as dominant products, good pricing, effective advertising, a good economy, and weak competitors. *Rep sales* are the sales resulting from the skill, knowledge, motivation, and effort of the sales force in the current year. For purposes of the incentive compensation discussion, the sum of carryover sales and franchise sales will be referred to as *free sales.*

Dan's territory has little carryover and franchise support; there would be no sales in his territory if he missed a day, a month, or the quarter. Sally's territory, on the other hand, would realize high levels of sales even if she were to miss the same amount of time. Her products are in demand, her customers have high switching costs, and she has a dependable reagent trail. Figure 10-14 contrasts Dan's sales with Sally's sales.

High-causality selling environments have large rep sales segments.

**Figure 10-14.** A Comparison of Free Sales and Rep Sales for Two Salespeople.

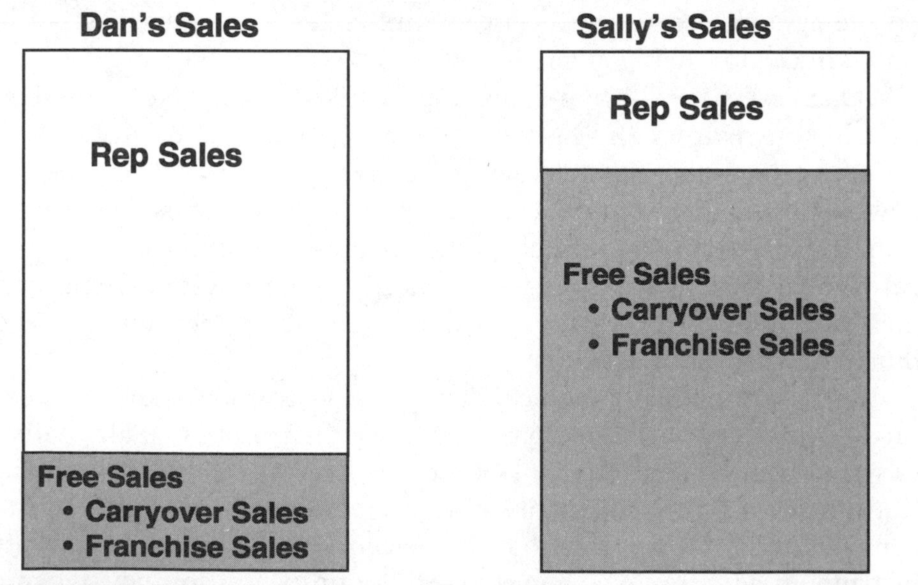

They are environments in which sales are determined primarily by the skill, knowledge, motivation, and efforts of the sales force. Dan's selling environment has high causality. His products are commodities, and his activity creates immediate sales for the bank. The salesperson is prominent in selling home mortgage loans. Sally's selling environment has lower causality. She has high carryover and a strong franchise, and her impact is longer term. The relationships she develops today will pay off significantly in future years.

Sales force causality is important in determining the salary/incentive mix. Incentives have a greater impact in high-causality environments. Incentives are motivational; people like to feel that their work effort will be rewarded. Work effort has high sales impact in a high-causality environment (where rep sales are large) and lower sales impact in a low-causality environment (where free sales are large). Sales increases in a high-causality environment are due to sales force effort. The sales force sees sales rise and feels a sense of accomplishment. Salespeople receive commensurate financial reward when a plan that includes high variable pay is adopted.

A low-causality selling environment has a different dynamic. Plans with high incentive pay will work only if the level of free sales can be estimated accurately. Otherwise, incentives are being used to pay for free sales. Paying incentives for free sales is the same as paying a "hidden salary." Not much is at risk with a highly incentive-based plan and low causality. Free sales are just that—they are free. Incentives need to be a reward for accomplishment; they lose their emotional impact if the sales force feels it cannot affect the outcome.

Some industries experience both high and low causality. The pharmaceutical industry sells both acute- and chronic-care products. An acute-care product such as an antibiotic has high sales force causality. Frequent sales calls to doctors during the flu season generate high sales volume for the firm. In contrast, products such as hypertensive agents serve the chronic needs of patients. Physicians are unlikely to switch to other products if they feel the products they are using work for their patients. Frequent sales force calls in a highly satisfied marketplace are wasted because the causality is low.

Several high- and low-causality environments are presented in Figure 10-15.

Team selling, market volatility, and sales force nonprominence are all threats to causality. They occur frequently and require a creative use of incentives.

The blood glucose monitor market is a good example of weak cau-

**Figure 10-15.** Selling Environments With High and Low Causality.

| *High-Causality Selling* | *Low-Causality Selling* |
|---|---|
| Acute-care pharmaceuticals | Chronic-care pharmaceuticals |
| Insurance | Consumer product merchandising |
| Real estate | Electric, gas companies |
| Financial services | |

sality resulting from team selling. Diabetics use blood glucose monitors to test their blood sugar daily. They purchase the monitor and testing strips in drugstores and health care outlets, and strips are not interchangeable between monitors. Consequently, the patient's choice of monitor is the critical decision for the manufacturer, since the purchase of a monitor generates many years of strip purchases.

Several people can influence the patient's choice of monitor. The patient can interact with up to four constituencies before making a final choice. First, the treating physician can recommend a product. Second, the disease is frequently diagnosed in a hospital. As a result, the hospital staff has an opportunity to recommend a specific product. Third, patients are usually referred to a diabetes nurse educator who provides information about the disease, treatment options, and lifestyle implications. The diabetes nurse educator is in a position to recommend a product. Finally, the patient acquires the product at a retail outlet. The pharmacist has the final influence. Patients can ask the pharmacist to describe the differences between monitors and make a recommendation.

None of these buying influences can be ignored. Manufacturers usually ask their sales forces to call on all of them. Typically, several independent selling teams are used, with each team calling on a different market segment. The individual influence and impact of each team are obfuscated by the complexity of the buying process. The whole team shares the total causality—members of all the selling teams share the rep sales component. Since an individual salesperson's impact is impossible to discern, an individually based incentive plan is difficult to construct.

Another common example of multilevel selling is national account selling with a local sales presence. This occurs when systemwide buying decisions are made at a headquarters location and the sell-in and pull-through is done at local sites. All consumer product firms are faced with this selling environment. They need to both call on Wal-Mart headquarters and service the individual stores. Sales force causality gets blurred across the various selling tasks.

Market volatility is another threat to sales force causality. For example, an advertising salesperson for a large national magazine happened to be in the office when the phone rang. She picked it up. A marketing executive for a global electronics firm was at the other end. The firm wanted to place thirty pages of advertising to launch a new product. The order made the salesperson's year. How much did she have to do to generate the sale? She had a windfall gain. Windfall gains are a result of market volatility. Volatility makes free sales very unpredictable, and it is difficult to separate the effects of causality and volatility. Unless the volatility is measured and accounted for in the incentive plan, it is better to treat a volatile market as having low causality.

Companies that ignore volatility and develop highly leveraged compensation plans incur two negative consequences. First, salespeople develop expectations of high income after a successful year in which they received significant windfalls. The sales force takes credit for the success and feels entitled to a similar income level the subsequent year. Second, there is a perception of unfairness when the windfall is not uniform across the entire sales force.

Sales force prominence is another important determinant of causality. A sales force is prominent when the competencies and effort of the salesperson are the primary determinants of sales. Other marketing instruments, such as product, pricing, advertising, telesales, and direct mail are more important than direct sales in some selling environments. Free sales can be quite large in this type of environment, but a highly leveraged incentive plan punishes or rewards salespeople for results that are beyond their control.

Dan earns more than Sally in most years. Why? Sales force compensation is usually higher and the incentive component is larger in industries with high sales force causality and high sales force prominence.

**Selling Process.** The selling process is another important consideration when determining the salary/incentive mix. A typical selling process can be divided into two components: selling activities and support activities. The activities making up these components are shown in Figure 10-16.

Salespeople in the United States spend between 15 and 20 percent of their time (depending on the survey) actively selling. Selling time is

**Figure 10-16.** Selling Process Components.

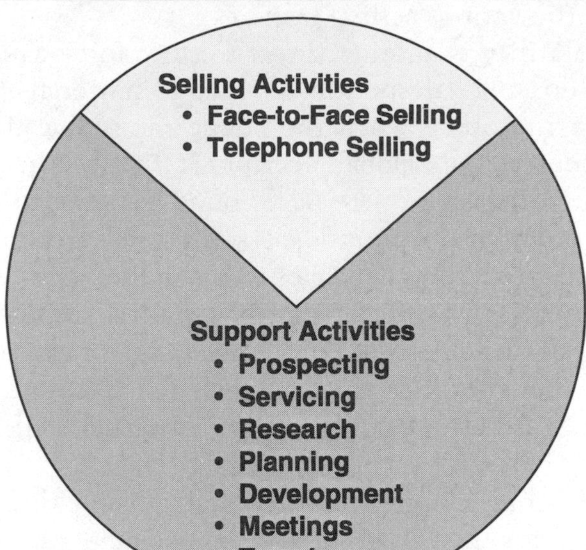


the actual time spent with customers pursuing sales. Incentive payments to the sales force are usually based upon territory results (e.g., sales) or the salesperson's activities (e.g., calls, developmental objectives). Effective incentive plans influence salespeople's activities. Incentive compensation plans with large components based on territory results or selling activities tend to increase the selling time component of the selling process. This is desirable in high-causality environments. However, in many other environments, support activities are also important, and excessive incentives can lead to behavior that may not meet customer needs or help the company achieve its objectives. The following list provides examples of selling processes that require significant support time.

- Customer service, customer training, inventory management, display maintenance, marketing research, report preparation, and forecasting are important activities.
- Selling requires creativity, problem-solving skills, or extensive technical, product, and application knowledge.
- Message control is essential because products can be misused.
- Relationship development is important, and overselling may create customer distrust.
- There is a long selling cycle, and consequently, sales force activities must be sustained for longer periods of time.

- Short-term incentives would be counterproductive.
- The firm wants to promote a career-oriented sales force.
- The firm is a learning organization and wants to encourage professional development.

**Sales Force Culture.** Finally, sales force culture should be considered when deciding the mix between salary and incentives. The culture can be thought of as the genes of the sales force. Culture guides salespeople as they encounter familiar or new situations. It establishes the baseline for the sales force's decision making and its acceptable behaviors. Values are a core component of the culture; they specify what is important, and they are the principles and standards that guide behavior. Frequently, values are evident in the way the sales force resolves its conflicts and dilemmas. The incentive compensation plan must be consistent with and should reinforce the firm's culture. Every sales force faces several common dilemmas. Figure 10-17 shows how the incentive/salary mix reinforces sales force choices in common dilemmas. The choices listed also suggest the type of people who will be attracted by each incentive plan.

## Measures of Performance: What Measures Should Be Used to Determine the Incentive Component of the Salesperson's Compensation?

Incentives are rewards for successful sales force performance. Performance cannot be judged without evaluative criteria. Performance criteria

**Figure 10-17.** Common Dilemmas and Their Impact on the Incentive/Salary Mix.

| ← Favor Incentives | Favor Salary → |
|---|---|
| Short-term results are rewarded. | Long-term results are rewarded. |
| The sales force focuses on results. | The sales force focuses on activity. |
| Hunters; selling new business is important. | Farmers; maintaining existing business is important. |
| Salespeople are empowered. | Strong controls are in place. |
| Individual orientation is favored. | Team orientation is desired. |
| The best talent is hired into the sales force. | The best talent is developed within the firm. |
| The sales force tries to be adaptive. | Stability is preferred. |
| Management views members of the sales force as company ambassadors who should receive incentives to produce measurable results. | Management does not value the sales force or feels that salespeople should be treated like everyone else. |

can be described in terms of four dimensions, as shown in Figure 10-18. Most firms use several criteria in their incentive plans.

*Metrics* are the performance attributes that get measured. Most firms use sales as their most important metric. Other common measures include gross contribution margin, market share, orders, collections (sales are counted when payment is received rather than when the order is taken), customer satisfaction, salesperson activities, and salesperson capabilities (e.g., skills and knowledge).

Metrics can be viewed from different perspectives, either as levels or comparisons. Sales, gross contribution margin, number of calls, and customer satisfaction scales are all examples of level metrics. Here, it is the precise level of the metric that is important. Alternatively, metrics can be stated as comparisons with some standard or level of expectation. Specifying the comparison within the measure itself enhances comparability. For example, metrics can be contrasted with the past (e.g. growth or decline), compared to a goal or target (e.g., percent of goal attainment) or compared to a peer group (e.g., district or region ranking).

*Focus* describes the emphasis, or level of aggregation, of the metric. For example, companies can evaluate product results, market segment results, or total company sales results.

**Figure 10-18.** Four Dimensions of Performance Criteria.

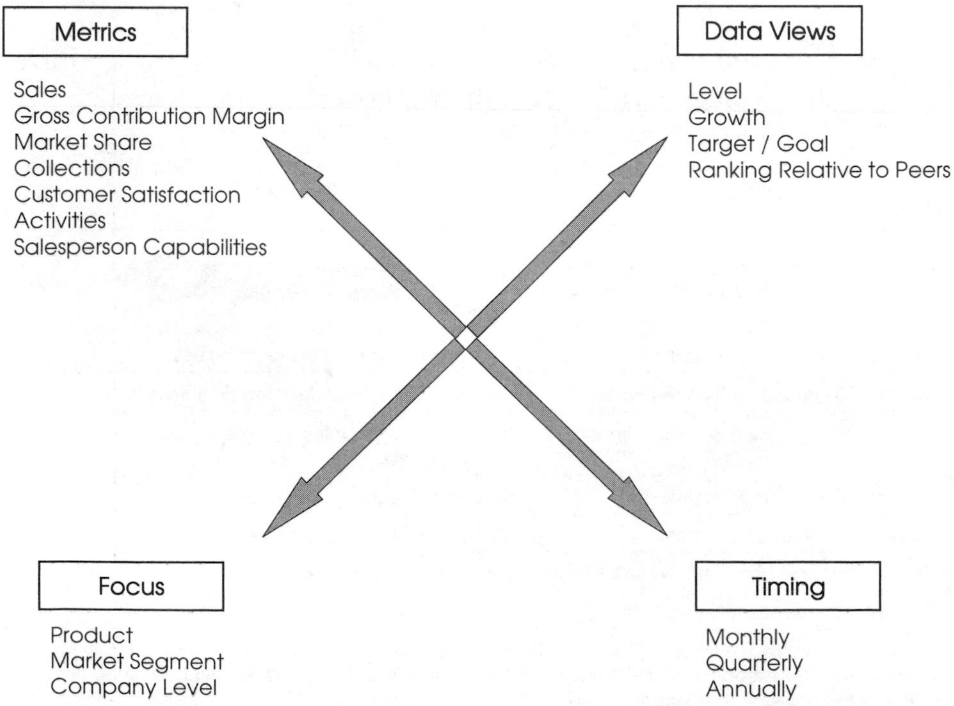

Finally, metrics have *timing*. They can be expressed daily, weekly, monthly, quarterly, or annually.

Several examples of how these four dimensions can be integrated to form incentive compensation measures are:

- Quarterly sales for strategic products
- Annual percentage of goal attainment for overall gross contribution margin
- Monthly ranking of salespeople on cumulative year-to-date sales of all products
- An average of ten calls per week
- Visiting "focus accounts" at least three times yearly
- Developing ten new accounts this year
- Attending Toastmasters training
- Reaching $2,000,000 in sales

Here are several recommended guidelines for selecting performance measures for incentive compensation:

- The measures should be important for the business and should be compatible with sales force strategy.
- The sales force should be able to influence the measures; there should be sales force causality.
- The measures should be objectively measurable; accurate data should be available.
- The measures should not favor any particular group of participant; they should be fair.
- The total number of measures should not exceed three; the incentive plan needs to be simple.

Measurement is highly salient, since the incentive plan affects everyone in the sales force. Here are four frequently asked questions about measurement, along with a few recommendations.

**Should Salespeople Be Paid on Results or Activity?** Recently, an experienced sales manager was asked this question. He did not hesitate for a moment before responding, "I never pay on activity. Salespeople will tell you that they have performed the requisite activity, but then the results are not there. I give a bonus only when I see results."

Sales force activity drives company results. Good activity generates incrementally better results. Poor activity generates incrementally poorer results. The firm benefits if the sales force successfully implements an effective selling process. If this is true, why not pay on activity? Because (1) the firm's investors reward the company for results, not activity, and (2) it is very difficult to measure activity accurately. However, there are situations in which activity measurement is more appropriate than results measurement. Figure 10-19 shows conditions favoring each type of metric.

**Should Incentives Be Paid When the Order Is Taken or When the Company Collects the Funds from the Customer?** The salesperson's main job is to get the order. Incentives are most motivating when they are granted soon after a successful sale. This argues that incentives should be attached to the order. However, in some industries there are time lags between the time the order is placed, when it is shipped, and when money is collected. The company does not acknowledge the sale until it receives payment. This creates a dilemma for compensation planners: Should payment occur when orders are taken or when monies are collected? An intermediate strategy is also possible: Pay some fraction of the total incentive at the time of the order and pay the rest at the time of collection. Figure 10-20 describes some of the conditions that favor each approach.

**Should Salespeople Be Paid an Incentive for High Customer Satisfaction?** The use of customer satisfaction measures for compensation pur-

**Figure 10-19.** Conditions Favoring Activity Versus Results Metrics of Performance.

| *Conditions Favoring Activity* ← *Metrics* | *Conditions Favoring Results Metrics* → |
|---|---|
| Company results are not measurable at the territory level. | Company results can be measured accurately at the territory level. |
| The company wants to control activity. | An empowered sales force culture is the norm. |
| Nonselling activities are important. | Sales are primarily determined by the skill, motivation, and efforts of the individual salesperson. |
| The firm has the best understanding of the most effective sales force activities. | The salesperson has the best understanding of the most effective sales force activities. |
| The company wants to build a highly professional selling organization. | Achieving the sales target is the highest priority. |

**Figure 10-20.** Conditions Favoring Payment of Incentives at Time of Order Versus Time of Collection.

| Conditions Favoring a Larger Incentive Payment at Time of Order ← | Conditions Favoring a Larger Incentive Payment at Time of Collection → |
|---|---|
| Collection is almost certain.<br>Long selling cycles exist.<br>The salesperson can become a nuisance for the customer. | There is a high risk of cancellation or nonpayment.<br>The company wants to accelerate the collection, and the salesperson can help achieve this goal.<br>High inflation rates exist in some countries, and it is important to collect money as quickly as possible. |

poses has been popular for many years. About 10 percent of all sales forces allocate some fraction of their incentive component to customer satisfaction. Salespeople are usually paid on the basis of their score on a customer satisfaction assessment.

There are at least two reasons why a customer satisfaction component should be added to the incentive plan. First, as William Hewlett of Hewlett-Packard put it, ''What gets measured gets done.'' If the company puts the customer first and wants a competitive advantage from customer satisfaction, then it makes sense to make the compensation plan consistent with this strategy. The logical consequence is to reward the salesperson on customer satisfaction.

Second, customer satisfaction may be a better measure of sales success than sales, gross contribution margin or market share. Company results are affected by many things that are not under the salesperson's direct control, such as the economy, market conditions, and competition. Well-designed customer satisfaction measures should isolate the true impact of the salesperson on customer satisfaction.

Unfortunately, there are several serious concerns that arise when survey-based customer satisfaction measures are used to compensate individual salespeople. First, the customer satisfaction goal needs to be assessed relative to the company sales and profitability goals. Obviously, customers will be very satisfied if they can have the product for free.

A second concern can be illustrated by the following story. One of the authors purchased an expensive European car and was presented with several papers to sign in order to take possession of the vehicle. One of the papers looked like a survey. When he looked closely at it, he observed that it was indeed a survey and that it was all filled out. The salesperson had taken the liberty of filling it out and now wanted the author's signature. The salesperson had given himself an "excellent" rating in all categories. Rewarding salespeople for customer satisfaction can change their behavior. In addition to selling products, the salesperson now has an incentive to influence survey results.

When told this story, the administrative assistant to another of the authors added a corollary. She said that the same thing had happened to her when she bought her car. However, she had said that she wanted something in return for filling out the customer satisfaction form. She negotiated and received $150 worth of merchandise. How many companies want their salespeople to give up customer equity to get high satisfaction ratings? Most companies prefer to retain that power for the next price negotiation. Careful survey administration and random sampling can partially avoid the problem of negotiating for ratings.

Unfortunately, there are two technical details that cannot be avoided even with careful administration. Customer satisfaction surveys can suffer from small sample size. In many industries, salespeople will not have enough customers for the results of the survey to be statistically valid. Small sample sizes result in wobbly or unstable measures, and one or two extreme respondents can have a big effect on the outcome. One quarter the rating is excellent, and the next quarter it is average. This kind of inconsistency leads the salesperson to believe that her or his efforts are ineffective. The only way to avoid this problem is to collect a sufficient number of surveys (more customers or prospects), either over a longer time period or for a more aggregate level such as a sales region or a sales district. Customer satisfaction works well for company and district evaluation, but it can be problematic for individual salesperson compensation in companies where purchases are infrequent or account lists are small.

The second technical detail concerns a selection bias. Frequently, the people who are most likely to fill out surveys are those who have had a bad experience with the salesperson. Consequently, the survey result may not be a true reflection of the overall customer base.

Survey-based customer satisfaction measures should be used cautiously at the individual salesperson level. These measures are more appropriate at the district and national levels, where sample size and salesperson "rating chasing" tend not to be large issues. Alternatively, companies should consider using measures such as the following:

- Number of customer complaints about the sales force
- Percentage of sales this year from existing customers

- This year's sales divided by last year's sales from existing customers
- Percentage of customers repeating
- Pay for the second sale to a customer

The reliability of these measures will become more evident as their use becomes more widespread.

**Can We Test the Impact That New Performance Measures Will Have on the Sales Force?** A company that wants to insert new metrics into next year's incentive plan can test to see what the incentive payments would have been had the metrics been incorporated into this year's plan. This test enables the plan designer to see how much pay disruption is likely to occur when the measures are modified. Incentive disruptions are very contentious unless they are warranted by performance. The northwest and southeast quadrants in the plot in Figure 10-21 are areas that

**Figure 10-21.** Testing New Performance Metrics by Comparing Payout by Salesperson—New Metrics Versus Current Plan.

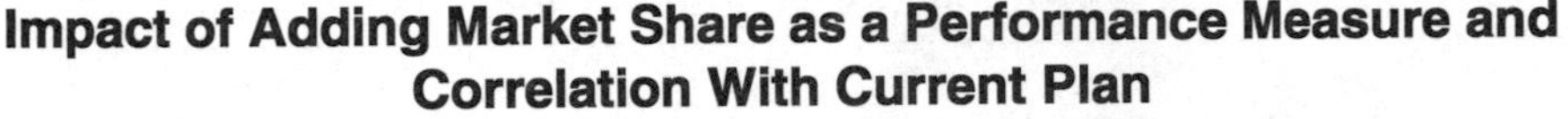


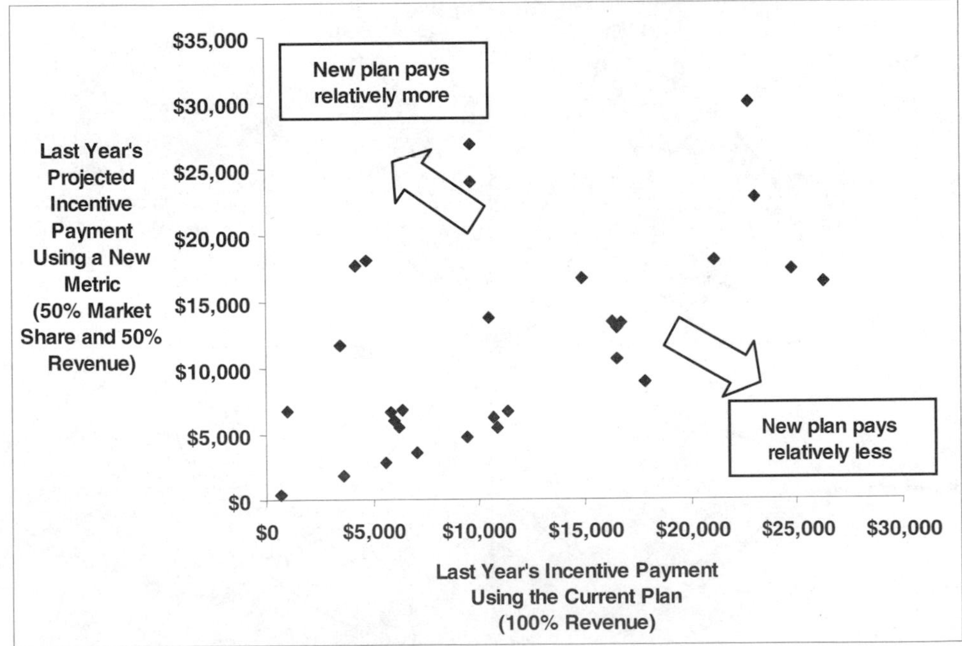


Each dot represents a sales territory.

need to be examined by the plan designer. He or she will certainly hear from the salespeople in the southeast quadrant.

## Performance-Payout Relationships: How Should Incentive Payment Vary With Measured Performance?

This is a complex decision with numerous alternatives and options. The Incentive Payment Design Wheel presented in Figure 10-22 provides an illustration of the decision process. The wheel shows eight important decisions that must be made in order to develop a viable incentive compensation plan. These decisions are shown on eight lines that intersect at the center of the wheel. The two extremes of each decision are described by the words outside the wheel; choices between the two extremes are also possible. Each of the decisions will be discussed in turn.

**Decision 1: Should the Incentive Compensation Plan Incorporate Goals for the Sales Force?** Some incentive plans are based on the achievement

**Figure 10-22.** The Incentive Payment Design Wheel.

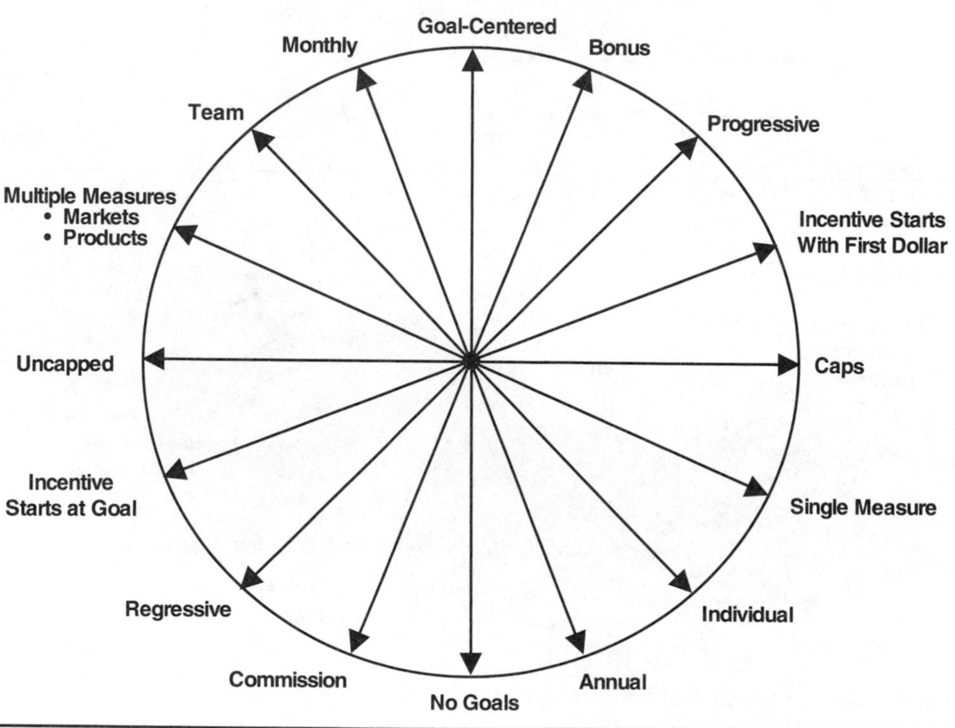

of specific goals or quotas; others do not depend on goals. About 85 percent of U.S. companies incorporate goals into their incentive plans. A comparison of these two approaches is provided in Figure 10-23.

Goals are used to communicate what is important. They:

- Measure accomplishment
- Increase motivation
- Assist in evaluation
- Reward performance
- Suggest effort allocation
- Ensure customer focus

Individuals and organizations that set goals achieve better results than those that do not. However, setting fair and realistic goals may not always be easy, or even possible. Data on revenue and market potential must be very specific and accurate or salespeople will view goals as unfair. For example, Knoll Pharmaceuticals decided that it was spending so much time managing and adjudicating complaints about quotas that it would be better to abandon them altogether. Instead, a firmwide bonus pool is now allocated to reps based on relative performance.

The table in Figure 10-24 contrasts conditions that favor a goal-centered approach and those that do not.

**Decision 2: Should the Incentive Compensation Plan Include Bonuses, Commissions, or Both?** Most incentive compensation plans can be repre-

**Figure 10-23.** A Comparison of Incentive Plans That Do and Do Not Include Goals.

| *Option* | *Description* | *Incentive Plan Illustrations* |
|---|---|---|
| Goals | A goal-centered plan establishes territory-level goals. They can be activity, customer satisfaction, or company results goals. There can be a single overriding goal or multiple goals. Chapter 11 provides an overview of this topic. | • Receive one month's salary at goal; get another month for every 10% beyond goal.<br>• 1% money up to threshold; 6% money beyond threshold.<br>• Bonus upon achieving activity and professional development goals. |
| No goals | There are no goals at the territory level. Salespeople are expected to sell as much as possible. | • 2% commission on every dollar sold. |

**Figure 10-24.** Conditions Favoring Goals Versus No Goals.

| *Conditions Favoring a Goal-Centered Approach* ← | *Conditions Favoring No Goals* → |
|---|---|
| Setting fair, realistic, and measurable goals is feasible.<br><br>It is critical for the company to hit its sales target.<br><br>Sales territories are out of balance in terms of market potential and earnings opportunity.<br><br>The market has high carryover—goals should exceed the carryover level to be motivational. | It is difficult to set fair and realistic goals because forecasting is unreliable as a result of new product launches, entry into a new market, or competitive markets with high volatility.<br><br>Sales territories have unlimited potential. ''The world is our oyster—go get it all'' is the attitude in the sales force.<br><br>Sales management wants to empower each salesperson to set his or her own goals. |

sented visually using a graph. The compensation graph enables quick recognition of the details of the performance-payout relationship. The graph's horizontal axis represents the performance measure, and the vertical axis represents the payment that the salesperson receives for each level of performance. Some different options for bonus and commission performance-payout relationships are shown in Figure 10-25.

Bonus and commission plans have fundamental differences. A bonus plan provides a big kick when a goal is attained. In contrast, commission plans pay out continuously. Bonuses encourage people to stretch for the big win. On the other hand, salespeople will be demoralized if they don't make the bonus. Commissions give continuous feedback when sales are made, and this can be highly motivational. However, big problems arise with commission plans if sales territories have unbalanced potential. Since some accounts and geography are better than others, territories must be balanced or a commission plan will be inherently unfair. Setting goals at the territory level can partially alleviate this concern.

Figure 10-26 provides several basic criteria for evaluating whether a bonus or a commission plan is more appropriate.

How are the rates or bonus numbers determined? The *amount at risk* is the fraction of the total compensation that is affected by the salesperson's effort. The *variable* component is the fraction of total compensation that comes from incentives. Although these terms are sometimes used interchangeably, they represent different concepts. For example, the variable component for a fully commissioned salesperson is 100 percent because the salesperson is paid entirely by commission. However, his or her at-risk component can be considerably less. For example, it would be 40 percent if 60 percent of territory sales is carry-over resulting from high switching costs and relationships developed in prior years. A useful rule of thumb is: *For any incentive to be effective, it has to be at least 15 percent of total compensation. To exert behavior control, the at-risk component should be at least 30 percent.*

**Decision 3: What is the Most Appropriate Performance-Payout Relationship?** An incentive plan can include many possible relationships be-

**Figure 10-25.** Alternative Bonus and Commission Performance-Payout Relationships.

| *Option* | *Description* | *Incentive Plan Illustration* |
|---|---|---|
| **Bonus** | A bonus is a one-time incentive payment for goal attainment. A salesperson could receive a single bonus or several bonuses for exceeding expectations. Multiple goals may be called gates, targets, or thresholds. | |
| | 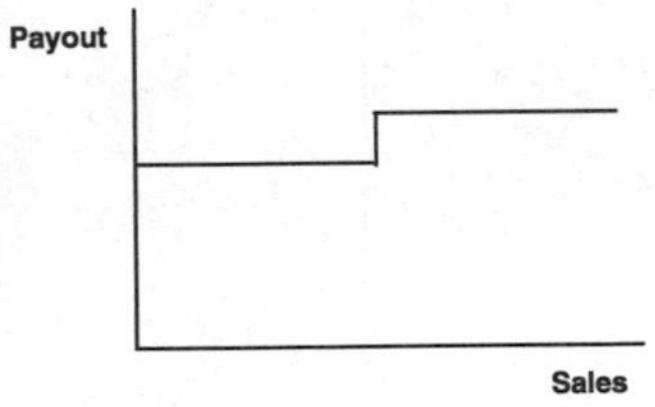 Payout / Sales<br>Single bonus paid upon goal achievement | • $10,000 bonus upon goal achievement |
| | 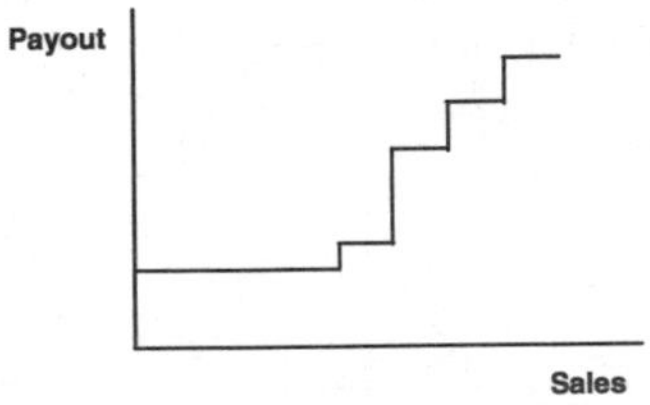 Payout / Sales<br>Multiple bonuses paid upon hitting several gates | • $2,500 bonus at 95% of goal<br>• $10,000 bonus at 100% of goal<br>• $5,000 bonus for each 5% above goal |

(continues)

**Figure 10-25.** Continued.

| *Option* | *Description* | *Incentive Plan Illustration* |
|---|---|---|
| **Commission** | Commissions are continuous incentive payments for achievement.<br>Payout / Sales<br>Commission from the first dollar of sales | • 3% commission for every dollar sold |
| | 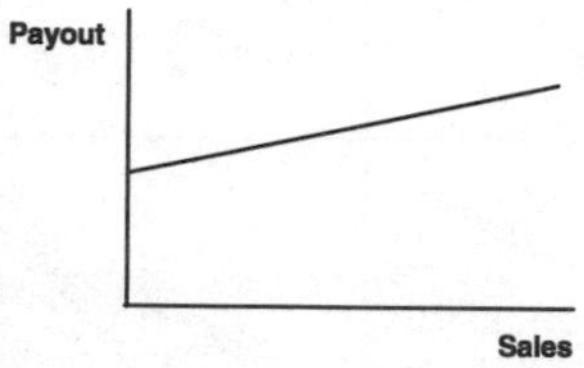 Payout / Sales<br>Salary plus commission | • $25,000 salary plus 2% commission for every dollar sold |
| | 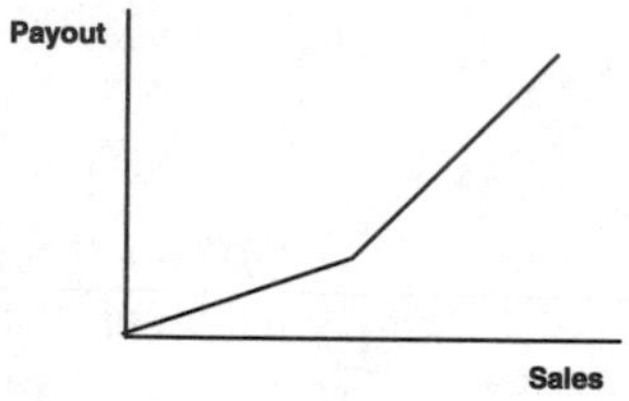 Payout / Sales<br>Multiple commission rates based upon target attainment | • 1% commission up to target<br>• 6% commission on every dollar above target |
| **Mixed** | A mixed incentive plan includes both bonuses and commissions. 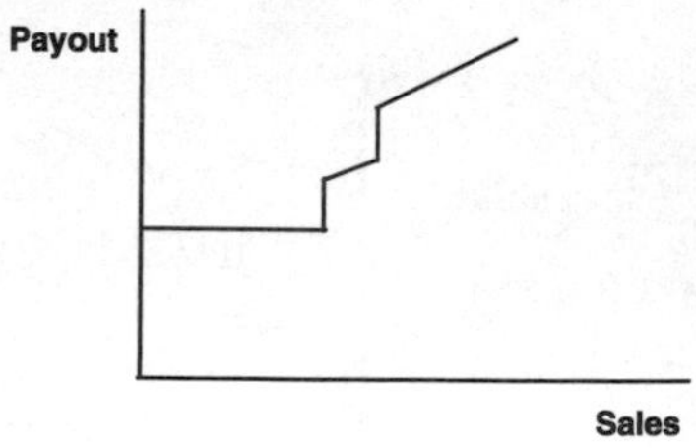<br>Payout / Sales | • Salary up to $1 million in sales<br>• $10,000 bonus plus 1% for sales above $1 million, and $12,000 bonus plus 2% for sales above $1.2 million<br><br>Another way to view this plan is:<br>• Salary up to $1 million in sales<br>• 1% on all sales once $1 million has been achieved<br>• 2% on all sales once $1.2 million has been achieved |

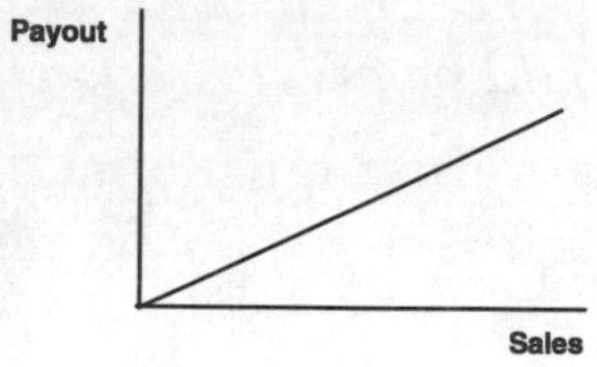

**Figure 10-26.** Criteria for Evaluating Whether a Bonus or Commission Plan Is Most Appropriate.

| *Perspective* | *Bonus Plan* | *Commission Plan* |
|---|---|---|
| **Selling Process** | The selling process is complex.<br>A team-selling environment exists.<br>A long selling cycle exists.<br>The marketplace has low to moderate sales force causality.<br>The product line has high carryover sales. | The selling process is simple.<br>An individual selling environment exists.<br>A short selling cycle exists.<br>The marketplace has high sales force causality.<br>The product line has low carryover sales. |
| **Sales Force Culture** | Sales effort control is possible and desired.<br>Cost control is not essential. | It is difficult to control the selling effort of the field force.<br>Cost control is needed. It is important to hold costs at a specified percentage of sales. |
| **Sales Management** | Performance measures are complex.<br>Multiple performance measures are used.<br>The company is able to set fair, realistic, and measurable goals.<br>Sales territories are inherently unequal. | Performance measures are simple.<br>A single performance measure is used.<br>The company has a strong revenue focus.<br>Sales territories are balanced or all territories have unlimited potential. |

tween performance and payout. The major types are described in Figure 10-27.

Each performance-payout relationship has advantages and disadvantages. Figure 10-28 compares performance-payout options and indicates the extent to which they help to achieve company sales force objectives. This ranking of the plans will be accurate in a majority of cases, but it is impossible to generalize accurately for all possible environments.

Here is a detailed look at how the various plans affect each objective.

*Objective: Rewarding Top Performers.* Progressive plans pay higher rates for higher sales, and high performers usually exceed goals and conse-

**Figure 10-27.** Types of Performance-Payout Relationships.

| *Option* | *Description* | *Incentive Plan Illustration* |
|---|---|---|
| **Linear payout** | The linear payout plan, or constant plan, pays the same rate for each level of achievement, e.g., each dollar of sales. The payout can begin with the first dollar or begin when a goal has been attained. It can be paid with or without salary. 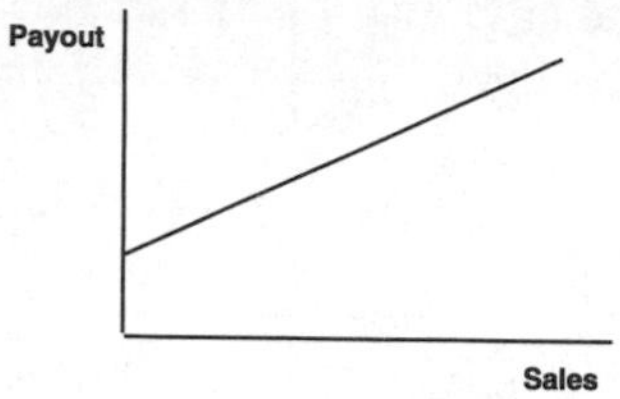<br>Payout / Sales | • Salary plus 3% commission on gross sales. |
| **Progressive payout** | Progressive plans pay different rates at different levels of sales, with the payout rate increasing as sales increase. 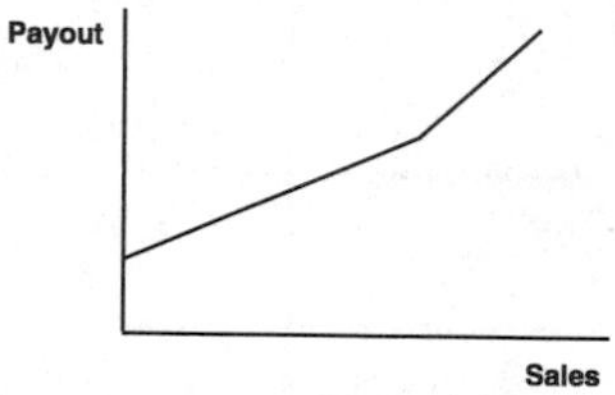<br>Payout / Sales | • Salary plus 2% commission to quota and 5% commission above quota. |
| **Regressive payout** | Regressive plans pay lower rates as sales increase. Plans that are capped (the salesperson can't earn more than a certain amount) are regressive plans. 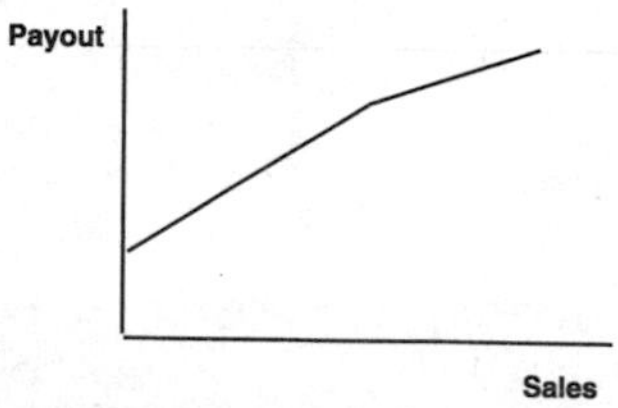<br>Payout / Sales | • Salary plus 3% commission on all sales up to $1 million and 1% commission on all sales over $1 million. |
| **Mixed** | Mixed plans have a combination of higher and lower rates as sales increase. The best mixed plans tend to be S-shaped, with the territory goal right in the center of the S. 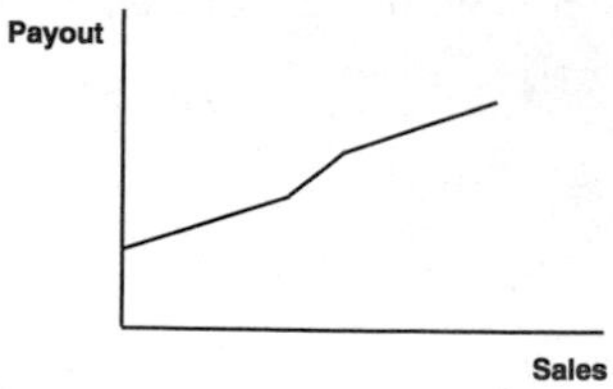<br>Payout / Sales | • Salary plus 2% commission for all sales up to $1 million, 3% commission on all sales over $1 million and less than $1.2 million, and 1% commission on all sales over $1.2 million. (The territory goal is $1.1 million.) |

**Figure 10-28.** Criteria for Evaluating Alternative Performance-Payout Relationships.

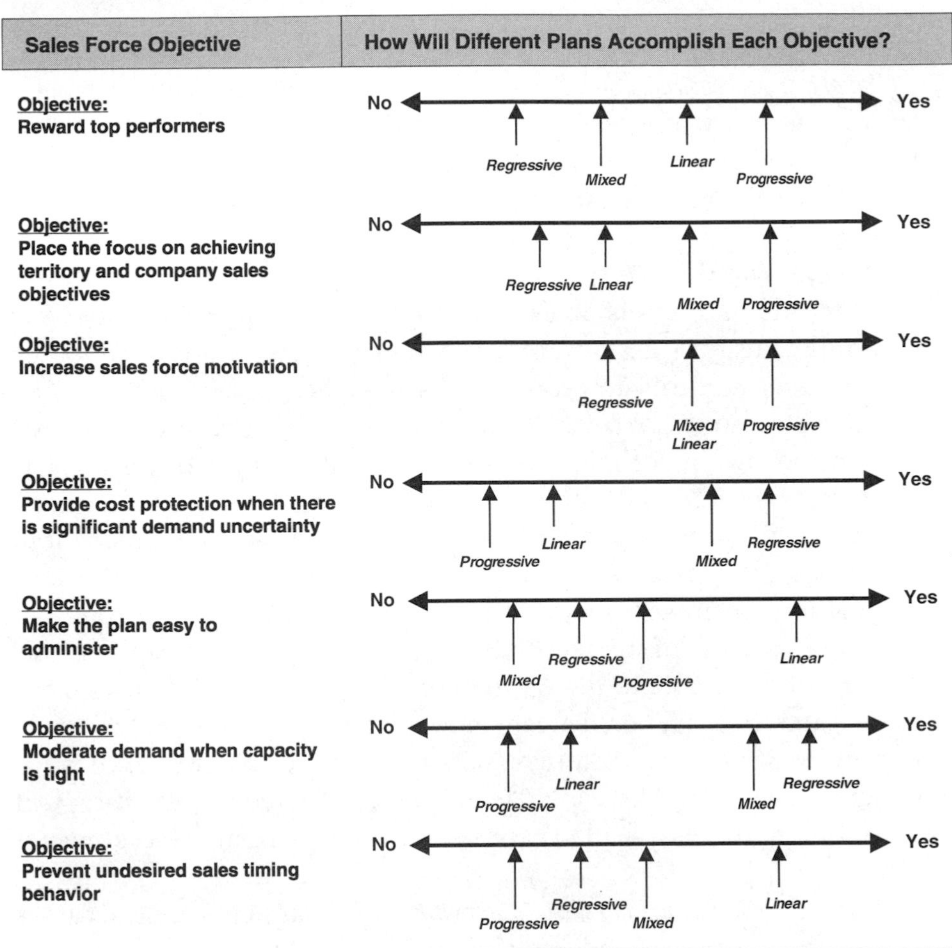


quently make more money. Regressive plans discourage the high performers, since they have to work disproportionately harder for less income. Why do it? Holding sales until the next period may be a better strategy.

*Objective: Achieving Territory and Company Sales Objectives.* Progressive plans and mixed plans encourage salespeople to reach gates where they receive higher payout levels. When territory gates are tied to company targets, the company is more likely to achieve its targets. The linear plan does not specify a territory goal, and salespeople will continue to sell if their commission rate is high enough. However, they may be unaware of their company's success or failure. Regressive plans encourage salespeople to hoard sales for the next period if they are in the regressive portion of the payout curve. This behavior lowers the likelihood of attaining company goals.

*Objective: Increasing Sales Force Motivation.* Progressive plans are the most motivating, while regressive plans are the least motivating. However, even progressive plans can be demotivating if imprecise quota setting leads to unreachable targets, making high payouts unattainable.

*Objective: Providing Cost Protection in Volatile Markets.* Goal setting in highly volatile markets is challenging. Goals that are set too low lead to windfall gains for the sales force when progressive plans are adopted. In linear plans, commission rates that are predicated on uncertain volume forecasts also lead to excessive earnings if the original volume estimates are too low. In both of these cases, the sales force can earn money well in excess of what their performance warrants. Regressive and mixed plans contain the company's exposure, and capped plans contain it even more dramatically.

Excessive earnings and self-funding plans are two conditions that can coexist. Even if progressive plans lead to excessive earnings, they are self-funding to an extent. As the company covers fixed costs, commission rates rise. Hence, salespeople earn more when the company can afford to pay more. Although costs may not be controlled, they can be covered. Also, since salespeople are likely to have diminishing utility for money, progressive plans encourage them as their interest wanes.

*Objective: Making the Plan Easy to Administer.* Linear plans are the easiest to compute, administer, and explain.

*Objective: Moderating Demand When Capacity Is Tight.* Regressive and mixed plans are best if there is a serious limitation on production or delivery capacity, and the company cannot deliver as much as the sales force can sell. Salespeople are discouraged if they generate a sale that cannot be consummated. Regressive plans discourage overselling.

*Objective: Preventing Undesired Sales Timing Behavior.* Progressive and regressive plans can lead to undesired sales timing behavior. Under a progressive plan, a salesperson who thinks she cannot make the quota or goal in one period can delay sales until the next period. Or, the salesperson may hustle at the end of the year when commission is high, then take a long "at-work" vacation in January and February because he hasn't earned his way to the next bracket yet. Even though a strong performance in January and February goes a long way toward improving the annual performance, salespeople frequently behave this way. This selling behavior can wreak havoc with production scheduling.

With a regressive plan, a salesperson who has made goal stops at the goal and hoards sales for the next period to receive a higher payout.

**Decision 4: When Does the Incentive Payment Begin?** The possibilities regarding when to begin incentive payments are described in Figure 10-29.

Typically, incentive plans that begin with the first dollar are highly commission-based. This type of plan is most appropriate in environments where the skill, motivation, and efforts of individual salespeople determine sales, and where the performance of each salesperson can be measured effectively.

For goal-centered compensation plans, the decision as to whether to begin paying at goal or at some fraction of goal is complex. Examine the situation from the following perspectives to reach a decision: the company perspective, the people and culture perspective, and the marketplace perspective.

**Figure 10-29.** Options for When to Begin Incentive Payments.

| *Option* | *Description* | *Incentive Plan Illustration* |
|---|---|---|
| Incentive payment begins with first dollar. | The incentive payment commences with the first sale. These plans are usually highly commission-based. They may or may not have a salary component. If they do not have a salary, the plans are called 100% commission. | • $1,500 for every unit sold.<br>• $20,000 salary plus $1,000 for every unit sold. |
| Incentive payment begins at goal. | The bonus or commission plan kicks in when the salesperson achieves his or her territory goal. | • Salary plus $15,000 bonus when goal is attained, plus 1% commission on all sales above goal. |
| Incentive payment begins at some fraction of goal. | The bonus or commission plan kicks in when the salesperson achieves some fraction of his or her territory goal. There are usually other incentive payments at goal and at other levels above goal. | • Salary up to 90% of goal, 2% commission on all sales between 90 and 100% of goal, and 3% commission on all sales beyond 100% of goal. |

*Company Perspective.* "The goal is the goal—we are not successful unless we make goal. So, why should we ever pay incentives if the goal has not been achieved?" This is a view that is expressed by many sales force managers. This logic suggests that incentives should be paid based on company success. If the company does well, the sales force shares in the success.

*People and Culture Perspective.* Since salespeople usually work alone, there are few opportunities for management to acknowledge their success. Receiving a bonus or reaching a higher commission gate is a visible and vital way in which salespeople are rewarded for their success. If the gates are set too high and only a few people achieve them, the message to the sales force is that it failed. If this failure is due to the goals being unattainable, the salespeople feel like victims. Even if the company hits its goal and the territory goals add up to exactly the company goal, half of the sales force will typically not make its target. Thus, half of the members of the sales force will view themselves as failures. People do not like to fail, and excessive unwarranted failure leads to a morale crisis. Behavioral science experiments show that groups perform better if they feel successful. A good rule of thumb is to make sure that at least 70 percent of the sales force receives some sort of incentive payout. If less than 70 percent of the sales force deserves an incentive payout, the problem is larger than an incentive compensation issue. It is likely that there are problems with hiring, training, or management.

Another perspective suggests that people should be rewarded for the skills, knowledge, and effort they bring to the job. A territory's sales can be divided into three parts. The first part is the free sales. These are the sales that would still exist if the sales territory went vacant for the year. (The concept of free sales was introduced earlier in this chapter.) The second part is the average sales. These are the sales that will exist if the salesperson applies average effort and has average capabilities. Average sales deserve a fair wage. Incentives should be paid on the third part, or sales above average. Figure 10-30 displays these concepts.

Based on the people and culture perspectives, incentive pay should commence at a level that takes into account free sales, average sales, and the objective of minimizing perceived failure. Incentives for free sales are merely "hidden salary." Average sales may be difficult to estimate—85 to 95 percent of goal is a good proxy. Remember, a sales force is likely to be motivated when at least 70 percent of its members receive an incentive payout.

**Figure 10-30.** A Perspective on Sales Force Incentives—Pay Incentives for Sales above Free Sales and Average Sales.

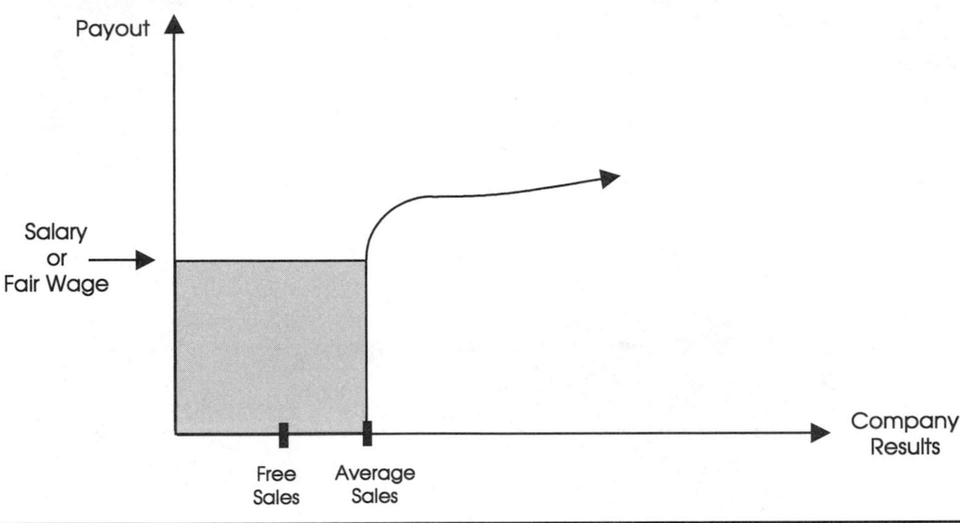


*Marketplace Perspective.* Marketplace volatility affects when incentive payments should begin. More salespeople are likely to perform below target in an uncertain market than in a certain market. This is due to the vagaries of the market rather than to a lack of skill, capabilities, and effort on the part of the salespeople. An intelligent incentive compensation plan acknowledges the statistical uncertainty in these markets; incentive pay begins at a lower level and rises more slowly than in a high-certainty market. This is how the advertising sales department of the *New York Times* addresses market volatility. The incentive plan gives each salesperson a goal, and the point at which the plan begins to pay varies by market team. Teams in the most predictable markets begin earning incentives at 95 percent of goal. However, teams in the most volatile markets begin earning incentives at just 80 percent of goal, but with a lower bonus rate. Thus, the same amount of money is spread across a wider target to compensate for the unpredictability. The payout scheme is shown in the graph in Figure 10-31. This sales force perceives this plan as fair and motivational. The company provides incentives successfully, despite volatility.

**Decision 5: Should the Incentive Compensation Plan Be Capped?** Some incentive plans place a limit on salespeople's earnings and others do not. Figure 10-32 provides a description of the options.

A capped incentive plan is a conspicuous example of a regressive

**Figure 10-31.** Incentive Payout Schemes That Acknowledge Uncertainty in Markets.

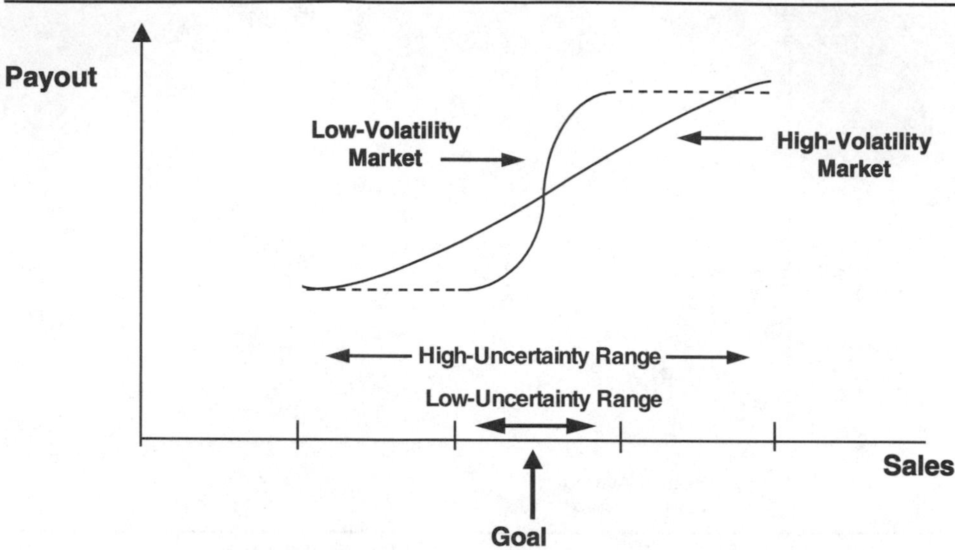


plan. Caps are most useful in a commission-based plan. Salary plans are capped by definition, and bonuses have a built-in cap because they usually stop at a high level of sales achievement.

A capped plan dampens the motivation of top performers. Salespeople will stop working hard if they feel that they can't earn any incremental income from their efforts, and they may hold sales over to the next period if they feel that those sales will earn incremental income in that period. In addition, if caps are reached too easily, the incentive plan becomes a salary plan.

Despite the danger of damaging the motivation of hard workers, income caps have several advantages. Using an income cap prevents

**Figure 10-32.** Capped versus Uncapped Incentive Plans.

| *Option* | *Description* | *Incentive Plan Illustration* |
|---|---|---|
| Capped incentive plan | The amount of money that a salesperson can earn in a single month, quarter, or year is limited to a specific amount called the "Cap". | • 1% commissions on all sales beginning with the first dollar up to 120% of goal; additional income stops at 120% of goal. |
| Uncapped incentive plan | A salesperson can earn an unlimited amount of money in a month, quarter, or year. | • 1% commissions on all sales beginning with the first dollar. |

unearned sales force windfalls. A sales force will make excessive income if the target income is set for a sales level that is easily attainable. This happens with poor forecasting or unanticipated market factors, such as market growth, weak competition, or significant product demand. When results are not clearly related to effort, rewards appear unfair and arbitrary.

Caps can moderate sales if product availability is limited. They also smooth income in highly volatile markets.

**Decision 6: Should Incentives Be Based on a Single Measure or Multiple Measures? How Can Multiple Measures Be Incorporated into an Incentive Plan?** Guidelines for selecting the most appropriate measures for incentive planning were presented earlier in the chapter. The guidelines contrasted activity, customer satisfaction, and company result measures, and stressed using no more than three measures in order to keep the plan simple. Several plan options incorporating multiple measures are described in Figure 10-33.

*The Weighted-Measures Approach.* The weighted-measures approach reduces multiple performance measures to a single measure by attaching weights to each independent measure and aggregating them. Since the individual metrics may be measured on different scales, taking a straight weighted average is usually not advised. For example, averaging sales and market share produces a number that is not meaningful. Individual measures need to be normalized first so that adding the weighted measures makes sense. Normalizing in terms of goal attainment is a good way to accomplish this when a goal-centered incentive plan is used. The example in Figure 10-34 shows how to calculate a weighted measure that integrates the sales of three products.

The approach is similar even if different measures are used instead of product revenue achievement for different products. Sales revenue, profit contribution, market share, and call activity could replace products A, B, and C in the table in Figure 10-34.

*The Matrix Approach.* The matrix approach integrates two measures into an incentive plan. An advantage of a matrix is that it can make complex plans concrete. The matrix in Figure 10-35 shows the payout that a salesperson will receive for different outcomes of the row and column measures.

In the matrix in Figure 10-35, the salesperson's payout depends on both the company's and the salesperson's performance. A matrix entry

**Figure 10-33.** Incentive Plan Options That Incorporate Multiple Measures.

| *Option* | *Description* | *Incentive Plan Illustration* |
|---|---|---|
| Single measure | The incentive compensation is based upon a single measure. | • Salary plus $5,000 bonus when the following gates are attained: 95, 100, 105, 110, 115, and 120% of sales goal. |
| Single measure with multiple qualifiers | A single measure drives incentive payout. The extent of payout depends upon the simultaneous achievement of product goals, customer goals, or activity goals. These subgoals are called qualifiers. | Salary plus a $5,000 bonus when the following gates are attained: 95, 100, 105, 110, 115, and 120% of sales goal. Three qualifier possibilities appear below:<br>• 25% increase in payout if the qualifiers for three product lines are achieved.<br>• 25% increase in payout if the qualifier for customer satisfaction is achieved.<br>• 25% increase in payout if several activity goals are achieved. |
| Multiple independent measures | The incentive compensation plan is based upon multiple measures. Incentives are calculated independently in terms of these measures. | Salary plus:<br>• $5,000 bonus when the following gates are attained: 95, 100, and 105% for Product A sales; and $3,000 bonus when the same gates are attained for Product B sales. |
| Multiple integrated measures | The incentive compensation plan is based upon multiple measures. These measures are used interdependently to calculate the incentive. | • The weighted-measures approach and the matrix approach are two methods for integrating multiple measures. Because of their complexity, they are discussed outside of this table. |

specifies the payout corresponding to the joint level of performance. The matrix entries are stated in terms of a multiplier that is multiplied by the target payout to determine the final payout. This is a conservative incentive plan; the company does not pay too much if it doesn't perform well—the company is protecting its downside.

The matrix plan in Figure 10-36 is designed to motivate salespeople to hold the line on price concessions to customers.

**Figure 10-34.** An Illustration of the Weighted-Measures Approach.

| *Product* | *Weight (Weights Used in the Incentive Plan)* | *Percent of Goal Attained (Example)* | *Weighted Goal Attained (Calculation)* |
|---|---|---|---|
| A | 50% | 110% | 55% |
| B | 30% | 90% | 27% |
| C | 20% | 105% | 21% |
| | | Overall Goal Achievement (calculated by summing the weighted goal attainment of the three products) → | 103% |

One of the most innovative incentive plans is a matrix suggested by Jacob Gonik for IBM in Brazil. The plan motivates salespeople to forecast territory sales accurately. The plan matrix is shown in Figure 10-37.

The rows represent the salesperson's forecast at the start of the planning period, and the columns represent the actual territory sales at the end of the period. The salesperson's payout depends on both his or her forecast and the actual sales. Having predicted sales, the salesperson is restricted to one of the rows. Notice that the numbers in each row are increasing. Therefore, the salesperson receives increasing compensation as he or she increases sales. Thus, the salesperson should be mo-

**Figure 10-35.** Incentive Payout Matrix Considering Both Salesperson and Company Performance.

| Company Performance (% of Objective) | Salesperson Performance (% of Objective): 80% | 90% | 100% | 110% | 120% |
|---|---|---|---|---|---|
| 80% | 0.2 | 0.4 | 0.8 | 1.2 | 1.7 |
| 90% | 0.3 | 0.5 | 0.9 | 1.3 | 1.8 |
| 100% | 0.4 | 0.7 | 1.0 | 1.5 | 2.0 |
| 110% | 0.6 | 0.8 | 1.1 | 1.6 | 2.1 |
| 120% | 0.7 | 0.9 | 1.2 | 1.7 | 2.2 |

Multiple of Target Payout

Target Payout = $25,000

**Figure 10-36.** Incentive Payout Matrix That Discourages Pricing Discounts.

Territory Sales ($ Millions)

| Pricing Discount (Coverage Across All Business) | 1.3 | 1.5 | 1.7 | 1.9 |
|---|---|---|---|---|
| 19.0% | 1.3 | 1.5 | 1.7 | 1.9 |
| 22.0% | 0.9 | 1.1 | 1.3 | 1.5 |
| 25.0% | 0.5 | 0.7 | 0.9 | 1.1 |
| 28.0% | 0.1 | 0.3 | 0.5 | 0.7 |

Multiple of Target Payout

Target Payout = $25,000

tivated to continue selling as much as possible. On the other hand, the columns are developed so that the largest payout appears in the row where the actual sales match the salesperson's forecast. Hence, salespeople earn the most when they forecast accurately.

With traditional incentive plans, salespeople do not have an incentive to forecast accurately because their incentive payout is tied to total sales volume. A salesperson is likely to forecast low so that he or she can earn more money and appear to be a star performer. With the Gonik plan, the sales force is rewarded for both performance and a good forecast. This plan is especially useful when the company relies on the sales force forecast in setting its production and manufacturing requirements. The plan also encourages the sales force to plan better.

The Gonik plan applies real economic costs to the sales force. Underforecasting results in stockouts, and overforecasting produces extra

**Figure 10-37.** Incentive Payout Matrix That Encourages Accurate Forecasting.

Sales Achieved ($ Millions)

| Sales Objective | 2.50 | 2.75 | 3.00 | 3.25 | 3.50 | 3.75 |
|---|---|---|---|---|---|---|
| 3.50 | 10.5 | 17.8 | 27.3 | 40.6 | **62.0** | 70.6 |
| 3.25 | 12.3 | 20.9 | 32.1 | **47.7** | 57.2 | 65.2 |
| 3.00 | 14.5 | 24.6 | **37.7** | 44.0 | 52.8 | 60.2 |
| 2.75 | 17.0 | **28.9** | 34.8 | 40.6 | 48.7 | 55.5 |
| 2.50 | **20.3** | 26.6 | 32.0 | 37.5 | 44.9 | 51.2 |

Payout Matrix
(Salesperson Picks the Objective)

inventory. The incentive payout differences down the columns incorporate some fraction of these costs. As a result, the sales force shares in the real costs of stockouts and inventory.

This is an innovative and useful type of plan; however, it has one disadvantage: It is complicated and can be difficult to explain to a sales force.

*The Impact of Aggregation.* When choosing between basing incentives independently on separate performance measures or aggregating the measures and basing the total incentive payout on the aggregate measure, consider the following: An incentive payout based on an aggregate measure almost always pays out less than the sum of the payouts of disaggregated measures for the same level of territory sales. The example shown in Figure 10-38 illustrates this point.

Plan A separates incentives for the two product groups. Plan B integrates sales from both product groups and uses total sales to determine the salesperson's payout. The impact of sales uncertainty multiplies as the number of independent plan components increases. In this example, $1,000,000 of sales could cost $55,000 in compensation under plan A, or it could cost $50,000 under plan B.

**Decision 7: Should the Compensation Plan Include Individual or Team Incentives?** A sales team is a cooperating group of individuals who work

**Figure 10-38.** A Comparison of Payouts Using Aggregated Versus Disaggregated Measures.

| *Plan A* | *Objective* | *Commission Below Objective* | *Commission Above Objective* | *Actual Sales* | *Payout* |
|---|---|---|---|---|---|
| Product Group 1 | $500,000 | 5% | 10% | $400,000 | $20,000 |
| Product Group 2 | $500,000 | 5% | 10% | $600,000 | $35,000 |
| Total | $1,000,000 | | | $1,000,000 | $55,000 |

| *Plan B* | *Objective* | *Commission Below Objective* | *Commission Above Objective* | *Actual Sales* | *Payout* |
|---|---|---|---|---|---|
| All Products | $1,000,000 | 5% | 10% | $1,000,000 | $50,000 |

synergistically to satisfy customer needs and sell the firm's products or services. *Dependence* and *synergy* are key words that describe effective teams. Dependence implies that individual team members are unable to perform all of the tasks that make up the most appropriate selling process. Team members need each other. A large systems sell may require software, hardware, applications, and customer and financing knowledge and capabilities. Synergy suggests that the team's success is greater than the sum of the individual team members' successes. Team members bring different skills and knowledge, they share the ownership of the outcome, and they enjoy their social interaction. High-performance teams also share best selling practices.

A team-based incentive plan and an option including a team component are described in Figure 10-39. Criteria for determining when team-based incentive plans are most appropriate appear in Figure 10-40.

Incentives awarded to the team need to be split among the members. There are at least three ways to split the team incentive. The equal-shares approach splits the team reward equally. It assumes that each team participant contributed fairly to achieve the team's goals. Alternatively, the sales manager can decide how to split the incentive. This approach assumes that the manager is close enough to the team to decide the apportionment. Finally, the team can decide. Each member votes on how to split the incentive among all team members. The sales

**Figure 10-39.** A Comparison of Individual and Team-Based Incentive Plans.

| *Option* | *Description* | *Incentive Plan Illustration* |
|---|---|---|
| Individual incentive plan | Rewards and incentive payments are based entirely on individual performance. | • The individual receives a $15,000 bonus upon goal attainment. |
| Team-based incentive plan | Rewards and incentive payments are based entirely on team performance. | • The team receives a $30,000 bonus upon goal attainment. |
| Combination incentive plan | Sales and profit creation are primarily due to the skills and effort of the individual salesperson. Individual measurement is also available. A team incentive is included primarily for knowledge and best practice sharing as well as job enrichment. | • The individual receives a $15,000 bonus upon goal attainment and a $5,000 supplement if the region achieves its goal. |

**Figure 10-40.** Conditions Favoring Individual Versus Team-Based Incentives.

| *Conditions Favoring an Individual Incentive Plan* ← | *Conditions Favoring a Team-Based Incentive Plan* → |
|---|---|
| Sales results are determined primarily by the skills, capabilities, and effort of the individual salesperson (high salesperson causality). | Sales results are determined primarily by the skills, capabilities, and effort of the sales team (high sales team causality), and it is hard to disentangle the contributions of individual participants. |
| Good performance measurement is available at the salesperson level. | Good performance measurement is available at the sales team level. Measures at the individual level are not very reliable. |
| The firm wants to encourage extraordinary individual effort, to hold the salesperson accountable for the performance of the sales territory, and to avoid the possibility of "free riders." | Teamwork and cooperation are part of the corporate mantra. Management feels that teamwork leads to improved service quality, staffing flexibility, employee job satisfaction, increased productivity, and a sense of unity. |
| Individual performance has higher variability (across time and across people) than team performance. An individual incentive plan allows for better discrimination between the top performers and the bottom performers. | Team performance has lower variability (across time and across people) than individual performance. This leads to more stability and security, as well as a perception of fairness and equity. |

manager then evaluates the responses to determine the final incentive split. This approach typically identifies the free riders and eliminates them from the team.

**Decision 8: How Frequently Should Incentives Be Paid?** Companies pay incentives semimonthly, monthly, quarterly, semiannually, and annually. Monthly, quarterly, and annual payments are the most popular. About one-third of all firms use each of these three methods. Commission-based plans usually pay more often while bonus-based plans pay less often.

Different levels of frequency have advantages and disadvantages, as displayed in Figure 10-41.

Year-to-date incentive plans can overcome some of the weaknesses associated with plans that pay frequently. These plans pay out on cumulative results as the year progresses. Salespeople have no incentive to hoard sales for the subsequent period. The cumulative plan smoothes

**Figure 10-41.** The Advantages of Frequent Versus Infrequent Incentive Payments.

| *Advantages of Frequent Payments (Monthly or Quarterly)* | *Advantages of Infrequent Payments (Semiannually or Annually)* |
|---|---|
| • Salespeople receive frequent feedback and rewards when the selling cycle is short.<br>• Rewards are in closer time proximity to the successes that spawned the reward.<br>• Successful behavior is reinforced. Motivation is increased.<br>• Sales force goals and incentive payments are adjusted quickly in volatile markets. | • Long selling cycles require long payment cycles.<br>• Payments at bonus time are larger and have greater impact.<br>• Administrative costs are lower.<br>• It is easier to set goals and quotas less often. Goal setting is more accurate for longer time periods.<br>• Sufficient time is allowed for the plan's objectives to drive sales force behavior.<br>• Performance is more stable because short-term sales variations are smoothed over the longer time horizon.<br>• Management ensures that it will not overpay the sales force, since incentive payments are not made until the annual revenues are computed. The company will not need to ask for a refund from the sales force.<br>• The company keeps the time value of money. |

the variability that occurs when short time periods are employed. Finally, early overpayment is avoided by holding back some of the payment until later periods. For example, a quarterly payment schedule may look like the one shown in Figure 10-42.

## A Compensation Adviser

As described so far in this chapter, compensation plan design includes decisions regarding the compensation level and mix (salary versus incentive), the measures of performance, and performance-payout relationships. Designing a good plan is a challenge. However, *implementing* a new plan is even more challenging. This section provides advice on how to implement successfully in a number of common situations.

**Figure 10-42.** Incentive Payout Schedule That Avoids Early Overpayment.

| *Payment Schedule* | *Cumulative Payment* |
|---|---|
| First-quarter payment | 15% of annualized incentive payment based on first-quarter results. |
| Second-quarter payment | 35% of annualized incentive payment based on first- and second-quarter results. |
| Third-quarter payment | 60% of annualized incentive payment based on first-, second-, and third-quarter results. |
| Fourth-quarter payment | 100% of incentive payment based on the year's results. |

## How to Change from One Compensation Plan to Another

Changing compensation plans can be difficult. The most important step is to involve the people affected. For a successful transition, communicate with the salespeople and solicit their input. If the new plan is based on new performance measures, put the new measures in place first, then three to nine months later attach the compensation plan. This gives the sales force and the sales support groups time to establish the veracity of the new measures.

Changing from a salary plan to a variable plan is particularly difficult. One way to make this transition is to hold back on raises and use the money saved for incentive pay. Another option is to cut salary and use the savings to fund incentives. When base pay is reduced, salespeople should earn more money under the new plan, as long as they make their sales goal. For example, the plan shown in Figure 10-43 gives back the lost salary plus some, as long as the objective is reached.

Letting the sales force vote on the amount of salary that is converted to incentives enhances buy-in. Finally, show the salespeople how much they would have earned last year with the new plan. If the plan has been designed well, the good salespeople should have made more money.

**Figure 10-43.** Example of a Plan That Eases the Transition From a Salaried to a Variable Compensation Plan.

| | *Year 1* | *Year 2* |
|---|---|---|
| **Salary Adjustment** | ($5,000) | ($5,000) |
| **Bonus Attainable at Territory Goal** | $6,250 | $12,500 |

Changing from a variable plan to a salary plan is easier if the plan is a flat commission with well-balanced territories. Bite the bullet and pay highfliers a guaranteed amount for a year, but do careful impact studies. It is useful to segment the salespeople (e.g., risk takers, risk avoiders, passives, assertives) to anticipate their reaction to the new plan.

Some compensation features are more permanent than others are. Changing compensation plans can be easy, if the right parts of the plans are changed. Salary levels are particularly difficult to decrease.

The following is a list of features, ranked from "most difficult to change" to "least permanent":

Total compensation levels
Commissioned plan
Bonus plan
Salary plan
Bonus levels
Commission rates

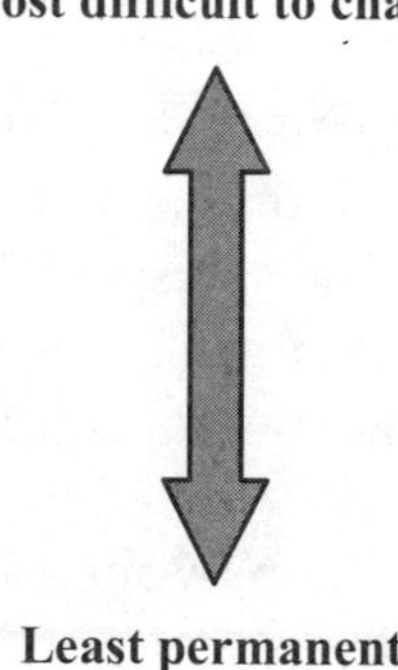


## Keep Compensation Plans Simple

As discussed earlier in this chapter, complex plans affect the salesperson's perception of causality by disassociating the selling effort from the rewards of selling. Complex plans also have large administrative costs, because someone has to do the work to determine the correct compensation for the sales force. Finally, complicated plans can cause salespeople to worry too much about the company's expectations, rather than taking care of the customer. Consider the two plans described in Figure 10-44. Which one communicates company expectations more clearly?

There may be many sales force objectives: product, customer, and professional. This leads to plan complexity. Complex plans are more likely to have varied interpretations that lead to undesirable behaviors. Additionally, complex plans create work for the sales force. Interpreting the plan is not the most productive way for salespeople to spend their time. A well-designed plan fits on a card small enough to be carried around in the salesperson's wallet.

**Figure 10-44.** A Comparison of a Simple and a Complex Incentive Plan.

**How clear is the link between performance and rewards?**

**Plan A**
The salesperson is paid 2.5% commission until the sales objective is reached. The commission rate for sales above objective is 7.5%.

**Plan B**
The district contains ten salespeople. If the district reaches 95% of objective, there is $5,000 in the bonus pool. If the district reaches 100% of objective, there is $30,000 in the pool. The pool increases by $2,000 for each additional percent achieved over 100% of goal. If the company fails to meet its profitability goal, the pool is reduced by $5,000. The pool is divided among salespeople at the district manager's discretion, subject to the national sales manager's approval.

## Contests

> "We work for money, but we strive for plaques."
>
> —Andy Anderson

Incentives often include contests. A good contest improves morale and results immensely without a large cost. A little variety and excitement go a long way. Of course, the bonus or commission plan can have contest elements as well. A bonus can be a vacation trip. A commission structure can have the feel of a contest if labels are given to each bonus level or change in commission rate. Achieving 90 percent of goal is "threshold" or "bronze," 100 percent of goal is "success" or "silver," and 110 percent of goal is "excellence" or "gold."

To make contests work, the key idea is focus. Contests must focus on revenue, product, region, and time. They must be tied to a specific event, over a specific area, and for a specific short time. Making sales contests effective requires organization and creativity. Contests are more of an art than a science. Figure 10-45 provides some guidelines to keep in mind.

### How to Deal with Windfalls

The sales force can never be too successful, but the compensation plan and forecasting can be very poor. If the sales force is blasting past plan and compensation is in the stratosphere, a big problem is on the way: next year. The euphoria of great success blinds a sales force to its dangers. Huge success one year sets expectations for compensation forever. Salespeople may feel entitled to $50,000 per quarter. Keeping a high cost structure makes the company noncompetitive in the long run. It may prevent needed expansion. Salespeople feel that management is

**Figure 10-45.** Guidelines for Successful Contests.

| | |
|---|---|
| **Themes** | Invent a fun theme for the contest. Keep the prizes and slogans consistent with the theme. |
| **Only a few per year** | Do not have too many contests in a year. More than quarterly is over the limit. Keep the selling cycle in mind. If the contest is too short, credit will be given to salespeople who earned the sale last year but who are getting the contract today. In addition, too many themes get confusing. Keep it focused. |
| **Many goals** | Consider several levels of goals. If an individual salesperson does not have the sales to win, perhaps she or he can help the district's or region's goal. |
| **Challenging goals** | Make the contest goals challenging. No one should win without effort. The number of planned winners depends on the company culture. Some companies may want everyone to win so that they feel included. Others may want only a handful of stellar performers to win. There is a delicate balance, since difficult goals may lead to high-pressure tactics and less concern for the customer's interests. However, the harder the goals, the higher the performance will be. People work harder with a challenging goal than if they are told to "do your best." |
| **Measure** | Measure results as well as possible. Look at a graph of sales before, during, and after the contest to see the full effects. People work better with feedback and a tracking system. |
| **Deliver on promises** | Be careful not to promise rewards that cannot be delivered. A lot of lead time is needed to plan a trip to Hawaii for a large group. |
| **Management involvement** | Management attention is crucial. Make sure that awards are public and given by important people in the organization. |
| **More than money** | Consider a wide range of incentives, not just money. Set unusual goals, such as a contest that pays for product knowledge. Examples include employee of the month, a special parking place, or recognition in a monthly newsletter. Other creative ideas include amusement park tickets for the entire family, tickets to a special concert or sporting event, gift certificates to a favorite store, and currency for an auction at the annual company picnic. |
| **Set goals carefully** | The sales force must accept the goals. Also, be sure the reward is something that is important to salespeople. |
| **Spread success around** | Everyone should have a chance to win, but winning should not be easy. There should be significant gaps in performance so that those who did not win understand why. |

stealing their territory. If sales are extremely high, salespeople will attribute the success to their own efforts, but other factors are also important. Poor forecasting, strong products, successful marketing execution, weak competition, growing markets, and luck are also factors. Try to avoid runaway success before it happens.

If windfall gains occur, consider the following strategies. First of all, reset quotas and goals. Generally, changing a quota or goal is not a happy event; it breaks an implicit contract with the sales force. If management has done a poor job of forecasting, and the salespeople are not doing well or are doing too well, the best remedy may be to change the quota or goal. Such decisions need to be symmetrical—goals need to be raised when the forecast is too low and lowered when the forecast is too high. Another option is to set quotas for shorter time horizons. Finally, consider anchoring salesperson compensation to a range.

If compensation adjustments occur in midstream in response to a windfall, they can jeopardize the quick growth and excitement that the windfall generates. As a result, it may be best to just share the gains with the sales force as promised. However, communication is key. Let people know that this is a windfall and that it is a "one-time" event that is not likely to occur in the future.

## Transition Situations May Require Transition Features

**New Salespeople.** New salespeople need time to learn the products and their territory before they can be fully effective. The compensation plan can provide a salary supplement in place of a portion of the incentive component until a salesperson is fully functional. Figure 10-46 presents an example of such a plan.

**Key Account Changes—Old Territory/New Territory.** In many industries, salespeople need in-depth customer knowledge in order to be effective. If an account is reassigned, this in-depth knowledge must be transferred to the new salesperson. Figure 10-47 shows an example of a compensation plan designed to encourage smooth account transitions between salespeople. With this plan, salespeople receive incentives

**Figure 10-46.** Sales Force Compensation Plan for New Salespeople.

| *Year* | *Base Annual Salary* | *Twelve-Month Salary Supplement* | *Target Twelve-Month Incentive* | *Payout Rate at 100%* |
|---|---|---|---|---|
| First year | $32,000 | $10,000 | $2,500 | $44,500 |
| Second year | $32,000 | $5,000 | $9,500 | $46,500 |
| Third year | $32,000 | 0 | $17,000 | $49,000 |

**Figure 10-47.** A Transition Compensation Plan.

| *Performance Measure* | *Weight* Q1 | Q2 | Q3 onwards |
|---|---|---|---|
| Current territory | 50% | 75% | 100% |
| Prior territory | 50% | 25% | 0% |

based on performance in their current andprior territories for a period of time. The "prior territory" component of the incentive phases out gradually as the transition is completed.

**Launching a New Product.** One company had an exciting new product. To assure a strong launch, the sales force received an extra large commission on sales of this product. The company's bread-and-butter products kept the old commission rate. The result? Sales of the new product were great, and most salespeople got huge commissions. However, sales of the existing products dropped precipitously, and since these products accounted for most of the company's sales, profits also fell.

Here are some ways to compensate salespeople when a new product is being launched:

- To launch hard, put the new product on commission for a short period. Use contests. Give everyone cash up front with the message that "we know you will make it happen."
- Use milestone bonuses. Give rewards for the first reorder or the first presentation.
- Compensate for forecasting difficulties by cutting the incentive interval. Use quarterly goals instead of annual goals.
- Change the incentive plan if it is not achieving desired results.

But make sure that there is plenty of incentive to protect strong existing products.

## Conclusion: An Incentive Plan Design Process

A good compensation plan is simple and predictable. It is easy to understand, so that people can link their performance with their pay. It is predictable, so that people can plan their efforts. A good plan is fair and flexible to accommodate new product launches and volatile markets. It is economical, yet competitive. Finally, it meets the needs of its three most important constituents: the customer, the sales force, and the company. The four-step process in Figure 10-48 shows how to develop the appropriate incentive plan.

**Figure 10-48.** An Incentive Plan Design Process.

| *Step* | *Description* |
|---|---|
| Collect information | • Develop and understand the most appropriate selling process.<br>• Establish plan objectives.<br>• Determine the advantages and limitations of the current plan.<br>• Understand labor markets and the market rate for the type of people that the company would like to attract.<br>• Talk to the sales force. Understand its concerns and its opinion of the current plan. Estimate the reaction to alternative plans. |
| Generate incentive plan options | Answer the following questions:<br>• How much should the salespeople be paid?<br>• What proportion of a salesperson's compensation should be incentive pay?<br>• What measures should be used to determine the incentive component of the salesperson's compensation?<br>• How should the incentive payment vary with measured performance? |
| Test the options | • Each option should be tested to estimate how the sales force will alter its behavior in response to the option, how customers will react to this behavior change, how each salesperson's pay will change with each option, and how the company's sales, market share, and profits will ultimately be affected. |
| Select the most appropriate option | • Keep it simple. Try to get it to fit on a single "incentive card." As an example:<br><br>Base Plan<br>Base Commission Rate: 4.2%<br>Rate Above Quarter-to-Date Objective: 6.7%<br>Quarterly Target Products Extra: 1.5%<br><br>Quarterly Bonuses<br>1% Discount Reduction: $1,200<br>Expense Control Target: $500<br>5 New @ $9,000 Each: $500<br>90% Retention: $500 |

# Chapter 11

# Setting Effective Goals and Objectives

This chapter focuses on setting sales force goals. Approximately 85 percent of U.S. companies establish formal goals for their salespeople. Experience shows that organizations and individuals who are goal-focused are more successful in the long run than those who do not set goals for themselves.

This chapter is designed to help you:

- Know when to set "soft" goals based on competencies and activities and when to set "hard" goals based on sales and profits
- Set goals in a volatile business environment with high uncertainty in predicting future performance
- Implement an objective, data-based process for setting territory-level goals that incorporates input from local sales management
- Realize the factors that correlate with territory sales and incorporate these factors into your goal-setting process
- Understand the best formulas and processes for setting territory goals using four potential goal-setting methods
- Involve field sales management in setting goals and tracking progress against those goals
- Ensure that goals are fair, realistic, and motivational

## Introduction

A vacationer who was in Vermont to see the fall colors was surprised to see dozens of targets painted on one of the traditional red barns. He stopped the car and got out to take a closer look. The vacationer was astonished to see a bullet hole in the center of each target. When the farmer came out of his barn holding his rifle, the vacationer said, "I've never seen shooting this good! How did you do it?" The farmer replied, "I shot first."

Unfortunately, we have to draw the target first when we set goals, objectives, or quotas for salespeople. Goal setting, like much of sales management, is part science and part art. Because goals are critical in performance evaluation and compensation, goal setting is a contentious business. It is difficult to develop a simple, fair, realistic, and motivational goal-setting system. Interestingly, both excellent and poor goals share a common feature: They reveal management expectations.

## What Do Goals Accomplish?

Goals energize salespeople and organizations. They signal direction and achievement. Organizations mobilize and extend themselves to achieve self-set goals for innovation, new product launches, productivity enhancement, and revenue or market share growth. Individuals strive to achieve their own goals and objectives. Organizations and individuals who are goal-focused are usually more successful in the long run than those who do not set goals for themselves. Michael Jordan, the famous basketball player, had a personal goal of scoring eight points in each quarter.

As Figure 11-1 shows, goal setting within the sales organization

**Figure 11-1.** The Impact of Sales Force Goals.

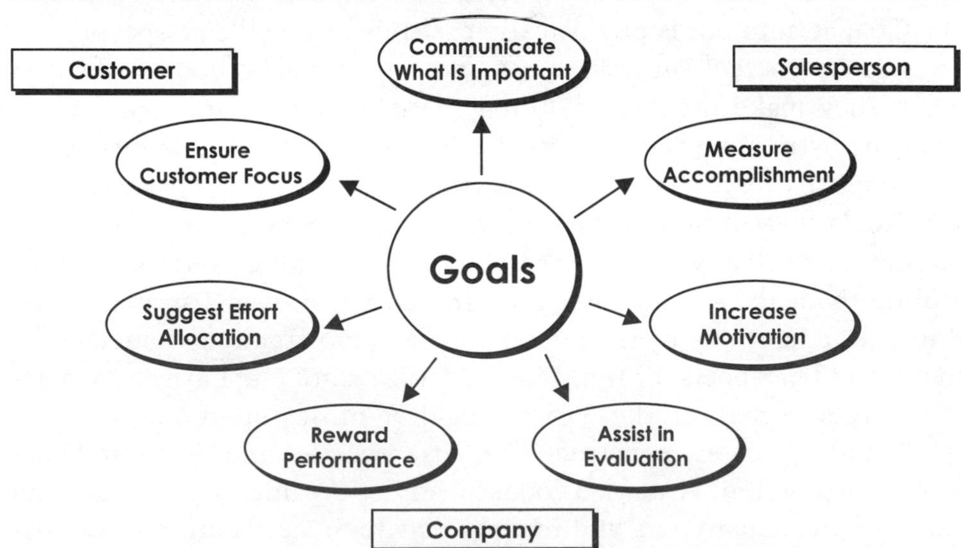

has an impact on the customer, the salespeople, and the company's results.

Organizations use goals to communicate their expectations and what they consider important. Typically, people take notice of goals. They receive special attention and treatment. By establishing a goal or an objective, management indicates that the dimension or outcome expressed in the goal is important for the firm.

Goals measure accomplishment. How does a person know if she or he is successful? Goals are a barometer; they signal achievement. People who achieve their goals are viewed as successful, and those who fail to achieve their goals are viewed as less than successful.

Everyone wants to be successful in some domain. Since goal achievement communicates success, goals are very motivating. They energize the selling organization, especially when they are realistic and attainable.

Goals help management evaluate performance. Individuals or teams who achieve their objectives have either met or exceeded expectations. The activities and behaviors that lead to goal attainment should be celebrated, encouraged, and continued. Reasons for failing to meet objectives can be analyzed to develop remedies.

Goal attainment leads to both extrinsic (tangible) and intrinsic (intangible) rewards. Incentive compensation plans reward individuals or teams with monetary payments for achieving or exceeding their goals. Other extrinsic rewards include recognition programs, such as High-Achiever Clubs, that provide trips and other incentives to high performers. Goal attainment is intrinsically rewarding as well. Salespeople and sales managers feel successful and have high levels of job satisfaction when they make their goals. Often the intrinsic rewards are derived from the extrinsic rewards. Money, trips, and other tangible incentives announce to everyone that a salesperson or sales manager is successful.

Goals suggest how the sales force should spend its time. Product, market, and activity priorities can be reflected in a goal structure that will motivate the sales force to allocate selling effort in a strategic way. Priorities among products, industries, large and small customers, customers and prospects, or hunting and farming are emphasized by placing aggressive goals on those that are judged most important.

Finally, goals are constructed to ensure a customer focus and customer satisfaction. A market-focused selling organization realizes the value of good customers and insures that their needs are met consistently. Customer-centered goals encourage the sales force to adequately support, service, and maintain the customer base.

As stated earlier, approximately 85 percent of U.S. companies establish formal goals for their salespeople.

## Types of Sales Force Goals

Sales force goals can be set for each of the five components of the selling organization shown in Figure 11-2. The responsibility for achieving particular goals varies with the job category within the selling organization. Senior sales management has the responsibility for achieving the higher-level goals, such as sales force investment and culture goals. Salespeople have direct responsibility for achieving local activity goals. Everyone has responsibility for customer and company results. Figure 11-3 suggests how goals are assigned to the sales team. The number of Xs in each cell signifies the importance of each type of goal at each level of the sales force team.

### Goal Relevance for Different Members of the Selling Organization

Senior managers have the primary responsibility for establishing the parameters of the selling organization. They are successful if the right people and the right number of people are hired, if the development and targeting programs enable the salespeople to be successful, if the compensation systems reward top performers, and if sales systems, such as territory alignment and goal setting, create an environment in which everyone has a fair chance to succeed. Poor company results, poor customer results, high turnover, low morale, inadequate product knowledge, poor selling skills, and unequal opportunity suggest that the senior sales managers are not meeting expectations.

First-level sales managers have direct responsibility for selecting and developing the sales team. Then, they must direct the team's selling effort to obtain customer satisfaction and sales results. Underperforming salespeople and poor company results suggest that the first-level sales managers are not meeting expectations.

Finally, salespeople decide what activities they perform. Their activities translate into customer and company results. Poor territory results or wasted activity signals that the salesperson is not meeting his or her objectives.

**Figure 11-2.** The Components of a Selling Organization.

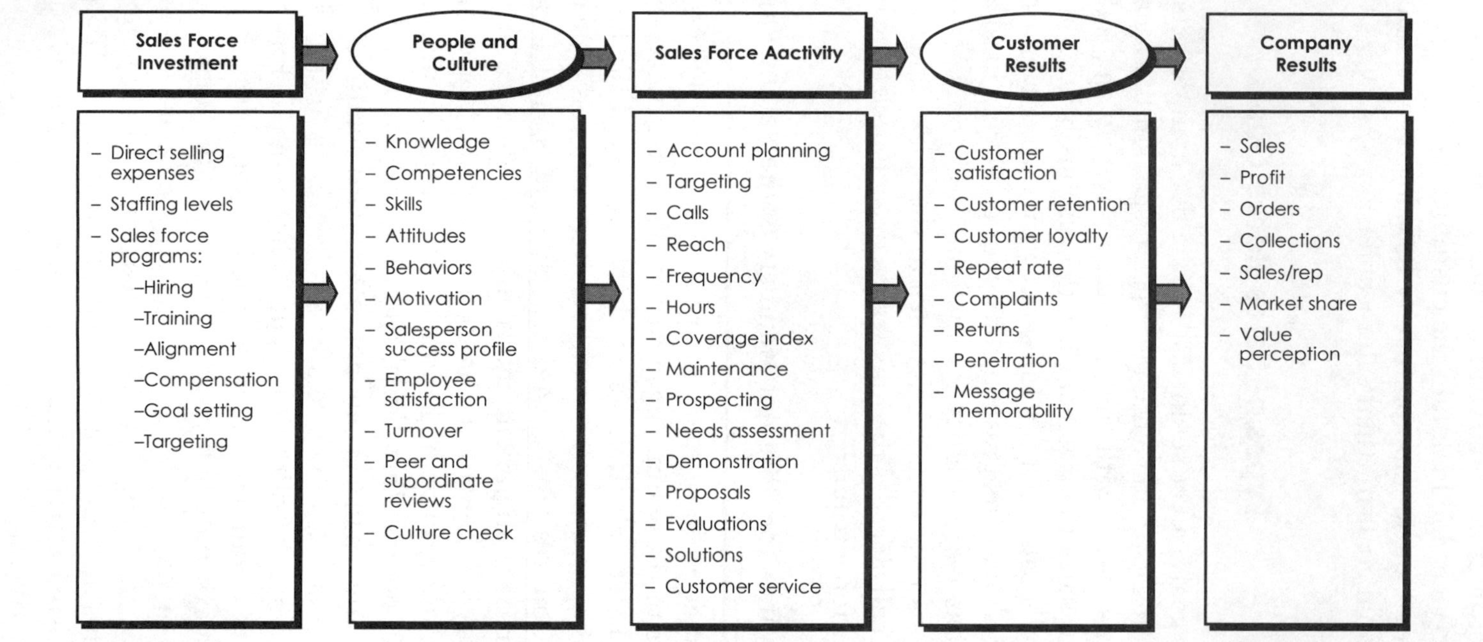

**Figure 11-3.** Goal Relevance for Different Members of the Selling Organization.

| | *Sales Force Investment* | *People and Culture* | *Sales Force Activity* | *Customer Results* | *Company Results* |
|---|---|---|---|---|---|
| **Senior Sales Management** | XXX | XX | | XX | XXX |
| **First-Level Sales Manager** | X | XXX | X | XX | XXX |
| **Salesperson** | | X | XXX | XXX | XXX |

## Goals and Objectives Reflect the Selling Environment as Well as the Culture and Values of the Sales Force

In Japanese schools, everyone is expected to reach the same level in every subject. It is not sufficient to study mathematics for the same number of years as everyone else; you must study mathematics until you have the required ability. In American schools, students study primarily the subjects that they like, which is often those subjects that they are good at. American and Japanese schools have opposing values. American schools develop student strengths, while Japanese schools remove student weaknesses. Should we set goals to improve our deficiencies, or should we set goals that capitalize on our strengths? These opposing strategies show how objective setting reflects culture and values.

A sales force culture, as described in Chapter 15, is defined as the unwritten rules that govern salespeople's behavior. Sales force goals establish what is important and valued. Hence, goals and culture are intertwined. Goals are an outgrowth of the sales force culture, and they, in turn, establish the parameters for the culture.

Certain cultures favor a focus on "people and culture" and "activity" goals, while other cultures favor strong "customer and company results" goals. This cultural dichotomy forms the basis of a major controversy in goal setting: Should goals be set in terms of people and activities (the softer side) or in terms of results (the harder side)? Sometimes the answer depends on the selling environment. Certain selling environments support only one type of goal. For example, goals cannot be set in terms of results if results cannot be measured accurately. How do we measure the impact of a retail merchandiser? Attractive displays sell merchandise—but how much? How do we measure the impact of an individual salesperson in a team-selling environment? The balance beam in Figure 11-4 suggests several of the environmental trade-offs that need to be acknowledged in setting goals.

Different sales force cultures produce different goals. A "results" culture holds that salespeople should be accountable for company results. Salespeople are closest to the customer and should be empowered to determine the appropriate activity. Pay is based on performance.

An "activity" culture suggests that goals should be set in terms of activities. Management feels that the right activities will lead to favorable results in the long term. Management determines the best way to sell, and everyone is expected to comply. Activities are customer-centered. Salespeople do not oversell; they carefully manage orders and customer service. There is a concern that if compensation is based on goal attainment, results-based goals could lead to inappropriate short-term income-maximizing behavior on the part of the salespeople at the expense of the customer. Activity goals require more management attention because they tend to be more complex and because activities are not easy to measure.

Activity-based goals assume that the company has the best understanding of the most appropriate activities for the salesperson. This can

**Figure 11-4.** Environmental Trade-offs in Goal Setting.

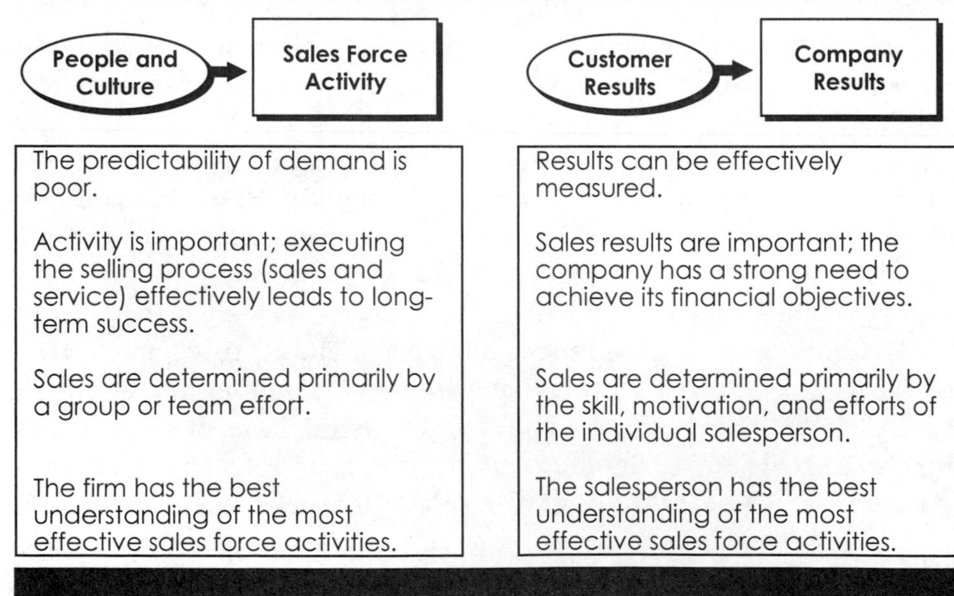

be the case when a company's databases enable it to perform cross-sectional analyses across salespeople to determine the most effective sales force activities. High- and low-performing salespeople can be compared to identify activities that lead to sales success. Selling strategies can be contrasted across different accounts to determine which ones produce better results. Company-developed prospecting and targeting systems reflect best practices learned by contrasting different salespeople and their selling approaches. The company assumes the risk for the attainment of results when it sets goals in terms of activity.

Results-based goals assume that the salespeople have the best understanding of the most appropriate activities for themselves and that the company is willing to empower them to achieve sales results in their own way. It is argued that highly qualified, well-trained salespeople know the best selling process for each of their accounts and prospects. Best practices are shared across the sales force so that salespeople do not become excessively myopic. Consequently, the salesperson assumes the risk for the attainment of results when the company sets goals in terms of company results. Many companies set both activity and results goals, thus sharing the risk.

The balance beam in Figure 11-5 summarizes these controversies.

**Figure 11-5.** Sales Force Culture Trade-offs in Goal Setting.

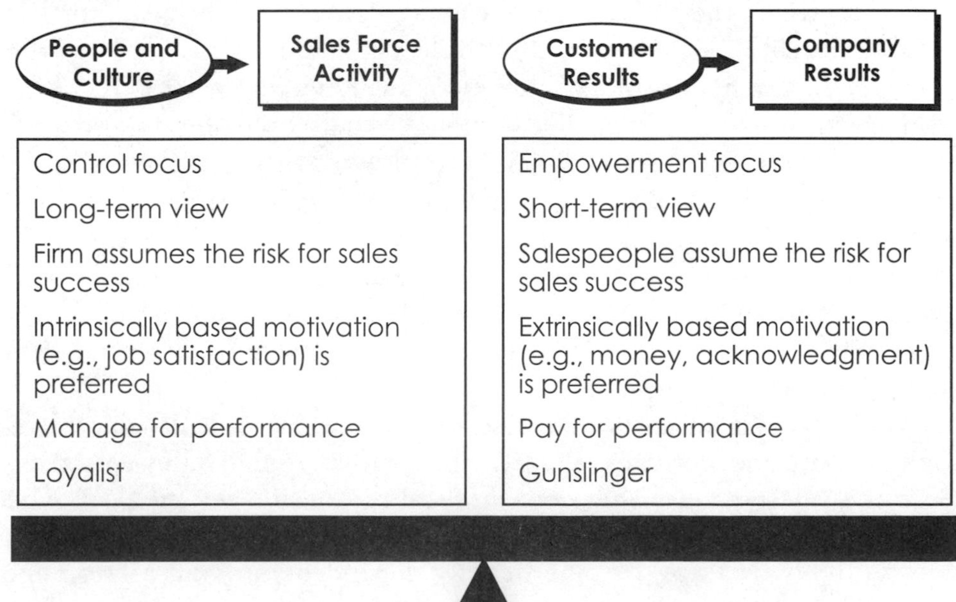

## Goal-Setting Observations

Goals that are challenging, attainable, and fair are motivational. Motivation is enhanced if there is a reward associated with achieving a goal. Rewards can be intrinsic or extrinsic; however, salespeople usually respond better to extrinsic rewards. Consequently, many companies link incentive compensation to goal achievement. This, of course, increases everyone's interest in how goals are set.

The company's objectives and salespeople's objectives do not always line up. The company needs to achieve sales and earnings targets. The salesperson wants to maximize his or her income. Consequently, the company wants to set high targets, whereas salespeople lobby for lower targets in order to increase their income. A goal-setting game results. Usually the company would like the sales force to participate in goal setting, since salespeople frequently have the best information regarding the opportunities in their territory, and because goals will have a higher likelihood of acceptance if the field is involved in setting them. The risk, of course, is that the field will low-ball the estimates. The best goal-setting process involves a data-based analysis of historical trends and market potential, in addition to field input.

Goal setting is difficult when there is high uncertainty in predicting future performance. New product launches illustrate this point vividly. Companies that underforecast the performance of a new product (and sometimes they do this intentionally) will set low goals for the field force. The sales force, in this situation, achieves goal early in the year and experiences windfall income gains when the year is finished. Nothing is wrong with that. The company is delighted about its success and has little problem in sharing its wealth with the sales force. Recall, however, that the success was due to a poor forecast rather than high performance. The company has now raised the income expectations for the sales force for the subsequent year—especially if the product continues to grow. The sales force feels entitled to the higher levels of income. How long can this last? What happens to motivation when a correction needs to be made?

Selling environments in which only a few large deals take place each year are another example of a situation with high sales volatility. Here the salesperson either gets the deal or doesn't get the deal. The salesperson's results vary widely, and precise goal attainment becomes very unlikely. Making income heavily dependent on goal attainment will contribute to either prosperous or disappointing years for salespeople.

Goal setting is challenging when random business comes in with no effort from the salesperson. A newspaper advertising salesperson may get a big order accidentally by picking up the phone when a new customer wants to place large volumes of newspaper advertising. This incident can make the year for the salesperson. Volatility-adjusted incentive compensation plans are the only way to deal with these environments effectively. These types of plans are discussed in Chapter 10.

Sales goals can be reset during the year. Resetting goals is reasonable if the current goals were not set accurately or if the selling environment has changed sufficiently to invalidate the current goals. Suppose that a company has an annual goal that is allocated down through the selling organization until it arrives at the salesperson level. When the company's annual goal hasn't changed, management may be reluctant to change a salesperson's annual goal. But what happens when a salesperson's largest account decides to move its headquarters to a new location serviced by a different salesperson? Many companies ask the salesperson who is losing the account to make up the business from new accounts, while the salesperson who is lucky enough to get this big account receives a huge windfall without effort. Fair goals are the most motivating.

As another example, what happens when a company's sales forecast is too high and individual salespeople realize that they cannot make goal? The sales force slowly loses motivation and exerts progressively less effort throughout the year unless the goals are adjusted to reflect the new economic realities. Goals have to be attainable if they are to be motivational.

Dynamic goal setting can be a two-edged sword. Increasing sales goals throughout the year because of a poor initial forecast is very unsettling and demotivating to a selling organization. A salesperson may think, "I exceeded my quarterly target and now they are raising my goal again—why do I work so hard?" The reasons for goal attainment are not always obvious. The achievement could be due to a low goal, or it may be due to high performance. It is clear what the salespeople will believe: They will attribute most of the overachievement to their effort. Consequently, a low forecast followed by an upward adjustment of the goal will be perceived as unfair. It is wise for companies to spend more time in developing their territory-level goals to avoid the need for goal adjustments.

The best goal-setting processes identify a realistic target area. Using this paradigm, goal setting can be thought of as forecasting a range, called the target area, rather than a single point estimate. Compensation plans can then be linked to goal setting using the "fair wage" concept, introduced in Chapter 10. This concept is that a fair wage should be paid for those sales that would exist if a salesperson with average capabilities applied average effort. Incentives should be paid on sales above this level. Figure 11-6 displays the target area and fair wage concepts.

The definition of the target area varies across companies. Some start the range at 100 percent of goal; others start it at 90 percent of goal. Some cap it at 120 percent of goal; others leave it uncapped. The range depends on the volatility of territory sales and the culture of the selling organization. High-volatility environments should have large ranges. Low-volatility environments should have tight ranges because goal setting can be quite accurate in these environments.

The sales force culture also helps resolve whether the target area starts at 90 or 100 percent of goal. Is it desirable to have a culture that rewards the true winners, the 30 to 70 percent of salespeople who beat their goal; or is it better to have a culture in which 50 to 90 percent of the salespeople feel successful because they achieved at least 90 percent of their goal? Academic studies suggest that the latter is more motivational and leads to better results. Goals need to be realistic and achievable. A sales force will be demotivated if goals are set too high and only a small number of superperformers achieve goal by the end of the year. If a salesperson is unlikely to make goal, he or she may delay business

**Figure 11-6.** Goals Can Be Set in Terms of a Target Range.

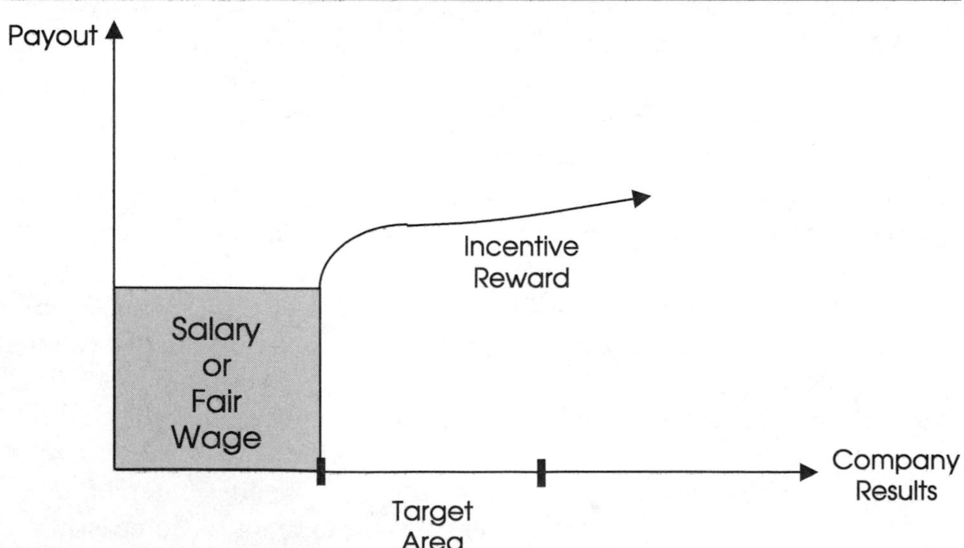

or check out well before the end of the fiscal year. Many companies like to have about 70 percent of their salespeople achieve goal. If the goals are realistic and achievable and less than 70 percent of the salespeople are achieving goal, then the problem is not a one of goal setting—it may be a hiring or development problem.

## An Example That Illustrates the Cost of Poor Goal Setting

Errors in goal setting can be expensive to the company, as seen in the following example. Assume that a company is using the incentive compensation plan illustrated in Figure 11-7.

The company pays a salary plus 2.5 percent commission on every dollar of sales up to a territory goal and 7.5 percent commission on every dollar for all sales that exceed this goal. This is a growth-oriented compensation plan because it aggressively rewards extra effort at a point where extra effort is required. If the salespeople beat quota, they benefit, and so does the company.

Using this example, it is possible to examine the cost of setting a poor goal. Assume that the fair wage concept is used to set the territory goal for each salesperson. Assume further that the fair wage goal is set at $1,000,000 for each of ten salespeople. That is, if each salesperson puts in a reasonable amount of work, he or she will sell $1,000,000 and earn $25,000 in incentive pay. This is the "perfect accuracy" scenario described in Figure 11-8. The goals are set accurately, and each salesperson achieves goal by performing a reasonable amount of work.

**Figure 11-7.** Example of a Growth-Oriented Compensation Plan.

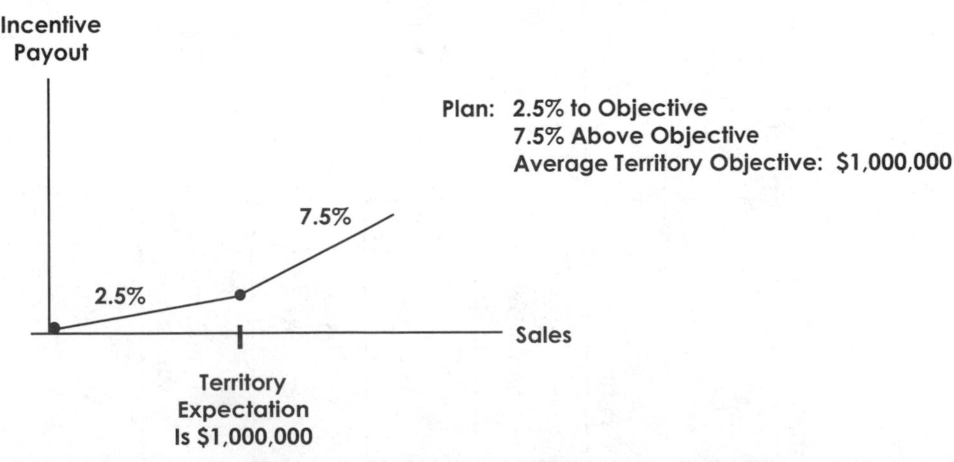

**Figure 11-8.** A Cost Comparison of Scenarios With Different Goal-Setting Errors.

| *Scenario* | *Sales Results* | *Company Sales* | *Individual Incentive Payouts* | *Company Incentive Payout* | *% Over the Cost of Scenario A* |
|---|---|---|---|---|---|
| **A**<br>**Perfect Accuracy** | 10 people sell $1,000,000 each | $10,000,000 | 10 @ $25,000 | $250,000 | 0% |
| **B**<br>**Some Error** | 1 person sells $1,100,000<br>8 people sell $1,000,000<br>1 person sells $900,000 | $10,000,000 | 1 @ $32,500<br>8 @ $25,000<br>1 @ $22,500 | $255,000 | 2% |
| **C**<br>**More Error** | 1 person sells $1,200,000<br>8 people sell $1,000,000<br>1 person sells $800,000 | $10,000,000 | 1 @ $40,000<br>8 @ $25,000<br>1 @ $20,000 | $260,000 | 4% |
| **D**<br>**Even More Error** | 2 people sell $1,200,000<br>4 people sell $1,000,000<br>4 people sell $900,000 | $10,000,000 | 2 @ $40,000<br>4 @ $25,000<br>4 @ $22,500 | $270,000 | 8% |
| **E**<br>**Significantly More Error** | 5 people sell $1,250,000<br>5 people sell $750,000 | $10,000,000 | 5 @ $43,750<br>5 @ $18,750 | $312,500 | 28.6% |

In Figure 11-8, four alternative scenarios are compared to the "perfect accuracy" scenario to reveal the cost of poor goal setting. Scenario B suggests that a goal of $1,000,000 was set for each territory, but that this goal was not accurate for two of the territories. Since the salesperson in one territory performed a reasonable amount of work and sold $1,100,000, that salesperson's goal should have been $1,100,000. The salesperson in the other territory did a reasonable amount of work and sold $900,000; accordingly, that goal should have been $900,000. The goals for eight territories were accurate. In this scenario, one person gets a windfall gain because the goals were not set accurately. The company's total payout is $255,000, or 2 percent above what it would have been if it had set its goals correctly. Scenarios C, D, and E demonstrate the extent to which the company's costs accelerate with increasing goal-setting error.

It is important to note that it may be difficult to determine whether a salesperson exceeded goal because the goal was too low or because the salesperson performed really well. The assumption for this example is that the goals were not set accurately. Inaccurate goals for a sales force with many overperforming and many underperforming salespeople will increase the cost of the forecasting error even further.

Finally, notice that in each scenario of Figure 11-8, the company sold $10,000,000. The company is pleased because it made its goal. However, its sales force costs can swing significantly depending on how accurately it set its goals.

Overall, this example describes the cost of annual goal-setting errors across territories. Companies that set quarterly goals may experience the same cost run-up when goal-setting errors occur over time. Salespeople receive windfall gains in quarters when the goals are set too low and lose motivation in quarters when they are set too high.

## Determining Successful Territory-Level Goals—A Five-Step Process

Many companies spend considerable time, energy, and money on determining quotas or targets. Territory-level goals are the most common goals established for a sales force. They can take many forms: sales revenue, units, profit, market share, sales growth, share growth, and profit growth. The appropriate type of goal and the right level for the goal depend on many factors, including the selling environment, the sales force culture, and data availability. The five-step process shown in Figure 11-9 can be used to improve goal setting in any selling environment.

### Step 1: Set National Goals and Objectives

Establishing a national objective is the first step in developing territory-level goals. The national goal can be determined either from the top down or from the bottom up. Top-down goals reflect market conditions, company strategy, and management's aspirations. Bottom-up goals sum individual territory, district, or regional forecasts to derive a total business goal. As mentioned in the last section, bottom-up goals may be understated because salespeople have an incentive to low-ball their forecast. Top-down goals may be aggressive or low depending on whether top management measures success in terms of growth or in terms of goal attainment. Many management teams integrate both top-down and bottom-up estimates to derive their final forecast.

National goals communicate management's strategy to the selling organization. Goals for revenue growth, unit growth, profit growth, share gain, sales retention, and market penetration are strong statements of strategy and intent. The company can further refine the objectives it communicates by stating goals by product line and customer segment.

Goal setting is enhanced by good forecasting. It is critical to consider historical sales trends, cross-sectional comparisons across sales territories, and the judgment of experienced sales and marketing people. Valuable forecasting techniques have been developed and refined over the last thirty years. Some use historical data (e.g., econometrics, time-series analysis), while others summarize judgmental data in the most objective way (e.g., Delphi forecasting). Systematic use of these techniques improves the accuracy of the national goal.

### Step 2: Understand Territory Expectations and Behavior

Understanding territory behavior and dynamics is important for determining appropriate territory goals. Territory results are directly affected by the performance of the salesperson. However, territory factors such as market potential and historical sales also have a significant indirect impact on territory performance. When measured, these factors provide a good benchmark for establishing territory goals. The factors that correlate highly with territory sales can be used to predict sales and are thus useful for goal setting.

Figure 11-9. A Process for Establishing Sales Territory Goals.

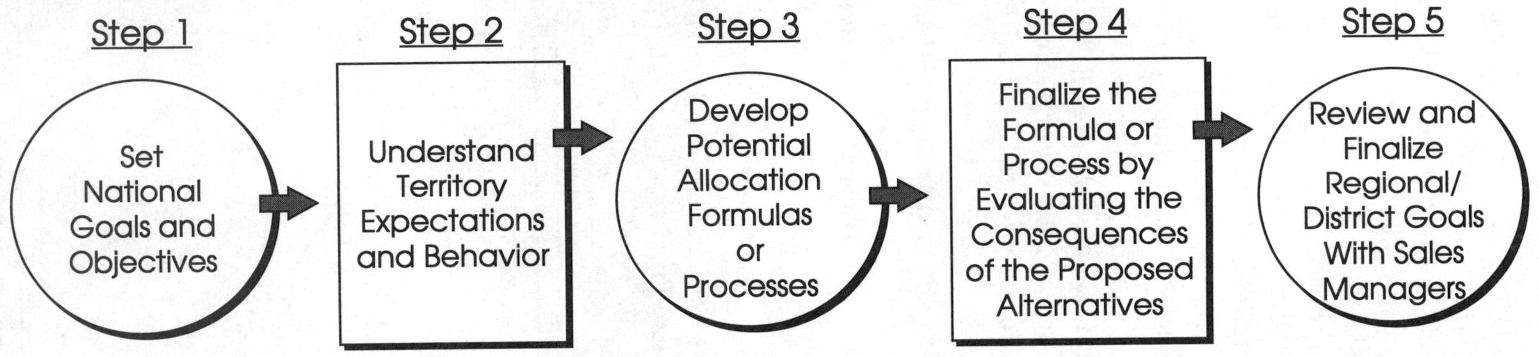

Factors that correlate well with territory sales are illustrated in Figures 11-10 through 11-15. Many selling organizations use these factors to establish territory sales quotas. These illustrations demonstrate two things. First, a statistical analysis for benchmarking territory goals is easy to do, and second, these analyses usually provide good results. The factors represented in this illustration are peculiar to one specific sales force—a sales force selling a medical instrument and test strips, purchased at retail by consumers who are influenced in their purchase decision by pharmacists, doctors, and nurses. Depending on data availability, other sales forces will employ other factors.

**Product Sales in Any Given Year Are Highly Correlated with Sales the Prior Year.** A good predictor of next year's sales is this year's sales. Figure 11-10 shows this relationship for the medical instrument company.

**Product Sales in Any Given Year Are Positively Correlated with Market Sales in the Prior Year.** Even though this relationship is not as strong as the one with the prior year's sales, market sales are usually a very good predictor of future sales. Figure 11-11 shows the relationship for the medical instrument company.

**Product Sales in Any Given Year Are Positively Correlated with Surrogates for Market Potential.** Precise market sales figures are often difficult

**Figure 11-10.** This Year's Sales Versus Last Year's Sales.

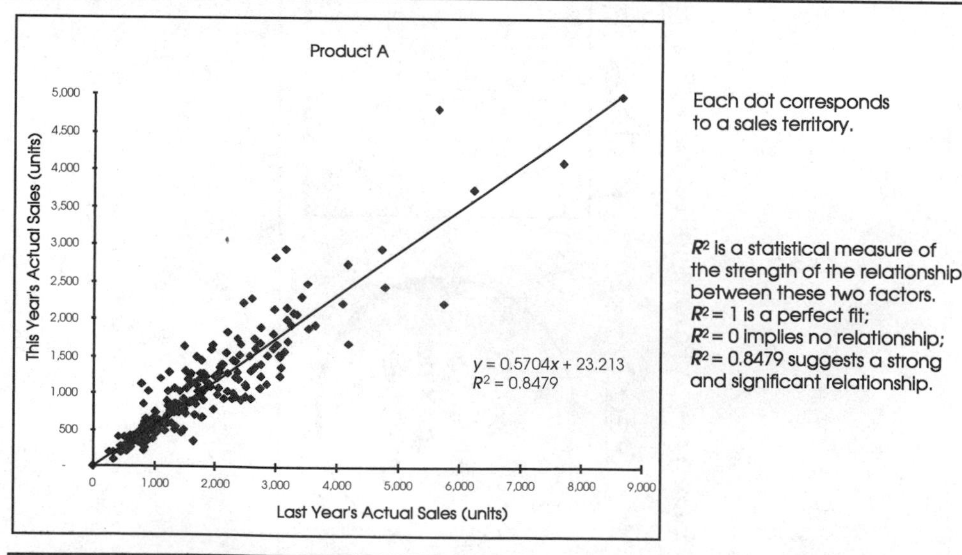

**Figure 11-11.** This Year's Sales Versus Last Year's Market Sales.

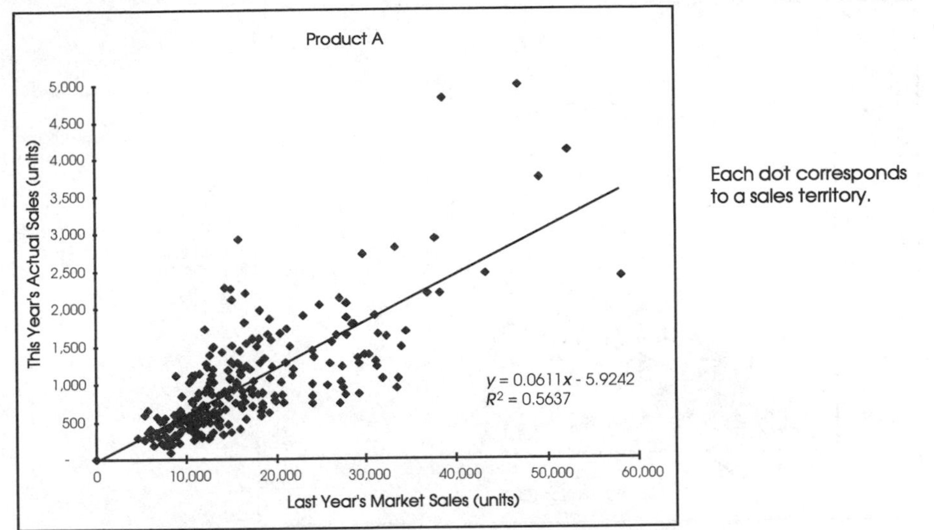


to obtain at the territory level. However, surrogates such as SIC sales, number of employees, building square footage, population, and consumer buying power index are usually available. Territory sales tend to be highly correlated with these surrogates. The relationship between territory sales and population for the medical instrument company is shown in Figure 11-12. The territories that fall significantly below the line in Figure 11-12 are usually underperforming.

**Product Sales in Any Given Year Are Positively Correlated with Competitors' Sales in the Prior Year.** Competitors' sales give a good indication of our product sales. This observation is especially useful when launching a new product into an established market—use competitors' sales to establish territory goals. The relationship between territory sales and a competitor's sales for the medical instrument company is shown in Figure 11-13.

**The Market Share Change Expected for Any Given Year Is Related to the Starting Market Share in That Year.** The traditional view of territory market share (or market penetration) is that low market shares suggest a large opportunity, whereas high market shares suggest penetration and so small opportunity for territory growth. This relationship is illustrated in Figure 11-14.

The starting market share has two important effects on the poten-

**Figure 11-12.** This Year's Sales Versus Population.

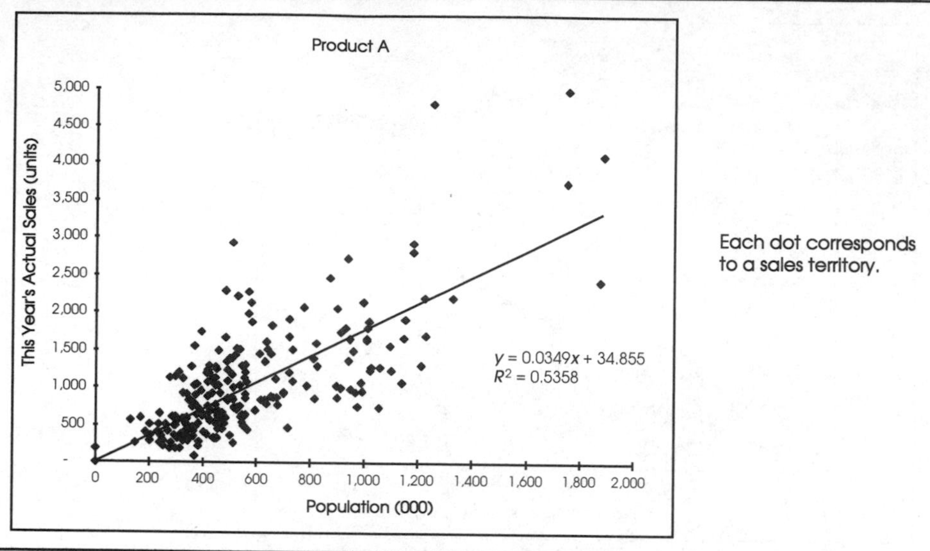


**Figure 11-13.** This Year's Sales Versus Last Year's Competitor 1 Sales.

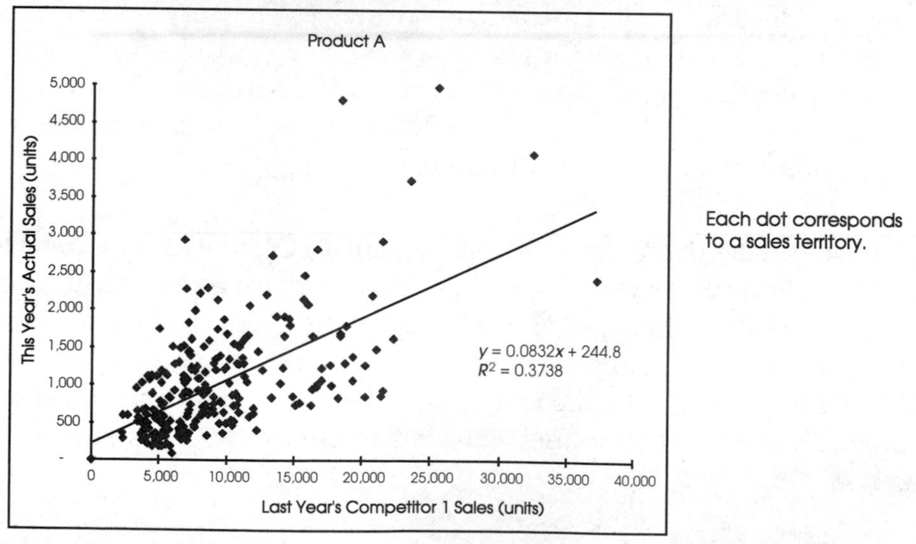

**Figure 11-14.** The Traditional View of Share Versus Growth.

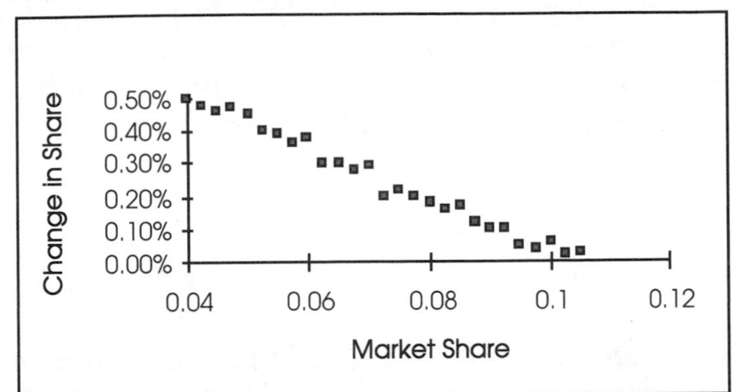


tial for territory growth. The first is the intuitive effect already observed: *A high growth rate is not sustainable forever.* No matter how much potential the territory has, sales cannot continue to grow rapidly forever, since we can sell to only 100 percent of the customers. Data for highly penetrated territories provide an indication of the limits to growth in other territories.

There is an emerging debate about what happens to sales territories with low market share. The traditional view is that low-market-share territories have high potential and are responsive to sales force effort. However, data do not always support this observation. In fact, low-share territories often do not grow as quickly as medium-share territories. An example is shown in Figure 11-15.

Data like those in Figure 11-15 lead to the counterintuitive conclusion that *small market share does not always imply an immediate growth opportunity.* Low share usually signals a problem. A competitor

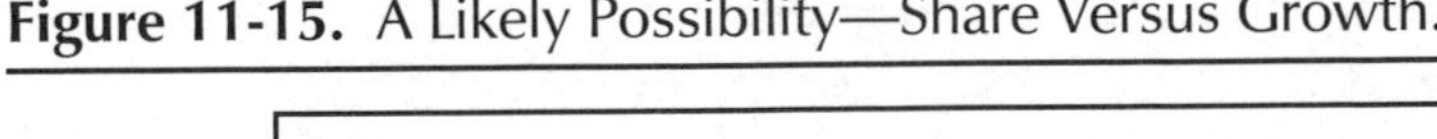

**Figure 11-15.** A Likely Possibility—Share Versus Growth.

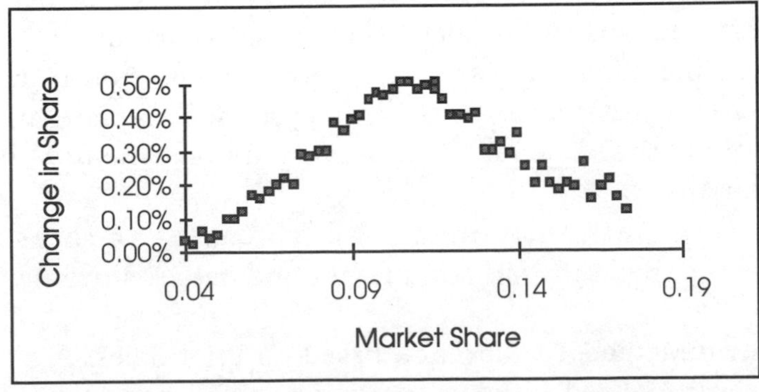

may be very strong, with a large, loyal customer base. Alternatively, there may be low awareness of the firm's product or service, and customer trial and repeat rates need to be developed. In either case, it takes time to realize the opportunity. Share gains will not be immediate. An exception to this threshold effect occurs when the market is growing quickly and the firm has not deployed sufficient sales resources to capture this growth.

## Step 3: Develop Potential Allocation Formulas or Processes

National goals need to be split among districts or regions and among sales territories. Some selling organizations derive territory-level goals using the subjective judgment of district and regional sales managers exclusively. Others rely on formulas (sometimes very complex formulas) to allocate the national goal among sales territories. Usually a combination of both approaches provides the best allocations.

Goal allocation formulas or procedures make the process explicit and fair. Salespeople are more likely to feel that their quotas are reasonable, realistic, and less arbitrary. Sales managers are liberated from the hassle of developing and justifying quotas. Even companies that use only the first-line sales manager's discretion to set territory quotas provide some guidelines to their managers (e.g., not less than last year!).

The best formulas and procedures are based on a solid understanding of territory expectations and behavior. This understanding is enhanced when accurate and reliable territory-level data are available.

Various goal-setting formulas and procedures have been developed and are being used by companies. Four alternative methods are illustrated for the district-level example in Figure 11-16. This sales district is made up of eight sales territories. Sales for the prior two years, territory market potential, population, and geographic area are provided for each of the territories. The market potential number is the best estimate the firm has for the total market opportunity in each territory. Population is included because it is felt that population is a good predictor of the latent demand for the firm's products. Square mileage is a good indicator of the expected travel time and the difficulty of covering the entire territory.

Several recommended formulas and approaches for goal setting are presented here. They differ in complexity and data requirements.

**Alternative Method 1: Allocation Based on Prior Sales.** A simple and straightforward method of goal setting is to use prior territory sales.

**Figure 11-16.** Territory Data for Goal Setting.

| *Salesperson* | *Sales 2 Years Ago $(000)* | *% of District* | *Sales Last Year $(000)* | *% of District* | *Market Potential $(000)* | *% of District* | *Population (000)* | *Land Area (Sq. Miles)* |
|---|---|---|---|---|---|---|---|---|
| Anderson | 1,840 | 18.3% | 1,920 | 17.9% | 8,890 | 15.6% | 2,041 | 1,806 |
| Brown | 1,600 | 15.9% | 1,680 | 15.7% | 8,730 | 15.3% | 2,121 | 9,045 |
| Carlson | 1,500 | 14.9% | 1,720 | 16.0% | 6,690 | 11.8% | 1,138 | 1,301 |
| Donahue | 1,300 | 12.9% | 1,450 | 13.5% | 2,950 | 5.2% | 613 | 61 |
| Everett | 1,220 | 12.1% | 940 | 8.8% | 8,490 | 14.9% | 1,785 | 4,239 |
| Fink | 1,120 | 11.1% | 1,140 | 10.6% | 4,990 | 8.8% | 1,048 | 6,524 |
| Good | 880 | 8.7% | 1,030 | 9.6% | 7,690 | 13.5% | 1,991 | 24,070 |
| Harper | 620 | 6.2% | 840 | 7.8% | 8,510 | 14.9% | 2,208 | 28,738 |
| **Total** | **10,080** | **100%** | **10,720** | **100%** | **56,940** | **100%** | **12,945** | **75,784** |

**The district goal for next year is $11,800,000, and the firm would like to develop territory quotas.**

Goals are allocated to territories based on the percentage of the total company sales they contributed in the prior year. For example, Anderson's territory contributed 17.9 percent of the district's sales last year. Therefore, this year Anderson is expected to sell 17.9 percent of the district goal of $11,800,000, or $2,113,000.

With this method, goals are determined objectively, and the calculation is easy to explain and accept. Unfortunately, this approach assumes that prior sales are consistent with territory potential. It places a greater burden on salespeople who are operating near their potential than on salespeople with untapped potential.

Using this rule, Figure 11-17 shows next year's territory goals for the district.

With this approach, every sales territory is expected to grow at the same rate as the district.

**Alternative Method 2: Allocation Based on Prior Sales and Market Potential.** A simple goal allocation process that improves on the prior sales approach can be used if market potential data at the territory level are available. In this approach, the goal allocation is split into two parts, as shown in Figure 11-18. The base allocation is simply the allocation of last year's sales. The growth allocation is defined as the allocation of any incremental growth in sales over what was sold last year. In our district illustration, the base allocation involves allocating last year's sales of $10,720,000, and the growth allocation involves the allocation of the incremental sales of $1,080,000.

Each sales territory is expected to sell at least as much as last year. That is, the base allocation replicates last year's sales. The growth in sales is allocated based on market potential. Each territory receives an

**Figure 11-17.** Goals Based on the Prior Sales Method.

| *Salesperson* | *Sales Last Year $ (000)* | *% of District* | *Next Year's Goal $ (000)* |
|---|---|---|---|
| Anderson | 1,920 | 17.9% | 2,113 |
| Brown | 1,680 | 15.7% | 1,849 |
| Carlson | 1,720 | 16.0% | 1,894 |
| Donahue | 1,450 | 13.5% | 1,596 |
| Everett | 940 | 8.8% | 1,037 |
| Fink | 1,140 | 10.6% | 1,252 |
| Good | 1,030 | 9.6% | 1,135 |
| Harper | 840 | 7.8% | 924 |
| **Total** | **10,720** | **100%** | **11,800** |

**Figure 11-18.** Next Year's Target Is Split Into Two Parts.

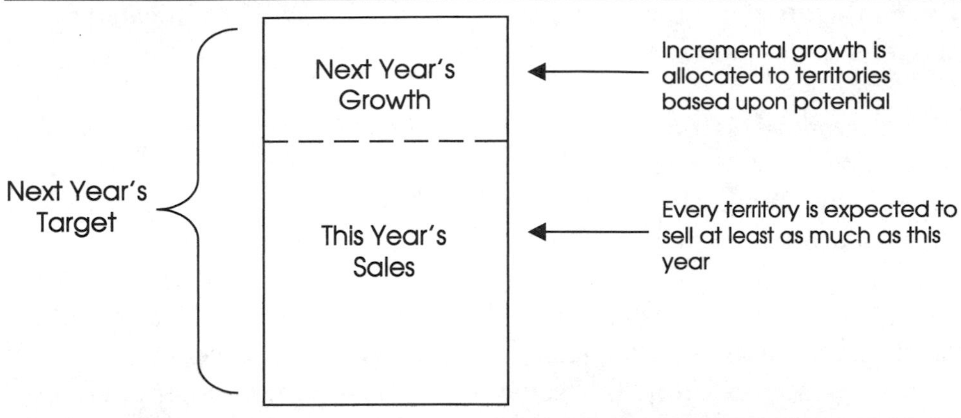


allocation of the incremental sales proportional to its share of total district potential. For example, the calculation of next year's goal for Anderson's territory is:

(Last year's sales of \$1,920,000) + (15.6% of district market potential × district growth allocation of \$1,080,000) = next year's goal of \$2,089,000

Figure 11-19 illustrates this approach for the eight territories in our example.

Notice that our discussion has assumed that there will be a growth in sales. If a decline is anticipated, this approach changes. Management would first need to estimate carryover sales—the level of sales that

**Figure 11-19.** Goals Based on the Prior Sales and Market Potential Method.

| *Salesperson* | *Sales Last Year \$ (000)* | *Base Allocation \$ (000)* | *Market Potential \$ (000)* | *% of District* | *Growth Allocation \$ (000)* | *Next Year's Goals \$ (000)* |
|---|---|---|---|---|---|---|
| Anderson | 1,920 | 1,920 | 8,890 | 15.6% | 169 | 2,089 |
| Brown | 1,680 | 1,680 | 8,730 | 15.3% | 166 | 1,846 |
| Carlson | 1,720 | 1,720 | 6,690 | 11.8% | 127 | 1,847 |
| Donahue | 1,450 | 1,450 | 2,950 | 5.2% | 56 | 1,506 |
| Everett | 940 | 940 | 8,490 | 14.9% | 161 | 1,101 |
| Fink | 1,140 | 1,140 | 4,990 | 8.8% | 94 | 1,234 |
| Good | 1,030 | 1,030 | 7,690 | 13.5% | 146 | 1,176 |
| Harper | 840 | 840 | 8,510 | 14.9% | 161 | 1,001 |
| **Total** | **10,720** | **10,720** | **56,940** | **100%** | **1,080** | **11,800** |

would be expected without sales force effort. Then the difference between the district forecast and carryover sales would be allocated to the territories based on market potential.

**Alternative Method 3: Allocation Based on a Weighting of Territory Factors.** Territory characteristics can have a significant impact on territory sales. A high-potential territory will have higher sales. A geographically dispersed territory will have lower sales. The weighted index method accommodates these observations. Goals are allocated to territories based on a weighted average of multiple factors. Typical factors include market potential, market share, market growth, percentage of total company sales in a territory, territory sales growth, number of targeted accounts, population, and geographic measures.

This method requires several calculations to develop territory goals. Our district example in Figure 11-20 illustrates the process. First, each important factor is assigned a weight. Sales management can determine these weights. Alternatively, the weights can be derived more scientifically using statistical methods such as regression analysis. In our example, management has selected two factors, last year's sales and market potential. It feels that these two factors are equally important, so each factor is assigned a 50 percent weight.

Once the factor weights are determined, a weighted share is calculated for each territory. Since there is a significant scale difference in the measurement of the two factors, they are normalized by dividing each territory factor value by the district total for the factor. For example, last year Anderson's territory contributed 17.9 percent of the dis-

**Figure 11-20.** Goals Based on the Factor-Weighting Approach.

| *Salesperson* | *Sales Last Year $ (000)* | *% of District Sales Last Year* | *Market Potential $ (000)* | *% of District Market Potential* | *50%–50% Weighted Territory Share* | *Next Year's Goal $ (000)* |
|---|---|---|---|---|---|---|
| Anderson | 1,920 | 17.9% | 8,890 | 15.6% | 16.7% | 1,971 |
| Brown | 1,680 | 15.7% | 8,730 | 15.3% | 15.5% | 1,829 |
| Carlson | 1,720 | 16.0% | 6,690 | 11.8% | 13.9% | 1,640 |
| Donahue | 1,450 | 13.5% | 2,950 | 5.2% | 9.5% | 1,121 |
| Everett | 940 | 8.8% | 8,490 | 14.9% | 11.7% | 1,381 |
| Fink | 1,140 | 10.6% | 4,990 | 8.8% | 9.8% | 1,156 |
| Good | 1,030 | 9.6% | 7,690 | 13.5% | 11.5% | 1,357 |
| Harper | 840 | 7.8% | 8,510 | 14.9% | 11.4% | 1,345 |
| **Total** | **10,720** | **100%** | **56,940** | **100%** | **100%** | **11,800** |

trict's sales and 15.6 percent of the district's market potential. The weighted shares are calculated by multiplying each territory's share of a factor by the factor weight and then summing across all factors. For example, the calculation for Anderson's territory is:

(17.9% of district sales × 50%) + (15.6% of district potential × 50%) = 16.7% weighted territory share

Finally, next year's goal is calculated by multiplying the district goal by the territory's weighted share of the goal. Anderson would receive 16.7 percent of the district goal of $11,800,000, or $1,971,000.

**Alternative Method 4: Allocation Based on Regression Analysis.** A regression analysis can be performed to derive weights that incorporate all of the factors given in this illustration. For this example, regression analysis determines the best regression fit to be:

---

Regression Equation

Sales this year = −697.78 + (1.85 × sales last year) + (−0.44 × population) + (0.04 × land area)

The $R^2$ is 0.973

The coefficients are statistically significant, exhibiting multicollinearity

---

The regression coefficients provide a good set of factor weights from a statistical goodness of fit perspective. These weights are used to develop territory scores, which are then used to develop territory shares and territory quotas. For example, a territory score for Anderson's territory is calculated using the regression equation as follows:

−697.78 + (1.85 × sales last year of $1,920,000) + (−0.44 × population of 2,041) + (0.04 × land area of 1,806) = territory score of $2,038,000

The territory scores are actually regression-based sales forecasts for each territory. However, they do not add up to the district goal for next year. In fact, the regression-based forecast of $11,906,000 for the district is a little higher than the district forecast of $11,800,000. Hence, the territory quotas must be adjusted to add up to the district goal. This is accomplished by determining each territory's share of the total of all territory scores and multiplying this share by next year's district goal. Figure 11-21 displays the scores, shares, and quotas for the eight territories.

Weighted-factor methods are likely to contain at least one component desired by each salesperson. Thus, these types of methods usually enhance the field's acceptance of the quotas. Additionally, the effect of data errors is reduced, since the allocation is not based on a single measure.

However, if factors and weights are determined arbitrarily or nonobjectively, the resulting allocation may be inappropriate. Analytical approaches, such as the statistical approach described above, usually provide the best weights in these situations.

### Step 4: Finalize the Formula or Process

Any recommended formula or process must be tested before it is implemented. This is especially true if the sales force's incentive compensation is tied to goal attainment. One valuable testing approach involves evaluating the consequences of the goals developed from the proposed process using historical data. This approach asks two questions: (1) What would the goals have been last year if the proposed goal setting process had been implemented a year earlier and the district sales goal was achieved, and (2) how do these goals compare to last year's actual sales? In short, the quota plan is tested by applying it to the year before last and observing how last year turned out. Figures 11-22 through 11-

**Figure 11-21.** Goals Derived From the Regression Equation.

| *Salesperson* | *Sales Last Year $ (000)* | *Population (000)* | *Land Area (Sq. Miles)* | *Territory Score (From Regression Equation) $ (000)* | *Territory Share of District* | *Next Year's Goal $ (000)* |
|---|---|---|---|---|---|---|
| Anderson | 1,920 | 2,041 | 1,806 | 2,038 | 17.1% | 2,020 |
| Brown | 1,680 | 2,121 | 9,045 | 1,877 | 15.8% | 1,861 |
| Carlson | 1,720 | 1,138 | 1,301 | 2,045 | 17.2% | 2,026 |
| Donahue | 1,450 | 613 | 61 | 1,722 | 14.5% | 1,706 |
| Everett | 940 | 1,785 | 4,239 | 442 | 3.7% | 438 |
| Fink | 1,140 | 1,048 | 6,524 | 1,240 | 10.4% | 1,229 |
| Good | 1,030 | 1,991 | 24,070 | 1,392 | 11.7% | 1,380 |
| Harper | 840 | 2,208 | 28,738 | 1,150 | 9.7% | 1,140 |
| **Total** | **10,720** | **12,945** | **75,784** | **11,906** | **100%** | **11,800** |

**Figure 11-22.** Testing Alternative 1: Prior Sales Method.

| *Salesperson* | *Sales Two Years Ago $ (000)* | *Goal for Last Year $ (000)* | *Sales Last Year $ (000)* | *Difference $ (000)* |
|---|---|---|---|---|
| Anderson | 1,840 | 1,957 | 1,920 | −37 |
| Brown | 1,600 | 1,702 | 1,680 | −22 |
| Carlson | 1,500 | 1,595 | 1,720 | 125 |
| Donahue | 1,300 | 1,383 | 1,450 | 67 |
| Everett | 1,220 | 1,297 | 940 | −357 |
| Fink | 1,120 | 1,191 | 1,140 | −51 |
| Good | 880 | 936 | 1,030 | 94 |
| Harper | 620 | 659 | 840 | 181 |
| **Total** | **10,080** | **10,720** | **10,720** | **0** |

25 show the results of this test for each goal-setting process described in step 3.

The credibility of the final goal-setting approach is enhanced when the difference between the new goal and actual sales performance has an intuitive explanation for each salesperson. For example, suppose management knows that Everett has had serious performance problems. The first three alternative goal-setting approaches are consistent with this knowledge, since all three show that Everett would have failed to make quota by a substantial margin. In addition, if management feels that Harper is a consistently strong performer whom they want to retain, alternatives 1, 2, and 4 work well, but alternative 3 does not because Harper would have missed his goal.

Testing the consequences of alternative goals using historical data

**Figure 11-23.** Testing Alternative 2: Prior Sales and Market Potential Method.

| *Salesperson* | *Sales Two Years Ago $ (000)* | *Goal for Last Year $ (000)* | *Sales Last Year $ (000)* | *Difference $ (000)* |
|---|---|---|---|---|
| Anderson | 1,840 | 1,940 | 1,920 | −20 |
| Brown | 1,600 | 1,698 | 1,680 | −18 |
| Carlson | 1,500 | 1,575 | 1,720 | 145 |
| Donahue | 1,300 | 1,333 | 1,450 | 117 |
| Everett | 1,220 | 1,315 | 940 | −375 |
| Fink | 1,120 | 1,176 | 1,140 | −36 |
| Good | 880 | 967 | 1,030 | 63 |
| Harper | 620 | 716 | 840 | 124 |
| **Total** | **10,080** | **10,720** | **10,720** | **0** |

**Figure 11-24.** Testing Alternative 3: Weighted-Factor Method Using Prior Sales and Market Potential.

| *Salesperson* | *Sales Two Years Ago $ (000)* | *Goal for Last Year $ (000)* | *Sales Last Year $ (000)* | *Difference $ (000)* |
|---|---|---|---|---|
| Anderson | 1,840 | 1,790 | 1,920 | 130 |
| Brown | 1,600 | 1,662 | 1,680 | 18 |
| Carlson | 1,500 | 1,490 | 1,720 | 230 |
| Donahue | 1,300 | 1,018 | 1,450 | 432 |
| Everett | 1,220 | 1,254 | 940 | −314 |
| Fink | 1,120 | 1,051 | 1,140 | 89 |
| Good | 880 | 1,233 | 1,030 | −203 |
| Harper | 620 | 1,222 | 840 | −382 |
| **Total** | **10,080** | **10,720** | **10,720** | **0** |

provides valuable insights. This test, however, makes a strong assumption: It assumes that the goal itself would not have motivated the salesperson to act any differently. However, goals are usually motivational, and therefore it is likely that this test understates the level of expected goal achievement. The test errs on the conservative side. For example, the test assumes that Anderson would have missed goal by $37,000 if alternative 1 had been used for goal setting. It is likely, however, that a goal of $1,957,000 for Anderson's territory would have motivated him to work harder to sell an additional $37,000 in order to make goal. Ultimately, however, testing is better than not testing, and each scenario should be evaluated after adjusting for bias.

**Figure 11-25.** Testing Alternative 4: Weighted-Factor Method Using a Regression Analysis.

| *Salesperson* | *Sales Two Years Ago $ (000)* | *Goal for Last Year $ (000)* | *Sales Last Year $ (000)* | *Difference $ (000)* |
|---|---|---|---|---|
| Anderson | 1,840 | 1,890 | 1,920 | 30 |
| Brown | 1,600 | 1,729 | 1,680 | −49 |
| Carlson | 1,500 | 1,637 | 1,720 | 83 |
| Donahue | 1,300 | 1,444 | 1,450 | 6 |
| Everett | 1,220 | 961 | 940 | −21 |
| Fink | 1,120 | 1,203 | 1,140 | −63 |
| Good | 880 | 1,114 | 1,030 | −84 |
| Harper | 620 | 742 | 840 | 98 |
| **Total** | **10,080** | **10,720** | **10,720** | **0** |

When evaluating the goal-setting process, management must consider who gets hurt and who is helped by each of the alternative goals. In addition to the individual analysis described in the previous figures, the graphs in Figures 11-26 through 11-30 expand our understanding of how the alternative goals affect the entire sales force.

The graph in Figure 11-26 compares the current distribution of goal attainment with the expected distribution of goal attainment using the goals developed from an alternative process.

Notice that with the alternative goals, all salespeople would have achieved at least 95 percent of goal. With the actual goals, three salespeople were below 95 percent attainment. Also, notice that with the alternative goals, a greater number of salespeople would have exceeded goal by 135 percent or more.

The graphs in Figures 11-27 and 11-28 illustrate what the income implications of an alternative goal-setting process might look like.

The graph in Figure 11-29 highlights the payout difference of two compensation plans, one based on the alternative goals and one using the actual goals. The territory numbers above the bars tell management who is helped and who is hurt by the new goals. It is important to consider who these salespeople are and whether or not the impact the alternative goals have on their bonus is desirable to management.

It is important to assess the impact that new goals have on various constituencies within the selling organization. Figure 11-30 lists groups to evaluate. Management certainly does not want to hurt the high-performing junior salesperson whose territory has low potential.

Once the goal-setting process has been finalized and goals have been developed, sales management must review the recommendations one final time for any circumstances that may have been overlooked in the process.

## Step 5: Review and Finalize Goals with Field Sales Managers

Field sales managers must be involved in the final quota decision because they have to live with the goals for the entire incentive period. Sales managers are allowed to adjust goals, since special circumstances can make a calculated goal unfair, unattainable, or not implementable. For example, regional differences caused by economic conditions or competitive situations may arise. New salespeople, vacant territories, sick leave, salespeople who are near retirement, and special relationships are factors that may need to be considered in calculating quotas. Recently filled territories that were vacant for an extended period of

**Figure 11-26.** A Distribution of Goal Attainment Comparison.

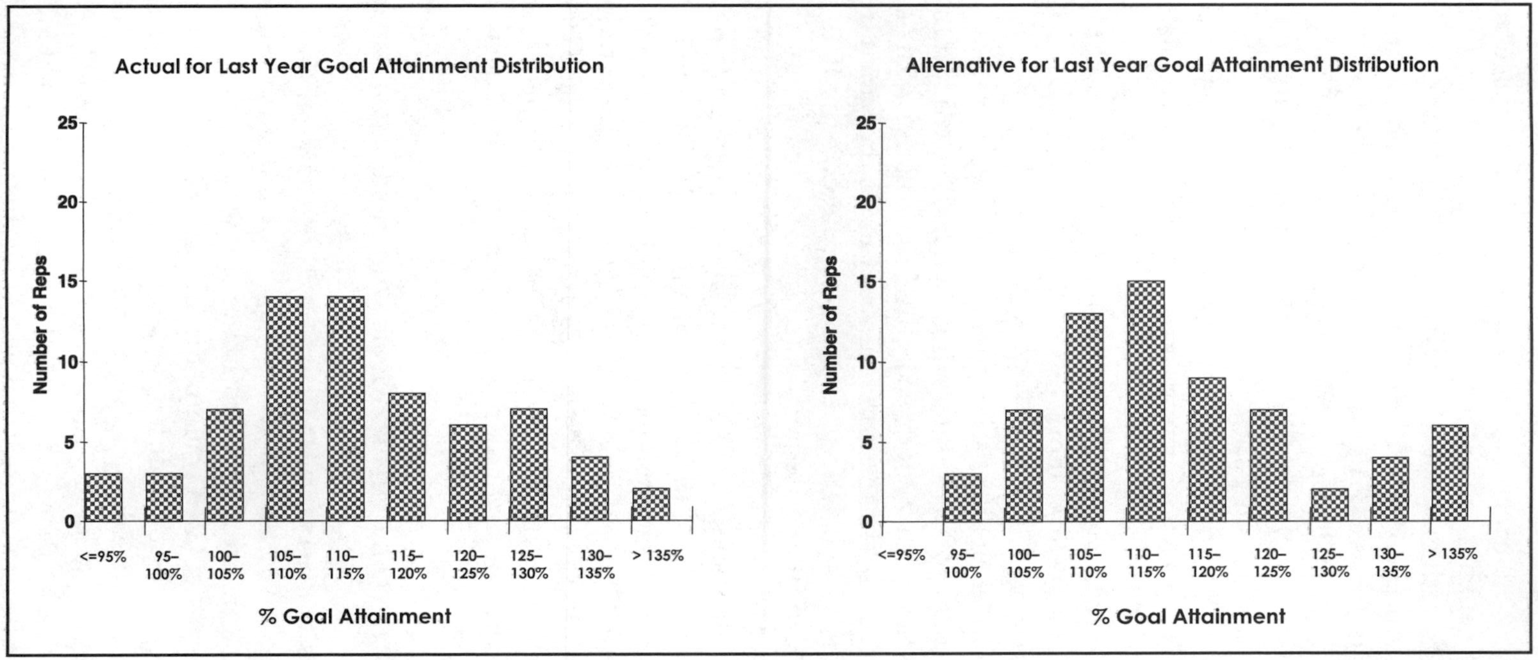

Actual for Last Year Goal Attainment Distribution

Number of Reps

25
20
15
10
5
0

<=95%
95–100%
100–105%
105–110%
110–115%
115–120%
120–125%
125–130%
130–135%
> 135%

% Goal Attainment

Alternative for Last Year Goal Attainment Distribution

Number of Reps

25
20
15
10
5
0

<=95%
95–100%
100–105%
105–110%
110–115%
115–120%
120–125%
125–130%
130–135%
> 135%

% Goal Attainment

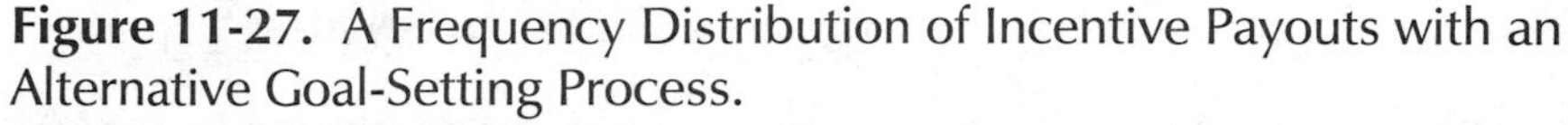

**Figure 11-27.** A Frequency Distribution of Incentive Payouts with an Alternative Goal-Setting Process.

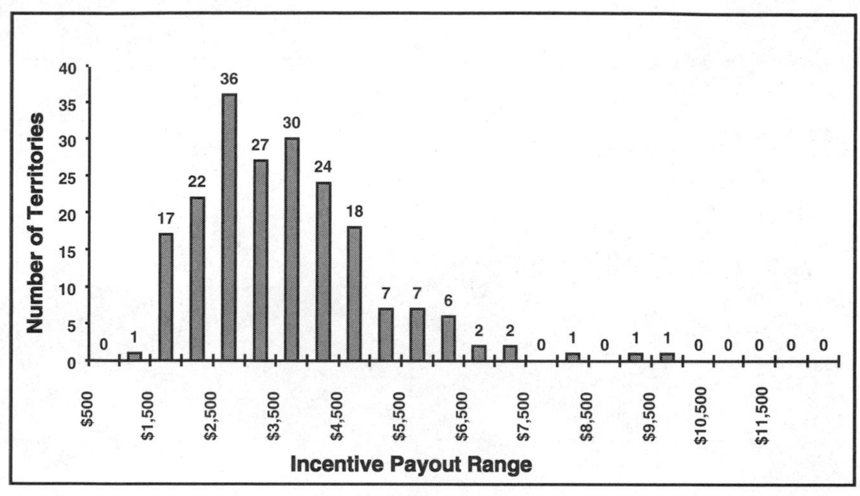


time may be less productive because of lost carryover. When sales managers are allowed to adjust goals, they feel motivated and comfortable with the goals.

Web-based systems can facilitate field managers' review of territory goals. For example, the OLIVE system developed by ZS Associates allows managers in the field to propose changes to territory goals based on local knowledge of special situations such as those described pre-

**Figure 11-28.** A Distribution That Rank-Orders the Territory Payouts That Would Result from an Alternative Goal-Setting Process.

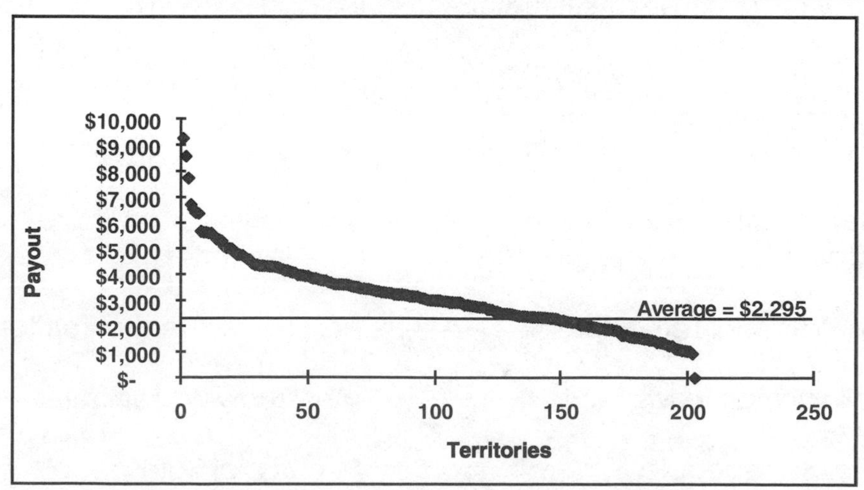

**Figure 11-29.** A Territory-by-Territory Analysis (Alternative Minus Actual Bonus)

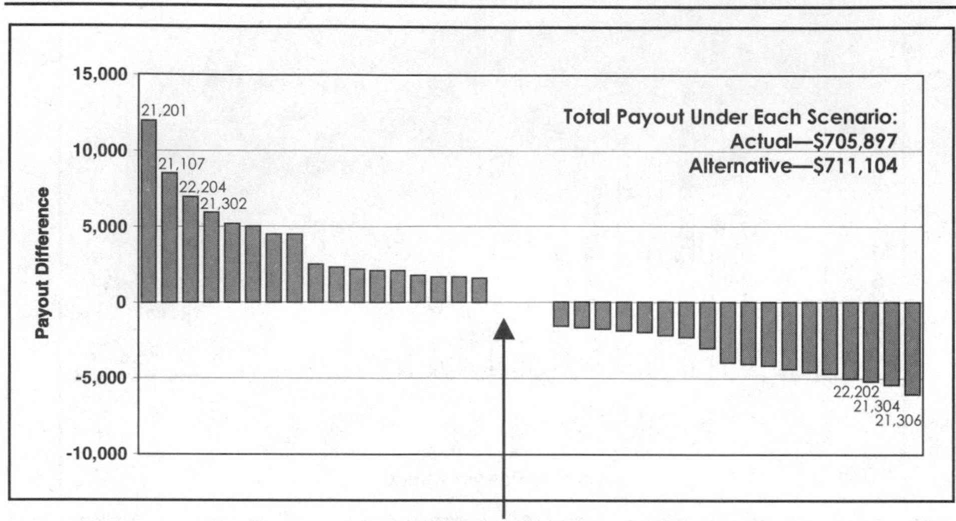


46 territories with change in payout < $1,500 not shown

viously. Managers can access a secure Web site via the Internet or a company intranet that provides historical performance data for their territories and the proposed goals for each territory. The managers then review these data and submit suggested adjustments to territory goals for approval by headquarters. Once approved, the changes can be entered into the system immediately. The Web-based system allows faster turnaround between goal creation and rollout. It also ensures greater accuracy, since the system enforces zero-sum changes and allocates revisions fairly down to subordinate territories. Finally, the Web-based

**Figure 11-30.** Groups That Could Be Affected Disproportionately.

| | | |
|---|---|---|
| High Performers | ↔ | Low Performers |
| High-Market-Share Territories | ↔ | Low-Market-Share Territories |
| High-Potential Territories | ↔ | Low-Potential Territories |
| Declining Territories | ↔ | Growing Territories |
| Senior Salespeople | ↔ | Junior Salespeople |

system provides an audit trail of changes, so all adjustments are properly documented and can be tracked easily.

The final quota adjustment by the district or regional manager concludes the goal-setting process. The final goals take into account territory behavior, an evaluation of the territory-level consequences of the new goals, and the manager's assessment of what is reasonable and fair. This process should develop goals that are attainable, fair, and motivational.

## Tracking Performance against Goals

As stated earlier, goals are an energizer. When implemented effectively, they can be great motivators for salespeople. However, in order for goals to motivate, feedback is necessary. Salespeople need to know how they are doing relative to a goal for the goal to affect their behavior.

Many sales forces provide performance feedback to salespeople in the form of hard-copy reports. These reports typically come out at regular intervals (monthly or quarterly, for example) and track territory performance against goals. In addition to hard copy, many salespeople can download performance data for their territory from headquarters onto a laptop computer. Spreadsheet or other analytical software on the laptop allows the salesperson to sort, graph, and manipulate data to track her or his performance relative to goal.

Some companies also use Web-based systems to track sales force performance against goals. Systems like OLIVE allow a salesperson to visit a secure Web site that provides the latest "scorecard" of performance for his or her territory. This scorecard provides immediate access to goal and attainment information, based on the latest available data. On the Web site, salespeople can use a "payout calculator" to compute their incentive payout for different goal achievement scenarios. For example, they can calculate how much incentive pay they will receive if they continue selling at the same pace. Alternatively, they can calculate how much more they would need to sell to make a desired higher bonus.

Web-based goal attainment tracking systems have many advantages. First, they give salespeople access to the latest data as soon as they are available. Next, they reduce the cost of producing hard-copy reports and shipping them to the field. Third, they provide a single place for salespeople to access performance data provided by different vendors. Finally, their interactive "what-if" features focus salespeople on the right activities and motivate them to get results.

## Concluding Goal-Setting Insights

### Poor Goal Setting Leads to Increased Costs and Low Morale

Salespeople may receive unearned income if their goals are set unrealistically low. Similarly, the sales force will lose motivation if goals are set so high that they are unachievable. "Management knows that we can't make it; they are just fooling themselves and us" may be the salespeople's point of view. Neither outcome is beneficial for the firm. It is important to strive to set realistic goals.

### Goals with Short Time Frames and Midyear Goal Corrections Are Appropriate in Volatile Business Environments

The business environment can present high levels of uncertainty. Under these circumstances, forecasting a national sales goal accurately is difficult. The uncertainty is amplified when territory-level goals need to be established. Goals with short time frames and processes that allow for midyear goal corrections are effective strategies for companies faced with volatile selling environments.

Decisions concerning goal adjustments need to be prudent and symmetrical. Raising goals when overachievement is evident and maintaining goals when they cannot be achieved is unfair and is not a good business decision. A management team that is known for trying to set the most realistic, fact-based goals (even if this means a midyear correction) will receive the support of the sales force.

### Goal Oscillation Can Be Tempered by Using Market Potential to Calculate the Goal

Sales managers and salespeople may lament, "I had a great year and what do they do? They significantly raise my goal for next year." Or, "I am not going to make my goal this year, so the best strategy is to hold back so that I can get a low goal next year." Goal oscillation, or alternating high and low goals, occurs when goals are determined entirely by sales in the prior planning period. Incorporating territory characteristics such as market potential into the goal calculation smoothes the oscillation. This, of course, assumes that the company has an estimate of or a good surrogate for territory-level market potential.

## The Most Suitable Goals Depend on Business Objectives and the Business Environment

Goals communicate what is important to the firm at the current time. The following four examples illustrate this point.

1. Profitability must be watched carefully in mature markets. Mature markets have limited growth opportunity, so quotas should favor profitability. A company will sacrifice profits if it generates too many sales at a reduced price.
2. Growth in sales or market share is a good measure for goal setting in growth environments.
3. Companies that are attempting to maintain and penetrate existing customers can state their goals in terms of customer service, customer satisfaction, and revenue growth.
4. Activity goals are useful when there are many new salespeople in the sales force. Activity goals double as a training device and are useful when the company wants to ensure that salespeople are doing the right things.

## Rank-Ordering Salespeople Is an Alternative to Goal Setting

Some companies find goal setting inaccurate, contentious, or frustrating, yet they need a mechanism for evaluating and rewarding their salespeople. Rank-ordering salespeople on one or more measures is an alternative to goal setting as a means of evaluating and rewarding. Salespeople who are ranked high, are viewed as top performers and those who are ranked low are regarded as low performers. Incentive pay is awarded to the top performers. Systems based on rank-ordering can work; however, their success hinges on an equitable and balanced sales territory alignment. Salespeople can be rewarded for having a good sales territory and not for their performance if the territories are not balanced.

Any organization that decides to abandon goals should have compelling reasons for doing so. Remember, you can't make goals if you don't have them. Opting to eliminate goals may hide a fundamental weakness.

### Limit the Number of Goals to Three

Too many goals confuse people and tend to scatter sales force effort and energy.

### The Process of Setting Goals Can Be as Beneficial as the Goals Themselves

Setting quotas allows the company to communicate its strategy in a tangible way. The company tells its salespeople what they can do to help the company make its corporate goal. Also, a well-administered process of quota setting allows the company to show its salespeople that they are being treated fairly. Web-based systems can streamline the process of incorporating field input and disseminating key information to salespeople.

### The Goal-Setting Process Must Recognize the Difference between Goals for Performance Evaluation and Goals for Rewarding

Monthly and quarterly quotas are useful for financial control and for rewarding salespeople quickly. However, there is too much variability in monthly and quarterly results for them to be useful for evaluating salespeople. Annual reviews based on annual goal attainment are more appropriate for evaluation.

# Chapter 12

# Precision Selling

Precision selling is a systematic process for segmenting customers and prospects and for developing and implementing segment-specific account coverage strategies. An effective precision selling program ensures that a sales force customizes its selling process for enhanced effectiveness. It also assures that best practices are part of the organizational knowledge of the company.

In this chapter you will learn:

- What the elements of a precision selling system are and how they are linked together to enhance productivity
- The different ways in which customers and prospects can be segmented using data on account profile, behavior, and needs
- The choices that have to be made with regard to how accounts in different segments are covered
- The implementation issues that arise with precision selling programs
- Useful insights that will help you ensure that the implementation of your precision selling program is successful

## Precision Selling

Customization is a sales force's distinctive weapon and a key driver of a salesperson's impact. Customization takes advantage of the fact that customers and prospects differ in many ways. They have different product and service needs; different sales, sales potential, buying influences, and buying processes; and different attitudes toward innovation, cost, and service. A salesperson is well positioned to exploit this diversity by delivering a customized sales program to each customer. A salesperson has the flexibility to adapt the company's approach and product/service offering for each customer and can adapt the sales process even as it is being executed.

## The Need for Precision Selling

Activity data compiled by the authors from numerous companies confirm a simple fact—salespeople do not naturally or instinctively allocate their effort in the firm's or in their own best long-term interest. Figure 12-1 shows one example of how a sales force allocated its time to customers with different sales opportunities. The graph shows the percentage of market potential contributed by ten customer segments, ranked from largest to smallest, along with the corresponding sales force effort allocated to each segment. This example is from an industry in which the salesperson had a reasonably good idea of sales potential at the account level.

In the example in Figure 12-1, even though the sales potential of the top 10 percent of the customers was, on average, nine times that of the bottom 10 percent, the sales force investment in the lowest-potential customers was 70 percent of the investment in the top-potential customers. A retrospective analysis of this situation established that the sales effort to half of the prospective buyers was unprofitable. Effort can be misallocated across customers, products, and activities.

The familiar 80-20 rule implies that 20 percent of the customers control 80 percent of the sales. Even though this is seldom literally true,

**Figure 12-1.** The Allocation of Effort to Segments with Different Market Potential.

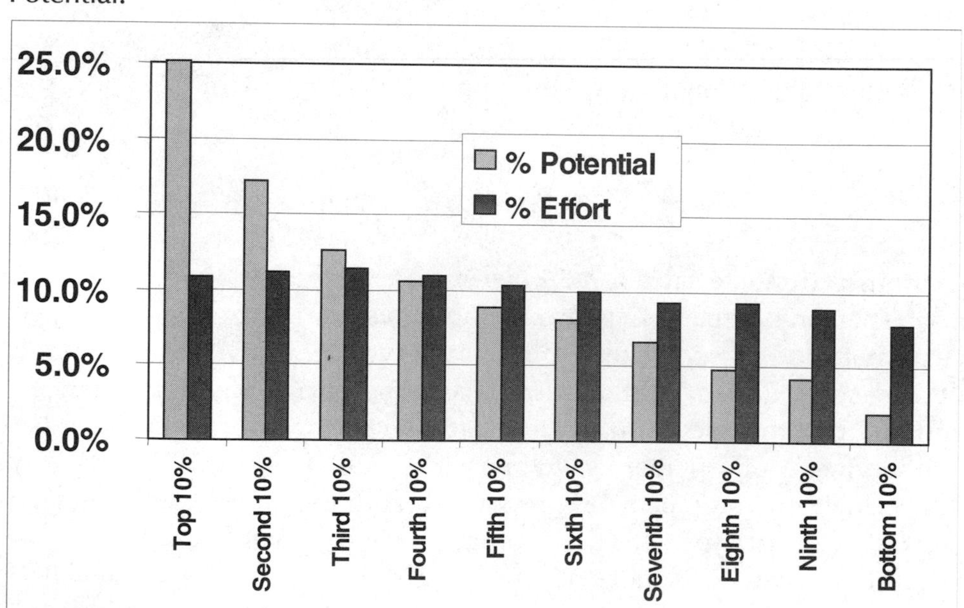

it reflects the accurate belief that sales potential and sales are concentrated. A variation of the 80-20 rule, i.e., the 80-20-30 rule, captures an even more powerful truth, i.e., that the typically high investment in the bottom 30 percent of customers can cut a firm's profits in half!

Figure 12-2 shows examples of systematic biases in whom a sales force sells to and how the sales force sells. The sources of systematic bias are the customer, the company, the sales manager, and the salesperson. A precision-selling process minimizes the impact of these biases.

**Figure 12-2.** Examples of Systematic Biases in Effort Allocation.

| *Source of Bias* | *Salespeople Who . . .* | *Are More Likely To . . .* |
|---|---|---|
| **Customer** | Have low-sales-potential, demanding customers | Spend too much time with them |
| | Have customers with high service needs or needs that the salesperson can't meet on his or her own | Focus on customers whose needs they can easily meet on their own |
| **Company** | Have territories with too many high-sales-potential accounts | Have low penetration or share as a result of poor coverage |
| | Have little information about the potential of different accounts | Spend their effort where the current sales are highest |
| | Have very little cash compensation at risk in the incentive plan | Expend too little energy customizing sales actions for individual customers |
| **Sales manager** | Are managed by the number of calls they make | Spend too much time with friendly customers irrespective of potential |
| | Are left alone to decide what to do | Have high variability in the quality of precision selling |
| **Salesperson** | Have difficulty handling rejection and customer objections | Shy away from difficult accounts |
| | Are concerned about making this period's quota | Seek the low-probability, high-volume account |
| | Are making good progress toward making quota | Seek the high-probability, low-volume account |
| | Have made quota relatively early in the period | Seek the low-probability, high-volume account |

There is a famous line from David Ogilvy, "I know for a fact that half my advertising money is wasted. What I don't know is which half." The first part of the statement is true for many sales forces too, but the second part is seldom true. Reallocating sales effort presents a significant opportunity for performance enhancement because although 20 to 35 percent of sales effort is typically wasted, it is possible to know which part this is, even before looking at the quality and nature of the effort.

A systematic precision-selling program pinpoints productive and unproductive uses of sales resources. Significant sales and profitability improvements are possible by making a transition from the intuitive approach that says "Just do it!" to a systematic approach to selling that considers account sales potential and other determinants of customer attractiveness.

Precision selling is strongly linked to three other chapters in this book:

- Chapter 1, which deals with defining the role of the sales force in a go-to-market strategy, in which segmentation drives the selection of different sales channels and processes for each segment
- Chapter 3, which focuses on sizing the sales force, with the level of activity in each segment determining the size of the sales force
- Chapter 4, which examines the issue of sales force structure, with the needs of different customer segments leading to sales force specialization

The segmentation frameworks of this chapter also apply to these other chapters. However, the focus here is on implementing a process for precision selling to assure the successful implementation of segment-specific sales actions.

## Two Key Questions: Whom to Sell to and How to Sell

Two key questions for precision selling are whom to sell to and how to sell. How to sell is important when the complexity of the buyer's decision-making process is high, and whom to sell to is important when there are many customers and prospects to choose from. Figure 12-3 shows the conditions under which each question becomes important.

If the number of customers and prospects is large, the first decision is who the target customers will be. This answers the whom to sell to question. A company selling business accounting software has 10 mil-

**Figure 12-3.** Determinants of the Importance of the Questions Whom to Sell to and How to Sell.

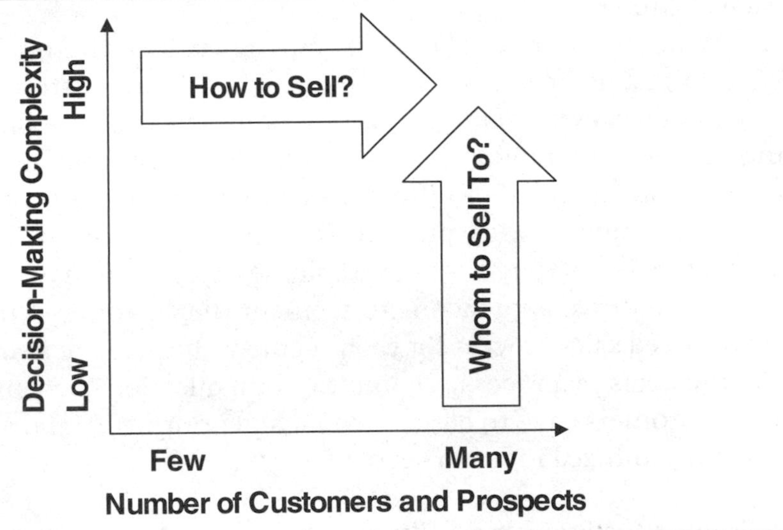


lion target businesses to choose from in the United States alone. The whom to sell to question can be multidimensional in scope: Small, medium, or large? Single site or multisite businesses? U.S. or multicountry businesses? Private or public companies? What industries? Which parts of the country? Are companies that are likely to buy using an accounting firm for advice or not? An office machines company selling copiers, printers, and fax machines has many of the same choices, and some new ones: Should the targets be current customers, competitive accounts, or both? Should the targets be companies that are price-sensitive or those that are feature-driven?

If the buyer's decision-making process is complex, the how to sell question is important. In many buying situations, buying centers with multiple points of influence have emerged. How to sell remains a key issue even when the customer selection task is simple. If a firm supplies gaskets to automotive manufacturers, the limited number of potential customers makes the whom to sell to problem trivial in nature. But the how to sell question is still relevant. How does each customer buy? Are decisions made globally or regionally? Does the buyer want to use the Internet to implement the transaction or to process a bid? Is the buyer interested in an exclusive arrangement, or will the order be split among multiple suppliers? Does the customer want to specify the product or codesign it? How much of the order is fixed and how much is variable?

If there are many customers and the decision process is complex, both questions become important. The customers have to be segmented and prioritized, and a selling process needs to be customized for each segment.

When the number of possible customers is limited, sales forces use customized approaches for each account. If the customer operates a buying center with many decision makers and a complex decision-making process, the how to sell question naturally leads a sales team to understand the roles of different people in the customer organization in the decision-making process. On the other hand, if the number of customers is very large—for example, several hundred for each salesperson—the normal approach is to segment the customers and use a more customized sales process for each segment. If there are many customers and the decision process is complex, both questions become important. The customers have to be segmented and prioritized, and a selling process is customized for each segment.

### A Process for Precision Selling

The precision selling process has four components:

1. *Segment customers and prospects:* Group customers and prospects into clusters with similar characteristics, behaviors, and needs.
2. *Develop account strategies:* Select target customers and determine the coverage approach for each segment.
3. *Implement:* Carry out the customized sales actions.
4. *Track and analyze:* Track and analyze actions and results to improve the precision selling process.

These components are shown in Figure 12-4. The remaining sections of this chapter describe each component in more detail. The first two steps are also the starting points for the development of a go-to-market strategy and for sizing and structuring the sales force.

## Customer Segmentation

Customer segmentation is the process of placing customers and prospects into groups with common characteristics. Good segmentation consists of identifying a small set of actionable segmentation characteristics or criteria and assigning customers and prospects to the seg-

**Figure 12-4.** Components of Precision Selling.

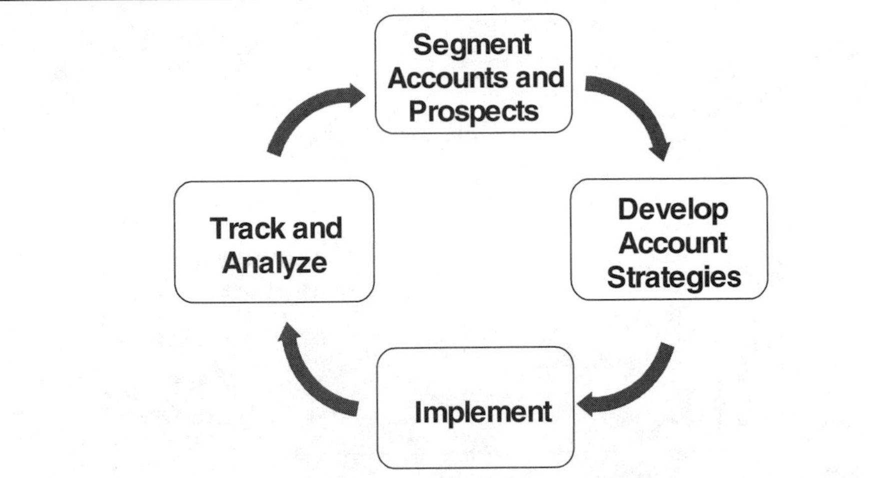


ments. Segment homogeneity ensures selling process similarity within a segment.

The same set of customers and prospects can be segmented in many ways. In order to develop actionable customer segments, *similar* sales actions should be appropriate for customers within a segment, and *different* sales actions should be needed for customers in different segments. The ultimate state of precision selling occurs when each customer is a specific segment, which is possible with a sales force and/or the Internet. Mass marketing, in which all customers are treated similarly, is the other extreme.

There are two stages to segmenting business-to-business markets for sales organizations. The first stage is to define a few meaningful, measurable, and actionable segments through a centralized or coordinated effort. If this stage leads to each segment's having just a few members, the segments are referred to as micromarkets. Figure 12-5 shows how varying levels of customer segmentation can affect sales results and the effort that is needed in order to perform the segmentation in the first place.

As Figure 12-5 implies, it takes incrementally more effort to make segmentation more granular, i.e., to have increased homogeneity in each segment at the cost of having many more segments. This granularity increases impact, since the segment strategies are precisely tailored for the homogeneous segments.

The second stage consists of an even finer formal or informal segmentation by the salesperson or sales team. Since a salesperson works

**Figure 12-5.** Balancing Impact and Effort of Centralized Segmentation.

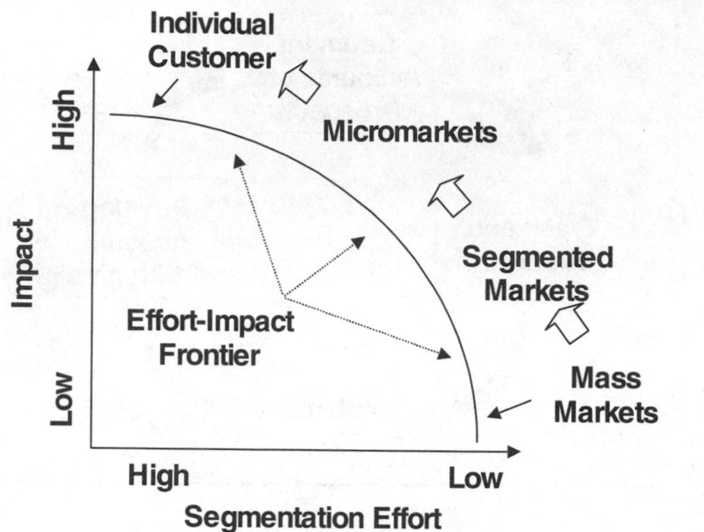


at the individual account level anyway, the second stage typically reaches either the micromarkets state or the ultimate state in which each customer is a segment. In many firms, in industries as varied as computer hardware, computer software, consulting, newspapers, and pharmaceuticals, salespeople develop a formal written plan *for each customer*. With sales forces, customer-specific sales actions exist naturally. The challenges are to ensure that:

- The centralized segmentation is compatible with the second action stage that takes place in the field.
- The customer-specific actions are the right actions.
- The firm benefits from cross-customer and cross-territory insights.

Customer segmentation uses variables of the types shown in Figure 12-6. Ideally, customer needs are understood in terms of products, services, and buying processes. Needs are expressed in terms of how a customer behaves, and the customer's profile is used as a surrogate for behaviors and needs. Customer segmentation in most firms tends to be fairly rudimentary. Significant improvement is possible by selecting from the best variables of the types shown in Figure 12-6.

There are two possible approaches to segmentation. The *a priori* approach begins with a set of identifiable customer/prospect character-

**Figure 12-6.** Categories of Segmentation Variables and Examples.

| *Categories of Variables* | *Profile* | *Behavior* | *Needs* |
|---|---|---|---|
| **Examples of Variables** | • Industry<br>• Geography<br>• Number of employees | • Sales<br>• Product category sales<br>• Sales growth<br>• Sensitivity to effort<br>• Loyalty<br>• Response to innovation | • Product criticality to buyer<br>• Price, technology, or service?<br>• Degree of centralization<br>• Buying influences<br>• Awareness<br>• Role of Internet in buying |

istics, such as industry and size, and works forward to see if the groups identified have distinct behaviors and needs. The *post hoc* approach begins with behaviors and needs, and works backward to see if the groups have identifiable characteristics. If the profile, behaviors, and needs are well understood for all customers and prospects, the best approach is to use behaviors and needs as the basis for segmentation. Typically, however, profiles are well developed, behaviors are partially understood, and needs are known for only a few customers based on research or customer interactions. In this scenario, the idea is to link the known needs and behaviors to the profiles, and then extrapolate this linkage to the accounts with unknown needs and behaviors.

## Sales Potential as a Basis for Segmentation

Segmenting on the basis of sales potential is important for three reasons.

First, accounts with larger potential typically require higher levels of investment. Second, information on the sales potential of customers gives a good indication of a salesperson's and a firm's performance in the marketplace. If a high-potential account has low sales, there is an opportunity to enhance performance. If a particular salesperson systematically underperforms with most high-potential accounts, the problem could be with the person. Finally, the extent of account penetration can also help define the selling process needed. For example, high-penetration accounts often need value-added programs to enhance stickiness, while low-penetration accounts need a targeted effort to study account needs and competitive vulnerability.

Figure 12-7 illustrates an example of potential-based segmentation for an industrial sales force. The five segments, A, B, C, D, and E, are defined in terms of average potential per account, as shown on the left side of Figure 12-7. On the right side is a comparison of the historical effort and the results per account in each of these segments. In this example, potential, effort, and sales are aligned.

Even though customer potential is a fundamental segmentation variable, most industries do not have information on market potential readily available. In such situations, diligence and work are required to assess potential; however, in most cases the effort is worth the cost. Often, surrogate measures of sales potential can be used. A copier sales force can use a surrogate such as the number of white-collar employees as a measure of copier potential. A Pitney Bowes sales force selling mailing systems needs to estimate the letter and postage volume to define customer potential. In this case, the number of employees and the industry will be used to estimate the potential of the customer. In the pharmaceutical industry, the sales of all products in a particular therapeutic class to a physician is used as a potential measure for that physician. These data are compiled from electronic pharmacy records. However, in countries where this information is not available, surrogates such as office size, physician specialty, the size of patient waiting areas, patient demographics, etc., are used to estimate potential. An Oracle sales force selling database products uses the installed number of different types of computers, such as personal computers, Unix servers, and mainframes, as a determinant of potential.

In general, firms use direct measures such as overall market sales or consumption figures when they are available. When these are not available, surrogates and markers are used. Customer size in terms of employees, office space, and overall sales are examples of surrogates. When the segmentation variable is categorical, it is called a marker. A customer's industry and the presence of a centralized buyer are examples of markers.

## Estimating Sales Potential Using Profile, Behavior, and Needs

Since sales potential is an important segmentation variable and direct or precise measures of sales potential are seldom available, processes for estimating sales potential are very useful. Figure 12-8 illustrates a four-step process that has been used successfully by several firms that have a large set of customers.

**Figure 12-7.** Segmentation Based on Sales Potential per Account.

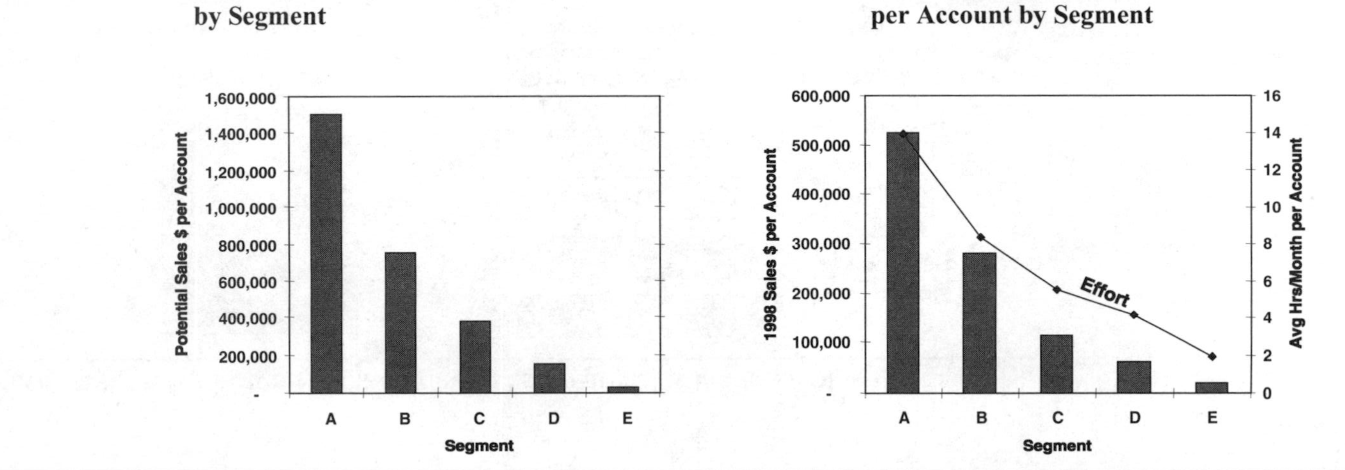

Figure 12-8. A Four-Step Methodology to Estimate Sales Potential of Accounts.

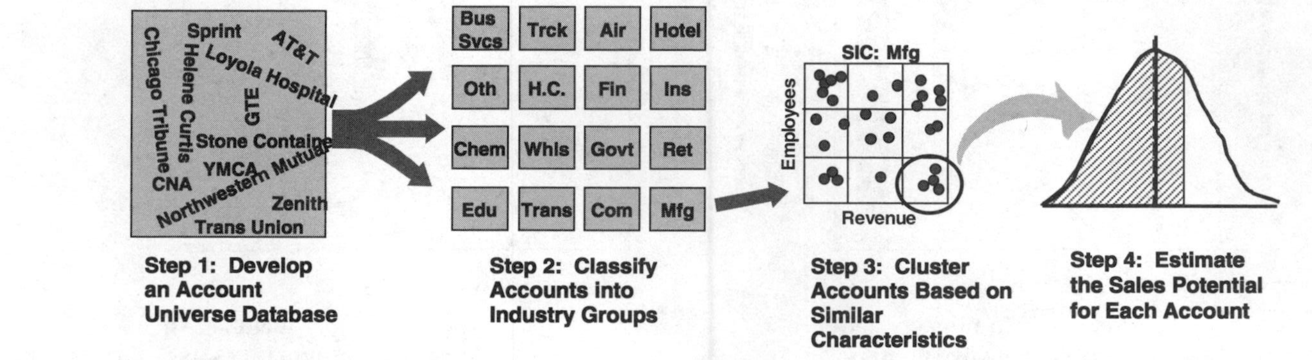

*Step 1: Develop an account universe database.* In this step, the set of customers and possible future customers is developed. Typical sources from which to create this list include the company's sales systems, salespeople, syndicated lists from firms such as Dun & Bradstreet, industry associations, and primary market research. Available data for each account are compiled. These data can include the types of variables discussed earlier, such as customer size, number of employees, company sales to the customer, customer loyalty, needs, and decision-making centralization.

*Step 2: Classify accounts into industry groups.* Industries are represented by their SIC codes. Since the number of SIC codes is large, the industries are grouped, and each account is assigned to an industry group.

*Step 3: Cluster accounts based on similar characteristics.* The accounts within each industry group are clustered on the basis of the variables deemed important for segmentation. In the example shown in Figure 12-8, the clustering is on the number of employees and the company revenue.

*Step 4: Estimate the sales potential for each account.* Analyze the accounts within each cluster and use an appropriate heuristic to estimate the sales potential for each account. One example of a heuristic is to use the eightieth percentile in terms of sales within each cluster as a proxy for what is possible with all accounts whose sales are lower than this percentile. This step yields a "potential" sales per account for each cluster. Another possible heuristic is to define the sales increase possible in an account as the difference between the account's current sales and 50 percent of the gap to maximum sales in its cluster. Different heuristics may be appropriate for customers and prospects, or for low-penetration accounts and high-penetration accounts. The best heuristic may also depend on the reason for the segmentation. In order to understand long-term potential, a high percentile, such as 90 percent, may be appropriate. To set goals for salespeople, some achievable distance from current sales to the maximum achievable is the right approach.

This four-step process is a systematic approach to estimating account potential. Such processes are approximate, yet they can be extremely valuable to sales organizations that wish to sharpen the focus of sales activity on the most attractive and responsive accounts.

**Segmentation Based on Account Profile.** The most useful segmentation variables depend on both the buyer and the seller. For a firm supplying restaurants with food or laundry services, surrogates could be the number of patrons per day and the average amount spent by each patron. For a supplier of floor-cleaning supplies, the surrogate would be the physical size of the restaurant.

A customer marker, such as industry, is more important if sales actions vary on the basis of that marker. For example, when Dell Computer Corporation sells to universities, it uses a different set of actions from those it uses when it sells to large corporations. With universities, Dell focuses on setting up buyers so that they can service themselves, with the university computer store playing a role in providing the order processing, billing, and installation functions. For corporations, it is a key-account sell. Dell is interested in becoming an approved supplier, then customizing the service offering with services such as keeping track of a customer's inventory. The sales process is different, and even the range of suitable products can be different. For universities, the Dell program is a well-standardized offering sold to all universities. For the corporate market, the program is highly variable and customized for the buying processes and the information technology infrastructure and management processes of the customer firm.

Figure 12-9 provides another example of using markers for segmentation. It shows a segmentation grid for a trade school. The trade school targets non-college-bound high school graduates for one- and two-year

**Figure 12-9.** Sample Segmentation of High Schools for a Trade School.

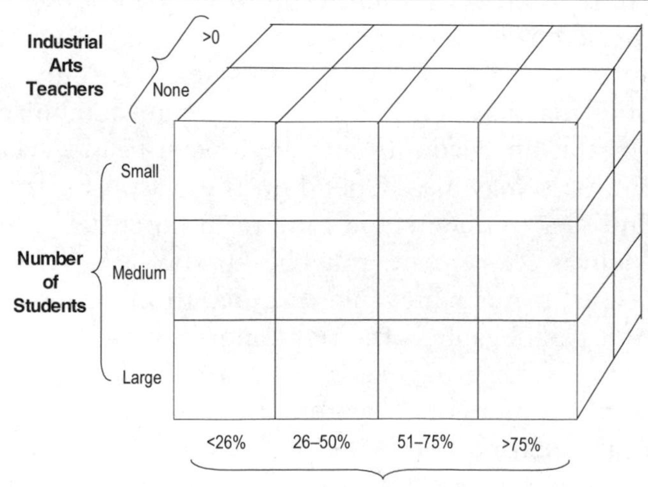

programs in fields such as data processing, manufacturing, and electronics. The attractiveness of a high school is enhanced if:

- The school is large.
- The school has industrial arts teachers.
- A smaller percentage of the student body is college-bound.

**Segmentation Based on Customer Profile and Behavior.** Whereas the account profile refers to *who a customer is* (industry, office space, employees), behavior refers to *what a customer does*. Common customer behavior measures include sales, sales growth, loyalty to a firm or its competitors, and response to innovation. Behavioral measures, when combined with measures of sales potential, naturally include the concept of a firm's competitive position. For example, market share can be used as a basis for segmentation in industries where competitive data are available or can be estimated at the customer level. Segmenting by customer behavior also provides insights into how the actions a sales force engages in should vary for different segments. For example, some companies in the computer industry use "hunters" to penetrate new accounts. The sales process used by these hunters is different from that used by the "farmers" who are responsible for maintaining and growing existing accounts. Behavior segmentation begins to provide a basis for determining the type of investment, not just the quantity of investment, that is appropriate for each segment.

Figure 12-10 shows an example of segmentation based on volume, growth, and sales effort. This type of segmentation raises interesting questions. If growth is low although effort is high, as for segment H, perhaps the effort devoted to the segment needs to be redirected. If the sensitivity of sales to sales effort can be estimated, this is a useful segmentation criterion.

It is often possible to use even richer behavior segmentation criteria to augment sales results and sensitivity to sales effort. Figure 12-11 shows an example of customer segmentation based on potential and loyalty. The clusters in Figure 12-11 are isolated in order to determine how the sales actions directed at the different segments should vary. In the figure, the size of the bubble indicates the number of accounts in the segment. This type of segmentation naturally leads to the issue of account strategy development. For example, the sales approach to fanatics would be focused on increasing customer stickiness and can include value-added services. The high-potential nonusers warrant either a watchful wait for a sales opportunity to present itself or an end run through a less visible department, product use occasion, or geographic area in which the customer operates.

**Figure 12-10.** Example of Behavioral Segments Based on Volume, Growth, and Effort.

| *Segment* | | *Accounts* | |
|---|---|---|---|
| *ID* | *Description* | *Count* | *Percent* |
| A | Enthusiasts | 249 | 7% |
| B | Consistently low volume | 1,145 | 33% |
| C | Moderate volume, high growth, high effort | 118 | 3% |
| D | Moderate volume, high growth, low effort | 88 | 3% |
| E | Low volume, high indirect sales/customer | 1,240 | 36% |
| F | Low and growing volume, high effort | 264 | 8% |
| G | Low and growing volume, low effort | 175 | 5% |
| H | High volume, slow growth, high effort | 70 | 2% |
| I | High volume, slow growth, low effort | 141 | 4% |

**Figure 12-11.** Example of Behavioral Segments Based on Potential and Loyalty.

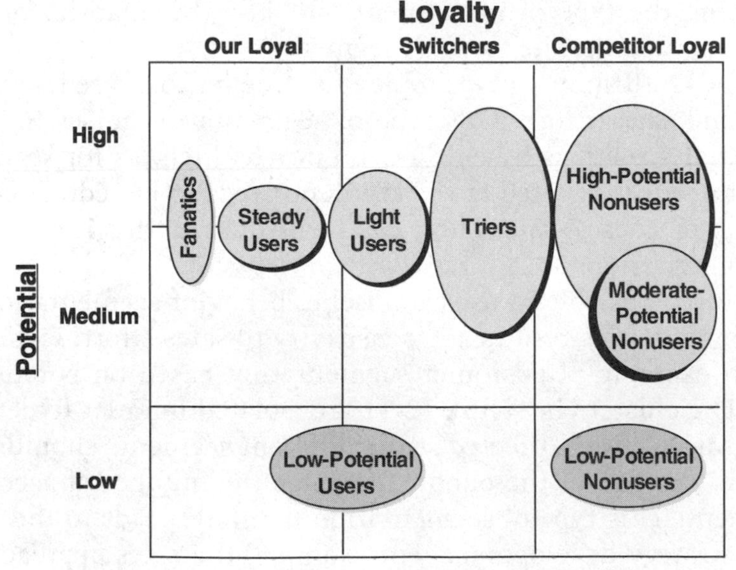

## Segmentation Based on Customer Profile, Potential, Behavior, and Needs

Customer needs drive potential, profile, and behaviors. To the extent that these needs can be understood, they are an even more powerful and practicable basis for segmentation.

An example of several customer-need-based dimensions for segmentation is illustrated in Figure 12-12. The rows refer to the customer's need for product and service. For example, consider a hospital supply customer, such as a large hospital system, that wants products from a supplier such as Baxter. In addition to wanting products, the hospital may want to form a partnership with Baxter to manage all the hospital's supply acquisitions. This is an example of a service-driven customer. The product-driven customer wants only the product, whereas the service-driven customer also sees value in the services surrounding the product. A product-driven FedEx customer is interested in getting packages to their destinations on time. A service-driven customer may be interested in having FedEx manage the customer's delivery logistics, tracking all shipments and allocating the costs to different departments and projects. A product-driven Sun Microsystems customer wants the Sun Server and Solaris software, whereas a service-driven customer also wants Sun's assistance in configuring and maintaining the system and in coordinating the customer's relationship with other suppliers of data storage, database, and system development products and services.

The columns of Figure 12-12 capture three common types of customer needs: cost, technology or product features, and relationship or trust. Such need-based dimensions are key determinants of the most appropriate sales actions for the customer.

Figure 12-13 illustrates segmentation based on three factors: volume, growth, and the degree of centralized decision making. The firm

**Figure 12-12.** Example of Segmentation Based on Customer Needs.

| | Cost | Technology | Relationship |
|---|---|---|---|
| **Product-Driven** | | | |
| **Service-Driven** | | | |

**Figure 12-13.** Example of Segmentation Based on Potential, Behavior, and Needs.

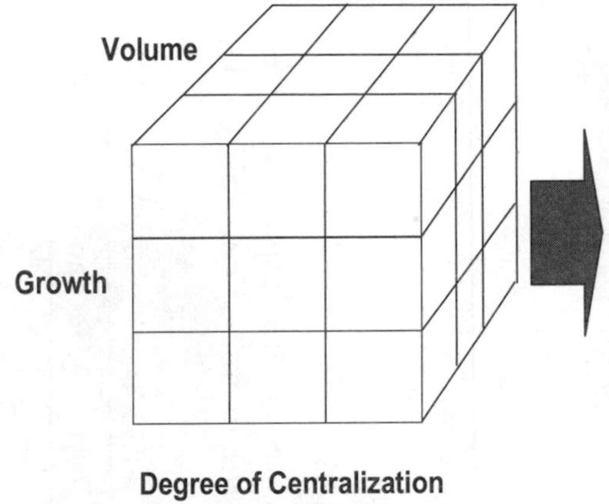

Volume

Growth

Degree of Centralization

| *Segmentation Variables* | *Range of Values* | | | |
|---|---|---|---|---|
| | *High* | *Medium* | *Low* | *Very Low* |
| *Volume* | >$200K | $125K–$200K | $50K–124K | <$50K |
| *Three-Year Growth Potential* | >100% | 50–100% | <50% | |
| *Degree of Centralization* | Single Point of Control | Shared Control | Decentralized | |

in this example is selling a consumer-industrial product through different types of stores. The volume and growth dimensions drive the quantity of sales investment the company makes in a customer. If a customer makes decisions centrally, key account coverage is warranted at the headquarters level. If a customer is decentralized, sales actions are aimed at a broader set of decision makers.

The sales force using the segmentation in Figure 12-14 sells medical devices to hospitals. The variables used include teaching versus community hospital, number of beds, and account status. The account status indicates whether the account is secure or vulnerable. In this example, a hospital that recently converted to the company's products is classified as *secure,* since the devices have a life of four to six years and are unlikely to be replaced in the interim. A *vulnerable* account in one in which the company's products are at the end of their useful life. The devices will be replaced soon, and the account is in play. An *opportunity* account is a competitor's vulnerable account. A mixed account is one in which different floors or departments are at different points in the product's life, and so while one hospital department is vulnerable, another one is secure.

This type of segmentation is also useful in the computer hardware and software industry. If a customer has recently installed a Hewlett-Packard Unix machine, it is unlikely that that customer will switch to an IBM or Sun Microsystems machine soon. The account is *secure* for the moment.

## Account Strategy Development

Segmentation lays the groundwork for account strategy development.

**Figure 12-14.** Example of Hospital Segmentation Based on Size, Type, and Vulnerability.

| *Segmentation Variables* | *Range of Values* | | | |
|---|---|---|---|---|
| | *Very Large* | *Large* | *Medium* | *Small* |
| *Size (Beds)* | >999 | 500–1,000 | 200–499 | <200 |
| *Type of Hospital* | Teaching | Community | | |
| *Account Status* | Vulnerable | Secure | Opportunity | Mixed, by Department |

This consists of:

- Developing one or more sales actions or coverage strategies for each segment
- Assessing the costs and benefits of each possible coverage strategy for each segment
- Selecting for each segment the most beneficial strategy that is within the capacity of the sales force.

Answering the following related questions will provide the best sales actions and coverage strategies:

- What is the nature of the customer interaction?
- Who performs the sales activities?
- What is the quantity of sales activities?

The answers to these three questions are not always separable.

Once a few meaningful, measurable, and actionable segments are defined, the value of segmentation can be realized only through action, as the salesperson interacts with customers and generates sales. It is expected that the actual sales actions delivered will be customized for each customer, and it is no accident that the word *customized* is derived from the word *customer*. As mentioned earlier in the chapter, in many firms salespeople develop a formal written plan for each customer.

The nature of the interaction between salespeople and customers/prospects is driven by:

- The status of the customer/prospect in the buying cycle
- The needs of the customer/prospect
- The role of the customer in the buying process
- The nature of the salesperson-customer relationship

Consider the sales funnel in Figure 12-15. The nature of a salesperson's interaction with an account varies depending on the account's position within the funnel. The salesperson has different goals for suspects, prospects, and customers. To achieve these goals, sales force activities range from qualifying to closing to providing service after the sale.

Suspects are accounts that *may* want to buy. Before putting a suspect into the funnel, the salesperson has to qualify the suspect by verifying that it intends to buy the kind of products the salesperson is

**Figure 12-15.** The Sales Funnel.

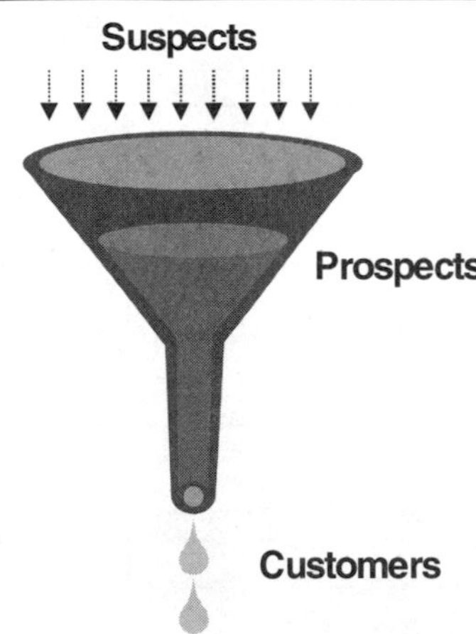


selling. The salesperson talks to the potential customer and assesses the account's situation. The activities at this stage revolve around verifying interest. Is a contract between another supplier and the potential customer expiring? Did the potential customer express interest by calling? Is the firm expanding its manufacturing capacity, which may mean that it needs more raw materials?

Once the possibility of a sale is established, the suspect becomes a prospect. At this stage, the activities center on understanding the buying center of the prospect. This includes understanding the buyer's needs and the roles different people play in the buying process. As mentioned before, effective segmentation will ensure that such selling process differences are considered in creating segments in the first place. A useful framework for understanding the different roles of buyers was developed by Robert Miller and Stephen Heiman.*

This framework defines three buyer roles: the economic buyer, the user buyer, and the technical buyer. The economic buyer controls the funds and is interested in the product's economic benefits for the buying firm. The user buyer is interested in the product working for the user, and the technical buyer ensures that the product meets specifications. The interesting role of the coach, who assists with the sale, can be played by a person from either the buying or selling organization.

Different buyers have different roles, and different customers can have different needs and motivators. Figure 12-16 illustrates the devel-

*Robert B. Miller and Stephen E. Heiman, with Tad Huleja, *Strategic Selling,* Warner Books, Inc., New York, 1986.

**Figure 12-16.** Account Strategies.

| | *Low Potential, Low Share* | *Low Potential, High Share* | *High Potential, Low Share* | *High Potential, High Share* |
|---|---|---|---|---|
| **Price-Driven** | Pull back | Low effort | Medium effort | Partner based on profitability enhancement |
| **Technology-Driven** | Pull back | Medium effort | Understand account needs | Partner based on technology delivery |
| **Relationship-Driven** | Low effort | Medium effort | Understand competition | Partner based on value-added services |

opment of account strategies based on account potential, the company's market share, and the buyer's primary motivation. For example, for the price-driven buyer, the partnership is based on enhancing the customer's profitability. For the competitive account that is technology- or relationship-driven, the strategy is to understand the account's needs and the competition.

In complex selling environments, many parts of a company touch many parts of the customer. The sales organization, marketing, manufacturing, research and development, and finance must all deal with the customer in a coordinated, multiplexed manner. The nature of the customer interaction is varied and complex, too. Usually, the account manager coordinates the effort across the various customer interactions.

## The Two Last Steps: Implementation and Tracking and Analysis

Segmenting and developing account strategies are the planning steps of precision selling. The implementation and tracking and analysis steps ensure that plans are executed and that there is institutional learning about what works and what does not. Capturing institutional learning ensures that energy is used effectively by utilizing the best practices across the sales force. At the micro level, it ensures that the precision selling process is resilient in the event of salesperson turnover or account reassignment.

In consumer markets, many promotional programs, such as advertising, are still broadly delivered. The marketer's challenge is to enhance a program's effectiveness by selecting the appropriate message, media, timing, frequency, etc. In sales force–intensive markets, there is frequently the opposite challenge. Each salesperson is delivering a customized, customer-specific program in the field on a regular basis. The organizational challenge is to put a conscious thinking framework behind the customization. If customers in Boise and Baltimore have similar needs, behaviors, and profiles, they should be getting the same proven set of sales actions: at the very least, what is discovered in Boise should be available to the company so that it can be tried in Baltimore. Customer relationship management systems and business planning systems are often used as tools to capture this learning.

The different components of a precision selling process can be centralized, decentralized, or somewhere in between. In a centralized process, the hub of the process is a headquarters-based organization or team responsible for precision selling. Some firms even have a position such as director of micromarketing or manager, precision marketing.

In a decentralized process, the salesperson is the hub of the precision selling effort. Information about the segmentation criteria and learnings are provided to the salesperson, and she or he decides what to do and how to do it. A hybrid process has both centralized and decentralized components. For example, the effort of defining the customer segments and broadly defining the account coverage strategies may be centralized. This is followed by a decentralized effort to define strategies for micromarkets or individual customers.

Figure 12-17 summarizes the pros and cons of centralization and decentralization, and the implications for the precision selling program.

## Seven Insights for Better Precision Selling Implementation

As is the case with many sales force programs, implementation may be the most important part of a successful precision selling program. Even the best-designed programs fail if they are not implemented in a way that allows the sales force to embrace them. Here are several insights regarding implementation.

**Precision Selling Programs Generate Institutional Learning.** Differences in customers and salespeople lead to hundreds of natural experiments being carried out every day between a firm and its customers. A systematic precision selling program creates a mechanism for capturing the learning from these experiments, which also minimizes the cost

**Figure 12-17.** Tradeoffs for Centralized and Decentralized Precision Selling Programs.

| | *Centralized Approach* | *Decentralized Approach* |
|---|---|---|
| Pros | • Allows development of a national program<br>• Provides the flexibility to change the program quickly<br>• Can effectively consider strategies for current and future products<br>• Can use cross-sectional data to uncover effective account strategies<br>• Makes knowledge about customers resilient to field turnover | • Is customer-driven by using local knowledge<br>• Is motivating for the salesperson<br>• Provides local flexibility |
| Cons | • May not be implemented by salespeople because they do not have ownership of the program<br>• Can't effectively consider local factors<br>• Typically is not able to deal with the details of micromarkets or individual customers | • Lacks control<br>• May not be consistent across the sales force because salespeople may not have a global picture<br>• May require more training resources and customized local programs<br>• Is vulnerable to field turnover |
| Implications | • Requires good information availability<br>• Requires the central group to understand the selling process, preferably by involving field members in the team<br>• Requires the central group to have credibility with the field<br>• Needs a strong "back channel," i.e., a feedback loop from salespeople to the central group<br>• Needs to transfer ownership through implementation process | • Needs focus on education and training<br>• Requires that information be made available to the sales force<br>• Needs a mechanism for sharing best practices<br>• Needs a customer relationship management system to capture learning and knowledge |

of relearning. Therefore, sharing best practices is a key ingredient of a precision selling program.

**Sales Support Resources Need to Be Customized for Salespeople, Too.** If management expects a sales organization to deliver customized sales actions to customers, the sales support program needs to be customized for the salesperson. For example, if a salesperson has difficulty cracking new accounts, the specific account development processes targeted at new accounts should be heavier in his or her territory. If a territory has few customers and many prospects, more telesales support for lead generation and qualification could be called for.

**Education and Involvement of Salespeople and Managers Is Essential.** Salespeople have to believe in and benefit from a precision selling program for it to be successful. Since salespeople are responsible for the implementation of any program, a program designed with field sales involvement is more likely to be field relevant and implementable in the field. Centralized efforts with an extreme command and control approach usually fail, since they are contrary to most sales cultures. Many people enter the sales profession because of the independence it provides.

**Precision Selling Is an Ongoing Process.** A firm may make a discrete change to its organization structure or its incentive plan, but precision selling is, by definition, an ongoing process. Therefore, it needs ongoing support systems for information capture, analysis, and dissemination and sharing of best practices.

**Quick Wins Are Important.** A virtuous cycle is created if success is shared and quick wins reinforce behavior. This is particularly critical if the predision selling process requires a significant investment of time and effort on the part of salespeople and sales managers.

**Identify Succinct Business Rules and Make Them Part of the Ongoing Dialog.** Successful precision selling programs define a few appealing sets of business rules that become part of the sales force dialog and culture. For example, one firm has each salesperson target five competitive accounts each quarter. In sales meetings and managers' interactions with salespeople, there is endless discussion of the status of the "T5 accounts" (the targeted five). Wins are shared and celebrated. Winning the T5 accounts has become a symbol of success in the firm.

**Data Are Necessary, but Having Data Is Not Enough.** In data-poor companies or industries, managers often believe that the only thing standing between them and a successful precision selling program is data availability. A database by itself is a cost item, not a revenue item. For precision selling to fulfill its promise, the program has to be useful to the people on the front line—the salespeople. Salespeople have to see the work they do to keep the process going as a help, not a burden.

## Conclusion

The sales force has the power to customize the sales process for each customer. This power comes at a price. On the one hand, variability in salespeople's capabilities and motivators creates variability in the sales actions. On the other hand, the customization itself makes the salesperson's company vulnerable to salesperson turnover. A precision selling program seeks to capture the benefits of customization, while bringing some discipline to the process to reduce the impact of the potential pitfalls. Beginning with a process for segmenting customers/prospects based on their profile, behaviors, and needs, and ending with a process for implementing, tracking, and analyzing activities and impact, precision selling helps close the loop between strategy, structure, size, and the tactics of delivering sales effort.

# Chapter 13

# Using Technology to Assist the Sales Force in Customer Relationship Management

This chapter focuses on the important role that technology plays in connecting a firm with its customers. Customer relationship management (CRM) systems help buyers and sellers store and share information, communicate, collaborate, and transact business.

In this chapter you will learn:

- How CRM systems enable improvements in efficiency and effectiveness that benefit customers, salespeople, and the company
- An effective process for designing and implementing a CRM system, including specific advice on setting goals, selecting a supplier, system design, implementation, and ongoing support
- Useful insights to ensure that your CRM system delivers the desired results

## Introduction

Customer relationship management is the set of tools and processes a firm uses to identify, attract, and retain customers and to leverage its relationships with its customers. Increasingly, CRM is becoming synonymous with *the use of technology* to manage customer interactions and transactions, and this is the focus of this chapter.

Most large firms have moved aggressively to automate the "back office," or systems for accounting, order entry, finance, and production.

The current frontier is automation of the "front office," which refers to functions such as sales, marketing, and customer service.

The combination of the speed and storage capabilities of computers with the connectivity of the Internet provides a powerful linkage among various customer-facing parts of a company, its partners, and its customers. Through this linkage, successful CRM implementations result in cost reduction, revenue increase, cycle time reduction, and enhanced customer satisfaction. However, unsuccessful attempts at CRM implementation waste time and money. Successful implementations are increasing, but in spite of many generations of CRM evolution, they are not yet the norm.

CRM systems range from simple contact-management systems that focus on assisting individual salespeople to complex enterprise-wide and cross-enterprise systems.

This chapter examines the role that CRM systems play in connecting suppliers and customers, and why many CRM systems fail. Additionally, the chapter explores the objectives of and opportunities provided by CRM systems and presents a list of core CRM components and implementation processes. The final section provides useful insights to steer CRM systems toward successful implementation and away from waste and failure.

## The Role of CRM Systems

As shown in Figure 13-1, the technology and terminology used to describe CRM have evolved over the years. In stage 1 of this evolution, *call reporting systems* focused on tracking activity and *sales force automation systems* tried to automate repetitive and error-prone sales tasks such as order processing. In stage 2, *electronic territory management systems* sought to increase the salesperson's effectiveness by assisting with targeting and customer profiling. This led to an evolution of the name to *technology-enabled selling* (TES) which implied a focus on the entire sales process. In stage 3, the term *customer relationship management* evolved, reflecting the realization that a firm's relationship with a customer is a many-to-many relationship. Numerous parts of a company, such as sales, service, marketing, finance, and product development, as well as a company's partners, need to collaborate and share information in order to meet customer needs. A major focus of current CRM systems is to ensure that customers have a consistent experience across multiple sales channels. If a customer gets product information

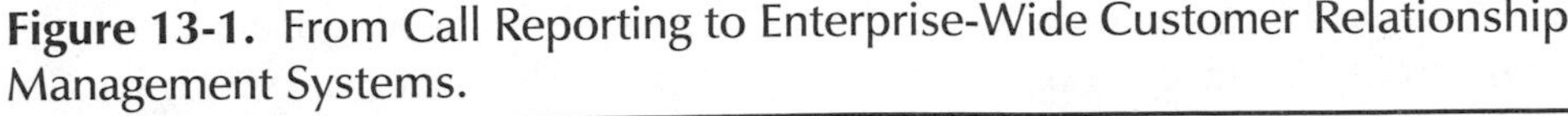

**Figure 13-1.** From Call Reporting to Enterprise-Wide Customer Relationship Management Systems.

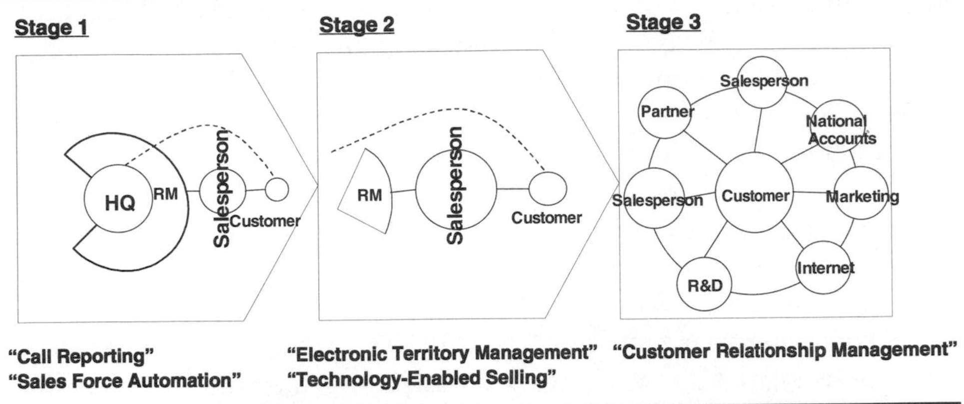


over the Internet, makes an inquiry over the telephone, sees a technical specialist for product design assistance, and sees a salesperson for pricing information, CRM systems seek to ensure that all the parties are integrated in order to ensure seamless collaboration and information sharing. This makes companies more effective in communicating with their customers and more efficient in transacting business. In addition, companies benefit from increased customer loyalty.

The term *partner relationship management* (PRM) is related to CRM, but focuses on optimizing relationships with business partners. PRM solutions focus on the special needs of indirect sales channels. For example, Cisco Systems, Great Plains, and Intel have invested heavily on customer-partner extranets.

Figure 13-2 illustrates how CRM systems connect sellers with their customers. The company and the customer are connected by many relationships. On the company side, every individual who interacts with a customer contributes to the sales process and is, in fact, "selling." The customer is typically a complex organization with a mix

**Figure 13-2.** The Role of Customer Relationship Management Systems.

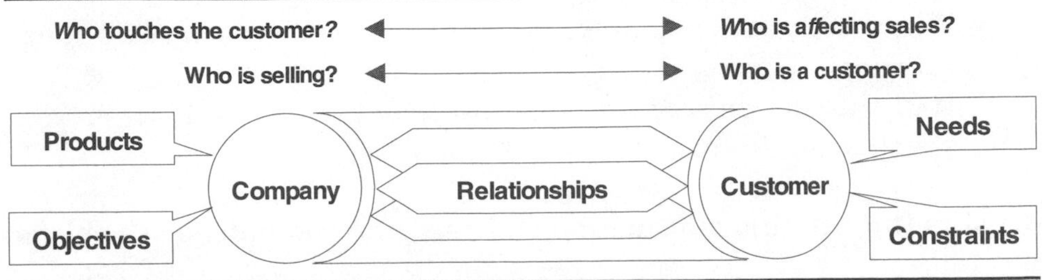

of decision makers, decision influencers, and users at different levels focusing on functional or economic aspects of the product or service. In such cases, the customer is not a single person, but a group of individuals who are collectively the "customer." Thus, many "sellers" touch many "buyers." Technology plays a pivotal role in helping buyers and sellers store and share information, communicate, collaborate, and transact business. This enhances the focus and value of the interactions for the sellers, partners, and buyers.

Here are some examples of how computer technology can help a selling organization be more effective or efficient in defining and meeting customer needs.

A computer network salesperson meets with a design engineer to audit the design of a new network connecting a customer's more than one hundred worldwide sites. They focus on hardware, software, space, power, and staffing needs within the customer's realm of operation and control. How have other firms organized their networks? Do the different components work with one another? Is the allocated physical space sufficient for the firm's evolving needs? They are assisted by a product configuration system provided over the Internet by the salesperson's firm.

An account manager for a soft drink manufacturer is discussing a special promotion with a grocery store chain representative. What was the impact on short-term volume, future volume, and category sales of a promotion implemented in demographically similar areas across the country? He taps into a presentation on his personal computer. Most of the work was done at headquarters, but it is captured convincingly and portably on the laptop computer.

A pharmaceutical sales rep reviews a potential list of more than six hundred physicians in her territory. As she plans her itinerary for the next quarter, she has the following questions:

- Who has requested what information?
- Who has been using her company's products? Who has not?
- Who are the innovators?
- Who has participated in recent market research studies and clinical trials?
- Will they see her, or are they interested only in a local professional symposium?

She sifts through this information on her laptop computer as she plans her time.

An automobile dealership has agreed to expand its advertising space in the Saturday paper. As the newspaper salesperson leaves, his colleague, the copy designer, remains to complete the layout design to the exact specifications he has just heard. The newspaper's sales team has just completed another successful sales cycle.

The office manager at one location of a *Fortune* 500 firm orders supplies from a customized Web site created by Staples. The one hundred products (out of thousands available on the general Staples Web site) that show up on the screen and their prices have been negotiated and approved by Staples' national account team and the customer's buying center. This self-service feature cuts the cost of processing orders by 26 percent. Both Staples and the customers benefit from the improved efficiency.

A product development team is in the early stages of testing a new concept. It needs a short list of loyal customers for a focus group. The customer database produces a list of seventy customers within seconds, and the list is e-mailed to the sales force for its input. The focus group is completed in seven days, a process that had a cycle time of a month before the sales force and the marketing department shared a common database.

The ten-year, $2 billion information technology outsourcing agreement is finally in place after eighteen months of specification and negotiation. Overall, more than eighty people from sales, legal, financial, technical, human resources, and general management, almost evenly divided between the buying and selling organizations, have been involved. A CRM system tracks their interactions and captures the processes that kept the project design moving forward and led to the successful agreement.

In these examples, there are three main CRM components, as shown in Figure 13-3. In order to make better *decisions*, CRM systems enable enhanced *processes* that rely on customer and product *data*.

This chapter focuses on how CRM systems affect salespeople. The most widespread use of technology in the sales function has been to assist salespeople in their jobs, not to replace them. Two terms commonly used by computer scientists provide a useful framework for understanding this distinction. *Artificial intelligence* (AI) is the effort to replace a human mind with a machine. *Intelligence amplification* (IA) is the development of systems that amplify the human mind by assisting it with tasks it finds difficult.

While an assembly line can be automated, it is difficult to automate most sales jobs. However, technology amplifies the intelligence

**Figure 13-3.** Examples of CRM System Components.

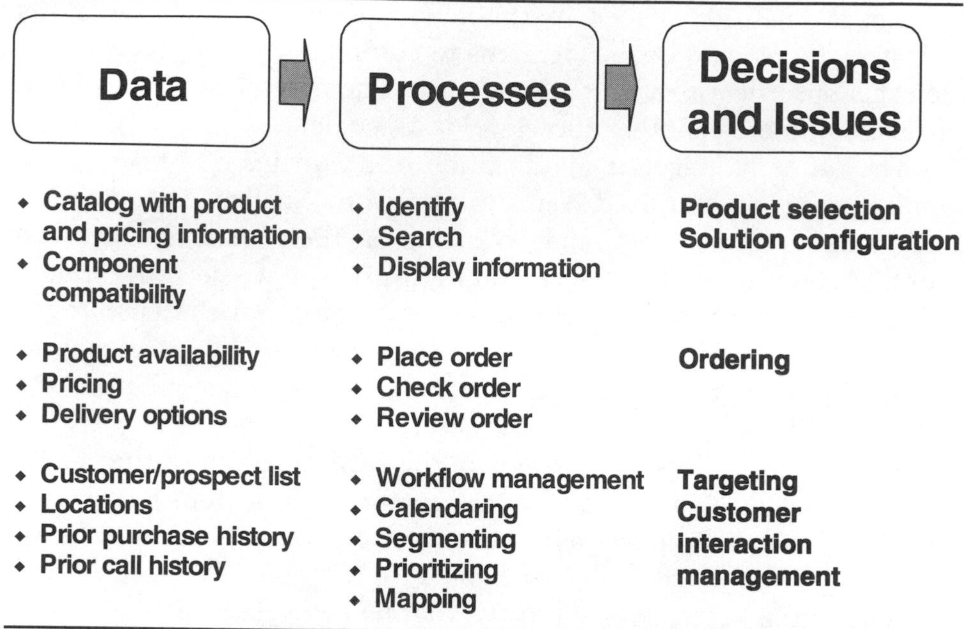


of salespeople and allows them to spend less time on mundane tasks and more time on understanding customers' issues and gaining new customers. Tasks that are difficult to perform manually, repetitive, or time-consuming should be automated. Sorting through a list of six hundred potential customers is a daunting task without a computer. A computer simplifies the task for the pharmaceutical salesperson.

A computer network salesperson had the difficult task of ensuring component compatibility across hundreds of devices. The computer assured high-quality execution, while adding tremendous value for the customer as well. On the other hand, creative work, such as solving a customer's problem by bringing together many skills and capabilities, or gathering intelligence on customers and competitors, is assisted by technology, not replaced by it.

As more firms use the Internet as a key channel for communication with their suppliers and customers, it is possible that customers will substitute an electronic system for the salesperson. Figure 13-4 represents the customer's point of view. If the value added by the salesperson is low and the value added by technology is high, the salesperson may be replaced. This is happening in some very specific segments of the markets for commodities such as plastics and steel, where the product is well understood by the customer. Customers find the value added by technology to be high when the intensity of information in the buying

**Figure 13-4.** Customer View of Salespeople and Technology.

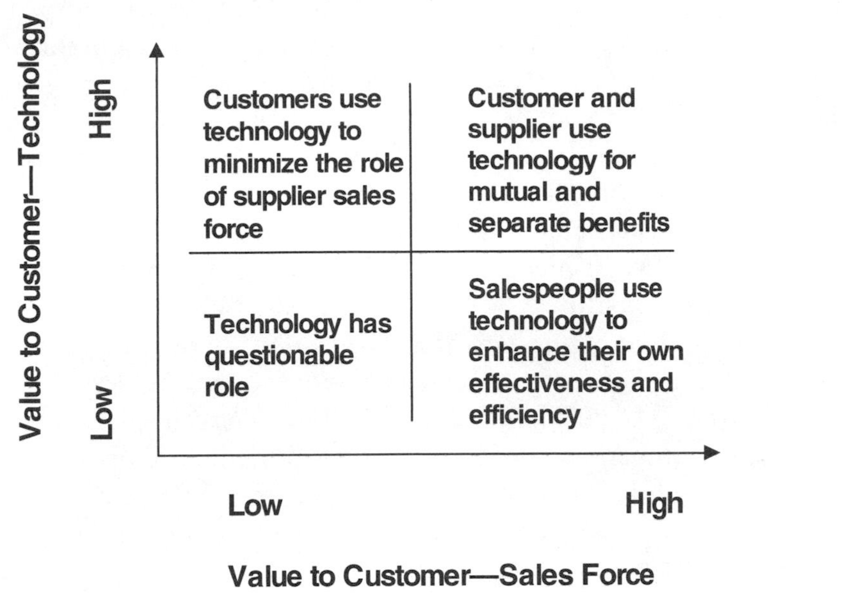


process is high. If both the salesperson and technology add value, technology will be leveraged by the customer and the salespeople.

Sometimes technology adds little value for the customer but can assist the salesperson. For example, a salesperson may use a computer system to target customers better or to track the decision influencers in a customer's organization. In such cases, the role of technology is to assist the salesperson, not to act as an interface between the supplier and the customer.

By assisting salespeople to do their jobs, CRM systems can bring significant benefits to a company. However, most studies indicate that a majority of implementations are not successful. The next section examines the reasons why so many CRM systems fail.

## Why CRM Systems Fail

Beginning with a *Harvard Business Review* article ("Automation to Boost Sales and Marketing") in 1989 by Moriarty and Swartz, successful implementations of sales force automation (SFA) systems have been widely reported. This article documented several successful implementations that provided a greater than 100 percent return on investment (ROI) within the first year of an SFA implementation.

A note of caution was sounded soon thereafter in a 1990 survey by The Conference Board, which found that "half of all companies with operational sales automation systems reported serious shortcomings with their systems, and nearly half, if they could start over again, would choose a different vendor." This theme has been consistently echoed by benchmarks run by the CSO Forum, a Boulder, Colorado, research firm. A 1999 report from the CSO Forum and Deloitte Consulting reported that 70 percent of firms had seen little or no improvement as a result of CRM implementation. While the opportunity to enhance productivity by using a CRM system remains significant, the possibility of losing money and wasting large amounts of time is also significant. Figure 13-5 indicates the reasons for failure of CRM systems.

A rigorous, well-planned, and well-executed implementation process helps companies avoid these risks. The details of such a process and many useful insights for avoiding failure are described later in this chapter. The next section explores the objectives of and opportunities for CRM systems.

## CRM Objectives and Opportunities

The objectives of any CRM project fall into two broad areas: enhancing effectiveness and improving efficiency. Effectiveness improvements

**Figure 13-5.** CRM Risk: Implementation Failure.

**General Reasons**
- The project objectives are fuzzy or continually changing.
- CRM project managers are technology-focused and not business-focused.
- Measurable business benefits are nonexistent or overestimated.
- Costs and effort levels are severely underestimated.

**Does Not Work**
- It's the first implementation of a new technology, and the pieces do not work at the scale needed in an actual implementation.
- The effort needed is severely underestimated.
- The project scope creeps upward until it is too heavy to function.
- It becomes impossible to coordinate the multiple suppliers.
- It is too complicated to move data from old systems to new systems.

**Not Used**
- Users do not know how to use it.
- Users see few concrete benefits.
- The infrastructure can't keep up with changes in people, systems, and business environment.

focus on increasing the top line, whereas efficiency improvements streamline processes to reduce cycle times and costs.

Effectiveness gains improve processes, and efficiency gains simplify processes. Effectiveness improvements help companies sell better, and efficiency improvements help companies sell faster, so that more time is left for crucial activities.

When a salesperson uses a computer system to price a proposal quickly, the added speed is an example of an efficiency gain. A task that would otherwise take a day can now be done in an hour. When a salesperson uses customer profiles to target better and therefore get more results from the same level of sales activity, this is an example of an effectiveness gain. Efficiency and effectiveness are useful in analyzing the value of CRM systems. These benefits are derived at the level of the salesperson, the team, the company, and even across companies. CRM systems can add value across enterprises by linking a customer with a supplier or multiple parties in a distribution chain, or multiple suppliers.

The productivity gains are realized by helping the three main stakeholders in the sales process: the customer, the sales force, and the company. Each of these is discussed in turn.

## Customer Benefits

Different types of customers seek different benefits. For example, in a *partnership* relationship, the goal is a seamless interface between buyer and seller. In this case, technology assists in coordination across multiple parts of the selling and buying organizations. For example, the salesperson, manufacturing, marketing, and finance can coordinate a proposal that commits the company to a multiyear supply and financing arrangement. In a *consultative* relationship, technology assists with product configuration, financing, and coordination with other suppliers. In a *transaction* relationship, the customer seeks efficiency through better order processing, better order expediting, and better price.

CRM systems affect a customer's evaluation and acquisition of a product. Access to information happens at a convenient time and place. Self-service and faster communications allow a customer to save time and money on a transaction.

CRM systems assist customers with many activities, including product selection, ordering, tracking and receiving, paying, and problem resolution. Technology can enhance the value that customers derive in several areas, and also can ensure the consistency of the customer's experience with different entities and channels of the supplier.

*Product selection*: An electronic or online catalog with up-to-date information and videotaped product "samples" make selection easier. Tools, which aid solution design, can check parts compatibility automatically and provide product mock-ups, increasing customer understanding of and confidence in the product. Finally, automated ways to communicate customer criticism of the product to designers can improve future products and therefore benefit the customer.

*Ordering*: Automation makes searching for and acquiring a product more convenient and efficient. Automated ordering and inventory allow quicker access to information and faster bids for the customer. The ordering process can include a check of parts compatibility as well as delivery dates and inventory levels. Finally, an automated system shortens the time from order to arrival and allows a customer to check the status of an order easily. The customer can still deal directly with a salesperson or can access an ordering system directly with a computer-to-computer hookup. Electronic data interchange (EDI) reduces the cost of inventory in the system, because finished goods inventory levels at supplier and purchaser sites are co-managed. In either case, automation benefits the customer because of an increase in information availability.

*Tracking and receiving*: Automation improves the customer receiving process. Bar code/scanning systems make checking of deliveries faster and more accurate for customers that receive large volumes of material. Automated systems help reduce shipping errors by keeping address information up to date throughout the system. Additionally, automated systems make sure that wrong picks and missing items in orders are infrequent. Good automation gives customers the right order with faster delivery.

*Paying:* Automation also improves the billing process. Electronic invoicing makes the process more accurate and timely.

*Problem resolution*: Remote diagnostics improve repair service; and with some types of products, repair can be done without a repair person ever having to come to the site. Problem resolution is also improved with an automated system. Tracking orders and customer records electronically is faster and more accurate than performing the tasks manually. E-mail or other messaging systems improve communication as well.

## Salesperson Benefits

The second focus of CRM systems is improving the effectiveness and efficiency of the salespeople. The company benefits from automation, but it also benefits from a better sales force.

CRM systems allow a salesperson to create a proposal quickly in order to close a sale or make a bid deadline that he or she might otherwise have missed. An ordering system reduces cycle time and costs, as it places the order, totals the bill, gives discounts, and does other detail work automatically.

Beyond these improvements, the Internet is also changing the sales process. With the Internet as a business address, salespeople have another communication channel that overcomes barriers of distance and time. They also have a handy research tool for keeping in touch with the company's and the customer's environment.

**Efficiency Improvement.** Automation to improve salesperson efficiency usually focuses on three areas: time management, administration, and communication. Scheduling and time management software reduces unplanned time. Automated tickler files organize and track leads and remind a salesperson to call on latent customers. Administrative chores such as reporting of expenses and calls are minimized through automated reporting. A good messaging system makes it easier for salespeople to contact customers and for customers to contact salespeople. Cell phones improve the accessibility of mobile salespeople. E-mail and faxes can be used to send large amounts of data quickly.

**Effectiveness Improvement.** Effectiveness gains for salespeople are derived primarily from the good use of information such as customer and product databases. Computerized prospecting systems provide access to prospects' corporate data, making it easier for salespeople to qualify customers. Leads and customer selection, as well as targeting information, are improved by the development or use of large customer databases. The selling process is improved with a computerized marketing encyclopedia, which contains product literature, presentations, and an electronic catalog that might contain a video of the product in action. A good selling database provides data about customers, product availability and specifications, and order status and profitability; it also improves forecasting.

An emerging source of effectiveness gains is the coordination of all parts of an organization that may touch a customer. This creates value in two ways. First, coordination increases overall customer satisfaction and engenders loyalty through better needs fulfillment. Second, coordination helps generate and convert leads and provides new opportunities based on a better understanding of current and future customer needs.

CRM system effectiveness gains for salespeople, focused on enhancing the top line, are realized from:

- Quicker decision making by allowing access to timely information
- Better allocations of sales actions across customers and prospects
- Delivery of training to salespeople without taking them out of the field
- Dissemination of new product information and best practices
- Better communication systems that enable teamwork and allow more effective contacts among customers and colleagues.

Figure 13-6 summarizes the range of salesperson-centered applications in CRM systems.

**Figure 13-6.** Salesperson-Focused Functions of a CRM System.

- Manage accounts and distributors
- Track sales by customer
- Plan and report sales calls
- Automate sales plans and tactics
- Answer requests for product literature
- Track leads; manage a tickler file
- Manage contacts
- Make computer-based presentations
- Access competitive intelligence on-line
- Enter orders
- Check inventory and order status
- Report and check expenses
- Calculate incentive earnings
- Write letters/do word processing
- Manage a personal calendar
- Get geographic information and routing
- Use electronic mail
- Access the Internet
- Receive training

### Company Benefits

For a company, the ultimate goals of a CRM system are to increase sales and/or reduce costs. These two goals are achieved mostly through the customer-centered and salesperson-centered CRM system functions discussed earlier.

CRM systems improve a sales manager's effectiveness, too. Figure 13-7 provides examples of management-centered uses of CRM systems.

CRM systems improve organizational learning through better communication and retention of institutional knowledge. Information and best practices are passed quickly to those who need them most by means of an intranet. Customer information remains in the company even if salespeople leave.

### Balancing the Needs of the Constituents

Thus far, discussion has focused on how a CRM system assists three parties: the customer, the salesperson, and the company. Which constituent's need is most critical? First, CRM must help the company, either by improving profitability or by maintaining its competitive position (the "automate or die" scenario). Next, CRM must not hurt the customer; if it does, this could affect profitability. Finally, the salespeople must want a CRM system and must benefit from it directly on a sustained basis. Otherwise, implementation will be difficult or the system will fall into disuse.

It is critical to understand who must do the work to make the system succeed and who benefits. If there is congruence between the party doing the work and the one benefiting, success is possible. For example, if the focus of the CRM system is on tracking salesperson activity and the salesperson has to track the activity for use by the manager, there

**Figure 13-7.** Management-Centered Functions of a CRM System.

- Report and forecast sales
- Communicate with salespeople and other company personnel
- Capture and disseminate best practices
- Report sales force activity
- Compare actual results with forecasts
- Design and manage sales territories
- Analyze marketing and sales programs by market, territory, product, customer type, price, or channel
- Enhance and streamline work flow and processes

is noncongruence. The salesperson does the work; the manager benefits. But if the focus of the CRM system is on better targeting and the salesperson benefits through reduced effort or increased sales, the system can succeed. The salesperson feels the texture of the customer and determines what information it is important that he or she collect. Company benefits are derived from salesperson and customer benefits, but there are added dimensions of company value, such as reduced costs. For example, the company has the ability to increase system value by adding external data about customers.

## The Components of a CRM System

A CRM system meets the needs of its three constituents, the customer, the salesperson, and the company, by using system elements in different ways. The core elements of any CRM system are listed in Figure 13-8.

## Nine Steps to Successful CRM Design and Implementation

The process shown in Figure 13-9 can be used to design and implement a CRM system.

The entire design and implementation process has three linked goals. First, the solution has to meet the firm's business needs. For example, a firm may use the CRM system to facilitate the transition to a team-based selling approach, in which customer representatives, technical specialists, and service personnel collaborate on acquiring and

**Figure 13-8.** Elements of a CRM System.

- **Customer Encyclopedia:** Customer and prospect profiles, needs
- **Product Encyclopedia:** Product profiles, product configuration tools, references
- **Pricing and Proposals:** Pricing, proposals, presentations
- **Ordering, Planning, and Tracking:** Orders, results, activities
- **Training:** Product, customer management, planning
- **Administration:** Expenses, commissions, general tools
- **Analysis:** Sales analysis, forecasting, office suite
- **Communication:** Electronic mail, intranet, internet, telemarketing tools
- **System Enhancement:** Configuration, maintenance, upgrade
- **Customer Support:** Frequently asked questions

**Figure 13-9.** CRM Design and Implementation Steps.

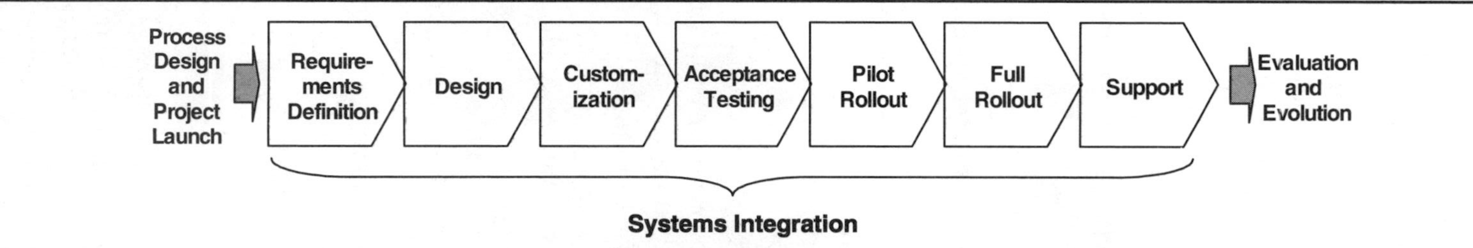

serving customers. Or, a firm may use the CRM system to make salespeople more productive through better targeting. Second, the implementation process must lead to a better understanding and enhancement of the firm's own capabilities. A CRM implementation is typically a complex task, and the firm must deal with the changes and the complexity. The pilot stage in most implementations assists significantly in achieving this goal. Finally, the stakeholders (customer, salespeople, service personnel, etc.) must have a commitment to and a stake in the CRM system so that they contribute to its adaptation and success.

The major issues and activities to be performed in each of the major design and implementation steps shown in Figure 13-9 are discussed next.

## Process Design and Project Launch

There are several questions to answer in the design phase: What are we trying to achieve? What processes are we trying to enhance? Is the focus on enhancing the salesperson's effectiveness, or is it on enhancing the efficiency of the company/customer interface?

Understandably, there is a focus on the ROI for CRM systems. ROI will be high only when users see a return on their investment of time and energy in using the system. If a customer uses the system and derives sustained value in the form of faster delivery times, the customer is more likely to spend the necessary time with the system. If a salesperson benefits from the system, he or she is more likely to invest the necessary energy to learn how to use the system and maintain the data within it. When users have a significantly positive ROI, the organizational barriers to success are removed and only technical ones remain. Stakeholders include the customer, the salesperson, service people, telesales people, the management team, and the information technology group within the firm.

Numerous activities are required in the design phase. Three of the major activities are setting goals, defining scope, and selecting suppliers.

**Setting CRM Goals.** Clear goals provide a framework that keeps a CRM project in focus and on track. Figure 13-10 shows examples of efficiency and effectiveness goals for a CRM implementation.

Before setting goals for the CRM system, a firm should do external benchmarking. What firms have achieved the benefits we seek? Are the

**Figure 13-10.** Examples of CRM Goals.

| | *Efficiency* | *Effectiveness* |
|---|---|---|
| **Process** | • Reduce travel time<br>• Reduce configuration error rates<br>• Increase proposal generation speed | • Improve customer selection for direct marketing programs<br>• Increase sales team coordination<br>• Improve sales forecasts<br>• Provide up-to-date information |
| **Outcome** | • Reduce costs<br>• Increase selling time | • Improve customer loyalty<br>• Increase sales |

goals realistic? Is the aim to be a pioneer, or is it to follow a proven track? Good sources of reliable information include other users, consultants, and conferences. Frequently, a firm wants to be the first with a CRM system, in the hope of getting a competitive edge through the system. However, being first usually turns out to be a competitive disadvantage; the pioneer makes the mistakes, and the followers learn from them and are more likely to succeed. The source of advantage is seldom the system itself. Most often, it is through system implementation and use that a firm derives gains in revenues or reduction in costs. In the CRM industry, uniqueness is a curse, not a blessing.

**Defining System Scope.** Once overall goals are established, the project scope and budget must be determined. Additionally, the users and uses must be specified, as shown in Figure 13-11.

Some firms limit the scope of the CRM to the sales organization. Others seek enhanced value by linking all areas of the firm that touch the customer. Typical areas linked include marketing, research and development, and service centers. Companies will also often link call centers, which are integrated inbound and outbound information sources,

**Figure 13-11.** Typical Range of CRM Users.

to the CRM. To decide on the parameters for the system, it is necessary to balance possible increases in complexity and the resulting increases in cost and implementation time with the possible benefits of an integrated customer view. External benchmarking provides valuable insights into other companies' successes and missteps.

**Selecting Suppliers.** After the scope of the system has been defined, the focus shifts to identifying suppliers that can meet the envisioned goals. The CRM industry is still in its growth stage, with new suppliers emerging on the coattails of every significant technology shift. Since many more waves of technology upheaval are likely in the future, a prudent approach to implementing a CRM system is to seek a fairly quick payback and to realize that the typical life span of a CRM system is three to five years. Not only is the *hardware* unlikely to last five years, but the *entire system* is likely to be obsolete after that period. With this in mind, using an experienced supplier company and, even more important, experienced people from a supplier is critical to the success of the project. Again, other users are a helpful source of information to supplement product demonstrations and implementation plan examples from suppliers.

## Requirements Definition

This step involves the formation of a project task force with a strong leader who has both business and technology credentials. CRM implementation is a perfect example of good judgment coming from experience, and experience coming from bad judgment. Typically, members of a project task force are representative of users and implementers such as sales, marketing, service, and information technology.

The task force on its own, or more typically with the help of a third party, maps data flows and analyses that will deliver the targeted efficiency and effectiveness gains. Who will own which data element? In addition to improving business processes, this step also examines the firm's ability to support all elements of the CRM system on an ongoing basis. For example, are there formal systems to control hardware and software acquisition? Are there processes for software and hardware upgrades and training? Is a communication infrastructure in place?

## Design

The design step will be considerably simpler if the prior steps are done well. In this step, data specifications, data views, and screen layouts are developed. The navigation from screen to screen is also specified. Cross-people processes, both inter- and cross-departmental, are defined (e.g., administrative approvals, handoff mechanisms for team selling, etc.). It is a good idea to have user groups audit this step to answer the following questions:

- Are the designs and navigation paths natural?
- When a user is performing one task, are other destinations easily accessible?
- Is the design intuitive, so that even an infrequent user will remember how to navigate the system?

Some useful criteria for evaluating the design include functional compatibility, ease of use, scalability, price, and implementation experience.

### Customization

In this, the technically most self-contained of all steps, the screens are used to configure the system. Most CRM implementations use third-party software modules and toolboxes to create a "customized" system for a company. Using off-the-shelf modules is advantageous because it cuts down on implementation time and because the systems and modules have been stress-tested by multiple organizations. In the customization step, the system is tested, support procedures are specified, and the operating environment for the CRM system is created.

### Acceptance Testing

At this step, the system is tested by users or their representatives before pilot rollout. Acceptance testing is the bridge between the technical development and customization and the user community.

### Pilot Rollout

Given the scale and complexity of CRM systems, it is essential to have a pilot rollout with a small group. The purpose of the pilot rollout is *not* to decide whether the firm wants a particular CRM system, but rather to ensure the success of the full rollout. In the pilot, a primary objective is to stress-test every element of system operation and upgrade. The goal is to see how the hardware, the software, the communication systems, the users, and the help desk work together to handle the routine and the exceptions.

A successful pilot rollout addresses problems that would otherwise show up in the full rollout. Fixes for problems and processes to handle unanticipated challenges are developed. The pilot rollout is as much a pilot of the people as it is of the technical system. At this stage, it is important to determine the variation in the skills of the people who will use the system so as to anticipate the training, handholding, support, and support staff needed.

Another purpose of the pilot group is to help generate enthusiasm for the project among peers. The spreading word of a successful pilot enhances demand for the CRM system among potential users. Also, members of the pilot group can be used as a resource for other salespeople who need help with the system.

The pilot rollout begins with training, followed by system installation and testing.

### Full Rollout

The full rollout consists of training, installation and testing, and system monitoring.

### Support

Software and design dominate hardware when it comes to CRM system effort and cost. The support infrastructure is also a significant investment and success factor. Figure 13-12 shows typical support roles.

The help desk assists users with any problems. For example, the help desk is available for support if the hardware malfunctions, all data are mysteriously lost, or a user does not know how to transfer a table from the CRM system into a presentation he or she is putting together for a customer. The help desk typically taps into other parts of the support infrastructure on an as-needed basis.

Facilities management is the infrastructure that keeps the hardware running. For example, the facilities management team is called upon if a computer needs to be repaired, a laptop is stolen and needs to be replaced and reloaded, or the communications lines are too slow and need to be speeded up.

Production support refers to the support needed to maintain system data. In a typical system, some data are generated or maintained in the system itself, but other data come from third parties such as Dun &

**Figure 13-12.** Example of CRM Support Infrastructure and Roles.

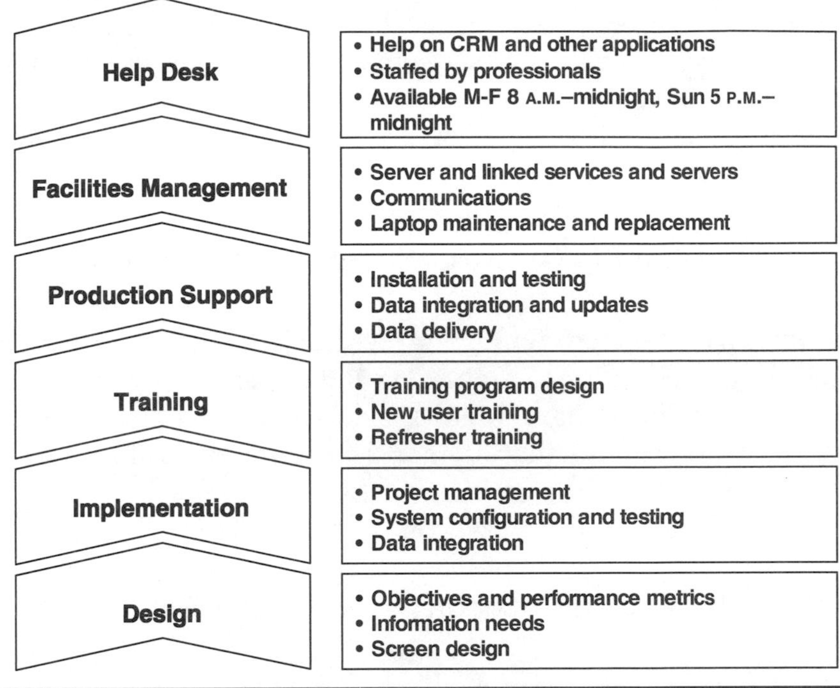


Bradstreet. The production support function ensures the quality and timeliness of data feeds.

Users have to be trained to use CRM systems, and training modules must be developed and delivered. Various levels of training include basic computer training, CRM system training, and, as the sophistication rises, training in maximizing the effectiveness gains created through the use of a CRM system. It is a continual challenge to have an effective system in place so that users do not have to be pulled from the field for training as system upgrades occur.

CRM systems are organic systems that evolve almost continuously. Implementation refers to the function that orchestrates the configuration and upgrade of a CRM system. The related design function articulates the objectives and success measures and specifies the system components.

### Evaluation and Evolution

To facilitate the ongoing success of a CRM system, the system's usage and impact need to be monitored. Are the processes that were redesigned working better? Are the effectiveness and efficiency gains being realized? Feedback from salespeople, customers, and other users should be encouraged. Through this feedback, companies often can identify further process improvements and opportunities to extend the system to other users. Ongoing assessment also helps in evaluating the project and ensuring that original and evolving objectives are achieved.

## Six Insights for Successful CRM Systems

Many firms have derived significant revenue gains and cost reductions through the successful implementation and use of CRM systems. However, even more firms have wasted significant amounts of time and money on CRM systems that did not deliver the desired results. This section provides some useful insights that will help to steer a CRM system toward success and away from waste and failure.

### Exercise Design Restraint—Overdesigned Systems Fail

It is not always easy to determine what to include in a system and what to leave out. Frequently, when a large committee uses a democratic process to decide on system features, the system that results is overdesigned. If a capability provides simple analyses quickly and is expected to be used frequently, make it available in the system. If it will be used infrequently, let an analyst at headquarters provide it in response to a field request. And if the capability is very complex, perhaps you need a project team. Figure 13-13 shows how to match features and capabilities of a CRM system.

Design restraint is a virtue. When deciding what to include in a CRM system and what to leave out, particularly when it comes to multiple views or screens, saying yes to too many decent ideas leads to a complex system with significantly diminished value. When any part of a CRM system is used infrequently, users forget how or when to use it. This is a serious problem when users have very different computer and analytical capabilities.

### Match the Implementation Cycle With the Technology Cycle

It is important to prototype rapidly because the traditional slower application development will be one generation behind the current technol-

**Figure 13-13.** Matching Features With Capabilities.

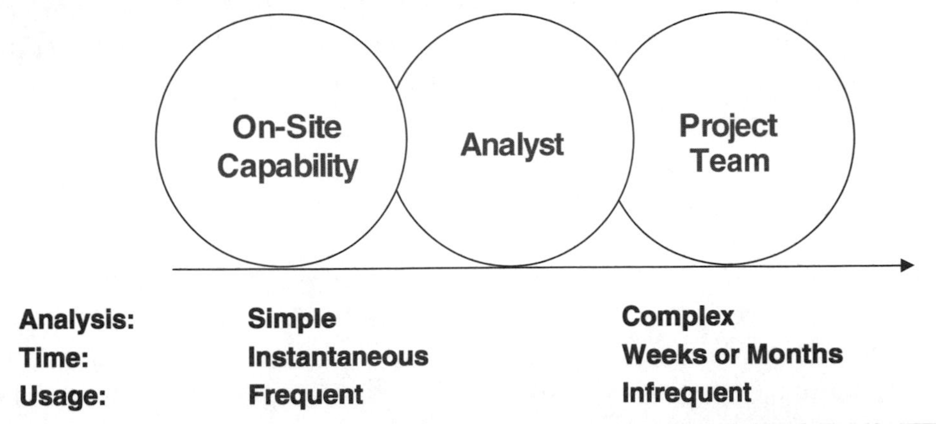


ogy. Figure 13-14 captures the problems raised by long implementation cycles and short technology cycles.

If the implementation is too slow, the next technology cycle will be well under way even as the implementation is being completed. Rapid prototyping is essential, and this is possible only with simple systems.

## Make Sure a CRM System Works at the Needed Scale

Often, custom-designed systems with great promise do not live up to their promise. An impressive small-scale demonstration falters under

**Figure 13-14.** Implementation Cycle and Technology Cycle.

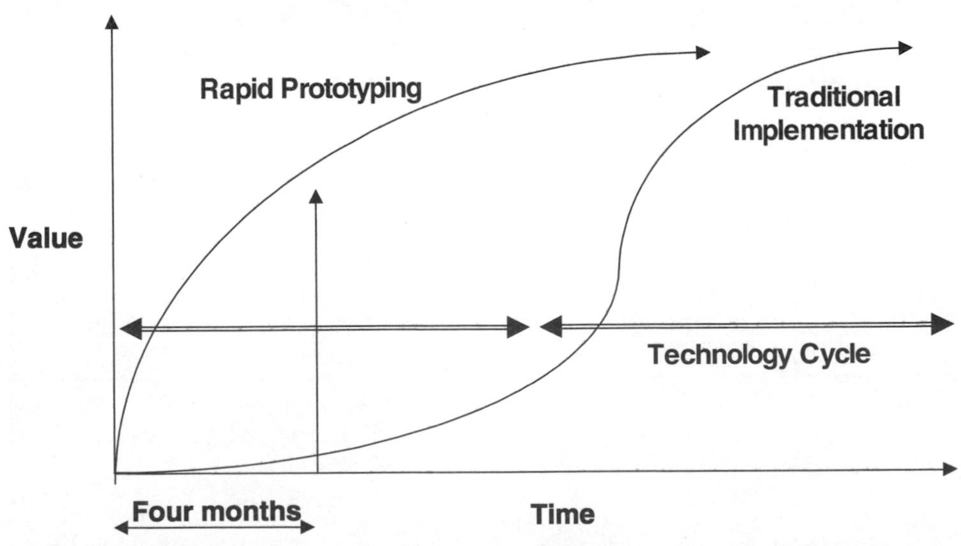

the rigors of a life-size customer database. Just because a system works in a demonstration does not mean that it can handle the scale and rigor of a real implementation. It is best to use a system that another company or division has tested and used successfully. A related good practice is to use a seasoned project team.

### Measure and Track Success at Multiple Levels

The performance of a CRM system should be assessed at multiple levels—qualitative and quantitative, direct and indirect. Direct measures are related to system usage and performance; indirect measures are the results due to the system. Figure 13-15 shows an example of one firm's success measurement categories.

### Pay Attention to Change Management and Training

The success of a CRM depends on its value to the users, which comes from its usage and its integration into the work processes of the stakeholders. A focused change management effort is essential when the system entails a significant change in work processes or necessary skills. Success depends on activities such as:

- User community involvement during design
- Creating excitement through newsletters, champion users, and ambassadors
- Addressing problems with current processes
- Training
- Support

**Figure 13-15.** Metrics for Measuring CRM Project Success.

| | *Direct* | *Indirect* |
|---|---|---|
| **Qualitative** | • User satisfaction<br>• Customer relationship quality<br>• Customer interaction quality | • Cross-organization communication quality<br>• Cross-organization customer coordination |
| **Quantitative** | • System uptime<br>• System usage<br>• Data quality<br>• Training time<br>• Administrative time | • Targeting effectiveness<br>• Customer retention<br>• Sales results |

Change management focuses on typical concerns salespeople have about CRM systems:

- Will it be difficult to learn and use?
- Will it replace me?
- Is my job going to change?
- Will I be expected to sell even more?
- Is it going to increase my administrative work?
- Is it going to be used to spy on my activities?

Lack of experience with CRM systems leads people to overestimate the benefits and underestimate the effort.

### Balance Customer-Centered, Salesperson-Centered, and Management-Centered Capabilities; Avoid Technology-Centered Thinking

Seek a balance between work and value—the constituents who make a CRM system operationally successful should also derive a major portion of the benefits. For example, it is a terrible idea to have salespeople feed data into a CRM system for the benefit of their managers. If a customer derives value by entering orders into a CRM system or using an inventory management capability, she is likely to refresh the databases necessary for these capabilities. If a salesperson benefits from a CRM system that assists with targeting, he will invest time to learn the system. Finally, technology-centered thinking is worthless. CRM systems do not succeed because they use the latest technology, they succeed because the technology enables stronger sales processes.

## Conclusion

Technology is both supplementing and supplanting traditional sales functions. The widespread use of CRM systems is focused primarily on the former by making the entire selling organization more productive. However, the success rate of CRM implementations remains disappointingly low. The single most important CRM lesson is to learn from history. A company must focus on clear process improvement goals, top management and user commitment, help from outside experts, and a phased implementation approach that helps the organization grow with a CRM system.

Technological barriers to CRM implementation success are falling rapidly because of the Internet. The application service provider (ASP) model, in which the CRM system resides on a server that is accessible over the Internet, is emerging as a good way to deploy a CRM system. This ASP approach provides several advantages:

- Customers, suppliers, and co-suppliers can link their systems.
- Access is available everywhere—geographically dispersed sales groups can easily share information; global account teams can interact seamlessly.
- Communication hassles are minimized.
- Implementation cycles are reduced.
- System upgrades can be done centrally and regularly.
- Maintenance and enhancement expertise can be centralized.
- Technology will be in the background, applications in the foreground.
- Paradoxically, the homogenization of CRM technology will take the focus away from the technology itself.

The ASP model could become dominant as wired and wireless communication bandwidth expands and system security issues are resolved.

# Chapter 14

# Performance Management

This chapter focuses on performance management, the control system of sales force productivity. Good performance management ensures that salespeople, working largely unsupervised, operate as a cohesive force, with aligned goals and consistent methods of achieving these goals.

In this chapter you will learn:

- How the components of a performance management system fit together to help you understand salespeople's performance and take action to change that performance
- The pros and cons of managing salespeople by input measures (capabilities, activities, and behaviors) or output measures (customer and company results)
- What situations warrant an empowerment (low-control) approach or a directive (high-control) approach to performance management
- Useful insights that will help you ensure that your performance management system is a source of power and strength for your sales force

## Performance Management: The Control Loop of the Sales Force

If a sales force is perfectly recruited, trained, structured, sized, motivated, deployed, and given incentives, should management just get out of the way? Not quite. Ongoing systems and processes to ensure that all the systems are aligned and stay aligned are essential.

Performance management is the control system of sales force productivity. It is the process a firm uses to leverage the other tactical sales productivity drivers. Management needs to get out of the salespeople's way, but actively manage the process at the same time. Performance management is important in all parts of the organization and is particularly critical in the sales function. Aside from the firm's culture, it is what ensures that salespeople, working largely unsupervised, operate as a cohesive force, with aligned goals and methods to achieve these goals.

Because of the inherent independence of the sales job and the natural variation in the situations and opportunities facing salespeople, many scenarios are played out in a sales organization. For example, one salesperson performs better than another does. Sales to seemingly similar customers are different. Sales in one territory exceed expectations, while sales in another territory are below expectations. Sales to existing customers are developing well, but the conversion of new accounts is lagging. A performance management system allows the company to understand the source of this variation in success and to apply continuous course corrections to enhance performance. A company expects a salesperson to be an effective link to customers. Salespeople are expected to understand customers, customize solutions and sales approaches, and create sales. In a cascade of responsibilities, the salesperson manages the performance of the customer, the first-line sales manager manages the performance of the salesperson, and so on to the top levels of the sales organization.

If a system is a little out of control and goes unmanaged, it is likely to veer off course quickly. In a sales force, this can happen in many ways. Consider the following salespeople and situations.

James does well one-on-one with customers, but when it comes to leveraging the entire team from the company—product specialists, manufacturing, R&D, and telesales—he feels that he loses power with the customer. Consequently, he underutilizes the other members of the team. His performance is good with the simple accounts and very erratic with complex accounts.

Susan had a great streak in the stock market and is now independently wealthy. She was intense and successful in the past, but now she is marking time until retirement, and her sales job has become a sideline.

Donna has personal problems. She is distracted, is intensely preoccupied with the personal issues, and is not focused on the job.

Sam shows exceptional results, but he does whatever it takes to make the sale. At times he goes beyond the firm's ethical guidelines.

Antonio once had a reasonable territory, but a huge customer no longer purchases locally. His quarterly goals have not been changed in response to the change in buying behavior, and as a result he has missed his goals for two successive quarters.

If left unmanaged, these problems have the potential to become disasters. However, most of them can be solved, and all can be managed, with the right performance management steps. For instance, if James has trouble with complex accounts, he needs coaching and training; he may need to observe a colleague or supervisor engaging in the activities and behaviors that lead to success with such accounts. Susan, for whom the sales job has become a sideline, and Sam, who has lapses of professional ethics, need to be dealt with firmly, put on probation, or even terminated from the job. Donna, who has personal problems, may need professional counseling. An effective sales manager can identify this problem and initiate the steps that may lead to a resolution. Finally, if Antonio has a poor territory or poor goals, the firm needs to improve his opportunities or reset his goals.

There are two key components to managing performance. First, performance management is about understanding the chain of drivers and outcomes that leads from a salesperson with skills and capabilities to tangible results such as sales and profits. Second, performance management is about making changes in the system in order to sustain and enhance performance.

Sales organizations use performance management to align the sales organization with company goals by:

- Establishing goals and priorities
- Developing plans to meet goals
- Monitoring progress
- Diagnosing problems
- Providing feedback and guidance to correct problems or change course
- Providing structured and ongoing guidance for salesperson development

This chapter focuses on managing the performance of the salesperson. However, the concepts apply at all levels in the sales force hierarchy. In fact, performance management processes can be used to align the goals of the entire sales organization and increase its effectiveness and efficiency.

## The Performance Management Process

Figure 14-1 shows the performance management loop and its consequences.

Goals lead to plans, which result in actions. Measurement is used to evaluate how well the goals are being met, how good the plans are, and the quantity and quality of sales actions. This leads to supportive or corrective consequences.

### Goals

Most sales organizations set sales goals for salespeople. Chapter 11 discusses the issues involved in establishing sales goals and the methods used to do so. A formal performance management system established goals for capabilities, activities, and behaviors—not just for customer results and company results.

### Plans

The plan specifies how the goals will be achieved. It has a salesperson-centered component and a customer-centered component. The salesperson-centered component focuses on how the salesperson will achieve his or her personal goals, such as improving certain skills or developing desired behaviors. The customer-centered component focuses on achieving the customer and company results through a set of

**Figure 14-1.** Components of a Performance Management System.

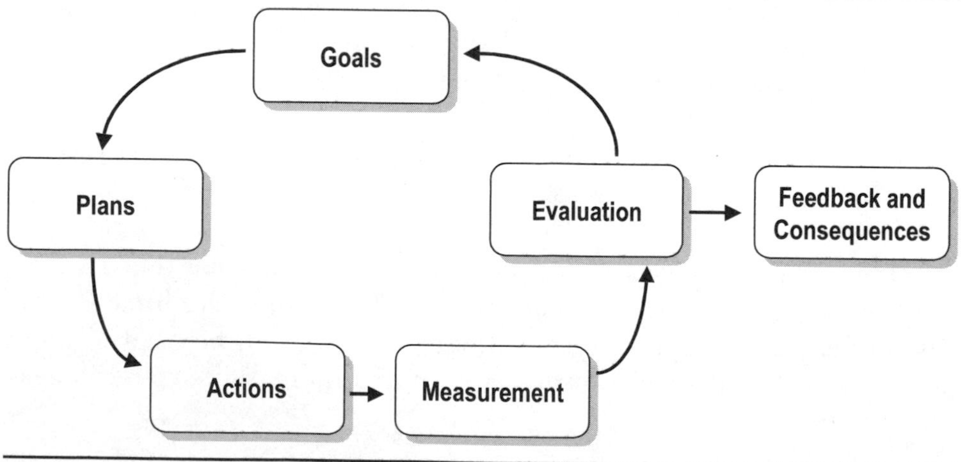

activities or sales actions. An example of a sales planning hierarchy is shown in Figure 14-2.

In Figure 14-2, a sales organization's mission drives the goals. The success factors that are necessary to achieve the goals are identified through an external analysis of customers, competitors, and the environment and through an internal analysis of the firm's salespeople and customer support systems. The plan identifies the sales strategies, other promotional strategies, and salesperson development strategies required to meet the goals. In this example, the personal development strategies are salesperson-centered, whereas the sales and promotional strategies are customer-centered.

## Actions

The actions to be taken to achieve sales goals include the entire spectrum of sales activities that the salesperson performs, such as prospecting, qualifying, needs analysis, promotion, closing the sale, and after-sale service. It also includes activities that the salesperson engages in to coordinate all company actions that affect the customer. For example, global account managers may be involved in ensuring that a customer includes the supplier's products in the design stage, the marketing group can be involved in pricing and configuration assis-

**Figure 14-2.** Example of a Planning Hierarchy.

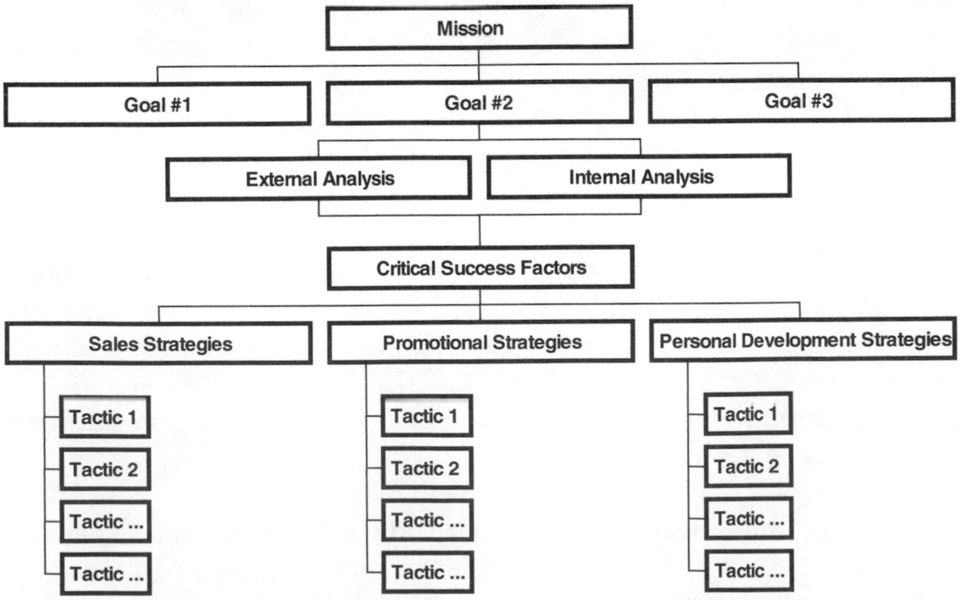

tance, and finance can be involved in negotiating payment terms. The performance management process operates horizontally if several parts of a functional organization are engaged in the sales process—different parts of the selling firm have expectations of each other.

## Measurement

The purpose of measurement is to assist with the evaluation of performance. Most organizations focus on measuring company results such as sales and profitability. Other levels of measurement follow the sales force productivity chain upstream. Customer results, sales force activities, and sales force skills are examples of measures that can help link the drivers of sales performance with the performance outcomes. If the quantity of sales activities is a key factor in generating sales, firms should track the quantity of activities directed toward each customer. If the quality of activities is more important in a creative selling environment, tracking the volume of sales activities will not be particularly fruitful. In such situations, a manager could still make a formal assessment of a salesperson's selling skills during a joint sales call.

## Evaluation

Evaluation of performance typically uses three types of measures: measures of results, measures of opportunity, and measures of effort or activity. Looking at these measures pair-wise provides insights into the various aspects of performance.

The measured result, whether sales or share, depend on the opportunity and effort of the selling organization. The link between effort and opportunity highlights the salesperson's ability to allocate selling effort appropriately to the best opportunities. The link between effort and results indicates how responsive or unresponsive to selling effort sales results are. This can be assessed by examining the relationship between sales variability and effort variability across territories or geographic areas. The final leg linking opportunity to results is a performance measure. It represents the salesperson's ability to penetrate the opportunity in his or her territory.

This evaluation framework helps managers evaluate performance by focusing on the factors that drive results and the methods that can be used to correct performance problems, reinforce good performance, and transfer best practices from one context to another.

## Feedback and Consequences

Since the goal of a performance management system is to enhance performance, feedback and consequences are critical to the process. The first line sales manager is an important participant in the process. Many firms recognize that the primary function of a sales manager is to manage the salespeople. The prior steps—setting goals, developing plans, and tracking activity—are designed to enable course correction. The consequences of a performance review can range from a reward and a revised goal to an improvement plan, probation, or termination.

A formal, active, and directive performance management system typically involves a series of prescribed steps, as in Figure 14-3.

In the *annual performance review,* past performance is assessed and goals for the future are laid out. The review has a retrospective component, assessing performance relative to plan, and a prospective component, creating goals and plans for the future. Once goals are determined, either alone or jointly with the sales manager, the salesperson must develop plans to achieve her or his goals.

The *periodic progress review* occurs two to four times a year and focuses on the recent past and on a success plan for the rest of the year. If course correction is needed, this step includes the creation of an

**Figure 14-3.** Prescribed Interactions Within a Formal Performance Management System During a Year.

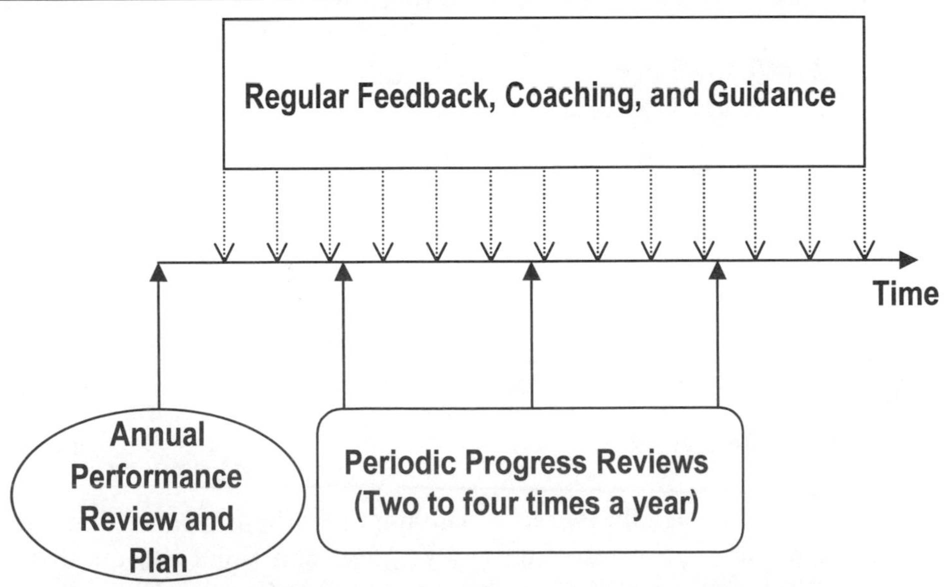

improvement plan. If performance standards have been seriously breached, this step can also lead to probation or the discharge of the salesperson.

The *regular feedback sessions* occur in person, during field rides, over the telephone, and via e-mail; they focus on assessment, coaching, and guidance.

## Performance Measures

The measures used in a performance management system are the same as those of the sales productivity framework, from *skills and capabilities* to *activities and behaviors* to *customer results,* and finally to *company results* (see Figure 14-4).

Performance management applies to all the links in the sales force productivity chain. Skills and capabilities drive the activities and behaviors, which in turn affect customer and company results. A performance management process evaluates the status of each link and then enhances it. The process includes the following measures.

### Knowledge and Skills

Do salespeople have the right knowledge, skills, competencies, characteristics, and values? What is the best way to enhance their knowledge and skills? Common performance measures are:

- Product knowledge
- Customer knowledge
- Market knowledge
- Selling skills, such as prospecting, targeting, needs identification, listening, presentation, persuasion, negotiation, and closing skills
- Computer skills
- Analysis skills
- Time and territory management skills

### Activities and Behaviors

Are the right activities delivered to the appropriate prospects and customers with the appropriate frequency? How can the type, quantity, quality, and allocation of activities be enhanced? If several people de-

**Figure 14-4.** Performance Impact of the Sales Productivity Stages.

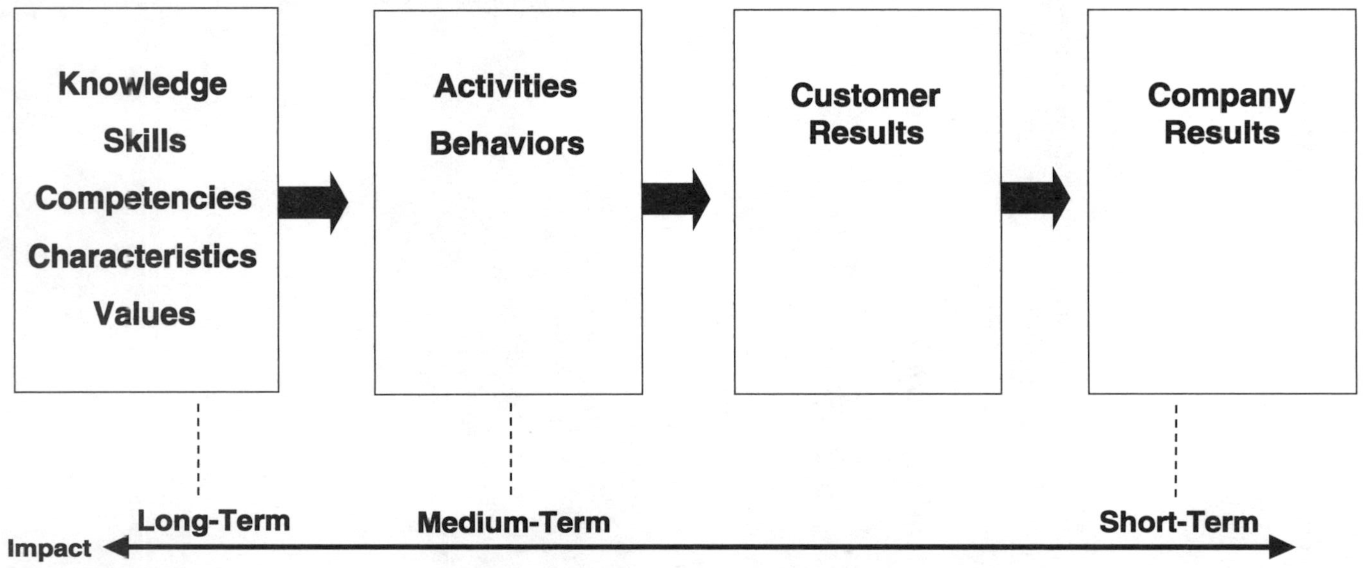

liver these activities, is the firm coordinating them? Many performance management goals are stated in terms of activities. For example, a quarter's goal for a salesperson can include successful completion of a training program on a new product or participation in a key account management workshop. Performance measures for *activities and behavior* will include:

***Work Activities***

- Calls
- Time spent with a customer segment, such as accounts in a particular industry or accounts of a certain size in terms of sales or potential

***Planning and Organizing***

- Business planning
- Territory planning
- Event planning and organizing
- Problem solving

***Behaviors***

- Initiative
- Teamwork
- Creativity
- Leadership
- Impact
- Flexibility

## Customer Results

Does the company achieve the highest level of customer satisfaction, retention, penetration, and results? Which customer segments are doing well, and which are underperforming? Examples of measures of *customer results* are:

- Satisfaction
- Retention
- Conversion
- Growth
- Repeat business
- Complaints

### Company Results

Is the company achieving its goals in the areas of sales, profitability, market share, and expense control? Some examples of sales performance measures are:

- Volume and growth
- Profitability
- Performance against quota
- Market share
- Expense control
- Rank

Goals, plans, actions, measurement, and evaluation (the elements of the performance management system in Figure 14-1) can be developed for any of the performance measures listed. Figure 14-5 provides some examples of various elements of the sales force productivity chain.

Figure 14-6 analyzes the pros and cons of managing by input measures (i.e., capabilities, activities, and behaviors) and by output measures (customer and company results). The time frame of impact is different if a person focuses on capabilities rather than activities or results. For example, when a person focuses on capabilities, he or she expects enhanced capabilities to result in improved activities and behaviors, which in turn will lead to better results. A focus on company results will have a short-term impact, whereas a focus on capabilities has a long-term impact. The goal of performance management is to ensure performance today, tomorrow, and for the future. Therefore, the focus is on the entire productivity chain, from capabilities to activities to customer results to company results. Most firms manage both inputs and outputs, but to varying degrees.

## Approaches to Performance Management

Two contrasting philosophical approaches to managing performance are shown in Figure 14-7. Most companies choose an approach that falls between these two extremes.

With the low-control approach, goals are set for a salesperson, and the company waits for results. The salesperson may or may not participate in the goal-setting process. The company provides information to

**Figure 14-5.** Examples of Measures and Performance Management System Components.

| | *Salesperson Capabilities* | *Activities and Behaviors* | *Customer Results* | *Company Results* |
|---|---|---|---|---|
| **Goals** | Improve ability to sell to complex customers | Increase time spent on new customer development | Increase satisfaction in large accounts | Increase territory profitability |
| **Plans** | Attend key account management course; seek best practice experience from peers | Track current time allocation and review weekly with field trainer | Spend 20% more time with large accounts | Focus flexible spending on key growth accounts |
| **Actions** | | | | |
| **Measurement** | Test product and market knowledge; solicit customer feedback | Call reporting | Customer satisfaction | Profitability and sales |
| **Evaluation** | Compare to ideal | Is coverage appropriate for strategic goals? | Compare to competitors | Compare to corporate financial goals |
| **Feedback and Consequences** | Remedial training, promotion | Refocus poor efforts | Enhance customer satisfaction | Improve in specific areas, rewards, probation, termination |

help the salesperson improve his or her performance. The primary basis of performance evaluation and success measurement is results compared to goal. Empowerment is part of the culture.

With the high-control approach, the firm attempts to control and influence every level of the productivity chain. High-control firms focus on the entire productivity chain, from capabilities to results. The firm influences the salesperson's capabilities through hiring and training, and controls her or his activities through direction and coaching. The organization, mostly through sales managers seeks to influence the results, rather than waiting for them. Control is part of the culture.

A "low control" environment focuses on hiring and results. A "high control" environment adds emphasis on coaching, training, and activity management.

**Figure 14-6.** The Pros and Cons of Focusing on Inputs and Outcomes.

| | *Input Measures: Capabilities, Activities, and Behaviors* | *Output Measures: Customer Results and Company Results* |
|---|---|---|
| **Pros** | • Greatest opportunity for behavior modification<br>• Encourages customer relationships<br>• Recognizes the difference between cause and effect<br>• "How you sell is as important as how much you sell" | • Keeps salespeople focused on results, which "pay the bills"<br>• Easy to apply<br>• Promotes initiative in a dynamic marketplace<br>• Consistent across different people in the organization<br>• Less time-consuming<br>• Protects from accusations of favoritism in assessing intangibles |
| **Cons** | • Requires manager's ability to observe and diagnose<br>• Requires time for observation, evaluation, and coaching<br>• Requires impartiality<br>• Likely to be inconsistently applied throughout the organization | • Focuses on ends rather than means<br>• Fails to stimulate growth of professionalism<br>• Short-term focused<br>• Difficult to broaden performance management areas as business matures |

As shown in Figure 14-8, the applicability of a particular performance management approach depends on two situational factors, the accuracy of measured results and the firm's knowledge of the most appropriate selling process. Does the firm (or the manager) know who the buyers are and how they buy? Does it understand what the most effective selling process is? Does it know what skills drive sales? These are all-important considerations in determining the best approach for performance management.

**Figure 14-7.** Contrasting Approaches to Performance Management.

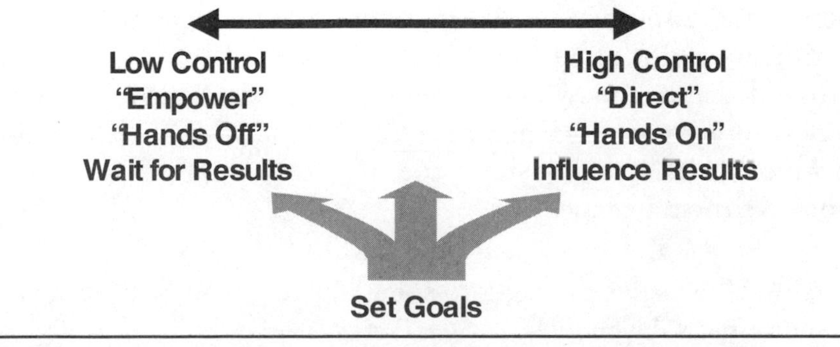

**Figure 14-8.** Determinants of Approaches to Performance Management.

| | | *Firm's Knowledge of the Most Appropriate Selling Process* | |
|---|---|---|---|
| | | **Perfect** | **Imperfect** |
| *Measurement of Results* | **Good** | Education<br>Empowerment<br>Direction | Empowerment |
| | **Poor** | Direction | Culture |

If the salesperson's results can be measured but the firm does not have a good understanding of the most appropriate selling process (Figure 14-8, upper right-hand quadrant), then the manager must rely on the salesperson's knowledge of his or her customers, empower each salesperson, and manage for results. On the other hand, if territory-level results measures are poor and the manager understands the activities that contribute to sales (Figure 14-8, lower left-hand quadrant), then a direction approach with activity control is a logical choice. When measurement and knowledge are both good (Figure 14-8, upper left-hand quadrant), any of a number of approaches can work. Firms typically use a combination of education, empowerment, and direction. In these situations, the approach is not as important as the consistency with which it is applied. Finally, if the measurement of results is poor and the firm's knowledge of the most appropriate selling process is imperfect (Figure 14-8, lower right-hand quadrant), culture is the strongest lever for sales force success.

Figure 14-9 gives various situational factors that determine whether an empowerment or a directive approach to performance management is more appropriate. The figure also includes some of the management implications of using either approach.

An added and somewhat related decision that a firm needs to address is whether the performance management system will be formal or informal. In a formal system, the steps are carefully laid out. For example, a firm may expect:

- A first-line sales manager to spend one day a month with each of his or her salespeople
- The sales manager to provide formal feedback on call planning

**Figure 14-9.** Drivers and Implications of the Empowerment and Directive Approaches.

| | *Drivers* | *Implications* |
|---|---|---|
| **Empowerment** | • The culture encourages empowerment.<br>• Management has poor knowledge of the sales process.<br>• Salespeople are domain experts.<br>• The selling process is complex, and there is high process variation across customers.<br>• Customer organizations are complex, and/or team selling is important.<br>• Results can be measured. | • Performance management systems are informal.<br>• Salespeople or sales teams have high information needs.<br>• The manager plays the role of facilitator.<br>• The manager ensures that adequate resources are available for the salesperson. |
| **Directive** | • The culture encourages control.<br>• Management understands the drivers of sales success.<br>• The sales process is uniform across customers.<br>• The sales organization is large.<br>• Results cannot be measured accurately.<br>• It is important to spread best practices across salespeople. | • Performance management systems are formal.<br>• The sales manager has high information needs.<br>• The evaluation function resides with the manager.<br>• The manager is expert and coach. |

and use of selling skills in at least three customer contacts a month

- Quarterly written and verbal performance assessments and annual performance reviews
- Forms and instruments to plan and track sales activities at every prescribed step of the performance management process

In an informal system, a performance management framework is used, but not every step is orchestrated and tracked; the system develops and changes organically. To ensure fairness in firing, careful documentation of bad performance is often maintained.

The firm's sales environment and overall culture are key determinants of whether the performance management process should be formal, informal, or somewhere in between.

## Seven Insights for Successful Performance Management

### Performance Management Works at All Levels in an Organization

Even though the primary focus of this chapter is on managing the performance of a salesperson, these processes work at all levels in the sales organization. First-line sales managers are more likely to take a process seriously and use it if a similar process is used to manage their own performance.

### Good Performance Management Reflects the Culture

A performance management system needs to be consistent with the sales force culture. A formal performance management system works in a formal culture. Using it in an informal culture will lead to confusion, conflict, or failure to use the system.

### Peer Influence Is Powerful in Helping Manage Performance

Most sales performance systems are hierarchical; the performance management dynamics occur between a salesperson and his or her superior. Organizations that use team selling have discovered a powerful horizontal (as opposed to vertical) lever to manage performance. Salespeople who work with peers naturally develop a system of horizontal dependence. They expect performance from one another and will perform for one another and support one another. Nonperformers may be subtly, or not so subtly, ejected from a team.

### Performance Management Must Leverage a Person's Motivators

Performance management must recognize that people are motivated by empowerment, goals, and positive feedback. The successful performance "manager" often takes the role of a coach rather than that of a boss and appeals to the achievement, social affiliation, power, ego gratification, and survival needs of the salespeople.

### Empowerment and Direction—It's Not Just a Question of "Either/Or," It's Also a Question of When

A person may need to be empowered in one area and directed in another. For example, a salesperson who has excellent selling skills can have poor computer skills. Performance management consists of a customized approach tailored to the individual.

### The Performance Management System Itself Must Be Dynamic

As an organization's products and markets evolve, success factors can change, and performance management systems and processes must also adapt. For example, a company that is entering a new market may need to use an empowering approach with its salespeople. However, as the market matures, a directive approach and sharing of customer strategies across people may become critical. Informal systems may have to give way to formal ones.

### Performance Can Be a Result of Built-in Attributes

Experience with many sales forces suggests that company results are most correlated with past results (primarily because of high carryover in most industries) and strongly correlated with market potential. Other salesperson or organization variables are weaker in predicting sales. This point is illustrated in Figure 14-10. The data are for a company selling blood glucose monitors. It shows a high correlation of sales to prior year sales, and even to competitive sales in each territory.

Evaluation of salespeople is complicated by the fact that exceptional results are frequently due to exceptionally high opportunity, not to exceptional ability on the part of the salesperson. In evaluating performance, one tries to control for the impact of factors such as potential and territory size. This problem is mitigated in situations in which organizations use balanced sales territories.

Estimates of sales potential provide a way to normalize a territory's performance. In Figure 14-11, territories above the "Expected" line are producing at a level that is higher than would be expected given the level of opportunity provided by the territory. The "High" line represents the best of what is possible in each territory. To set goals for the future, identify the "Headroom," or the gap between actual and best, and expect the salesperson to move toward the best in steps over a given period of time.

**Figure 14-10.** The High Correlation Between Past Sales and Current Sales and Between Market Potential and Current Sales.

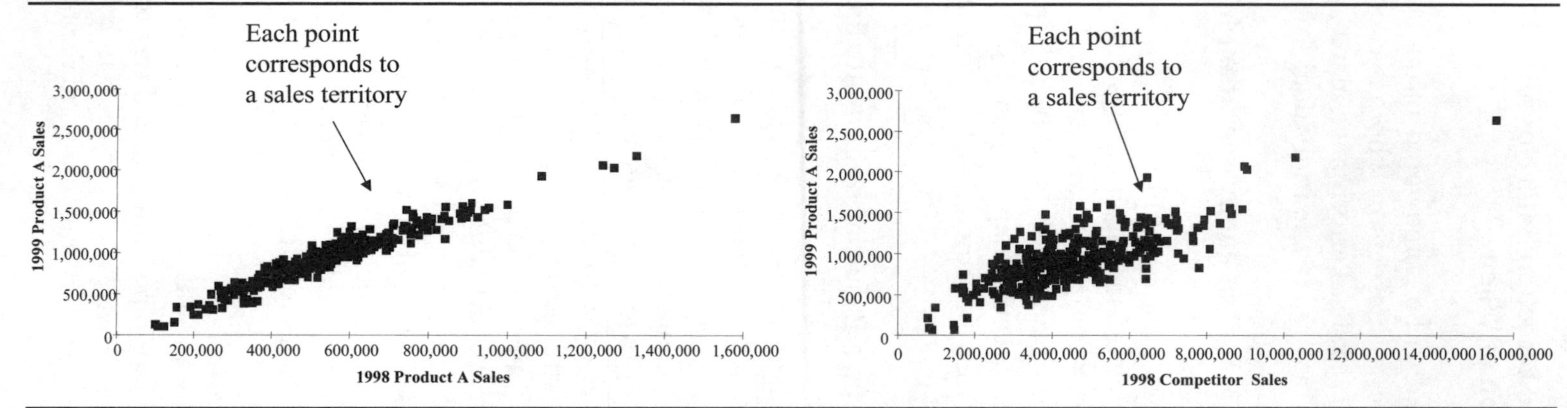

**Figure 14-11.** The Performance Frontier.

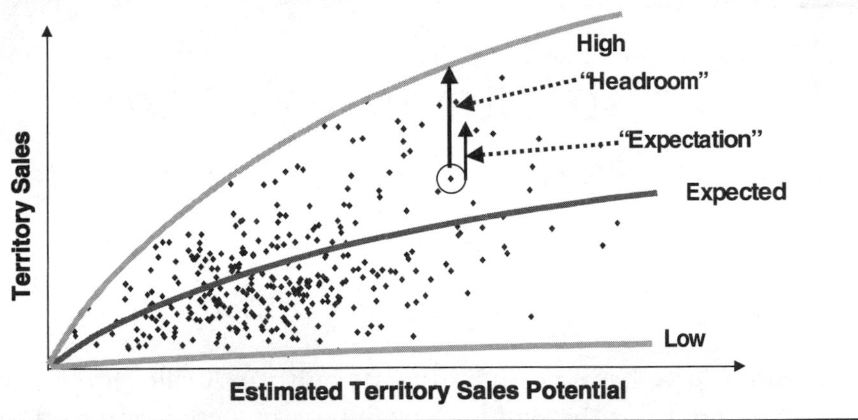


## Conclusion

The strength of a performance management system is a surprisingly frequent differentiator of successful and unsuccessful managers, and of even successful and less than successful companies. Without such a system, strong people and systems can go awry. Performance management is a critical job of a sales management team, one that can be a source of power and strength for a firm.

# Chapter 15

# Building a Potent Sales Force Culture

Every sales force has a personality—its culture. A sales force culture is the unwritten rules that guide the behavior of a company's salespeople and sales managers. Culture is shaped continuously by the decisions made by management. This chapter will help you:

- Understand the elements of a successful culture
- Develop and implement a plan to change a sales force culture through vision, communication, action, and rewards
- Maintain a successful sales force culture at your firm

## Introduction

A lot can be learned about a sales force by listening to salespeople's stories. For example, upon graduating from college, four friends—Eric, Julia, Matthew, and Natalie—joined different sales forces in diverse parts of the country. A year later, they reunited at a friend's wedding. They all had stories to tell about their new careers and the companies they worked for. The most interesting stories showed the contrasts among the different sales force cultures they had experienced.

Eric went to work for a very large business-to-business distributor. His company was in the maintenance, repair, and operating (MRO) supplies business. He sold supplies to buildings and work sites. The company's catalog had more than 500,000 items including numerous brands and types of tools, fans, motors, pumps, lighting equipment, and fixtures.

Eric described some of his experiences when he first joined the company: "We had a two-week new employee orientation. They talked about the history of the company, the product line, the company's suppliers, and the customers. On the last day, we met Jeff—a company legend. He never let a customer slip through his hands. When Jeff started with the company, he was given a territory that included parts of Kentucky. The rural section of the territory included several coal mines that had never bought products from Jeff's company. In fact, the last company sales representative to call on the mines had been run off by someone with a shotgun. Jeff viewed the mines as a challenge. He backpacked into the mines, set up camp, and refused to leave until the superintendent of the mines bought product from him. It took him a week, but he came back with an order. The mines have been customers ever since.''

Julia went to work for an office supplies distributor. Her firm sold all types of office supplies, such as paper, pens, and folders, to small and medium-size businesses in a large city in the Midwest. Her product catalog also included several thousand items. Here is how Julia described her sales force: ''People can earn a lot of money at my company. People who have been with the company for a long time have lots of accounts that continue to buy from them. I suspect that the NBA and NFL games we take them to helps to cement the relationships. Hot and cold leads come into the company on a regular basis, and new leads are distributed among the salespeople. Regrettably, the person who distributes them gives the best leads to the established salespeople because he believes that they are better at closing new business. Once the account is closed, it stays with the closer. The rich keep getting richer, and some of us are wondering if we can make enough money as we try to build our own account base.''

Matthew went to work for the consumer division of a tool manufacturer. He called on large and small retail accounts describing company promotions, training the retail salespeople about the company's products, making sure that the company's merchandise was displayed effectively, and taking orders whenever possible. Matthew talked about one of the people in his sales district: ''Zeke is really a great guy. All the salespeople love his attitude. His real estate investments have made him a lot of money. Consequently, he works when he wants to, usually three or four days a week, and he takes long vacations. Management leaves him alone because he has a number of large accounts, usually people whom he includes in his investments. The guy has it made.''

Natalie went to work for a bank in the commercial lending group. Her story was very brief: ''We are bankers—we are not salespeople.''

Stories about companies' sales forces say a lot about the culture of the selling organization. Jeff and Zeke are heroes in their companies. They communicate cultural norms. Jeff's company was very impressed with his ambition, work style, and sales results. The MRO distributor would like other salespeople to emulate Jeff. As a result, it communicates his values and activity whenever it can. What better time than at new employee orientation? Zeke, on the other hand, has evolved as a grassroots hero. He is well liked and admired for his financial success. His peers do not seem to be too concerned about his lackadaisical approach to his job and the tool manufacturer has done little to undercut his hero status. Sales force heroes like Jeff and Zeke communicate what is expected and/or tolerated. They tell us about the corporate norms, values, and work styles. We can expect Eric's and Matthew's behaviors to differ as a result of the different role models at the two companies.

Julia recognized the selling culture at the office products distributor quite quickly. She noticed that the best leads went to people who already had rich territories. Since the compensation plan for the sales force was 100 percent commission with a small draw, it would be a long time before she could accrue significant earnings. She would need to work hard, build her business, and expect to earn most of her money in the future. She also observed that a number of young salespeople were getting discouraged and leaving the firm. Unfortunately, the firm attributed its high turnover to a tight labor market when, in fact, it was due primarily to the entrepreneurial or greedy (depending upon the perspective) culture.

Natalie experienced a very different culture. Her colleagues viewed themselves as bankers and denied that selling was a large part of their job. Critical job skills are underdeveloped when organizations do not define the roles for their people properly.

Each company has its own culture, and their differences are quite obvious, as can be seen from these stories. The daily lives of Eric, Julia, Matthew, and Natalie are affected by their company's culture. The company's acceptable values and work styles shape their activity, behaviors, and attitudes. Even their professional development is affected by the norms that the company adopts. Since the culture affects everyone in the sales organization, it is important to understand its components and what can be done to change it.

## Norms, Values, and Work Styles—The Elements of a Sales Force Culture

Every sales force has a personality—its culture. The culture can be thought of as the genes of the sales organization. It is the unwritten rules that guide the behavior of the firm's salespeople and sales managers as they encounter familiar or new situations. The culture establishes a baseline for the firm's decision making and for its acceptable activity.

Cultures are defined in terms of appropriate choices. Salespeople face numerous choices every day. Often the choices lead to opposite behaviors and activities, which can create a tension. Salespeople look to their culture to suggest the appropriate choice. Several common choices are presented in Figure 15-1. In each case, neither choice is right or wrong—just appropriate or inappropriate, depending on the selling environment and the culture the firm wants to establish. A strong culture provides guidance for salespeople, so that they make appropriate choices almost automatically.

All cultures are based on norms and values. Norms and values are fundamental to the culture because they guide organizational choices and hence affect sales force activity. A norm describes how an individual should behave when faced with a choice, whereas a value expresses how an individual should aspire or desire to behave when faced with a choice. Cultures make statements about both norms and values.

Norms and values are rooted in organizational history, are continually modified or reinforced, and are overhauled from time to time by visionary management teams. They can be communicated explicitly through mission statements and mottoes, through public announcements and proclamations such as "we are bankers, not salespeople," and through heroes such as Jeff, the person who landed the big mining account. Alternatively, norms and values can be communicated implicitly through "water-cooler" stories, such as the story about Zeke, the part-time salesperson whose outside business success was the envy of the tool manufacturing sales force.

Figure 15-2 provides a list of culture-defining choices. Management should make a clear value statement regarding each choice.

Cultures fail when there is a "disconnect" between management's stated values and management action. Figure 15-3 gives examples of how management can appear inconsistent when implementing its culture.

Values must be supported by management action. The sales force productivity drivers described in the Sales Force Productivity Framework, developed in Chapter 2, provide a list of sales management decisions that ensure that appropriate values are established and maintained. Figure 15-4 reviews the relationship between the sales force productivity drivers and culture formation.

**Figure 15-1.** A Sample of Sales Force Choices.

| *One Choice* | *An Alternative Choice* |
|---|---|
| Visit existing customers. | Call on prospects. |
| Be customer-centered. Do whatever is best for the customer. | Be sales-centered. Do whatever it takes to make the sale. |
| Get a quick hit. Today's sales are important; we need to make our goal. | Attempt to penetrate a very large competitive account even though it requires a considerable investment of time with an uncertain outcome. |
| Sell existing and familiar products and services. | Sell new products and services. |
| Call on lots of customers and prospects—a "reach" strategy. | Call frequently on a few targeted customers and prospects—a "frequency" strategy. |
| Control costs; keep overnights to a minimum. | Stay in touch with customers even if it means traveling to the edges of the sales territory. |
| Hold price. | Get sales. |
| Telephone customers; use the call center more extensively. | See customers regularly in person. |
| Discuss call planning with your manager, incorporating him or her into difficult selling contexts. | Be independent; take care of everything yourself. |
| Compete, individually, to become part of President's Club. | Cooperate, as a team, to meet customer needs. |
| Attend professional development workshops regularly. | Sell whenever possible. |
| Be a salesperson. | Be a consultant. |
| Embrace e-commerce. | Deny e-commerce. |

The sales force culture is shaped continuously by the decisions made by sales management. The hiring process says something about the kind of people the firm wants to attract. The training program says something about the skills, knowledge, and attitudes that the firm deems essential for achievement. The criteria in the performance management and evaluation systems identify the dimensions that salespeople should regard as important. The reward and recognition programs define success and show how the firm recognizes accomplishment. The level of balance in the territory assignments demonstrates the organiza-

**Figure 15-2.** A List of Culture-Defining Sales Management Choices.

| | |
|---|---|
| **Short-Term**<br>Decisions are made to maximize short-term operating results. | **Long-Term**<br>Decisions are made to increase the long-term welfare of the company. |
| **Cost**<br>The cost of the sales force has high salience. Sales force efficiency is very important. | **Market Opportunity**<br>The revenue-generating potential of the sales force has high salience. Sales force effectiveness is very important. |
| **Customers**<br>Customers are viewed as the most important asset. Customer satisfaction is top priority, even at the expense of the sales force. | **Employees**<br>Employees are viewed as the most important asset. Satisfied employees will take good care of customers. |
| **Control**<br>Management wishes to control the activity in the field. | **Empowerment**<br>Management wishes to empower the field to solve problems and select the most appropriate activity. |
| **Activity**<br>Activity measurement is included in the performance management system and the incentive compensation plan. | **Results**<br>The performance management system and the incentive compensation plan utilize financial measures, such as sales, profits, or market share, exclusively. |
| **Individual**<br>Individual success is valued over team success. A little competition gets the juices flowing. | **Team**<br>Team success is valued over individual success. A cooperative environment enhances performance. |
| **Adaptive**<br>Selling organizations need to adapt quickly to environmental changes. The sales force needs to be able and willing to change to conquer the competitive landscape. | **Stable**<br>Customer relationships are critical. Disruption should be minimized so that customers don't have to see new faces all the time. |
| **Hunting**<br>The organization's growth and market share objectives can be achieved only if it continually converts new accounts. | **Farming**<br>It is much more expensive to convert a new account than it is to maintain an existing account. Never lose an account. |
| **Hiring**<br>Hire the best. | **Training**<br>Develop people so that they can succeed. |
| **Extrinsic Reward Systems**<br>Financial rewards and acknowledgement drive performance. | **Intrinsic Reward Systems**<br>Survival, achievement, social affiliation, power, and ego drive motivate people. Appeal to these to increase motivation. |

**Figure 15-3.** Examples of the Potential Inconsistency Between Management's Stated Values and Management's Actions.

| *What Management Asks For* | *What Management Does* |
|---|---|
| Profitability | Pays for achieving sales goals |
| Increased attention to hard-to-get accounts | Rewards for short-term success |
| Sales force commitment and loyalty | Reduces headcount when profitability is threatened |
| A skilled, knowledgeable, and technically savvy sales force | Postpones investment in sales force training and expects salespeople to self-diagnose deficiencies and correct them |

tion's view on fairness. The organizational structure reveals management's opinion regarding the importance of sales force effectiveness versus sales force efficiency.

Norms and values are unambiguous when the sales force drivers are consistent. Figure 15-5 shows how four distinct cultures can be reinforced by sales management decisions.

As Figure 15-4 shows, there are dual causalities: First, the sales force driver decisions affect the culture of the sales force, and second, the sales force culture affects sales force activity. Consequently, cultures can be understood by observing the work style of the sales force. Work style refers to how people act, how they make decisions, how they interact with one another, and how they interact with customers. The work style can be organic, encouraging creativity, flexibility, and spontaneity, or it can be mechanical, encouraging control, order, and inflexibility. A culture may reward individualism or teamwork; it can be empathic or cutthroat.

Work styles are also based on choices. The work-style wheel in Figure 15-6 presents a spectrum of work-style choices available to sales management.

There is no right or wrong work style—there is just an appropriate or inappropriate work style for a particular situation. Which work style is most appropriate usually depends on the firm's products, markets, and selling environment, as well as on the philosophy of the management team. Different industries frequently display different work styles. Stereotypical work styles for the insurance and pharmaceutical industries are presented in Figure 15-7.

The pharmaceutical culture needs a conservative, controlled work

**Figure 15-4.** The First Three Sections of the Sales Force Productivity Framework.

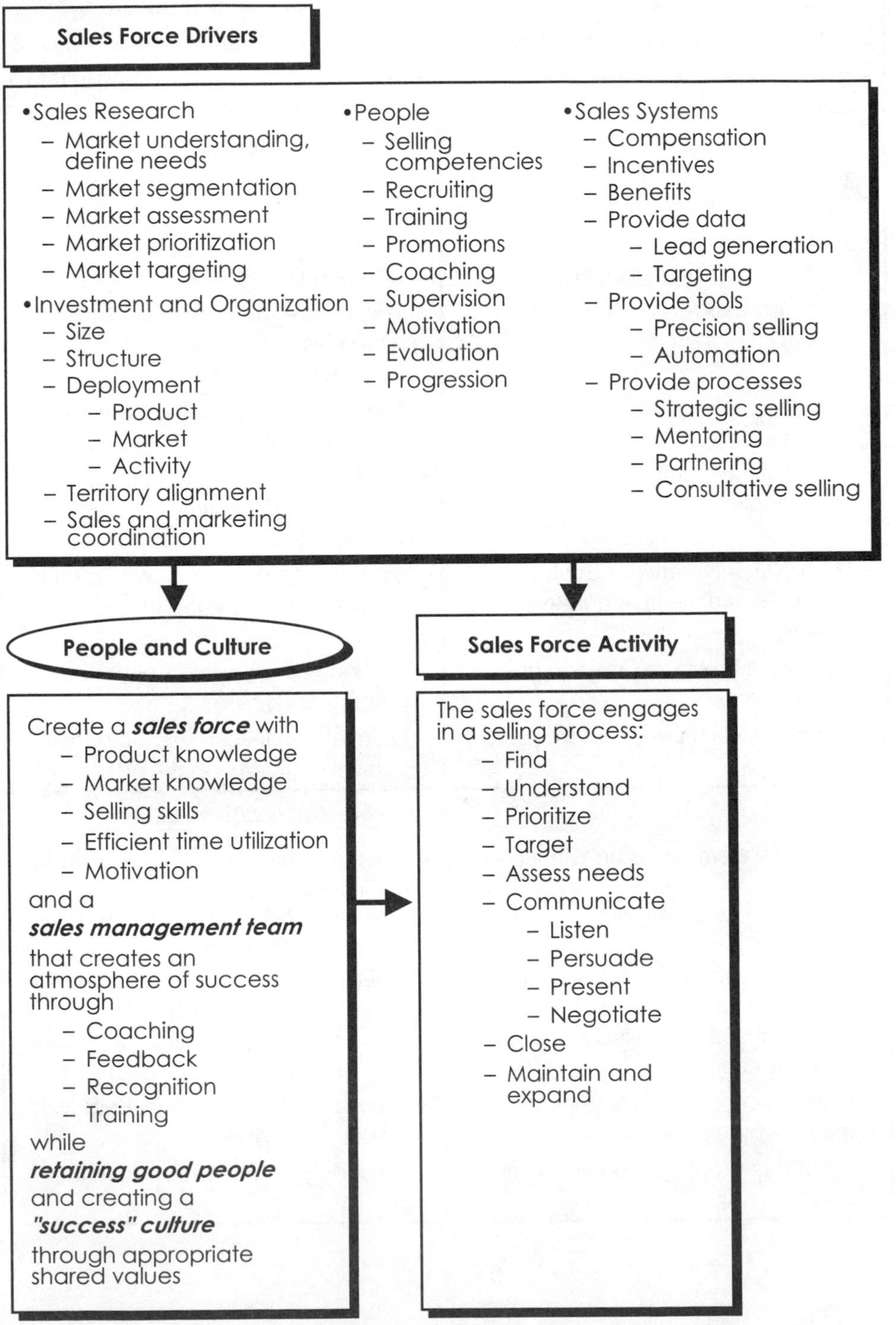

**Sales Force Drivers**

- Sales Research
  - Market understanding, define needs
  - Market segmentation
  - Market assessment
  - Market prioritization
  - Market targeting
- Investment and Organization
  - Size
  - Structure
  - Deployment
    - Product
    - Market
    - Activity
  - Territory alignment
  - Sales and marketing coordination
- People
  - Selling competencies
  - Recruiting
  - Training
  - Promotions
  - Coaching
  - Supervision
  - Motivation
  - Evaluation
  - Progression
- Sales Systems
  - Compensation
  - Incentives
  - Benefits
  - Provide data
    - Lead generation
    - Targeting
  - Provide tools
    - Precision selling
    - Automation
  - Provide processes
    - Strategic selling
    - Mentoring
    - Partnering
    - Consultative selling

**People and Culture**

Create a ***sales force*** with
- Product knowledge
- Market knowledge
- Selling skills
- Efficient time utilization
- Motivation

and a
***sales management team***
that creates an atmosphere of success through
- Coaching
- Feedback
- Recognition
- Training

while
***retaining good people***
and creating a
***"success" culture***
through appropriate shared values

**Sales Force Activity**

The sales force engages in a selling process:
- Find
- Understand
- Prioritize
- Target
- Assess needs
- Communicate
  - Listen
  - Persuade
  - Present
  - Negotiate
- Close
- Maintain and expand

**Figure 15-5.** Decisions for the Sales Force Drivers Can Establish and Maintain a Consistent Culture.

| *Control Culture* | *Empowerment Culture* |
|---|---|
| • Salary/incentive mix favors salary. | • Salary/incentive mix favors incentives. |
| • Activity goals are incorporated into territory objectives. | • Territory, objectives are stated in terms of sales and profits. |
| • Calls are reported by salespeople, and activity data are maintained and analyzed at headquarters. | • There is no call reporting. |
| • Headquarters provides information on the best accounts to call on. | • Headquarters lets the field determine whom to call on. |
| • The customer gets a controlled message. | • The salesperson determines the content of his or her interaction with the customer. |
| • There is a low span of control (ratio of salespeople to sales managers). | • There is a high span of control (ratio of salespeople to sales managers). |
| • Sales managers travel frequently with salespeople. | • Sales managers are available to the sales force, but travel with salespeople infrequently. |
| • Hiring decisions involve the human resources and the headquarters groups. | • Sales managers know how to recruit and are empowered to hire. |
| • The hiring profile favors good businesspeople. | • The hiring profile favors entrepreneurs. |
| • Training is centralized and frequent. | • Field sales managers are the primary trainers of their people. |
| *Competitive Culture* | *Cooperative Culture* |
| • Reward systems focus on winners and losers.<br>—Only a few people qualify for President's Club.<br>—Salespeople are ranked in terms of performance.<br>—Incentive plans reward individual performance. | • Reward systems focus on teamwork and cooperation.<br>—Many individuals qualify for the President's Club.<br>—Territory performance is evaluated against territory goals.<br>—Incentive plans reward cooperative behavior. |
| • Team meetings have a competitive spirit—winners are announced. | • There are lots of team meetings with best practice–sharing sessions. |
| • The hiring profile favors ego-driven people. | • The hiring profile favors empathic people. |

**Figure 15-6.** The Work-Style Wheel.

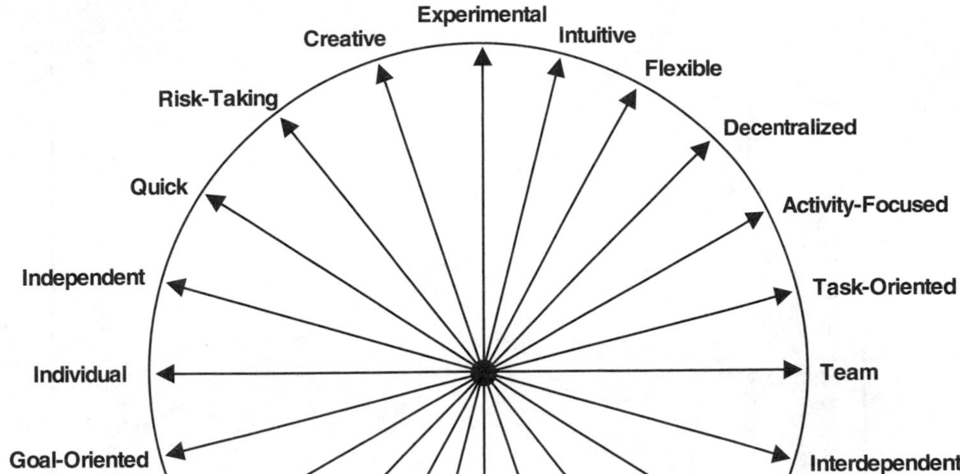


style. Product misinformation can have dire consequences; salespeople cannot exaggerate product benefits. Product information is developed centrally and is reviewed by the FDA. Salespeople are deliberate, consistent, and activity-focused. The incentive component of the compensation plan is lower than in most other industries. Salespeople are more analytical, since their products have a scientific basis. Teamwork is important for coordination, since multiple sales forces from the same company usually call on the same targeted physicians.

The insurance culture is quite different. Since most insurance products are commodities, sales success is primarily due to the skill, knowledge, motivation, and individual effort of the salesperson. Most companies pay their salespeople entirely through commissions; hence salespeople tend to be very goal-oriented. They work on their own and are inclined to be more experimental and risk-taking than salespeople in other industries.

Several aspects of the sales force work style set it apart from other functions within a company:

- Salespeople usually work alone. Their sales manager travels with them only infrequently, and they meet other salespeople primar-

**Figure 15-7.** The Insurance and Pharmaceutical Work-Style Wheels.

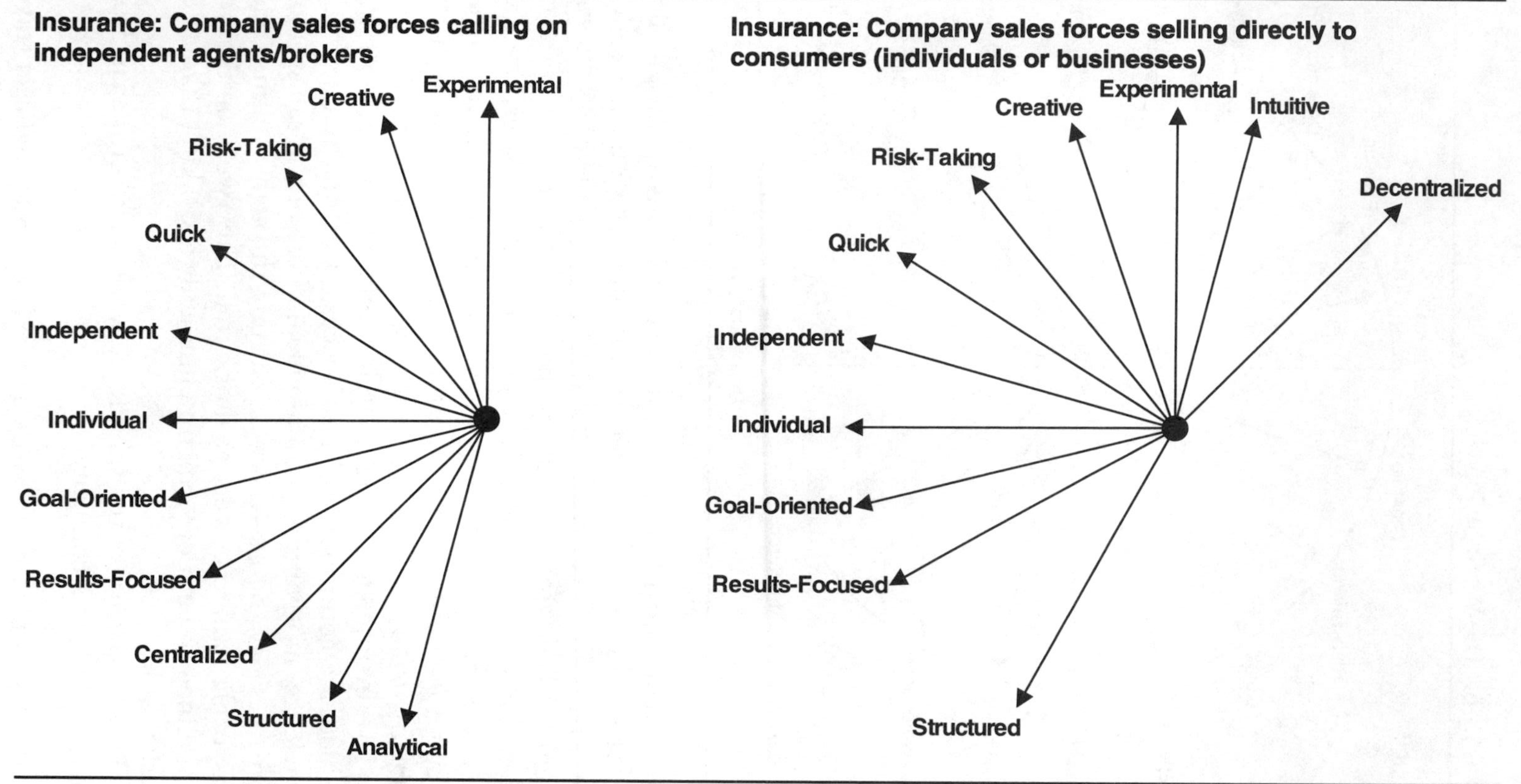

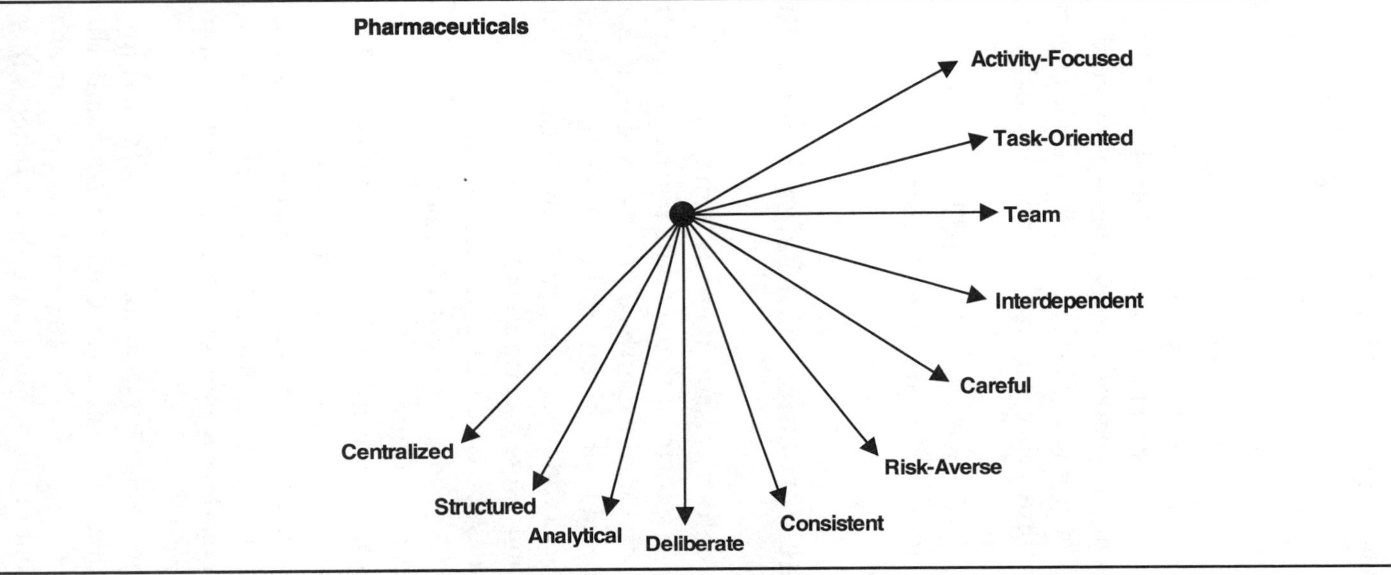
Pharmaceuticals
Activity-Focused
Task-Oriented
Team
Interdependent
Careful
Risk-Averse
Consistent
Deliberate
Analytical
Structured
Centralized

ily at regional and national sales meetings throughout the year. Unlike other people in the company, who develop strong ties to those they work with, salespeople have many weak ties to other individuals in the organization. Consequently, they look to rules, values, and norms to help them make choices in the field.

- Even though their work is largely unobservable, salespeople's results are usually measurable, and their performance is public. This feeds a competitive spirit. As a result salespeople have a hard time being collaborative.
- Sales forces tend to be nonhierarchical.
- Salespeople are boundary spanners—they connect the company with its customers. Further, most of their energy is directed externally into the marketplace, not internally within the company.
- The sales job involves considerable rejection. Consequently, rewards and recognition are important.

## The Formation of a Sales Force Culture

A sales force culture, at any point in time, is the union of the sales force's history, its environment, and its people. The culture is anchored in its history and is constantly evolving as norms, values, and work styles are adjusted by members of the sales force. Cultural components that contribute to the success of the selling organization are reinforced. If teamwork and value creation lead to success, they become cultural norms. The sales force's culture attracts compatible people and rejects nonconformists. A sales force culture shapes its people, even as its people are shaping the culture.

New sales force cultures are initiated when a sales force is created. This may happen when a new company assembles a sales force for the first time, or when an established company determines that it needs to add another selling organization. Mergers and acquisitions also result in sales force creation. A new sales force is crafted from the pre-merger selling organizations.

When a new sales force is formed, a new culture begins to form almost immediately. A sales force leader is usually the first person recruited. He or she is typically given the title of National Sales Manager or Vice President of Sales. The new culture reflects this leader's personality. New organizations typically select an external candidate as leader—since sales is a new function for the company, it usually does not have resident expertise.

An internal candidate is almost always chosen as the sales force leader when selling organizations are merged. Too many people will lose their jobs if the merged company looks externally for candidates. The chosen leader is usually associated with the stronger selling organization or the acquiring firm. Internal candidates have some further advantages: They are available, they understand the politics, and they have a working knowledge of at least one of the pre-merger organizations. These are critical advantages because the merged organization usually wants to complete the integration as quickly as possible.

New selling organizations within existing companies may choose either an internal or an external candidate for the sales leader position. An internal candidate brings knowledge of the organization and the organizational culture. An external candidate usually brings knowledge of the markets the new sales force will serve.

Whatever the source of the new sales force leader, he or she has preferred values, norms, and work styles. The new leader usually has many years of experience in sales. He or she has developed an understanding of what works and what doesn't and is eager to build the culture for a new selling organization. It is very important to recruit the right person for the initial sales force leader role. This should not be a temporary or "acting" position.

The new sales manager is faced with many decisions. Whom do we hire? How many people should we hire? What should the training program look like? Whom do we select for key sales management positions? How much should we pay people, and what should the pay plan look like? What systems do we initiate? How will we know if we are successful? All sales force driver decisions need to be made.

The leader begins to develop his or her team. The team shares challenges and develops solutions. These solutions reflect the team members' best understanding of the environment, marketplace, products, business model, and sales force strategy. The sales force culture emerges from these initial decisions and the shared experience of the initial team members.

The sales job is largely unsupervised. Consequently, the sales force culture becomes a conglomeration of subcultures. Each sales district establishes a culture of its own. National account teams and product specialists may have cultures that are different from those of the rest of the field force. Hunters and farmers have their own subcultures. In tight overall cultures, the subcultures have very similar values, norms, and work styles. In loose cultures, renegade sales teams are allowed to exist. The overall sales force culture includes an indication of whether it is tight or loose.

Cultures evolve over time, and their roots are frequently forgotten. The following story demonstrates the impact that cultures have on the behavior of members of a community.

---

Five apes are placed in a room. A cluster of bananas hangs from the ceiling. A ladder is placed underneath the bananas. The bananas are reachable only by climbing the ladder. The experiment is set up so that any time an ape starts to climb the ladder, the whole room is sprayed with ice-cold water. In a short time all the apes learn not to climb the ladder.

Then, one ape is removed from the room and is replaced by a sixth ape, and the water sprayer is disabled. The new ape (number six) starts to climb the ladder. He is attacked unmercifully by the other four apes. He has no idea why he is being attacked. Another old ape is replaced by a new ape. The same thing happens, with ape number six doing the most hitting. This pattern continues until all the old apes have been replaced. Now all of the apes stay off the ladder, attack any ape that attempts to climb it, and have absolutely no idea why they are behaving this way.

---

Cultures survive as long as the sales force is successful. Sales force achievement, usually measured in terms of sales and profit goal attainment, reinforces the cultural norms, values, and work style: "If it ain't broke, don't fix it." Change takes work. Small changes in the culture occur constantly as the management team revises the recruiting process, the training program, recognition and rewards programs, performance management systems, and other sales force programs. Large changes in the culture usually require a critical incident such as a major market shift, a severe earnings shortfall, or a significant market share loss. The next section describes how a sales force culture can be changed.

## How to Change a Sales Force Culture

Cultures have momentum; they roll along if there is no need for them to change. Culture change is hard work. On occasion, however, a culture becomes a liability for a sales force. Environmental forces can prevent a culture from succeeding. For example, a relationship-oriented culture is difficult to maintain if customers interact with suppliers primarily over the Internet. A sales force culture may also be incompatible with a new sales force strategy. Salespeople who for years have allocated their time among a few reliable customers will have difficulty if a new management team initiates a sales force strategy focusing on new business development.

Inappropriate sales force cultures need to be changed. People are the change agents—they are the only ones who can change cultures. If the culture is very strong, it may take a very strong individual to initiate the change process. The change initiator is typically at the top of the organization—a divisional president or a vice president of sales. On occasion, a company will bring in an outsider to set the change in motion. The outsider usually replaces the current sales force leader. Outsiders bring a new perspective; they can make objective choices because the current culture is not ingrained in them. However, an outsider is an outsider. He or she needs to learn the organization quickly in order to be effective. Strong insiders who separate themselves from the current sales force culture have a very good chance of being successful. They know the organization, its people, and the subtleties of the current culture. In this case, the sales force is more likely to view the change agent as "one of us."

As shown in Figure 15-8, a culture change process has at least four components: vision, communication, action, and rewards. The following sections discuss each of these components. In addition, the culture change process is illustrated using the changes that occurred at Guidant, a medical device company.

**Figure 15-8.** A Culture Change Process.

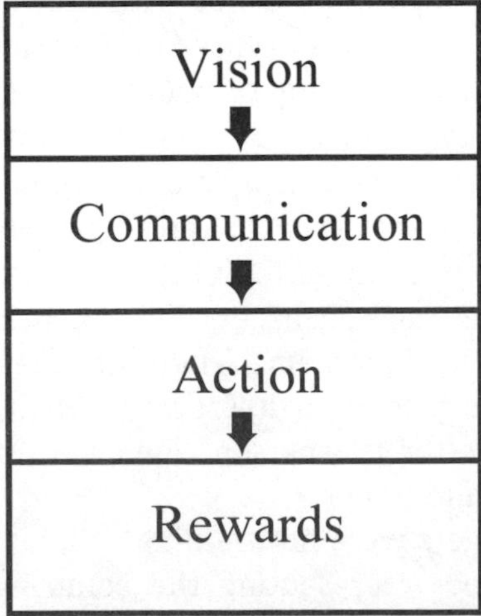

---

### The Culture at Guidant—Jay's Story

At the time of this story, Jay Graf was president of the Cardiac Rhythm Management Division at Guidant. Guidant is a medical device company engaged in the design, manufacture, and sale of implantable cardiac rhythm management devices. These devices are indicated for the management of patients with slow and fast heart rates and patients with heart failure. Jay became president in 1992. He was immediately faced with a corporate culture that disappointed him. Even though the following discussion revolves around the sales force, most weak cultures are endemic to the entire organization. Jay was faced with inappropriate values and work styles in R&D, manufacturing, marketing, and sales.

Jay changed the entire culture of his organization. This is his story of how the sales force changed. Here is a quick description of the pre-1992 culture:

> "The company was not offering competitive products. Customers believed that Guidant was years behind in technology and couldn't catch up.
>
> "After many years of failure, there was no trust and confidence in the organization. The attitude was, 'We will never get out of this; things are not going to change; the company cannot design its way out of a paper bag.'
>
> "There was no accountability. No one could depend upon anyone to do what he or she had promised to do.
>
> "The sales organization was not making plans. Expenses were not under control.
>
> "There was a large group of people who sold virtually nothing—the 'slugs.' They were satisfied with a low level of performance. There were numerous excuses for low sales.
>
> "There was a small group of people who had lots of sales, made lots of money, and were arrogant about it—the 'gunslingers.' They intimidated the management of the division and held it hostage. Their attitude was, 'If I don't get what I want, I will leave.' They were not committed to the company.
>
> "The regional sales managers did not lead. They did not confront performance problems. Their attitude was, 'Five pacemakers a month is good enough; it's better than none. I may not be able to get a better salesperson, and even if I do, it will take too long to train him or her.'
>
> "Sales managers were not training and coaching their people. They were not representing the company adequately to their people.

"Regional sales managers were emasculated. Top management communicated with salespeople over their heads and never gave them an opportunity to look smart in front of their people.

"The marketing group was a target of sales force criticism. It lacked credibility and did not have a good understanding of selling. In general, it did not provide useful materials to the sales force."

## Vision

Assume that a decision has been made to change the current sales force culture. How should it change? The company must develop a vision of how the norms, values, and work style need to change so that sales force behaviors are aligned with the requirements of the company's current product line, selling environment, and business model. A vision identifies what the company wants to achieve. It directs the renewal process.

Figure 15-9 presents a process for establishing a culture vision. There are three pertinent cultures. The *ideal culture* is a statement of the values, norms, and work styles that are most appropriate for the selling organization, in light of the company's current product line, selling environment, and business model. The ideal culture is an expres-

**Figure 15-9.** A Process for Developing a Culture Vision.

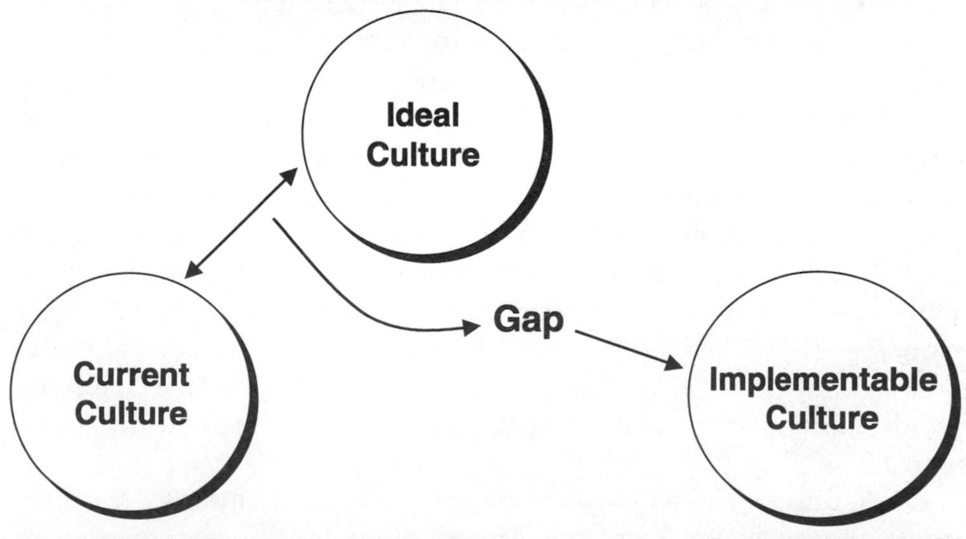

sion of where management would like to be. Some companies will rely on a powerful leader to define the ideal culture. This is especially common if a company is in distress. Other companies will use a consensus approach. In this approach, a group of high-performing sales managers and salespeople convene with the Vice President of Sales and the Division President for a two-day workshop to hash out the appropriate value system, sales force norms, and work styles. A group consensus is the objective of the workshop.

Once an ideal culture has been determined, it is compared to the current culture. Many companies use upward feedback surveys to assess their current culture. An upward feedback survey elicits opinions about the current culture from the sales force. Managers may have their own beliefs about what the culture looks like, but they are frequently surprised by the values, norms, and work styles that are assumed by the sales force.

The difference between the current and the ideal sales force cultures is called the *gap*. The gap can be narrow or wide. Wide gaps require bold moves. Narrow gaps can be tightened by incremental changes.

Organizational barriers frequently prevent quick attainment of the ideal culture. For example, if the work style suggested in the ideal culture is incompatible with the skills and competencies of the current sales force, then the ideal culture is not feasible. The *implementable culture* is the culture that comes closest to achieving the ideal, given organizational constraints. The implementable culture is the best candidate for the culture vision.

When there has been a drastic change in an industry, the gap between the current and ideal cultures can be very large. For example, in the late 1990s the utility industry experienced a significant sales force transition. In the past, utility companies were monopolists; they did not need to sell. Their customers were captive. In many cases their sales forces were made up of engineers on a two-year rotation before their next promotion. Sales training was nonexistent. The sales force was paid 100 percent salary. Deregulation brought change and competition. Large accounts now needed to be sold because there now were many suppliers who could meet their energy needs. The sales force did not know how to sell, so it needed a new culture. Figure 15-10 presents the ideal and pre-deregulation work style wheels for many utility companies.

At Guidant, the wide gap between the current and ideal cultures had developed slowly over time. Management had allowed this to happen, and Jay decided that it was time to change it. He developed a vision of an implementable culture to support his business goals.

---

Guidant Vision

Some important components of Jay's vision included the following:

"Trust and confidence in the organization need to be rebuilt.

"Accountability—People are going to be held accountable for results. Individuals who need resources to generate their results will be given resources. This eliminates excuses.

"Predictability—People are expected to deliver on their commitments. Everyone can count on it."

---

## Communication

Cultures rely on communication to disseminate their values, norms, and work style. High-level sales managers spread the culture through mottoes, proclamations, and public statements. "Customer satisfaction is priority 1" and "we will be the market leader in three years" are examples of culture-influencing statements. Sales managers communicate the culture through coaching, mentoring, and performance appraisals. Training managers spread the culture in training modules. Information specialists convey the culture through information formats and speed in getting information into the hands of the salespeople. Salespeople communicate the culture in their daily interactions with peers. Eric, Julia, Matthew, and Natalie each shared their culture with their friends when they met at the wedding.

Any change in culture must be communicated quickly and forcefully. Top managers need to repeat the message constantly. For example, a new vice president of sales took over a sales force that had been mismanaged for years. He was instituting a new culture. He delivered a forceful message at the annual sales meeting. It was not the first time he had delivered the same message. Feeling that he was being monotonous, he asked one of the authors if he was overdoing it. It was the author's opinion that his message needed to be delivered repeatedly. The vice president was bored, but his constituents were not because he was communicating his vision to a different subset of people each time. In other words, he was repeating the message frequently, but any one individual had heard the message only a few times. Nonetheless, it was beginning to take shape in their minds.

**Figure 15-10.** Utility Industry Pre-Deregulation and Ideal Post-Deregulation Work-Style Wheels.

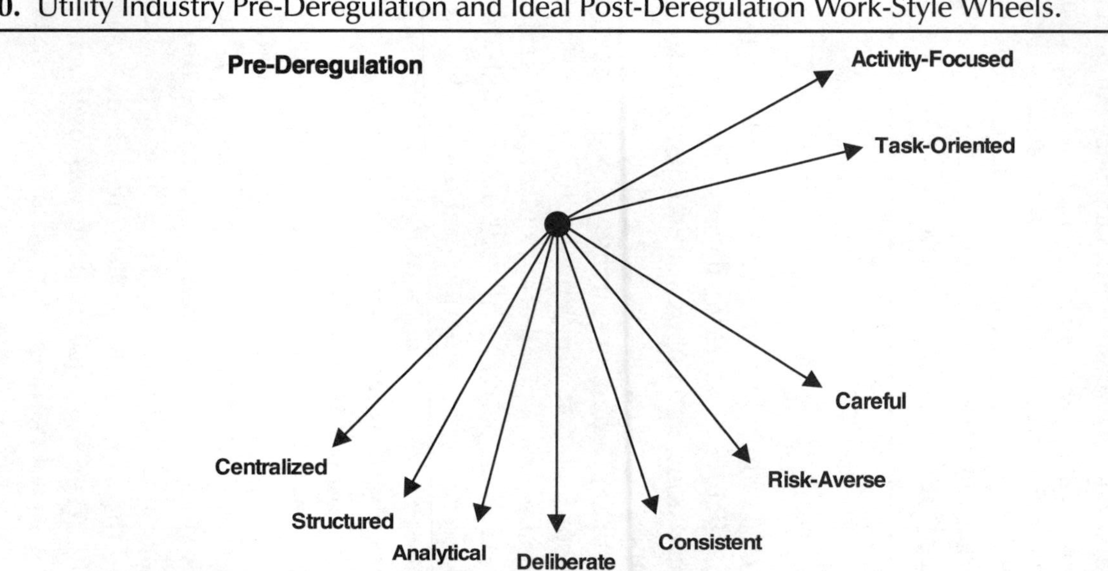

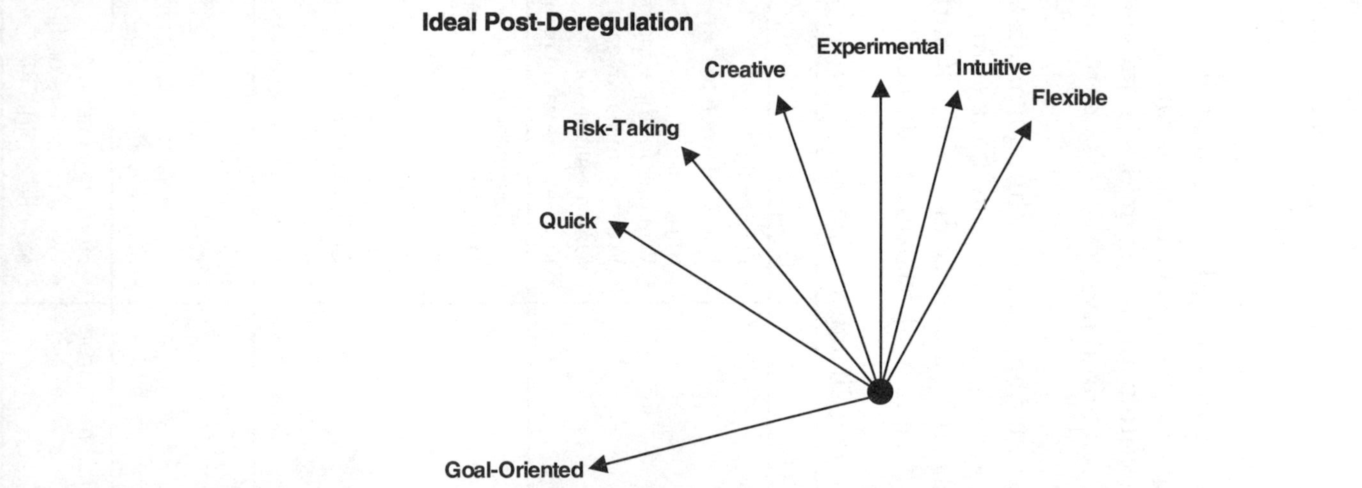
Ideal Post-Deregulation
Quick
Risk-Taking
Creative
Experimental
Intuitive
Flexible
Goal-Oriented

Stories, legends, and myths are useful in communicating a new culture. The story about Jeff, the salesperson who finally got the mining sale after camping out for a week, is a very powerful communication about what it takes to be successful. Most sales forces can pinpoint individuals or events that embody the values the management team wants to reinforce. These individuals become the heroes and these events become the substance of the legends that reinforce a cultural change.

Metaphors are used frequently to communicate within a sales force culture. They help to explain and illustrate complex concepts and often communicate unwritten rules. Figure 15-11 presents some common metaphors. Sports and military metaphors are the most common ones used in sales.

Compared to other functions within the organization, sales forces have very strong rituals that reinforce their culture. Some examples include "the sales call," "the cold call," "the golf outing," "the motivational meeting," "the annual recognition dinner," "president's club,"

**Figure 15-11.** Common Culture Metaphors.

| *Metaphor* | *Examples* |
|---|---|
| Sports metaphors | • Playing team ball<br>• Knowing when to carry the ball and when to pass<br>• Win one for the Gipper<br>• We're in this as a team<br>• One for all, all for one<br>• Knowing the game plan |
| Military metaphors | • It's a new battle for us<br>• The fight is on a different front<br>• We're the front line<br>• First line of defense<br>• Storm the castle<br>• Cut off their reinforcements<br>• It's a behind-the-lines fight<br>• Hand-to-hand combat |
| Family/nurturing metaphors | • We take care of you<br>• We help each other grow<br>• We're all one happy family<br>• Be one of us |
| Weather/meterological metaphors | • Storm front approaching<br>• We're in the eye of the hurricane<br>• No one could have forecast this one |

and "the customer relationship." New rituals help establish new cultures.

At Guidant, communication was a critical part of Jay's culture change strategy.

---

Guidant Communication

"It is more a question of what you do than of what you say. The former president of the organization had not planned to speak at the first national sales meeting—but I did. I told people that we were not an accountable organization and that that was going to change. I also told them that we were going to work hard to become a predictable organization. We were going to change our work style. I gave them my list of ten measurable personal objectives for the next year and said that we were going to review them again at our next meeting. I wanted the entire organization to start talking about what they were going to accomplish and then show the results."

---

### Action

Actions are the most powerful communication medium. Managers must "walk the talk." A manager who discourages overselling, even at the risk of missing a revenue goal, has credibility when he or she tells the sales force that customer satisfaction is the number one priority. Words and actions need to be consistent. Managers who tell the sales force that they are empowered yet insist on counting calls develop a nontrusting culture. The salespeople will ignore the words and make sure that they make lots of calls, even if the calls are not very productive. Consistent and forceful words and actions are required if values and work styles are to become part of cultural memory.

The sales force productivity drivers provide an agenda for the actions that need to be taken to bring about a culture change. The change process is likely to start with new role definitions for all levels within the selling organization.

Some people will be unable to adapt to the new vision. They like the current culture. They grew up in it, they nurtured it, they are comfortable with it, and they do not want to change it. Some individuals are going to be incapable of adapting to the work style of the new culture. As an example, perhaps relationships were important in the past, but now pricing, technical expertise, and value creation have become important in a new consultative environment. Such a transition may be impossible for some.

People who cannot adapt to a new culture should leave the company. Outplacement requires some tough decisions, and current leaders many not be up to the task. They may be unable to make all of the tough decisions required to move the organization forward. They have too many friends within the sales force. Hence, outplacement frequently begins at the top.

The organization should begin recruiting, promoting, and training as soon as the roles and responsibilities have been defined. The recruiting and promotion criteria should reflect the values and work style of the new culture. The training organization has an important role in the culture transition process: It emphasizes the new culture to new employees. Remember that Jeff, the man who converted the mines, came to new employee orientation. Training also helps the sales force implement the culture shift. An investment in understanding the process of change management and the skills required to implement change facilitates a smooth transition. It also says that employees and their professional development are valued, which is a positive statement about the new culture.

Success metrics must reflect the norms, values, and work style of the new culture. They form the basis for a revised performance management system and revised reward and recognition programs. For example, a shift from sales to market share as a measure of performance establishes the importance of developing new business and sets a more competitive tone. An emphasis on goal attainment encourages accountability. The power of these programs during a culture transition should not be underestimated.

Benchmarks are also important to the transition process. The sales force should know when it is on track. Quick and long-term wins must be defined. New role definitions, a new hiring profile, a new training initiative, a new compensation program, and a successful sales meeting are all examples of quick wins. Every quick win needs to be recognized and celebrated.

The culture change process is more effective if there is urgency. Quick wins need to have aggressive deadlines. Poor sales results, an outside threat, or a significant event can be used to create urgency.

At Guidant, Jay took action steps that supported the new culture.

Guidant Action

"The compensation plan changed; it became growth-oriented. Growth became the expectation; five units per month was unacceptable. Top performers had higher upside opportunity under the new plan. Individuals who were top performers and demonstrated leadership received company stock. This created a group of people who were eager to help the company.

"We heightened recognition for good performance. The first sales banquet was a big success. There were numerous visible symbols of selling success. There were lots of awards—top salesperson, rookie of the year, statesman's club, etc. Trophies and medals abounded. 'Next year I'll be on stage' was a comment heard from several people who didn't receive an award. Positive values and work styles were affirmed at this meeting.

"Marketing support improved. Everyone in marketing now has some sales experience. Now, everyone knows that everyone else knows what he or she is talking about. Sales and marketing are on the same page. They meet regularly to discuss relevant issues.

"The regional managers have become an integral part of the communication process. Top management must go to them first. Salespeople get information from their managers. Salespeople feel that the company trusts its managers. The regional managers are forced to manage.

"Marketing people used to run the national sales meeting. Now regional managers run the meeting. They run the seminars and the discussion groups. This helps with implementation. Managers can refer to discussions at the national meeting when questions arise in the field.

"The Vice President of Sales left the company shortly after my arrival. His replacement came from within Guidant. The new vice president was chosen because of his 'integrity, judgment, courage, and ability to make things stick.' A number of regional sales managers were unable to adapt to the new culture, so they left the organization.

"The sales force size stayed the same in spite of the financial stress that existed in those first few years. More people were added as the organization began to thrive. In fact, acquisitions were made later, which required further modification of the sales force culture."

### Rewards

The selling organization needs to provide both extrinsic and intrinsic rewards for the behaviors that are suggested by the values, norms, and work styles of the new culture. Money, recognition, and status are powerful communicators. When Mary Kay presents a pink Cadillac to the outstanding performers at the annual sales convention, the company makes a statement about what it values. The story about Jeff's initiative at the mining company makes a statement about the preferred work style. Behaviors that are rewarded visibly are viewed as successful. Shared success becomes the fabric of the culture.

At Guidant, rewards and recognition were critical to the success of the new culture.

---

Guidant Rewards

"We changed the compensation plan and passed out lots of hardware.

"You can't run an army without medals."

---

## How to Maintain a Successful Culture

A sales force culture is formed by the intersection of the sales force's history, its environment, and its people. The culture shapes its people at the same time as the people shape the culture. Only people can maintain a strong culture or change a weak culture. Here are some suggestions for maintaining a successful culture.

1. Constantly assess the current values, norms, and work style using an upward survey. Revise the culture vision if the product line, selling environment, and business model suggest that the company is not as successful as it could be because of the current culture. Identify an implementable culture and begin the change process.
2. Constantly reward acceptable behaviors. Behaviors will be adopted if they are tried and found to be successful.
3. Cultures are shared. Practice effective communication to give the sales force advice on what is preferred.
4. Use heroes, legends, myths, and parables to communicate the

culture. Stories are remembered better than concepts. Begin employee indoctrination at the very first training session or orientation.

5. Ensure that the sales force heroes embody the appropriate values, norms, and work style. Never let Zeke be a hero; always look for the Jeffs in the sales force.
6. Ensure that actions and words are compatible. "Walk the talk."
7. Urgency and strong leaders are necessary for a successful culture change.

# Index